AIRCRAFT *of the* RAF

Warners Group Publications,
The Maltings, West Street,
Bourne, Lincolnshire PE10 9PH
Tel: 01778 391000
Fax: 01778 392422

Publisher
Rob McDonnell
robm@warnersgroup.co.uk

Editor
Stephen Bridgewater
steve.bridgewater@gmail.com

Sub Editor
Charlotte Bailey

Head of Design and Production
Lynn Wright

Designer
Mike Edwards

Advertising
Kristina Green
kristina.green@warnersgroup.co.uk
Tel: 01778 392096

Elizabeth Ridge
elizabeth.ridge@warnersgroup.co.uk
Tel: 01778 395059

Advertising Production & Design
Nicola Lock
nicola.lock@warnersgroup.co.uk
Tel: 01778 392420

Marketing Executives
Katherine Brown
katherine.brown@warnersgroup.co.uk
Tel: 01778 395092

Luke Hider
luke.hider@warnersgroup.co.uk
Tel: 01778 395085

Distribution
Warners Distribution, Andy Perry
Tel: 01778 391152

Cover image
Hawker Hurricane Mk1 R4118
© Darren Harbar Photography

All Images via Awyr Archives or by the Editor (SDB) unless stated

Crown Copyright

Welcome

Great Britain was by no means the first nation to see the military value of airpower; but it was the first to form a truly independent air force, separate to that of the Navy and Army. As such, on April 1, 1918, the British Royal Flying Corps (RFC) and Royal Naval Air Service (RNAS) merged to form the Royal Air Force (RAF).

Since then, the RAF has remained on constant readiness to protect Britain from attack and to defend the freedom of UK citizens and those in need. However, the RAF has always been more than just a 'fighting' force. Whether it is delivering humanitarian aid during times of natural or manmade tragedy or rescuing civilians in distress from desolate mountains or frigid seas, the RAF's aircraft and aircrew are a welcome sight to those in need.

Increasingly, the RAF finds itself in a position of 'preventing' conflict. The Cold War days of Mutual Assured Destruction (MAD) have given way to an era of electronic warfare. In today's 'cyberage', reconnaissance and surveillance aircraft scan the airwaves for tell-tale communications that can enable the RAF to stop an attack before it has even begun.

From trainers to fast jets and support helicopters to refuellers and reconnaissance machines the RAF in 2020 operates a diverse fleet of more than 800 aircraft. Behind the scenes, more than 30,000 personnel keep the RAF functioning on a day-to-day basis; from intelligence analysts and cyberspace communications specialists to chefs, drivers, aircraft technicians and, of course, pilots; there are more than 60 'trades' in today's RAF.

This special publication is a tribute to all those who have served – and continue to serve – in the world's oldest air force. In a little over a century, hundreds of different aircraft types have served with the RAF and in the following pages we tell the stories of some of the most iconic as well as some of the more unusual. Of course we include the 'legends' such as the Spitfire, Hunter, Harrier and Vulcan – but we also turn our attention towards the unsung types as well as some 'what might have beens'. We also feature a series of 'Fast Facts', with trivia and lesser known annecdotes about the RAF's aircraft and people.

I hope you enjoy reading the following pages as much as my team and I have enjoyed putting them together.

Steve

Stephen Bridgewater
Editor, *Aircraft of the RAF*

RAF Chronology

Running throughout these pages you will find a chronology of aircraft types that have been operated by the RAF since 1918. For the sake of 'completeness' we have also included some of the more important prototypes and experimental aircraft that have flown in RAF markings and played a vital role in developing its airpower. Where an aircraft has served the RAF in a number of very different variants (such as the Spitfire, Hunter or Harrier) we have included the most numerous and important versions in our timeline. Aircraft are listed in chronological order according to the date they entered RAF service and 'eagle-eyed' readers will note the appearance of some Naval aircraft. This is because the 'Fleet Air Arm of the Royal Air Force' was formed in 1924 to encompass RAF units embarked on ships. It was only in 1939 that the FAA was returned to Admiralty control. Heroes, icons, lesser known oddities, 'what ifs' and downright 'flops' are given equal coverage.

Contents

The Force Awakens

Although it was formed at the height of warfare, the fledgling Royal Air Force was equipped with a ramshackle fleet of hand-me-down ex-Army and Navy aircraft

From the outbreak of Great War in 1914 the Royal Flying Corps (RFC) and the Royal Naval Air Service (RNAS) had both defended Britain and taken the fight to the enemy in mainland Europe.

However, by 1917 German Gotha bombers could easily penetrate British air defences and a series of deadly attacks on London and other cities began to rock the public's confidence.

One such raid on Purley, London, in which 162 people were killed – including 18 children in a school – caused an outcry and it was decided that something had to be done. As such, in early 1918, the government commissioned a review into British air power.

This was entrusted to Lt Gen Jan Smuts, who - somewhat controversially - recommended that aviation be treated as its own force.

The six-page 'Smuts Report' noted: "The day may not be far off when aerial operations with their devastation of enemy lands and destruction of industrial and populous centres on a vast scale may become the principle operations of war, to which the older forms of military and naval operations may become secondary and subordinate."

Smuts' suggestion to amalgamate the RFC and the RNAS was accepted by Prime Minister David Lloyd George and the Royal Air Force (RAF) was formed on April 1, 1918.

Prior to this all military aviation had been conducted by air arms of nations' armies or navies – the newly formed RAF would become the world's first dedicated, standalone air force. It was also the largest, with more than 20,000 aircraft and 313,000 men at its disposal.

Of these, the RNAS contributed 55,066 officers and men and 2,949 aircraft; the remaining personnel and machinery provided by the RFC.

By the end of March 1918, the RFC comprised some 150 squadrons; the majority of which kept their squadron numbers in the RAF whereas those of the RNAS were renumbered from 201 Sqn onwards.

1

'Knights of the Air'

While the early years of aviation were seen by many as romantic and daring it was, in reality, a risky occupation. It attracted eccentric risk-takers whom the media referred to as 'Knights of the Air', but the memoirs of those who served during what was intended to be the 'war to end all wars' make for sobering reading.

What started as almost chivalrous aerial battles quickly descended into a dog-eat-dog affair, with pilots employing purer animal instincts in an attempt to stay alive. In his seminal work *Sagittarius Rising*, pilot Cecil B Lewis wrote that aircrew were "either in the stretch or sag of nerves. We were either in deadly danger or we were in no danger at all."

The everyday risks were all too real. Pilots and observers were not permitted to fly with parachutes (which were thought to inspire cowardice!) and lived in constant fear of losing control or burning to death in their aircraft. Some even resorted to carrying a service revolver to end their lives in the event of fire.

RAF Fast Fact

The RAF motto, "Per ardua ad astra" ("Through Adversity to the Stars") was coined by Frederick Sykes. Although pretty much forgotten these days, Skyes – who succeeded Trenchard as Chief of the Air Staff in 1918 – was an experienced pilot and had written numerous operations manuals for the RFC. He was also a meticulous administrator without whom the RAF might not have made it through its first year of independence.

1918

Airco DH.4 Considered by many to be the best single-engined bomber of its era the Airco DH.4 was easy to fly and could operate at relatively high altitude and speed. The RAF inherited a fleet of DH.4s and from June 1918 they formed part of the Independent Air Force, carrying out strategic bombing of Germany. After the Armistice, DH.4s were used to transport passengers to the Paris Peace Conference.

Airco DH.6 Created by Geoffrey de Havilland as a dedicated training aircraft, the DH.6 was simple and cheap to both build and maintain. It was designed to be safe and simple to fly; although it was often criticised for being 'too safe' as it failed to prepare students for more the advanced fighter types they would go on to fly. A handful of DH.6s served in the fledgling RAF but were soon retired.

Airco DH.9 The DH.9 was a development of the DH.4 fitted with an all-new and much improved fuselage. It served as a bomber with the RFC and RAF and the type's last combat use was in support of the final campaign against Mohammed Abdullah Hassan (the so-called "Mad Mullah") in Somalia in February 1920. A handful of DH.9s survive and this Puma-engined example returned to the skies after restoration in 2019. **SDB**

Airco DH.9A A development of the DH.9 featuring an American-built Liberty V-12 in place of the unreliable Siddeley Puma engine. The prototype flew on April 19, 1918 and deliveries started in June – making it the RAF's first 'new' type. The RAF went on to operate 1,730 examples and five post-war squadrons served in the Middle East, carrying out raids against rebellious tribesmen until 1930. In total, 1,997 DH.9As were built.

Airco DH.10 Amiens A development of the DH.3, which had been rejected by the War Office in 1916 because it believed that strategic bombing would be ineffective. It could carry twice the bomb load as the DH.9A and entered service in November 1918. DH.10s flew a single bombing mission the day before the war ended. Postwar, DH.10s were deployed to Egypt and India and also provided an air mail service between Cairo and Baghdad.

2

1. The Royal Aircraft Factory S.E.5A was one of the most advanced fighters of the Great War but it was soon obsolete in the postwar period. **SDB**
2. The Bristol M.1C Monoplane Scout was a formidable weapon but was relegated to predominantly second line duties because of unjustified mistrust of monoplane designs. **SDB**
3. Perhaps the most famous British fighter of the Great War was the Sopwith Camel; so named because of the 'hump' over its two Vickers .303 machine guns. **SDB**
4. The Royal Aircraft Factory B.E.2c was a major redesign of the earlier B.E.2 and was a more inherently stable aeroplane. This helped the crew focus on their reconnaissance duties as less time had to be devoted to actually keeping the aeroplane flying in a straight line! **SDB**

3

4

Hand-Me-Downs

Despite being a new force the RAF would have to wait a long time before it received its own independently allocated aeroplanes. Rather, it relied on a mismatched fleet of former RFC and RNAS machinery.

From ageing flying boats such as the Fairey Campania, Felixstowe F.3 and Short 184; to bombers including the Airco DH4 and Handley Page O/400, and scouts as various as the Bristol M.1C and Sopwith Pup, this ramshackle group of aircraft soldiered on until the end of the war but in many cases were completely unsuitable for the role at hand.

The first 'new' aircraft to join the RAF was the Airco DH.9A bomber; itself a modified version of the DH.9 which in turn traced its history back to the DH.4 of 1917. Although the DH.9A was much improved, not least because of its more powerful and reliable American engine, it was still unsuitable to the changing face of warfare in the latter months of the war – let alone the emerging interwar period.

The end of the Great War in November 1918 brought with it inevitable defence cuts. The RAF would have to wait nine months before learning it would be retained, but its manpower would be cut to a strength of just 35,500 including 6,500 officers on permanent commissions.

Superlative Snipe

Among the new generation of aircraft that bolstered the fledgling RAF's ranks was the Sopwith Snipe.

The aircraft traces its history back to April 1917 when Sopwith's Chief Designer, Herbert Smith, began to design a replacement for the company's successful Camel fighter.

The Snipe was slightly smaller than the Camel and the centre-section of the upper wing was uncovered, providing better visibility from the cockpit.

The first prototype, powered by a Bentley AR.1 rotary engine was completed in October 1917 and a second, powered by a more powerful 230hp Bentley BR.2 engine, flew a month later.

The Snipe was evaluated by the Air Ministry and an order for 1,700 airframes was placed in March 1918. The type entered service with 43 Sqn on August 30, 1918 and also saw service with 4 Sqn Australian Flying Corps (AFC) from October 1918. The RAF's 208 Sqn (previously 8 Sqn RNAS) converted onto the Snipe from Camels in November, too late to see action.

At the cessation of the war Snipes formed an important part of the British Army of Occupation and many did not return to the UK until September 1919. Meanwhile, Snipes replaced Camels in four home defence squadrons and the type was selected to be the RAF's standard postwar single-seat fighter.

In 1919, RAF Snipes supported the White Russians during the Russian Civil War against the Bolsheviks, with twelve examples being used by the RAF mission in northern Russia.

Although it was quickly superseded by more modern machinery, the RAF did not retire its final Snipe until 1926.

Policing the Empire

Even the more 'cutting-edge' designs such as the Snipe and Royal Aircraft Factory S.E.5a were hard-pressed to meet the requirements of the RAF in the 1920s and beyond. It was obvious that new aircraft were desperately needed; not least to help the RAF in the important role of

Armstrong Whitworth F.K.8 A general-purpose biplane designed by Dutchman Frederick Koolhoven as a B.E.2c replacement. It was fitted with dual controls so the observer could control the aircraft if the pilot became incapacitated. The F.K.8 entered service in January 1917 and the RAF inherited 694 examples when it formed. The last examples - in service with 150 Sqn in Greece - retired in September 1919.

Avro 504K & N The first Avro 504 flew in 1913 but the type was constantly modernised throughout the Great War. The '504K was also the RAF's standard training aircraft for many years. The new Armstrong-Siddeley Lynx radial-engined '504N variant was introduced in 1925 and 592 airframes were built for the RAF's five flying training schools, with whom they served until 1933. Today, a handful of originals and several replicas still fly. **SDB**

Blackburn Kangaroo Envisaged as a twin-engine reconnaissance aircraft and torpedo bomber the Kangaroo first flew in 1916 in seaplane form but was later redesigned as a landplane. However, the rear fuselage was prone to twisting, causing control problems. As such, the order for 50 was cut to 20. Kangaroos of 246 Sqn sank one U-boat (UC-70 off Scarborough) and damaged four more by the end of the war.

Bristol F.2B Fighter The 'Brisfit' proved to be agile and rugged and could hold its own against German single-seat fighters. At the end of the war the RAF had 1,583 F.2Bs in service. Postwar, the F.2B was adopted as the RAF's standard army cooperation machine and continued to operate throughout the British Empire. The last example was retired by 20 Sqn in India in 1932. Today, two F.2Bs still fly; one in the UK and one in New Zealand. **SDB**

Bristol M.1C Monoplane Scout The only British monoplane fighter to reach production during the Great War. It first flew in July 1916 and was 43kts (50mph) faster than contemporary German monoplanes. However, the institutional mistrust of monoplane aircraft meant only 130 were built. The RAF inherited a handful of M.1Cs in 1918, mostly located at training units in Britain. This faithful replica flies with the Shuttleworth Collection. **SDB**

Founding Fleet

At its inception in 1918 the RAF was equipped with a disparate fleet of aircraft, all of which were inherited from the RFC and RNAS. These consisted of: *Airco DH.4, Airco DH.6, Airco DH.9, Airco DH.10 Amiens, Armstrong Whitworth F.K.8, Avro 504K & N, Blackburn Kangaroo, Bristol F.2B Fighter, Bristol M.1C Monoplane Scout, Fairey Campania, Fairey Hamble Baby, Fairey III, Felixstowe F.2A, Felixstowe F.3, Felixstowe F.5, Handley Page 0/400, Handley Page V/1500, Martinsyde Buzzard, Nieuport Scout, Norman Thompson N.T.2B, Royal Aircraft Factory B.E.12, Royal Aircraft Factory B.E.2, Royal Aircraft Factory F.E.2, Royal Aircraft Factory R.E.8, Royal Aircraft Factory S.E.5A, Short 184, Short 320, Short Shirl, Sopwith 1½ Strutter, Sopwith Camel, Sopwith Cuckoo, Sopwith Dragon, Sopwith Pup, Sopwith Salamander, Sopwith Snipe, SPAD S.XIII, Vickers Vimy*

5

policing the British Empire from the air.

Chief of the Air Staff, Sir Hugh Trenchard, argued that airpower would be a more cost-effective way of controlling large areas than using land forces. His theories were put into practice in 1920 when the RAF aided ground units to defeat rebel Somaliland dervishes.

With its first success on the board the RAF was given responsibility for all British forces in Iraq in 1921, with the task of 'policing' the tribal unrest. RAF airmen would also see service in Afghanistan in 1925 and 1928.

A series of newer, more capable, aircraft would join the force over the decades to come, but these were ordered in ever smaller numbers.

Naval Aviation

The creation of the independent RAF in 1918 effectively took away control of maritime aviation from the Royal Navy. Although the aircraft and personnel now fell under the control of the RAF, the Admiralty retained responsibility for aircraft carriers.

Trenchard famously argued that "air is one and indivisible" and naval aviation was therefore properly the responsibility of the RAF. Needless to say, the Admiralty took the opposite view and lobbied hard for the return of naval aviation to their control.

Six years after it was formed, the RAF created the 'Fleet Air Arm of the Royal Air Force' (FAA) on April 1, 1924. It still consisted of RAF units

6

1918

Fairey Campania A reconnaissance and patrol aircraft that was the first aeroplane created specifically for carrier operations. It was designed to fly from the deck of the Campania (a converted liner) and for take-off, the aircraft used jettisonable, wheeled 'bogies' fitted to the floats. It could also take off from water when needed. It then landed on water and was hoisted back onto deck. In total, 62 were built but the last retired in 1919.

Fairey Hamble Baby Fairey licence-built Sopwith Baby floatplanes but in October 1916 it began modifying the type with its own improvements. This included hinging the entire trailing edge of each wing along the rear spar, which could be lowered to create extra lift. The aircraft was named the Fairey Hamble Baby and boasted longer wings, a new fin and modified floats. The last 72 of 180 built were built with wheeled undercarriage.

Fairey III Designed in 1917 to meet an RNAS specification, the Fairey III was powered by a 260hp Sunbeam Maori. It was ordered in both floatplane and wheeled versions as the Fairey IIIA and IIIB respectively.
In total, 50 IIIAs and 28 IIIBs were completed before the Rolls Royce Eagle-powered IIIC was available. This led to the much improved IIID, of which 207 were built for the RAF.

Felixstowe F.2A The Felixstowe flying boats trace their history back to the RNAS' Felixstowe F.1 created by Lt Cmdr John Cyril Porte RN. Working at Felixstowe, Porte created the new aircraft based upon the US-designed Curtiss H-4 but incorporated an advanced hull. The F.2A was based on the larger H-12 and was used as a patrol aircraft over the North Sea until the end of the war.

Felixstowe F.3 Larger and heavier than the F.2A, the RAF received around 100 F.3s. They had greater range and a heavier bomb load, but poorer agility. The F.3 was used extensively in the North Sea where they were used to fight German patrol aircraft as well as hunting U-boats and Zeppelins.
The lack of manoevrability compared to the F.2A meant the type was not as popular with its crews.

and airmen, who operated RAF owned aircraft embarked on the decks of Navy ships.

Perhaps as a result of this inter-service rivalry, the FAA was seemingly at the back of the queue when it came to new aircraft. As such, by the late 1930s the service was still equipped with outdated and outmoded airframes such as the Fairey Swordfish biplane.

The Admiralty maintained its campaigning for the return of naval aviation to their control and eventually proved successful, taking responsibility for the administration of the FAA on July 30, 1937. Two years later, on May 24, 1939, the FAA was returned to full Admiralty control and renamed the Air Branch of the Royal Navy.

War on the Horizon

Just two decades after it was formed, the RAF found itself on the brink of war once again. Years of under-investment and poor decision-making left it under-equipped and overstretched.

When it had formed in April 1918 it inherited more than 22,000 aircraft. At the outbreak of World War Two in September 1939 the RAF's operational strength in Europe had diminished to a mere 2,000 aircraft.

This did not bode well for the almost six years of conflict that lay ahead. ■

5. At the end of the war Snipes formed an important part of the British Army of Occupation in Europe and the type was also selected to be the RAF's standard postwar single-seat fighter. **SDB**
6. The RAF was formed by merging the RNAS and RFC in April 1918. In the process it inherited a myriad of types during the chaos of war. **SDB**
7. Where it all began; officers of the RAF's 1 Sqn at Clairmarais near St Omer, France with their S.E.5a aircraft, shortly after the air force had been formed.
8. Among the few surviving Sopwith Pup variants is G-EBKY, preserved in flying condition by the Shuttleworth Collection in Old Warden, Biggleswade, Bedfordshire. Delivered in 1919 as a two-seat Sopwith Dove it was converted to Pup configuration in the 1930s by Richard Shuttleworth. Powered by a Le Rhône 9C rotary engine it is painted in the colours of 9917, which flew with the RNAS aboard HMS *Manxman*. **SDB**

Felixstowe F.5 Developed in a bid to regain the F.2A's manoeuvrability the F.5 was completely redesigned. However, the decision to incorporate as many elements of the F.3 as possible to help reduce costs diluted any benefits. Nonetheless, it became the RAF's standard flying boat. Although it didn't see active service during the war, the last F.5s were retired in 1925 and replaced by Supermarine Southamptons..

Handley Page O/400 A development of the earlier O/100 strategic bomber, the O/400 entered service in April 1918. The type played an important role in the latter days of the conflict and could drop the new 1,650lb (750 kg) bombs on targets in Germany. After the war, O/400s remained in service until the end of 1919. Eight were fitted with VIP interiors to carry officials to Paris to negotiate the Treaty of Versailles.

Handley Page V/1500 A night-flying heavy bomber created to bomb Berlin from East Anglian airfields. The V/1500 entered service with 166 Sqn in October 1918 and the first examples were taxiing out for their debut mission when news was received that the Armistice had been signed. The type later carried out a bombing raid on Kabul during the Third Anglo-Afghan War. V/1500s were eventually replaced by Vimys.

Martinsyde Buzzard Developed as a fast and powerful fighter, but the end of the war meant less than 400 were produced. Although originally powered by a Rolls Royce Falcon engine these were needed for Bristol F.2 Fighters, so the Buzzard was re-engined with the 300hp Hispano-Suiza 8. The RAF received 57 Buzzards before the end of the war, but these did not reach operational squadrons.

Nieuport Scout This sesquiplane fighter entered French service in March 1916 and demonstrated outstanding manoeuvrability and an excellent rate of climb. Considered one of the best fighters of the war it was used by many operators and entered service with every Allied power; including the RFC and RNAS. A few transferred to the RAF and remained in service in Palestine until July 1918.

Advanced Fighters of the Roaring 20s

Two aircraft epitomise the advancing technology and performance of the 1920s RAF more than any other; the Gloster Grebe and the Armstrong Whitworth Siskin

The Armstrong Whitworth Siskin (a siskin being a smallish yellow-tinged finch) was one of the earliest aircraft designed specifically for the RAF (as opposed to an aircraft it inherited from the RFC). It was also the air arm's first 'all-metal' fighter and proved so capable that it would see service into the 1930s. Famed for its aerobatic prowess, the Siskin perfectly sums up the seemingly carefree era of flying in aviation's 'Golden Years'.

The design of the Siskin can be traced back to 1919 when the RAF issued 'Air Ministry Specification Type 1' calling for a single-seat fighter to utilise the newly developed 320hp ABC Dragonfly radial engine.

Maj F M Green, formerly of the Royal Aircraft Factory but now working for the Siddeley-Deasy Motor Car Company, created the S.R.2 Siskin to meet this specification and the all-wooden machine flew for the first time in May 1919. It proved to be a high performing aircraft but the Dragonfly engine was both temperamental and unreliable. It also was also lackin in power so the 325hp Armstrong Siddeley Jaguar was selected to replace it as the Siskin's powerplant.

The new combination – dubbed the Siskin II – took to the air on March 20, 1921, by which time Siddeley-Deasy had merged with the Armstrong Whitworth firm.

1

All-Metal

By now the British Air Ministry had become concerned that another war could quickly deplete its stocks of wood, so a decision was made to concentrate on all-metal aircraft. As such, the Siskin was redesigned in 1923 to incorporate an all-metal aluminium alloy frame. The new Siskin III first flew on May 7 of that year and the RAF ordered six for evaluation.

By the beginning of 1924 the type was showing great promise and the RAF ordered an initial production run of 64 airframes – these becoming the air arm's first all-metal fighter when they entered service with 41 Sqn at RAF Northolt near London in May 1924.

The new fighter boasted a top speed of 136kts (156mph), a range of 280 miles (450km) and a service ceiling of 27,000ft (8,230m). After an initial rate of climb of 2,953ft/min the definitive Siskin IIIA (powered by a 385hp Armstrong Siddeley Jaguar IV) could reach 10,000ft (3,048m) in just over seven minutes.

Siskins were also flown by Nos 1, 17, 19, 23, 24, 25, 29, 32, 43, 54, 56 and 111 Sqns and served until 1932 when the last examples were retired and replaced by the Bristol Bulldog.

Grouse to Grebe

Whereas the majority of the RAF's first generation of biplane fighters utilised upper and lower wings that were generally of similar size and configuration it was Gloster Aircraft Company Chief Designer Henry Folland who first demonstrated an alternative.

The Armstrong Siddeley Jaguar engine was not only unreliable but also prone to catching fire

Folland realised that by using a thick upper wing – to create high levels of lift – teamed with a thinner, medium lift lower wing he could create an aircraft that combined the advantages of the low drag monoplane with those of a high lift biplane.

1918

Norman Thompson N.T.2B The RNAS' standard single-engined flying boat trainer was powered by a 160hp Beardmore engine in a pusher configuration. The pupil and instructor sat side by side . The type entered service in July 1917 and the RAF inherited 79 ex-RNAS examples in 1918. They were flown from Felixstowe, Calshot and Lee on Solent. After the war they were sold to friendly overseas nations.

Royal Aircraft Factory B.E.2 Early versions of the B.E.2 entered RFC service as a reconnaissance aircraft in 1912 but constant development meant it remained operational throughout the war in the 'recce', bomber and night fighter roles. From the B.E.2c variant on it had been adapted to be 'inherently stable', making it ideal for aerial photography. This stability came at the cost of manoeuvrability. The final examples were retired by 1919. **SDB**

Royal Aircraft Factory B.E.12 Essentially a B.E.2c with the front cockpit replaced by a large fuel tank, the B.E.12 also had a 150hp RAF 4a engine in place of the earlier aircraft's 90hp RAF 1 powerplant. Later B.E.12b versions had a 200hp Hispano Suiza powerplant and a small number remained in service long enough to join the RAF's 37, 75, 76 and 77 Home Defence Squadrons. This example was downed in Bulgaria in October 1917..

Royal Aircraft Factory F.E.2 Introduced as a two-seat fighter in late 1915 the 'Fee' was made obsolete by the introduction of more modern German fighters by the end of 1916. It was re-tasked as a night-fighter with home defence squadrons on anti-Zeppelin patrols and F.E.2s were also used as night bombers. The RAF inherited seven squadrons of them in 1918 but these were retired by March 1919.

Royal Aircraft Factory R.E.8 The two-seat reconnaissance and bomber aircraft replaced the B.E.2 and became the standard British reconnaissance and artillery observation aircraft from mid-1917 to the end of the war. More than 4,000 were produced and saw service in Europe as well as Italy, Mesopotamia, Palestine and Russia. By November 1918, the R.E.8 was regarded as obsolete and it was quickly retired after the Armistice.

2

3

RAF Fast Fact

Two Gloster Grebes were modified for suspension beneath the R33 airship on a 'trapeze'. These were used to trial the 'parasite' fighter concept where an airship would carry its own defensive fighters.

1. A trio of Armstrong Whitworth Siskin IIIAs of 43 Sqn, aloft from their base at RAF Tangmere, Sussex in 1930.
2. A member of groundcrew assists the pilot of this Siskin as he boards for a sortie.
3. Siskin J7147 of 41 Sqn. This aircraft was lost on October 9, 1924 when it dived into the ground during a formation loop at RAF Netheravon - killing Sgt Harold George-Taylor.
4. A pair of Gloster Grebe II from 25 Sqn taking off from their base at Hawkinge.
5. The Gloster Grebe II prototype J6970 at Martlesham Heath, Suffolk in 1923.

4

5

He demonstrated the new configuration to great effect on his one-off Gloster Grouse II, which proved the wings would create high levels of lift for take-off but low drag at a higher cruise speed. The Grouse was a modified version of the Gloster Nighthawk, which was itself a derivative of the RFC's Nieuport fighters used during the 1914-1918 Great War.

Impressed by what they saw, officials at the British Air Ministry ordered three prototypes – to be called the Nighthawk (Thick Winged). Based on the Grouse II, these would be fitted with more powerful 350hp Armstrong Siddeley Jaguar III engines. After successful performances during trials at RAF Martlesham Heath, Suffolk the Ministry went on to order the new fighter – by now called the Grebe and powered by a 400hp version of the Jaguar powerplant. The RAF would go on to receive 108 Grebe fighters and an additional 21 two-seat training variants.

All of a Flutter

The Grebe entered service with 111 Sqn in October 1923, replacing the Sopwith Snipe. The type immediately proved popular with pilots as it was faster and more agile than the Snipe, but early versions suffered a tendency for the outer section of the wing to 'flutter' at high speed. Following trials Gloster came up with a modification to the ailerons and additional v-struts to help brace the outer wing panels. This cured the complaint, although the later Gloster Gamecock would incur similar problems.

Like the Sopwith Snipe it replaced, the Grebe was of fabric-covered wood construction. The fuselage had ash longerons and spruce stringers, while the wings had spruce spars and ribs. Two synchronised .303in Vickers machine guns were mounted on the fuselage top decking.

Another issue experienced was with the Jaguar engine, which was not only unreliable, but also prone to catching fire - particularly problematic given the combustible composition of the airframe itself!

The Grebe would go on to serve with Nos 19. 25, 29, 32, 56 and 111 Sqns in the RAF but the last examples were retired in 1929, less than six years after they entered service – such was the pace of aircraft development. The type was replaced, in part, by the Gloster Gamecock, which in itself was developed from the Grebe. ■

Royal Aircraft Factory S.E.5A The RAF S.E.5A is considered by many to be the 'Spitfire of the Great War.' Designed by Henry Folland, John Kenworthy and Maj Frank Goodden, it was one of the fastest aircraft of the war but was also both stable and manoeuvrable.
The outstanding fighters equipped 22 squadrons of the RAF in April 1918 and remained in frontline use with 18 units until late in 1919. **SDB**

Short Type 184 This two-seat reconnaissance and torpedo bomber seaplane was designed for the RNAS by Horace Short in 1915.
The Type 184 became the first aircraft to sink a ship with a torpedo and nearly 1,000 were built. The Type 184 was still in production at the end of the conflict and postwar RAF duties mostly entailed spotting mines. Most were finally retired in late 1920 but some flew on until 1922.

Short Type 320 Designed to meet an RNAS requirement for a seaplane to carry a Mk IX torpedo. The first examples entered service in April 1917 and it was the most advanced British seaplane of the war - but construction problems delayed its deployment and meant it never launched a torpedo in action. More than 50 transferred to the RAF in April 1918 but the last was retired by October 1919.

Short N.1B Shirl Intended to carry the heavy Mk VIII torpedo from early aircraft carriers, the Shirl entered production too late to see service during the Great War. The first aircraft flew in May 1918 and while it could lift heavier torpedoes than the Sopwith Cuckoo it lacked its agility to escape once the weapon was dropped. Nonetheless, an order for 100 was placed but the German surrender meant just four were delivered.

Sopwith 1½ Strutter When it entered service in 1916 the 'Strutter' was first British two-seat tractor fighter and the first British aircraft with a machine gun synchronised to fire through the propeller. It gained its name because of the mix of long and short cabane struts that supported the top wing. Strutters were obsolete by 1918 but a handful served the RAF as trainers or Home Defence fighters.

From Record Breaker to Flying Ambulance

Vickers' range of twin-engined aircraft served as bombers, transports and even flying ambulances, but are best remembered for their record breaking flights

The Vickers Vimy was developed as a heavy bomber during the latter stages of the Great War. The large aircraft came from the drawing board of Vickers' Chief Designer, Reginald Kirshaw-Pierson, and the prototype first flew on November 30, 1917 - just four months after the project was started.

The aircraft was sent to Martlesham Heath, Suffolk for official service trials in January 1918: it immediately gained the attention of the Air Ministry by lifting a heavier payload than its main competitor, the Handley Page 0/400, despite only having half the power.

Unfortunately for the Vimy, it came too late to see operational service and only three examples were delivered before the Armistice was signed.

Over 1,000 Vimys had been ordered but postwar cutbacks meant only around 230 were actually completed; 147 of these built by Vickers and the remainder by subcontractors including Clayton & Shuttleworth Ltd, the Metropolitan Wagon Co, and the Westland Aircraft Works.

It would be July 1919 before the type finally entered squadron service (with 58 Sqn in Egypt) but Vimys formed the backbone of the RAF's heavy bomber force throughout the '20s.

Pioneers

Perhaps the most significant use of the Vimy was that of establishing long distance air routes. In June 1919 Capt John Alcock and Lt Arthur Whitten-Brown made the first non-stop crossing of the Atlantic Ocean in a Vimy. The same year, the Australian government offered £10,000 for the first all-Australian crew to fly an aeroplane from England to Australia.

Keith and Ross Macpherson-Smith along with mechanics Jim Bennett and Wally Shiers completed the journey from Hounslow, London to Darwin on December 10, 1919. Their aircraft was registered G-EAOU, which some suggested stood for 'God 'Elp All Of Us'!

Vernon

Postwar, Vickers developed a civilian airliner variant of the Vimy which it christened the Vickers Vimy Commercial. More than 50 were made and it also formed the basis for the Vickers Vernon – the RAF's first dedicated troop transport.

Vernons were introduced in 1921 and in February 1923, examples belonging to 45 Sqn and 70 Sqn airlifted nearly 500 troops to Kirkuk, Iraq after the town had been overrun by Kurdish forces. This is thought to have been the first ever strategic airlift of troops.

1

Virginia & Victoria

Such was the pace of development that work on a Vimy replacement began as early as 1920. The resulting Vickers Virginia was broadly similar to its predecessor but was larger and had a greater wingspan. It also had a lowered 'pulpit' in the nose to give the front gunner a better field of view.

The Virginia entered squadron service in 1924 and a total of 124 were delivered in a number of variants. The Mk I to VI had straight wings but the Mk VII had swept outer wing sections. The Mk VII also saw the rear fuselage gunner moved to a purpose built tail turret.

At a time of 45 minutes, the same journey by land would have taken some three days to complete

While the early examples were built from wood and fabric the Mk X had a duralumin and steel structure covered in a mixture of fabric, aluminium and wood.

The Virginia quickly became obsolete as a bomber but the type remained in service until the late 1930s being used for reconnaissance, parachute training and even to develop the techniques needed for aerial refuelling.

1918

Sopwith Camel The replacement for the Pup, the faster and more heavily armed Camel entered service in 1917. A fairing over the gun breeches (designed to stop them freezing) created a 'hump', which led to the Camel name. The RAF gained 33 squadrons but by 1919 just six remained. That year they were deployed during the Russian Civil War but the RAF's Camels had retired by October. This reproduction flies at Old Warden. SDB

Sopwith Cuckoo The first wheeled aeroplane designed specifically for carrier operations; the Sopwith Cuckoo torpedo bomber was completed too late for service in the war. Deliveries began in August 1918 but it was November before 185 Sqn embarked on HMS Argus. A total of 232 were built but the final unit (210 Sqn) disbanded in April 1923 and the Cuckoo was replaced by the Blackburn Dart.

Sopwith Dolphin The Dolphin entered RFC service in early 1918 and despite concerns over its radical 'back stagger' wings (needed to maintain the centre of gravity) it proved to be an impressive fighter. Four new RAF squadrons were equipped with Dolphins but the type was retired after the war. The last RAF unit to operate Dolphins was 79 Sqn, which retired the type in September 1921.

Sopwith Dragon A development of the Snipe, the Dragon was fitted with a 320hp ABC Dragonfly radial engine in place of the earlier rotary powerplant. In November 1918, the RAF changed an order for 300 Sopwith Snipes to Dragons. Almost 200 were built but problems with the engines meant only a handful of powerplants were delivered. The Dragons were therefore placed in storage and never entered service.

Sopwith Pup Almost 1,800 Pups were built as single-seat scouts for the RFC and RNAS from the autumn of 1916. Within a year it had been outclassed by newer German fighters but remaining airframes were relegated to Home Defence and training squadrons. A few of these remained in service long enough to join the fledgling RAF in April 1918 and were mostly used as trainers (or personal runabouts by instructors).

RAF Fast Fact

Some Vimys and Valentias were also fitted with loudspeakers used for 'sky shouting.' This could be used for conveying instructions or propaganda to unruly tribesmen whilst policing the Empire.

1. Vickers Victoria V K2344 showing the swept wings the variant inherited from the Vickers Virginia X.
2. Vickers Valentia K3611 of 216 Sqn is prepared for flight at Tobruk, Libya. The aircraft soldiered on until 1941 when it was lost in an accident at the Haft Khel landing ground in what is now Iran.
3. A 45 Sqn Vickers Vernon transport aircraft is loaded with the body of a fallen serviceman in Iraq in 1921.
4. Vickers Victoria J7924 lumbers back to land at the end of a sortie.

The Virginia bomber was developed in parallel with the Vickers Victoria transport aircraft. The latter mated a fuselage similar to the Vernon with the more advanced wing from the Virginia. The aircraft could house 24 troops on collapsible canvas seats arranged along the sides of the fuselage, and power came from a pair of 450hp Napier Lion engines with large frontal radiators.

Like the later Virginias the Victoria benefited from metal structure; something that proved much more suitable for the hot and humid areas where the Victoria often served. Deliveries began in February 1926, with the aircraft replacing the Vimys of 70 Sqn in Iraq and 216 Sqn in Egypt.

In the winter of 1928-29, a number of Victorias from 70 Sqn helped evacuate diplomatic staff and their dependents from Kabul together with members of the Afghan royal family endangered by a civil war.

A total of 97 Victorias were built and the type served until 1935, although many were later converted into Valentias.

Valentia

By the mid-30s the Napier Lion engines in the RAF's Victoria fleet were tired and in need of overhaul. The decision was therefore made to upgrade the aircraft with more powerful Bristol Pegasus engines. A total of 56 aircraft were so converted; becoming known as the Valentia in the process.

The aircraft was such a success that the RAF ordered 28 new-build Valentias to boost the cargo carrying force.

Compared to the earlier Victoria the Valentia also benefitted from a strengthened airframe and wing, wheel brakes and a tailwheel in place of a tail skid.

The Valentia first entered service with 70 Sqn at Hinaidi, Iraq in 1934 and would also equip British forces in India, Iraq and Persia.

Although they were mostly used as transport aircraft the Valentias could be used for offensive operations with bomb racks under the wings. Some were also fitted with loudspeakers used for 'sky shouting' – to address rebellious tribes during air policing flights.

Air Ambulance

The first recorded air ambulance flight in the world was a Royal Flying Corps Airco DH.9, which flew an injured soldier from the Camel Corps to medical facilities in Turkey in 1917. At a time of 45 minutes, the same journey by land would have taken some three days to complete.

Throughout the 1920s and 30s the Vickers Vimy, Vernon, Victoria and Valentia were used extensively by the RAF as air ambulances, transporting wounded troops to safety.

These paved the way for the world-leading aeromedical service the RAF has provided for more than a century – from the Vimy to today's Boeing C-17 Globemaster III. ■

1919

Sopwith Salamander Based on the Snipe, the Salamander was created 'trench fighting' (ground-attack) missions. It first flew in April 1918 and had an armoured forward fuselage to protect the pilot from ground fire. Although two aircraft arrived in France by October 1918, they did not see service before the Armistice. Only around 210 of the 1,400 airframes ordered were completed and, beset with problems, they were retired.

Sopwith Snipe Created as a replacement for the Camel the first Snipe reached the Western Front in September 1918 and 100 were in service by the end of the war. It would become the RAF's standard postwar single-seat fighter and between 1919 and 1926 Snipes served with around twenty squadrons at home and abroad. At one point the RAF had more than 500 Snipes, although 400 of them were in storage. **SDB**

SPAD S.XIII Developed in France by Société Pour L'Aviation et ses Dérivés (SPAD); S.VII and S.XIII Scouts had been delivered to the RFC while it waited for the first Sopwith Dolphins to arrive. The SPADs proved popular fighters and while they saw limited RAF service on the Western Front the S.VII was used to good effect by 30, 63 and 72 Sqns in Mesopotamia (modern-day Iraq. Kuwait, Syria and Turkey).

Vickers Vimy Had the Great War continued the new breed of heavy bombers, such as the Vimy, would have been used to bomb Germany. The first example flew in November 1917 and while it would not obecome perational until July 1919 the Vimy would become the backbone of the RAF's heavy bomber force throughout the 1920s. Vimys also conducted long-range proving flights, including the first ever transatlantic flight in 1919. **SDB**

Parnall Panther TThe Panther carrier-based reconnaissance aircraft was built by the Bristol Aeroplane Company from 1919. Unusually, the plywood fuselage could be folded for shipboard storage (it was hinged aft of the cockpit). Some 150 were built and they served with Spotter Flights aboard HMS Argus and HMS Hermes. The last examples were replaced by Fairey IIIs in 1926.

Beardmore Inflexible

Big, heavy and underpowered – the all-metal Inflexible tri-motor proved to be far from impressive

The improbable looking Beardmore Inflexible traced its roots back to the equally unusual Rohrbach Ro IV flying boat.

German-born Dr Adolf Rohrbach worked for the Zeppelin-Staaken company during the Great War and set up Rohrbach Metall-Flugzeugbau in 1922 to design and build all-metal stressed skin aircraft.

In order to evade the restrictions of the Treaty of Versailles (which prevented Germany developing warplanes), Rohrbach set up a Danish subsidiary to assemble aircraft. In turn, his designs came to the attention of Scottish shipbuilders William Beardmore and Co and in 1924 they signed a licencing agreement to produce the Ro IV flying boat as the Beardmore ReBo.2 Inverness.

The twin-engined aeroplane was unusual not just because of its all-metal (duralumin) construction but also because it incorporated a mast and sails for use in case of engine failure or running out of fuel!

Two almost identical prototypes were built, however testing in 1925 showed the aircraft to have poor handling both in the water and in the air; therefore the project was cancelled.

Inflexible

Undeterred by the flying boat's failings, William Beardmore and Co saw potential in the stressed skin construction methods pioneered by Rohrbach. Having acquired the licence for the technology the team at its Dalmuir factory in Scotland used plans for the Rohrbach Ro VI landplane to create a massive all-metal three-engined transport aircraft, which it christened the Beardmore Inflexible.

Unusually, in addition to being constructed of metal it was also designed as a mid-wing monoplane – this at a time when most large aircraft were still wood and fabric biplanes.

The aircraft was built in sections and sent by sea from Scotland to Felixstowe, from where they were then transported by road to the Aeroplane & Armament Experimental Establishment (A&AEE) at Martlesham Heath, Suffolk for assembly.

Following final assembly the Inflexible performed its maiden flight on March 5, 1928 and demonstrated generally good handling qualities. Power came from three 650hp Rolls-Royce Condor II engines, but even these struggled to overcome the aircraft's all-up weight of 37,000lbs (16,783kg). Prior to the flight, concern had been expressed about the aircraft's available power and it was decided to extend the runway by 400 yards (366m) before allowing testing to begin. As it happened the aircraft was airborne well within the space available and the flight passed without incident – although the climb rate and cruise speed left a lot to be desired.

However, with a top speed of just 95kts (109mph) the aircraft was next to useless as a transport aircraft and with no formal interest from the Air Ministry the prototype was dismantled in 1930. Nevertheless, it still had an important role to play as its decay was carefully monitored to investigate the effects of corrosion on light-alloy stressed skin structures. ■

1. The Inflexible was a behemoth. With a staggering span of 157ft 6in it was 15ft wider than a Boeing B-29.
2. All that remains of the Inflexible is one wheel; exhibited at the Science Museum, London.
3. The one-off Beardmore Inverness proved unstable both in the air and on the water.

1920 **1921** **1922**

Nieuport Nighthawk Developed by Nieuport & General towards the end of the Great War, the Nighthawk was to see only limited RAF service due to unreliability of its ABC Dragonfly engine – which got so hot they sometimes charred the propellers! Created as a Snipe replacement, the new fighter was eventually re-engined with the Armstrong Siddeley Jaguar or Bristol Jupiter powerplants.

de Havilland DH.29 Doncaster The Doncaster was ordered by the RAF as an experimental long-range monoplane. Built of wood and fabric, the two-seat aircraft had a 54ft span wing and a 450hp Napier Lion IB engine.
The two DH.29 Doncasters built proved useful test and trials aircraft for the RAF, particularly in the field of thick-section cantilever wings.

Westland Walrus Created as a cost-effective three-seat reconnaissance aircraft and built from surplus DH.9A parts. An observer's position was fitted and a ventral panier also allowed the observer to view downwards. Arrestor gear was also provided. The first joined 3 Sqn in 1921 and the type served in the Fleet spotting role until 1925 when it was replaced by the Avro Bison.

Avro Bison The carrier-based spotting aircraft had a distinctively 'tubby' fuselage constructed of steel tube. The pilot sat in an open cockpit forward of the wings while an enclosed cabin was provided for the navigator and radio operator. There was a cockpit for a Lewis gunner in the rear fuselage. The first of 55 joined the RAF in 1922 and the type remained in service until 1929.

Bristol Bullfinch Designed as a parasol-wing monoplane fighter, which was convertible to a two-seat biplane. This meant it met the RAF's requirements for both a single-seat interceptor fighter and a two-seat reconnaissance-fighter. The Bullfinch flew in monoplane form on November 6, 1922. Three were built but the two-seater was overweight and the project was abandoned. and the project

Water Birds

The interwar RAF maintained a sizeable fleet of flying boats and seaplanes, paving the way for their extensive use by Coastal Command during World War Two

The RAF had experimented with flying boats during the Great War but it was during the 1920s when they really came to the fore.

More than 70% of the planet is covered by water, so an aircraft that could operate from lakes and seas gave tremendous flexibility; especially when the RAF was involved in policing the far-flung extremes of the Empire.

The first RAF flying boat to be designed after the Great War was the Supermarine Southampton, which was notable for the very fact that it went on to serve for over a decade.

Designed by Reginald J Mitchell, the aircraft was based on the civilian Supermarine Swan, which had been evaluated by the Air Ministry in 1924.

The Southampton was a biplane powered by a pair of Napier Lion engines. The aircraft had triple fins and rudders, and early Mk I examples had wooden hulls. Using a metal hull on the Mk II reduced weight and, combined with improved engines, gave the Mk II a range of more than 500 miles (805km).

The Southampton entered RAF service in August 1925 and conducted various long-distance flights; the most famous of which lasted for over a year and saw four aircraft travel 27,000 miles (43,451km) to circumnavigate Australia as well as visit Hong Kong, Indo-China and Burma before ending the journey in (appropriately) Singapore.

Other large RAF flying boats – of varying degrees of success – included the Blackburn Perth and Iris, Short Singapore and Rangoon, and the Supermarine Scapa and Stranraer.

'Shagbat'

Supermarine also produced the single-engined Walrus, which would be the mainstay of RAF Coastal Command's air-sea rescue fleet for the majority of the war.

It was created as a single-engined amphibian that was capable of being catapulted from warships and was initially designed by Supermarine as a private venture project.

Affectionately known as the 'Shagbat' to those who flew it or were rescued by it, the Walrus first flew in 1933. Most of the airframe was made from metal as experience had shown that wooden structures deteriorated rapidly under tropical conditions. The wings could be folded, giving the machine a stowage width of just 17ft 6in (5.33m), and power came from a 750hp Bristol Pegasus II radial engine that was mounted in the 'pusher' configuration.

Supermarine had built 285 by the time the factory began concentrating on Spitfires and flying boat production moved to Saunders-Roe. Most of the early airframes were delivered to the FAA and it was not until 1941 that the type entered RAF service as an air-sea rescue aircraft.

By the end of the war Walruses had rescued over a thousand downed aircrew, with 277 Sqn alone responsible for 598 of these. A more powerful replacement, the Supermarine Sea Otter, was introduced from 1942 – but the Walrus soldiered on and it would be April 1946 before the last example was finally retired. ■

1. Supermarine Walrus I K5783 was built as part of the first production batch. It was operated by 720 Sqn, New Zealand Division and embarked on HMS *Achilles* but was lost on July 15, 1939 when it slipped from the crane while being recovered aboard the ship after a flight. It sank in 300 fathoms of water but the crew, Pilot Lt Sykes and Telegraphist Lt Trent were uninjured. ***State Library of Victoria***

2. A pair of Southampton flying boats from 210 Sqn. The unit operated the type until 1936 when they swapped them for Saro Londons. In 1939, these were swapped for Supermarine Stranraers but by April 1940 the squadron was operational on the Short Sunderland. It operated the big flying boats until it finally disbanded in February 1957.

1922

de Havilland DH.27 Derby Designed as a long-range heavy bomber. It was a large, single-engined biplane, with wings that lacked both sweep and stagger. It was mostly built of wood and power came from a 650hp Rolls-Royce Condor III driving a four-bladed propeller. Two were built but the Air Ministry awarded the contract to the Avro Aldershot, which had an internal bomb bay.

Gloster (Nieuport) Nightjar When Nieuport closed down the rights to the Nighthawk were purchased by Gloster, which produced the Nightjar shipborne variant. Some 22 surplus Nighthawks were fitted with Bentley BR2 rotary engines and arrestor gear and served with 203 Sqn from 1922 to 1924.

Vickers Vernon The Vernon biplane [see also p12] was the RAF's first dedicated troop carrier and the first of 55 entered service in 1921. It was a development of the Vickers Vimy Commercial (itself a passenger variant of the Vimy bomber) and was powered by either Napier Lion or Rolls-Royce Eagle VIII engines.

1923

Blackburn Blackburn A carrier-based reconnaissance and gun spotting aircraft that used the wing and tail surfaces of the Dart bomber. The first of 44 was delivered to the RAF in April 1923. Some Blackburns were used as dual-control trainers but all were obsolete by 1931, when they were replaced by the Fairey IIIF.

Blackburn Dart A carrier-based torpedo bomber that was a development of the unsuccessful Blackburn Swift. It had a wide track undercarriage that allowed a torpedo to be carried below the fuselage. It entered service in 1923 and would be the standard single-seat torpedo bomber until 1933.

Fairey's Long Range Monoplane

The Long Range Monoplane was designed to be as simple as possible. So much so; if you ask a child to draw an aeroplane there's a chance it would look something like this!

When an RAF crew flying Hawker Horsley bombers failed to break the long-held absolute distance world record for the third time the Air Ministry issued Specification 33/27 in December 1927.

This called for a machine designed not just for a specific record, but as a serious research aircraft aimed at increasing the range of all aeroplanes. To help get the funding approved by government the specification was also claimed to be for a future postal aircraft.

Fairey answered the requirement with a simple single-engined monoplane. The wood and fabric wing was mounted high so that fuel could be stored within it and gravity-fed to the lower fuel tanks. The aircraft had a total fuel capacity of 1,043 Imp Gal (4,742 lit) and other concessions to long-range operations included a pair of parallel oil filter circuits (allowing one filter to be removed and cleaned while the other remained in use) and even a pneumatic bed for the reserve pilot to sleep in between 'shifts'.

Power came from a 570hp Napier Lion XIA engine, which was tested in both a Fairey IIIF and Airco DH.9A before being mounted onto the prototype (J9479) in mid 1928.

1. The Fairey Long Range Monoplane would ultimately earn Great Britain the absolute world long distance record by flying from England to South Africa non-stop.

Tests & Trials

Named simply as the Fairey Long Range Monoplane, the aircraft performed its maiden flight on November 14, 1928 from RAF Northolt near London and immediately began testing and trials work for the RAF. These would soon include a number of flights in excess of 24 hours in duration.

The aircraft's first long-distance sortie was from England to India and on April 24, 1929, Sqn Ldr Jones-Williams and Flt Lt Jenkins departed RAF Cranwell, Lincolnshire. They landed in Karachi after and incredible 50 hours and 48 minutes in the air.

It was the first non-stop flight between the two countries but the distance of 4,130 miles (6,646km) was short of the world record, which had recently been increased to 4,912 miles (8,007km) by the French.

Tragedy Strikes

It was therefore decided to make an attempt at a non-stop flight from England to South Africa and the aircraft departed on December 16 with the same crew aboard.

Unfortunately, the aircraft struck the ground south of Tunis in bad weather and was destroyed. The crew were killed in the impact. The aircraft's log was recovered from the wreckage and at 6pm the crew had logged an altitude of 5,000ft (1,524m). However, the aircraft struck a hill that was just 2,300ft (701m) above sea level. The onboard barographs showed the aircraft was actually lower than 3,000ft (914m) at 6pm so either the crew had entered the wrong figure in their log, the altimeter had failed or the crew had become confused and believed they were higher than they were.

Undeterred, the Air Ministry ordered a second airframe (K1991) and this flew on June 30, 1931. It differed from the first aircraft in a number of ways, most notably the addition of an autopilot and wheel spats.

Between February 6-8, 1932, K1991 was flown by Sqn Ldr OR Gayford (the officer in charge of the RAF Long Range Development Unit) and Flt Lt GE Nicholetts non-stop from Cranwell to Walvis Bay, South West Africa. This was a world distance record of 5,410 miles (8,540km). On its return to England the aircraft was deemed surplus and, sadly, unceremoniously scrapped. ■

RAF Fast Fact

The Fairey Long Range Monoplane was one of the first aircraft to be fitted with a bed for crew to sleep in mid-flight.

1923

de Havilland DH.42 Dingo The DH.42 Dormouse and Dingo were almost identical, wooden, two-seat biplanes designed for fighter-recce and army cooperation roles respectively. The Dormouse had a 360hp ASJaguar II and the Dingo had a 410hp Bristol Jupiter . Both were written off during trials and the project halted.

Fairey Flycatcher Designed as a carrier and floatplane fighter to replace the Nightjar. Powered by a Bristol Jupiter engine, the Flycatcher had flaps along the entire trailing edges of both wings. These reduced the landing and to just 50 yards. Some 192 were built and the type was flown from all British carriers of the day both at home, in the Mediterranean, East Indies and China Seas.

Gloster Grebe The Grebe [see also p10] was the RAF's first all-new interwar fighter. The prototype flew in May 1923 and the type began replacing Snipes from October. It was popular with pilots but prone to wing flutter, which led to additional struts being fitted to support the upper wing. The RAF received 108 Grebe fighters and 21 trainers. The last examples were retired in 1929.

Parnall Plover Designed by Harold Bolas to meet the RAF's specification for a replacement for the Nightjar. The Plover was a conventional wood-and-fabric biplane but was fitted with full-span flaps and could operate from either wheels or amphibious floats. Although 13 Plovers were ordered in 1923, these were retired in favour of Fairey Flycatchers when the FAA took over naval flying a year later.

Short Springbok An experimental all-metal reconnaissance biplane. Developed from the 1920 Short Silver Streak – which was the first British all-metal aeroplane. It first flew in April 1923 and was truly 'all metal' with a duralumin fuselage and metal skinned wings. This made it heavy so the Springbok II had fabric-covered wings. Six were built but none entered service.

Bristol's High Flying Monoplane

The one-of-a-kind Bristol 138 set a number of altitude records and played a vital part in developing the RAF's high altitude capabilities

The Bristol Type 138 came about during a period of intense rivalry between nations and the aircraft manufacturers themselves.

There was both international prestige and commercial success at stake for the aircraft that could fly the furthest, the fastest or the highest. In the case of the Bristol 138 the world altitude record was the sole goal.

However, by the 1930s it was becoming obvious that the resources needed to establish ever greater records were fast becoming out of the reach of independent manufacturers – and the Bristol Aeroplane Company realised they would need government support if they were to fulfil their dream.

Between 1929 and 1934, there were a number of altitude records established by rival aircraft from Germany, Italy and the USA as well as the first flight over Everest by a pair of Westland Wallaces in 1933. However, it was not lost on the Air Ministry that all of these aircraft had been powered by Bristol-produced or Bristol-designed engines.

Government Backing

So it was, in November 1933, that Bristol's designer Frank Barnwell proposed a purpose-built high-altitude research aircraft. He had observed the interest the British Air Ministry had shown in the successful Everest flight and seized the moment.

Barnwell's Type 138 was a large single-engine, single-seat monoplane, equipped with a supercharged Bristol Pegasus engine. Although interest was initially considered 'lukewarm', the men at the Ministry really began to take notice when Italian pilot Renato Donati achieved a new world altitude record in April 1934.

With public opinion swinging in favour of a government-sponsored record attempt by a British team the Air Ministry issued Specification 2/34 in June 1934: calling for an aircraft capable of achieving the hitherto unreached altitude of 50,000ft (15,030m).

1. With a 66ft wingspan the Bristol 138 was one of the largest single-engined aircraft in the world when it first flew in 1936.

In order to cope with the extreme altitudes flown at, the pilot was provided with a revolutionary pressure suit made of rubberised fabric. Coupled with a helmet and closed-circuit breathing apparatus this enabled the pilot to withstand the lack of oxygen at height.

The Type 138 was powered by a Bristol Pegasus engine which featured a high performance two-stage supercharger, a critical component to provide power at such extremely high altitude.

Record Breaker

Built of wood to minimise weight the Bristol Type 138A (K4897) performed its maiden flight on May 11, 1936 with test pilot Cyril Unwins at the helm.

The aircraft then passed to the Royal Aircraft Establishment (RAE) for high altitude testing and on its very first trial, on September 28, it achieved a new record of 49,967ft (15,230m).

However, the pilot (Sqn Ldr Swann) suffered from oxygen deprivation when supplies ran low on the two-hour flight. He had to break the window of his pressure helmet after descending to a safe height.

After modifications to reduce weight and improve the pressurisation system, the aircraft then returned to 50,000ft (15,240m) on six further occasions.

In early 1937 Italy recaptured the record so, on June 30, the Bristol 138 was flown again and increased the record to 53,937ft (16,440m). However, the flight nearly ended in disaster when the canopy cracked.

The pilot, Flt Lt Adams, only survived by virtue of his specially adapted suit and helmet.

Further research flights were flown but there were no more record attempts. The Bristol 138 programme had gathered invaluable flight data and led to the future of pressurised aircraft. ■

RAF Fast Fact

Between 1928 and 1938, the altitude record was broken ten times; six of them by aircraft using Bristol engines.

1924

Supermarine Sea Lion II Developed in 1922 for that Schneider Trophy, the Sea Lion II flying boat was as a modified version of its Sea King II amphibious fighter with a 450hp Napier Lion 'pusher' engine. It won the race and in 1923 was passed to the RAF and re-engined with a 550hp Napier Lion. That year it came third behind American Curtiss CR-3s but would be retained as a hack.

Armstrong Whitworth Siskin The Siskin [see also p10] was another fighter aircraft designed around the promising Dragonfly engine. It first flew in May 1919 but the engine was so disappointing that it would be 1924 before the RAF ordered the Siskin, by which time it had an AS Jaguar engine and an all-metal airframe. Siskins were used by eleven squadrons until replaced by the Bulldog in 1932.

Avro Aldershot Designed as a long-range day and night bomber with a range of 500 miles and a bombload of 2,000lbs. The RAF ordered 15 for use with 99 Sqn and the first entered service in July 1924. In 1925 the Air Ministry decided that heavy bombers needed multiple engines, so the Aldershot was unceremoniously retired by the RAF by March of 1926.

Avro Andover The Andover used the biplane wings, undercarriage and tail of the Aldershot bomber combined with a new fuselage and large over-wing fuel tanks. This created a cabin which could hold twelve passengers or six stretchers. Four were built; three used as flying ambulances and one as a transporter – all based at St Mary's RAF Hospital at RAF Halton.

de Havilland DH.53 Hummingbird Created for the *Daily Mail* Light Aeroplane Competition of 1923 and powered by a Douglas 750cc motorcycle engine. The RAF ordered eight in 1924 as training aircraft. Two were used for 'parasite aircraft' trials; being launched and retrieved from an airship by means of a pylon that hooked onto a trapeze lowered from the airship.

On Silver Wings

Like flying Art Deco sculptures, the stylish Hawker biplane fighters and bombers epitomise the glamourous 1930s

The analogy that "if it looks right, it'll probably fly right" can apply to a number of aircraft in the RAF's history and is often used when discussing the Hawker Hunter jet fighter of the 1950s. However, it is equally as apt for a much earlier range of Hawker designs.

The Hawker Fury is, perhaps, one of the prettiest aircraft ever to fly in RAF markings. It was also the first operational RAF fighter to exceed 175kts (200mph) and its perfectly harmonised controls made it the ideal aerobatic platform. It stole the hearts not just of pilots, who loved its handling and performance, but the British public with its regular display appearances at airshows.

The Fury actually began life as the Hawker Hornet; itself a development of the company's F.20/27 prototype fighter. The Hornet performed its maiden flight at Brooklands, Surrey in March 1929 but soon its 420hp Rolls Royce F.XIC engine was replaced by a 480hp Kestrel.

Following evaluation by the Air Ministry the type was ordered for the RAF, although the service insisted on a name change to something more 'ferocious' – thus the Fury was born.

The prototype Fury I flew from Brooklands with chief test pilot George Bulman at the controls on March 25, 1931 and the first examples entered service with 43 Sqn in May of the same year. The production aircraft were powered by a 525hp Kestrel II but later Fury II airframes benefited from the 640hp Kestrel VI.

A total of six squadrons were equipped with the Fury and they remained on strength with Fighter Command until January 1939.

Hart

The Fury was not Hawker's first glamourous biplane of the era, however. In 1926 the RAF issued a requirement for a new all-metal, two-seat high-performance light day-bomber.

In response, Hawker designed a single-bay biplane powered by the Rolls-Royce Kestrel. They called the new aircraft the Hart and the prototype (J9052) first flew in June 1928. During testing it demonstrated good handling and could reach 153kts (176mph) in level flight. The Hart competed with the de Havilland Hound, Fairey Fox IIM and Avro Antelope and, upon finding it was cheaper to operate, an order for the first of 992 to be delivered to the RAF was placed in the summer of 1929. The Hart would become the most widely used light bomber of its time and the design proved so adaptable that it spawned an entire range of 'spin-offs'.

The Fury had perfectly harmonised controls, which made it the ideal aerobatic platform

Harts entered service with 33 Sqn in 1931 and the type was deployed to the Middle East during the Abyssinia Crisis of 1935–1936. Examples also saw service on the North-West Frontier of British India during the inter-war period and some aircraft flew on as late as 1943 in communications and training roles until being declared obsolete in 1943.

Audax & Hardy

The Hawker Audax was derived from the Hart but specialised for army co-operation duties with a hook below the fuselage to pick up messages. Over 700 Audaxes were produced and some examples saw service during World War Two; notably in Africa where the Audax flew against Italian troops on the Kenya–Abyssinia border. Some airframes were modified to carry a 250lb bomb during the Anglo-Iraqi War of 1941.

The Hardy was a general-purpose variant of the Hart and was 'tropicalised' for use in the Middle East. The prototype was simply a production Hart that had been modified with a bigger radiator, a message pick-up hook, water containers and a desert survival kit.

Demon & Hind

The Demon was developed as an interim fighter variant of the Hart bomber. While it did not boast the performance of the Fury the two-seat Hind was available in larger numbers and provided fighter cover until more modern successors could be developed. Armament was a single .303in Lewis Gun in the rear and two fixed .303in Vickers guns in the nose. A total of 232 Demons were built for the RAF.

1924

Fairey Fawn A light day-bomber and army cooperation aircraft designed as a replacement for the DH.9A. Fawns entered service with 12 Sqn in March 1924 and also flew with 11 and 100 Sqns. It would only serve on the frontline for two years before being replaced by the Hawker Horsley and the Fairey Fox. Royal Auxiliary Air Force squadrons would retain the type until 1929.

Handley Page Hendon Created as a two-seat torpedo bomber, the Hendon lost out to the Blackburn Dart. However, the RAF ordered six examples as test and evaluation machines. These were used to investigate various configurations of leading edge slots/slats and how they affected slow flight. It was found that a 'slotted and slatted' Hendon could land on a carrier without using arrestor gear.

Vickers Virginia The Virginia [see also p12] was created a replacement for the Vimy. It was very similar but had a lowered front gunner's 'pulpit', a greater wingspan and a longer fuselage. The Mks I-VI had straight wings and the Mk VII introduced swept outer wings. Some 124 Virginias were built, of which 50 were metal built Mk Xs. Virginias served from 1924 to 1938.

1925

Bristol Beaver Envisaged as an army co-operation aircraft to replace the Bristol F2B, the Bristol Boarhound first flew in 1925. It lost out to the Armstrong Whitworth Atlas but in 1928 Bristol modified it into the prototype Beaver, which was allocated an RAF identity and competed with various types to replace the DH.9A. In this case it lost out to the Westland Wapiti.

Fairey Ferret Designed to meet an FAA need for a reconnaissance aircraft, the Ferret was Fairey's first all-metal design. It failed to interest the FAA so attention turned to the RAF, with whom it was touted as a general-purpose biplane. Three examples of the Ferret were built and although they performed well in trials the RAF also failed to order the type into production.

1. The Fury was considered by many pilots to be a sportscar of the skies. Only one example survives today; K5674 was delivered to 43 Sqn the RAF in 1935 and following restoration it flew again in July 2012. **SDB**
2. Hawker Hart K2467 of 57 Sqn's C Flight aloft in the 1930s.
3. The sole surviving airworthy Demon is K8203. The aircraft was initially assigned to 64 Sqn, whose livery the restored aircraft now wears. It is now based at the Shuttleworth Collection. **SDB**
4. The Shuttleworth Collection's Hind was one of 20 delivered to the Afghan Air Force in 1938. In 1968, it was donated to the collection and after an epic road journey from Kabul it was restored to flying condition. **SDB**
5. Hardy K4308 from 6 Sqn at RAF Ramleh in Palestine in the late 1930s. The aircraft was destroyed in Sudan in 1940 during an air raid.

RAF Fast Fact

The basic Hawker design can be traced from the Fury biplane to the World War Two Hurricane and even the post-war Tempest - such was the success of Sydney Camm's design.

The Hind was conceived as a replacement for the Hart but was based on the earlier type; the main difference being a larger Kestrel V engine and the inclusion of the cut-down rear cockpit that had been developed for the Demon.

Hinds entered service in November 1935 and would eventually equip 20 RAF bomber squadrons. However, by 1937 the Hind was being phased out of frontline service and being replaced by monoplanes such as the Fairey Battle and Bristol Blenheim. Surplus Hinds were then used as intermediate training aircraft, providing students with experience in aircraft more advanced than the Tiger Moth.

Osprey & Nimrod

The Hart family also went to sea, with the Osprey being a navalised carrier-borne version of aircraft that could be used in both fighter and reconnaissance roles.

It entered service in 1932 and 103 served with the Fleet Air Arm of the RAF. In late 1936, Ospreys of 701 Sqn were deployed to RAF Kalafrana, Malta in an anti-submarine and anti-piracy role.

The single-seat Fury was also adapted for use by the Navy, albeit indirectly. The Air Ministry wanted a replacement for the ageing Fairey Flycatcher fleet and Hawker's designer Sydney Camm was approached to adapt his radial-engined Hoopoe biplane for the contract. However, Camm had been so impressed with the Kestrel V-12 engine in his Fury design that he recommended the Ministry opted for that powerplant instead.

The new fighter flew in early 1930 and was christened the Norn, but upon receiving a production contract it was renamed the Nimrod.

The Nimrod was very similar to the Fury but had a cross-axle type undercarriage with trailing struts and compression legs to absorb the impact of carrier landings. A headrest was also added to ease pilot neck strain during catapult launches and the entire airframe was anodised to help supress corrosion.

The first production Nimrods entered service with 408 Flight embarked on HMS *Glorious* in 1932 but the type was ultimately replaced by more modern designs before the start of World War Two.In 1933 Camm designed a monoplane version of his Fury. The aircraft was not developed until Rolls-Royce began producing its famous Merlin engine, by which time the Fury monoplane was revised and became the prototype Hawker Hurricane .

In recent years a number of Hawker biplanes have returned to flight with examples of the Fury, Nimrod I Nimrod II, Hind and Demon all gracing British skies. ■

Gloster III The Gloster II was created for the 1924 Schneider Trophy but as there were no other competitors, the contest was postponed to 1925. The aircraft was updated to the Gloster III with a 700hp Napier Lion VII and special radiators on the leading edge of the lower wings. Two were built and shipped to the USA. One was damaged during taxi trials and the other finished second.

Gloster Gorcock Gloster received an order for three experimental fighters to explore the concept of all-metal-framed (but fabric covered) aircraft. Power came from the water-cooled Napier Lion engine that had been used in the Gloster III. The resulting Gorcocks bore a strong resemblance to the later Gamecock and all three were used for various research projects for several years.

Handley Page Handcross Developed in response to a requirement for a single-engined day-bomber. The Handcross was a wood and fabric biplane powered by a Rolls Royce Condor V-12 engine. Three prototypes were ordered and following trials, the Hawker Horsley won the contract. One Handcross remained in use as a trials aircraft until at least 1928.

Handley Page Hyderabad Developed from the Handley Page W.8 airliner to be the RAF's last wooden heavy bomber. Created as a replacement for the Vimy, it was fitted with a single fin and rudder and two Napier Lion engines. The Hyderabad entered service with 99 Sqn in December 1925, replacing the Avro Aldershot. It also served with 10, 502 and 503 Sqns; the latter operating them until 1933.

Hawker Woodcock Designed as a night-fighter in 1922 but rejected due to a lack of manoeuvrability and serious wing flutter issues. The aircraft was redesigned and flew again in July 1923; by now armed with a .303in Vickers gun either side of the cockpit. The first of 63 aircraft entered service in May 1925 but they began to be replaced by the Gloster Gamecock in 1928.

The Need for Speed

As part of its desire to win the prestigious Schneider Trophy the RAF formed the High Speed Flight in 1927

Announced in 1913, the Schneider Trophy was awarded annually (and later, biennially) to the winner of an outright speed race for seaplanes and flying boats.

Jacques Schneider was a French financier and hot air balloonist who saw competition as an ideal method of encouraging advancements in technology. He offered a prize of approximately £1,000 (equivalent to approximately £33,000 in today's money) to the pilot of the fastest aircraft around a 280km (174 miles)– later 350km (217 miles)– triangular course. If a club or country won three consecutive races it would retain the Schneider Trophy in perpetuity.

The first race was held in Monaco on April 16, 1913 and was won by a French Deperdussin at an average speed of 39.72kts (45.71 mph). The following year Britain's Howard Pixton flew to victory in a Sopwith Tabloid at 75.45kts (86.83 mph). In just a year, the competition had seen speeds nearly double. The contests proved incredibly popular and some attracted crowds of over 200,000 spectators.

1

High Speed Flight

Fast-forward a decade and the British public was taking an ever keener interest in the Schneider Trophy. Team GB had lost the 1925 race, with the poor result blamed on "technical inferiority." The following year the British were so disorganised that they failed to arrange a team in time to compete in the race, so for 1927 the Air Ministry stepped in and created the High Speed Flight with the sole aim of bringing home the trophy for good.

Pilots were drawn from the RAF and the 'Flight' (as it was generally known) was based at Marine Aircraft Experimental Establishment at Felixstowe, Suffolk. Training began using a Gloster Mars I, which was designed by Henry Folland as a racing derivative of the Nighthawk fighter and fitted with a 450hp Napier Lion II engine. It had already broken the British speed record in 1922 (170.67kts/196.4mph) and, after being fitted with floats, was sold to the Flight.

Venice - 1927

The 1926 race had been won by the Italians, so according to the rules they hosted the following year's race. Venice was chosen as the venue and the Flight arrived in force with a pair of Supermarine S.5s and two Gloster IVs.

The team also took their Short Crusader to Venice with the intention of using it for training, but it crashed after it was incorrectly rigged following shipping from England.

The Gloster IV was a wooden biplane designed by Henry Folland with a monocoque fuselage. Both the upper and lower wings were 'gull' shaped to reduce the drag where the wing met the fuselage. Power came from a 900hp Napier Lion VIIA with radiators built into the surfaces of both the wings and the floats to aid the aircraft's streamlining.

Three were built, all differing in the size of the wings and tail. The two with the shortest wingspans (the IVA and IVB) were sent to Venice and the IVB was chosen to compete.

The Supermarine S.5 was designed specifically for the 1927 race and was a new monoplane from the pen of Reginald J Mitchell. The fuselage was built mainly from duralumin while the wing was spruce with a plywood skin.

Three were built, one with a direct drive 900hp Lion VIIA engine, and the other two with

Stainforth became the first person in history to break the 400mph mark

a geared 875hp Lion VIIB engine.

On the day of the race (September 26, 1927), the Gloster IVB piloted by Flt Lt Samuel Kinkead retired after five laps due to a cracked propeller shaft but the two S.5s came home in first and second place. Flt Lt Sidney Webster flew S.5 N220 to victory at an average of 244.76kts (281.66mph) and, as such, Britain would host the next race. However, to allow more time for development it switched to a biennial schedule.

Calshot - 1929

Although there was no race in 1928, Samuel Kinkead made an attempt on the world air

1925

Parnall Peto A small submarine-carried spotter seaplane. Two prototypes were built, the first with mahogany floats and the second with metal floats. The aircraft was launched using a catapult and recovered using a crane. The first crashed and was rebuilt with modified floats – but was then lost when the submarine it was aboard flooded and sank. No orders were placed by the Ministry.

Supermarine S.4 Designed by R J Mitchell for the 1925 Schneider Trophy. The aerodynamically 'clean' monoplane had a 680hp Napier Lion VII engine and raised the world seaplane speed record to 226.752mph. It was shipped to the USA for the race but crashed during practice due to wing flutter. The S.4 was the progenitor of a line of racing aircraft that ultimately led to the Spitfire.

Supermarine Southampton The original twin-engine biplane flying boat had both its hull and its wings manufactured from wood. The later Southampton Mk II had a metal hull that lowered the weight and increased range. Southamptons entered RAF service with 480 Sqn in August 1925 and the type would serve until 1936, when 201 Sqn swapped its examples for Saro London flying boats.

1926

Armstrong Whitworth Ape Perhaps one of the most unusual aircraft to fly with the RAF. The Ape was an experimental biplane built to explore new ideas in aerodynamics. The length of the fuselage could be changed and different tails could be fitted. The wings' stagger and dihedral could also be altered. The Ape was underpowered but it would provide valuable service throughout the 1920s.

Fairey Fox Developed by Fairey, to prove that the Fawn (which had been hampered by the constraints of the RAF's spec) could be bettered. The Fox bomber was designed around the Curtiss D-12 engine and clever aerodynamics meant the Fox proved to be faster than the fighters of the day when it entered service in 1926. Sadly, budgetary restraints meant only 28 Foxes were ordered.

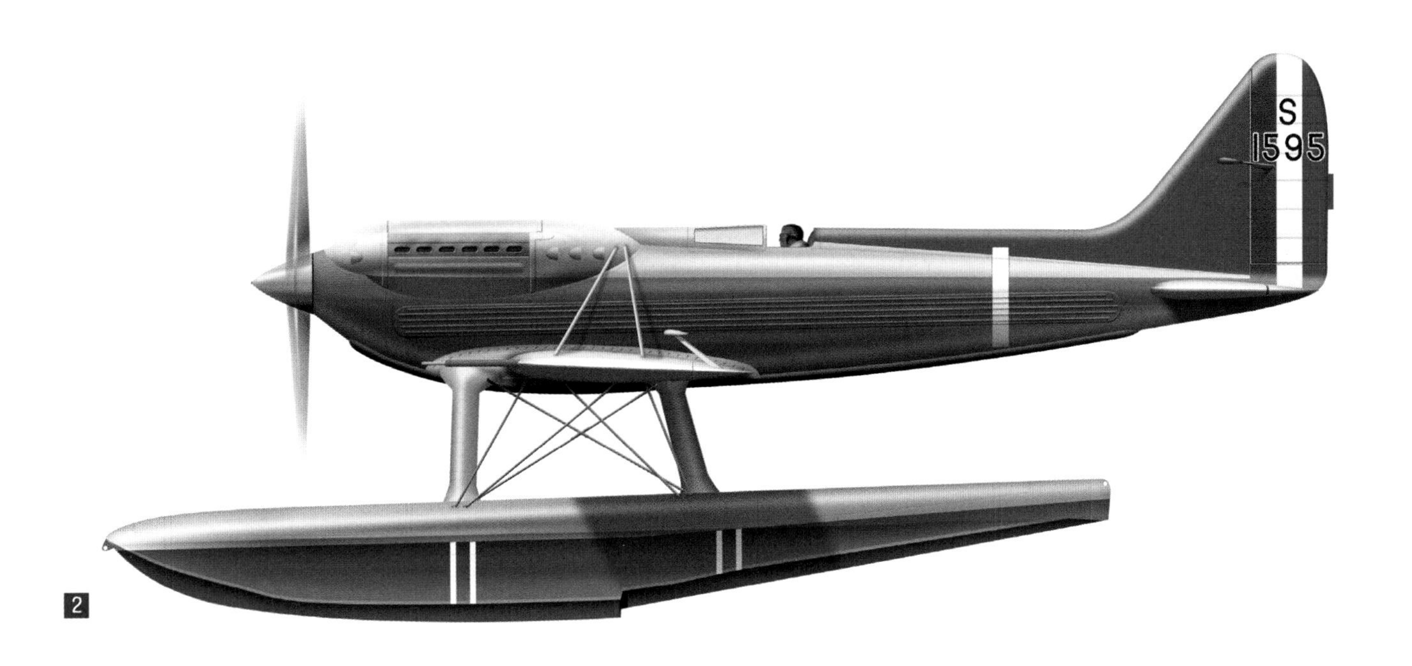

speed record using Supermarine S.5 N221. However, as he approached the start of the course the aircraft plunged into the water, killing him.

Although funding was more restricted than in 1927 the Flight was determined to perform well on home territory in 1929.

Mitchell had decided the Napier powerplant had been pushed as far as it could, so for 1929 he developed the new Rolls-Royce powered Supermarine S.6. This was a refined version of the S.5 with an all-metal construction and the 875hp Lion engine replaced by a monstrous, supercharged 1,900hp Rolls-Royce R powerplant. Two aircraft (N247 and N248) were delivered to the Flight in August, a month before the race.

The Gloster VI, created for the 1929 races, was Gloster's ultimate floatplane. It was a low-winged monoplane similar to the S.6 and was powered by a supercharged Napier Lion.

1. The Gloster IV biplane was designed by Henry Folland. Both the upper and lower wings were 'gulled' to reduce the drag where the wing met the fuselage.
2. Supermarine S.6B S1595 was victorious in the 1931 Schneider Trophy. **Andy Hay/www.flyingart.co.uk**
3. Two Supermarine S.6 racers at the 1927 Schneider Trophy at Calshot.
4. The Supermarine S.5 was designed by Reginald J Mitchell specifically for the 1927 race. The fuselage was built mainly from duralumin while the wing was spruce with a plywood skin. Power came from a 900hp Napier Lion engine.
5. The Gloster Napier VI did not compete in 1929 due to problems with its fuel supply; but it set a speed record of 336.3mph the day after the race. Hours later the Supermarine S.6 edged the record up to more than 350mph.

Two were built but while the aircraft showed promise it had problems with fuel supply in turns, which led to the engine cutting out. This was an unacceptable risk during low altitude air racing and the aircraft was forced to withdraw from the competition.

As such, the High Speed Flight entered Supermarine S.5 (N219) along with the two S.6s in the Schneider Trophy, which took place at Calshot, near Southampton.

Flt Lt D'Arcy Greig flew the S.5 home in third place in 56 minutes and 15 seconds behind an Italian Macchi M.52 in second place and F/O Richard Waghorn in the winning S.6 (N247).

The second S.6 – flown by Sqn Ldr Richard 'Batchy' Atcherley was disqualified for turning inside one of the marker poles, but nonetheless, set world speed records for 50 and 100 km during a later run.

The rules of the Schneider Trophy decreed that a third win would result in Britain keeping the trophy for ever and after the 1929 victory Prime Minister Ramsay MacDonald announced "We are going to do our level best to win again."

1927

Gloster Gamecock Originally dubbed the Grebe III the new fighter differed sufficiently to earn a new name. It dispensed with the Jaguar engine in favour of a Jupiter and also had better ailerons, aerodynamics and internally mounted machine guns. The first joined 23 Sqn in May 1926 and although six units would operate Gamecocks it was 23 Sqn that was last to retire them, in July 1931.

Handley Page Harrow Although the Harrow lost out to the Blackburn Ripon in the contest to replace the Dart torpedo bomber it played a significant role in the development of automatic slats and slots. The second prototype continued the research begun by the Hendon in 1924 and tests proved that automatic wingtip slats could help prevent an inadvertent stall/spin accident.

Vickers Victoria The Victoria [see also p12] had an enclosed cabin for 24 troops on collapsible canvas seats along the sides of the fuselage. The type first flew in 1922 but it would be three years before the RAF ordered the first of 97 examples, by which time the Victoria had gained the Virginia's swept-back wing design. Deliveries began in 1926, replacing Vernons and Vimys in Iraq and Egypt.

Westland Westbury Created as a twin-engined Home Defence night-fighter, the large Westbury was designed around the 37mm Coventry Ordnance Works (COW) gun. Although it had good flying characteristics it was not put into production as the performance was too poor for a fighter aircraft. However, it did serve for several years as an armament trials platform, mostly for the COW gun.

Armstrong Whitworth Atlas Another attempt to create a replacement for the DH.9A, this time in the army co-operation role. It was evaluated against the Bristol Boarhound, de Havilland Hyena, Vickers Vespa, and Short Chamois and selected for production. The first entered service with 13 Sqn in 1927 and the RAF also received the two-seat Atlas Trainer version. The last Atlas was retired in 1935.

1. S1596 was the second Supermarine S.6B. It had been due to make the speed record attempt but sank following a minor accident.

However, with the Wall Street Crash of 1929 funding for such an event became scarce to find. The RAF suggested disbanding the High Speed Flight as it was felt that technological development would continue whether or not the UK competed.

Lady Lucy

Elsewhere the Schneider Trophy had become a source of huge national pride. Italian leader Mussolini was aggrieved by his nation's poor showing in the 1929 race and dedicated a huge amount of resources to the team's Fiat-engined Macchi aircraft for the 1931 contest.

Meanwhile, Britain's Labour government did the complete opposite and withdrew all funding. Furthermore, the Air Ministry forbade the use of the aircraft that competed in the 1929 race and told the pilots, who had been eagerly training to fly the aircraft, they were not permitted to compete in the contest. At the same time it refused to police the racecourse, which was scheduled to take place over the busy shipping lanes in the Solent.

The Royal Aero Club sent a statement to the Cabinet on January 22, 1931, offering to raise £100,000 (£6.7 million today) if the Government would rescind the Air Ministry's decrees on planes, pilots and policing.

The lack of official support caused a public outcry and an appeal was placed in Lord Rothermere's *Daily Mail* group of newspapers to back the national team. Help came from the most unexpected of areas, in the form of a wealthy 74-year-old widow.

Fanny 'Lucy' Radmall was the daughter of a wool-warehouseman and draper. The ninth child of ten children, as a young woman she worked as a professional dancer and a chorus girl known as 'Poppy.' Aged 16, she eloped to Paris with Frederick Gretton (the married heir to the Bass brewery fortune). Despite never marrying, he left her £6,000 a year (£709,000 today) for life when he died in 1882. She became an active suffragette while married to Lord Byron, a descendant of the poet. Widowed, she married again – this time to shipping magnate Sir Robert Houston. He died in 1926, leaving her £5.5 million (£330 million today) – of which she donated £100,000 to the High Speed Flight.

As a staunch Conservative the gift gave Lady Houston an opportunity to attack the Labour government, with the declaration "Every true Briton would rather sell his last shirt than admit that England could not afford to defend herself."

Calshot - 1931

With the financial burden removed, the Air Ministry allowed the RAF to compete again and preparations began for the 1931 race. However, there were less than nine months left to design and prepare the aircraft. The High Speed Flight was reformed while Mitchell and Rolls-Royce set to work.

In reality there was no time to design a new aircraft so, instead, the S.6 design was modified to S.6B standard and the output of the engine was increased to 2,300hp. Other than the engine, the main difference from the S.6 were redesigned floats which provided additional cooling. Other aerodynamic refinements were aimed at reducing drag.

Two all-new aircraft (S1595 and S1596) were built to this specification and the two existing S.6s were upgraded and renamed S.6A.

The race itself proved to be quite the anti-climax with Italy, France and the USA failing to field any competitors. Undeterred, Britain decided to run the race as planned – the lack of any opposition guaranteeing victory.

The High Speed Flight brought a total of six Supermarine racers to the contest; S.5 N219 (which had come second in Venice in 1929), S.5 N220 (the winner in Venice in 1927) the two refurbished S.6s (S.6A N247 that won at Calshot in 1929 and S.6A N248 which was disqualified in 1929), and the newly built S.6Bs.

RAF Fast Fact

Just 18 days after the Schneider triumph the Air Ministry issued Specification F7/30, which called for a modern all-metal land-based fighter aircraft. The Ministry specifically invited Supermarine to participate – and thus the Supermarine Spitfire was born.

The plan was to beat the previous race time then to make an attempt at establishing a new absolute speed record.

Tragically, N247 was destroyed in a take off accident resulting in the death of Lt G L Brinton. However, on September 13, 1931, Flt Lt John Boothman flew seven perfect laps of the course in S1595 to win the race at a top speed of 295.52kts (340.08mph) – 10kts (12mph) faster than the winning speed in 1929.

Attention then switched to the record attempt. This initially got off to a bad start when a minor accident led to S1596 sinking, but on September 30 Flt Lt George Stainforth took off in S1595, which had been fitted with a highly tuned 'sprint' version of the Type R engine.

He would go on to achieve a record of 354.12kts (407.5mph) and become the first person in history to break the 400mph mark.

The RAF's High Speed Flight was wound up within weeks of the 1931 victory. Britain had secured the Schneider Trophy but, more importantly, the Supermarine S.6B would go on to directly influence the development of the Spitfire fighter and the Rolls-Royce R powerplant would evolve into the war-winning Merlin engine. ■

1927

Bristol Bagshot Designed as a large, twin-engined, night-fighter to the same requirement as the Westbury. The Bagshot was a high-wing monoplane with an unusual triangular-section fabric-covered steel fuselage. It was to be armed with the COW gun but the wing was found to flex in flight and it was grounded. It was handed to the RAF, briefly tested, then scrapped.

de Havilland DH.60 Genet Moth Geoffrey de Havilland created his DH.60 Moth as an affordable light aircraft for private pilots. It had folding wings to allow it to be stored in the average council house garage and could be towed behind a car to the airfield. Although originally powered by the Cirrus engine the RAF ordered six Armstrong Siddeley Genet radial engined versions for display flying.

Fairey IIIF The most prolific of the Fairey III [see p8] was the IIIF, which was designed as a three-seat reconnaissance aircraft for the FAA and a two-seat general purpose aircraft for the RAF. The Fairey IIIF entered RAF service with 47 Sqn in Khartoum in December 1927 and during the interwar period only the Hawker Hart family was produced in greater numbers.

Gloster IV To compete in the 1927 Schneider Trophy, the Air Ministry ordered aircraft from Gloster, Supermarine and Shorts. The Gloster IV was a development of the Gloster III of 1925. Both wings were gulled to minimise drag and radiators were built into the surfaces of the wings and floats. Three were built, differing in the surface area of the wings.

Hawker Horsley The last all-wooden Hawker aircraft, the Horsley and served as a medium day bomber and torpedo bomber. The first examples were delivered to 100 Sqn, replacing the Fairey Fawn. It could carry up to three times the bomb load at higher speeds and over further distances. Horsleys remained in service in the day-bombing role until 1934 and the torpedo bombing role until 1935.

Queen Bee: Mother of all Drones

Today, the word 'drone' conjures up images of sophisticated UAVs spying from beyond the horizon. However, in the 1930s it symbolised something completely different

In 1932, the Air Ministry saw a need for a new gunnery target for anti-aircraft training. The requirement called for an 'aircraft' that could take off, fly around while being shot at and then be recovered and reused if it had not been destroyed. Towed targets had been in use for some years, but the risk of shooting down the tow aircraft meant gunners needed to be somewhat 'restrained' in their practice.

Fairey Queen

The first aircraft to be developed for the role was the Fairey Queen, which was essentially a radio-controlled pilotless version of the Fairey III biplane. Its wing had an increased angle of dihedral to improve its lateral stability for remote control. Only three were built and all were launched from HMS *Valiant* – the first two crashing after 18 and 25 seconds respectively! The third was successful and flew several times before it was 'dispatched' by the gunners aboard HMS *Shropshire*.

This proved the concept but the Fairey Queen was a large and expensive aircraft. The decision was therefore made to develop the first cost-effective, full-sized, reusable, unmanned target.

Queen Bee

At first glance the de Havilland DH.82B Queen Bee looked identical to the Tiger Moth, which had been in RAF service as a trainer since early 1932. However, the airframe was quite different; combining the engine, wings, undercarriage and tail of a Tiger Moth with the wooden fuselage of a Moth Major. The latter was cheaper and offered buoyancy (in the event of a ditching) compared to the Tiger Moth's metal-framed fuselage.

The Queen Bee was remotely flown by an operator using a control panel either in another aircraft or on the ground. It was also designed to operate from runways or be fired from a catapult (to then land at sea on floats).

The aircraft retained its own 'manual' controls and if required it could also be flown from the front cockpit.

1. Winston Churchill and the Secretary of State for War waiting to see the launch of a de Havilland Queen Bee on June 6, 1941.
2. A Queen Bee launches from a steam catapult.

Remote Control

When flown remotely the Queen Bee was controlled via a panel that used a simple rotary dial. Numbers on the dial corresponded to commands such as 'turn left' or 'pitch down' and the pilot would simply dial in his instructions. Upon receiving the signal the aircraft's radio would send a command to servos that moved the flight controls.

Similar radio controls were housed in the front cockpit, enabling a test pilot to calibrate their function in flight.

Interestingly, the ailerons on the Queen Bee were permanently locked and control was restricted to the rudder, elevator and throttle.

The Queen Bee was first flown (manned) at Hatfield in 1935 and then remotely-controlled at Farnborough later the same year – although the Air Ministry demanded that a safety pilot was aboard for the testing.

A total of 412 Queen Bees were constructed (360 on floats) and the type represented a major step forward in radio-control technology, leading the way for the modern-day Unmanned Aerial Vehicles (UAVs) in service around the globe today. She is indeed the Mother of all Drones. ■

1928

Short Crusader For the 1927 Schneider Trophy, Short created the Bristol Mercury-powered Crusader. Although beset with engine problems the Crusader was shipped to Venice for the race but it was to be used only as a practice aircraft. Unfortunately, when it was reassembled the control wires to the ailerons were crossed and the aircraft rolled into the water and crashed on its first test flight.

Supermarine S.5 Designed for the 1927 Schneider Trophy, the S.5 differed from the earlier all-wooden S.4 by virtue of composite wood and metal construction. Three were built, one with a direct drive 900hp Napier Lion VIIA and two with a geared 875hp Lion VIIBs. The S.5s came 1st and 2nd in the 1927 race in Venice; the winning aircraft flown by Flt Lt Webster at an average speed of 281.66mph.

Beardmore Inflexible The Inflexible [see also p14] was built by William Beardmore and Co to demonstrate the use of the Rohrbach principle for stressed-skin construction. The gigantic all-metal, three-engined transport suffered from being overweight and underpowered. Therefore, the aircraft was dismantled in 1930 and used to investigate the effects of corrosion.

Boulton Paul Sidestrand A twin-engined medium bomber that first flew in 1926 and entered service in 1928. Only 20 were built and they served solely with 101 Sqn. The crew of three consisted of pilot, nose gunner and a gunner who could move between the dorsal or ventral positions. Capable of loops, rolls and spins the Sidestrand was designed to be able to evade enemy fighters.

Bristol Bullpup In 1924, Frank Barnwell started work on a series of fighter designs that eventually led to the Type 107 Bullpup biplane. Power came from a 480hp Bristol Jupiter and the structure was all-metal with a fabric covering. It was pitched for the F.20/27 competition and while performance was respectable it lost out to the Hawker Fury. Just one Bullpup was therefore built.

The RAF's Last Biplane

The Gladiator was obsolete by the time it entered service. Undeterred, brave crews took their biplanes to war in Europe, Scandinavia, Africa and the Mediterranean

In the early 1930s the Gloster Aircraft Company realised that its Gauntlet could be significantly improved to meet a specification for a new fighter capable of 217kts (250mph).

Chief Designer Henry Folland modified the Gauntlet to create an aircraft that transcended two very different aviation eras. The resulting SS.37 prototype retained the biplane wings, radial engine and wood-covered fabric construction familiar on 1920s fighters but combined them with an enclosed cockpit and a raised aerodynamic rear fuselage. It also had a low-drag cantilever undercarriage with internally-sprung wheels and powerful landing flaps below both the top and bottom wings.

Armament consisted of four .303in Browning machine guns; two of which were mounted in the fuselage with synchronisation allowing them to shoot through the spinning two-bladed propeller. The other two guns were mounted in bulges below the lower wings.

For expediency, the prototype (K5200) first flew in an open cockpit configuration – taking the skies for the first time on September 12, 1934 with Gloster Chief Test Pilot Gerry Sayer at the helm. Subsequent production versions of the aircraft – by now dubbed the Gladiator – would all boast the enclosed cockpit, although many pilots still preferred to fly with the canopy slid open to aid visibility.

The aircraft was powered by an 850hp Bristol Mercury engine and the prototype reached 210kts (242mph) whereas the production versions could attain 223kts (257mph): some feat for a radial powered biplane.

1

Wartime Service

The fighter was produced in two main variants, the Gladiator I and Gladiator II; the latter almost identical to the former apart from the use of a Fairey fixed-pitch three-blade metal propeller and a slightly more powerful (by 10hp) Mercury engine.

All Gladiators were manufactured at Gloster's Hucclecote Factory near Gloucester with the first production Gladiator I (K6129) being accepted into service by 72 Sqn at Tangmere, Sussex on February 16, 1937.

By September, eight squadrons had achieved operational status and these formed the backbone of London's air defences until Spitfires and Hurricanes arrived a year later.

In reality the Gladiator had been obsolete by the time it entered service, but by the time World War Two began the type was heavily outmoded by the new breed of monoplane fighters. However, a need to defend Britain's trade routes throughout the Empire meant that Gladiators were redeployed overseas.

Battle of Britain

Two squadrons of Gladiators were despatched with the British Expeditionary Force to France in 1939 during what is now known as the 'Phoney War.' Sadly, most of the aircraft were destroyed on the ground by a German air raid on May 18, 1940 and the remainder were flown back to Britain shortly afterwards.

The Gladiator also saw operational service during the Battle of Britain with 247 Sqn, 239 Sqn and 804 Naval Air Squadron. No combat sorties took place at the height of the battle but in late October 247 Sqn Gladiators intercepted a Heinkel He 111. Unfortunately, it escaped.

During this period, most of the British-based Gladiators were located in the north of England and Scotland; on October 17 the type scored its first success when a 607 Sqn machine shot down a Dornier Do-18 over the North Sea. Even further north, Gladiators from 23 Sqn took part in the Norwegian Campaign, flying from a frozen lake. Numerous Luftwaffe aircraft were downed during the campaign.

RAF Fast Fact

During the Anglo-Iraq War of May 1941 RAF Gladiators frequently found themselves in dogfights with Royal Iraqi Air Force Gladiators.

Malta and Africa

Perhaps the Gladiator's most celebrated service was in defence of Malta. A fleet of Sea Gladiators (similar to the standard aircraft but fitted with arrestor hooks and a dinghy) were delivered to the island by HMS *Glorious* and

1928

Fairey Long-Range Monoplane The Long-Range Monoplane [see also p18] was designed for record breaking distance flights. The first performed its maiden flight on November 14, 1928 and the following year it set off on a flight from England to India. A second long-range flight in December 1929 ended in tragedy when the aircraft fatally crashed into high ground. A second was built and used for several record attempts.

Gloster Gnatsnapper Created to meet a need for a Bristol Mercury-powered carrier fighter. The prototype (fitted with a Jupiter as the Mercury proved overweight and unreliable) flew in February 1928. Two years later the Air Ministry asked Gloster to redesign it with the Jaguar VIII. The aircraft was badly damaged in a landing accident during trials and the contract was therefore given to the Hawker Nimrod.

Vickers Valiant Vickers' civilian Vixen biplane had wooden wings and these were found to suffer in extreme temperature and humidity. It therefore designed a set of metal wings for the Vixen; creating the Vickers Vivid. The company felt this would appeal to the RAF as a general purpose biplane. The resulting Valiant was evaluated against the Bristol Beaver, Fairey Ferret and Westland Wapiti; with the latter awarded the contract.

Westland-Hill Pterodactyl Geoffrey Hill developed the Pterodactyl series of tail-less designs in an attempt to create an aircraft that was incapable of stalling or spinning. Initially flown as a glider in 1924 it was later given an engine and in 1928 gained Air Ministry backing. Subsequent machines were built by Westland Aircraft and went from a 35hp Cherub power-plant to a 600hp Rolls Royce Goshawk engine over the next few years.

Westland Wapiti A general-purpose biplane designed to replace the DH.9A. To reduce cost the Wapiti used the same wing and tail as the DH.9A. A total of 565 were built and the type remained in production until 1932. Wapitis could carry up to 580lb of bombs under the wings and fuselage and were equipped with cameras and a radio. The Wapiti equipped 20 RAF squadrons at home and in India and Iraq.

1. Today, just a pair of Gloster Gladiators remain in airworthy condition. G-AMRK (foreground) is operated by the Shuttleworth Collection and G-GLAD belongs to The Fighter Collection. **SDB**
2. Gladiators of 94 Sqn, guarded by Arab Legionnaires, refuel during their journey from Ismailia, Egypt, to reinforce the Habbaniya garrison in Iraq during the Ango-Iraq War of May 1941.
3. Gladiator II N5903/G-GLAD was delivered in 1939 and served with 141 Sqn at Grangemouth near Edinburgh. In 1994 the airframe was sold to The Fighter Collection at Duxford and following restoration it flew again for the first time in 2008. It is painted in the markings of 72 Sqn; the first frontline RAF squadron to be equipped with Gladiators. **SDB**
4. L8032/G-AMRK was the last production Gladiator I, built in 1937 and is currently painted as K7985 of 73 Sqn, the aircraft flown by 'Cobber' Kain at the 1937 Hendon Air Pageant. Here, the aircraft demonstrates the low-drag cantilever undercarriage with internally-sprung wheels, powerful landing flaps and enclosed canopy that were so revolutionary for their day. **SDB**

flown from RAF Hal Far.

During the Siege of Malta in 1940, the few remaining Gladiators held off the Italians for ten days until Hurricanes could arrive to take over. The well-told story that just three Gladiators – named *Faith, Hope* and *Charity* – undertook this work alone is simply a myth. More than three aircraft were operational (though not always at the same time) and the names were not given to the aircraft until after the conflict – but the bravery and resilience of their crews remains remarkable.

Meanwhile, in North Africa, Gladiators also faced Italian Fiat CR.42 Falco biplanes in the Desert War. Here, the RAF fighters' good low-altitude performance helped the Gladiator to a 1.2:1 kill ratio over the CR.42. Marmaduke 'Pat' Pattle claimed 15 kills during the campaign, making him the highest-scoring RAF biplane ace of the war.

Further afield in East Africa, Gladiators duelled with Italian fighters over Ethiopia as well as protecting Allied shipping in the vicinity. It was during the latter role that a 94 Sqn aircraft flown by Gordon Haywood was responsible for the surrender of the Italian sub *Galilei Galileo*.

Greece, Iraq and Syria

In October 1940, after war broke out between Greece and Italy, Britain despatched 80 Sqn's Gladiators to assist the Greeks. Again, a number of victories were scored against Italian Fiat CR.42s.

The Royal Iraqi Air Force (RoIAF) had been equipped by the British prior to independence and its main fighter squadron was equipped with Gladiators. In May 1941, Iraq rebelled and a skirmish broke out between the RoIAF and RAF units at RAF Habbaniya near Baghdad. On May 5, P/O Watson shot down an Iraqi Gladiator over Baqubah – it was the only recorded Gladiator-on-Gladiator kill. Later in the war the remaining RAF Gladiators in Iraq would also see extensive combat against Luftwaffe and Regia Aeronautica (Italian Air Force) aircraft in the region.

In June-July 1941 the British also decided to invade Vichy French-controlled Syria to prevent the area from falling under German control. The French in Syria had supported the Iraqi rebellion and allowed Luftwaffe aircraft to use their airfields for operations over Iraq but quickly surrendered when Gladiators began dogfighting with French Dewoitine D.520 monoplane fighters.

Despite its seemingly archaic appearance, the Gladiator biplanes still offered up some surprises for the Axis forces during the early campaigns of World War Two. ■

1929

Westland Witch A high-altitude day bomber with a parasol wing. The Witch had a bomb bay inside the front fuselage and this meant it needed a complicated split-axle undercarriage, meaning the bombs could fall unhindered by the landing gear. During testing the Witch suffered from structural weaknesses, including a number of landing gear failures. As such the project was very quickly abandoned.

Westland Wizard Westland's first attempt at a monoplane fighter. In 1925, the company's engineers drew up plans (in their spare time) for a racing aircraft. The racer was damaged during testing and rebuilt as a fighter. Renamed the Wizard, it was delivered to the RAF for testing but the pilot's view was criticised. The later Wizard II had a modified wing but lower performance; so the project was cancelled.

Bristol Bulldog One of the most famous RAF fighters of the inter-war period. The Bristol Bulldog was the result of a series of fighter designs from the pen of Frank Barnwell and replaced the Siskin and Gamecock in squadron service. For some years 70% of all RAF fighters were Bulldogs and the 312 aircraft equipped nine units. The last examples were retired in September 1937 and remained pilots' favourites.

de Havilland DH.77 Created as a fast climbing interceptor, the DH.77 was a lightweight monoplane powered by a 300hp Napier Rapier engine. Developed as a private venture, the company decided to concentrate on civilian aircraft so the DH.77 was passed to Gloster. The DH.77 demonstrated excellent performance. However, the contract was awarded to the heavier and more powerful Hawker Hornet.

Fairey Firefly IIIM The Firefly II was a private-venture fighter design that lost out to the Hawker Hornet. The aircraft was predominantly built of wood but was later rebuilt as the all-metal Firefly IIIM and pitched against the Hawker Nimrod in the contest to replace the FAA's Fairey Flycatcher. It lost out again but one was fitted with floats and used as a trainer by the RAF's High Speed Flight pilots ahead of the Schneider Trophy races.

Camouflaged & Impressed

At the outbreak of World War Two the RAF was in need of all the aircraft it could get; so a variety of civilian aircraft were commandeered and painted in camouflage

With World War Two well underway the British Government established the Ministry of Aircraft Production (MAP) in 1940 to take over the responsibilities for planning wartime aircraft procurement from the Air Ministry.

Over the coming years the British aviation industry would build up to a peak of delivering more than 2,500 machines a month to the RAF and Fleet Air Arm.

However, in those early months of war the RAF needed all the aircraft it could muster. At the outbreak of the conflict private flying was effectively suspended so a vast network of civilian aircraft sat idle in hangars the length and breadth of Britain, and the MAP saw these as an ideal source of stop-gap airframes.

Aircraft that were deemed to be of use to the RAF – primarily in training, transport and liaison/communication roles – were commandeered and 'impressed' into military service. These airframes were often given a coat of camouflage paint, RAF insignia and allocated service serial numbers.

Ferry Pilots

Some of the larger aircraft were used by RAF Ferry Command and the Air Transport Auxiliary (ATA) to transport pilots who had delivered new aircraft from the factories to operational units around the country. In the case of the ATA the aircraft were also used to fly service personnel on urgent duties from one place to another and on occasion even performed air ambulance work.

Training Fleet

Many of the civilian aircraft that were impressed into service had previously flown with flying schools around the country; as such they were ideal to bolster the RAF's fleet of trainers.

More than 150 de Havilland Tiger Moths as well as numerous examples of the Gipsy Moth, Moth Major and Hornet Moth were also allocated to training units. These were boosted further by more than 30 Blackburn B-2s and a similar number of Avro Cadets – the latter very similar to the RAF's pre-war Avro Tutor.

Geoffrey de Havilland's Moth family saw extensive service in other areas of the RAF with 25 impressed examples of the Hornet Moth being used for coastal patrol duties, 45 Leopard Moths and 47 Puss Moths allocated to various units to act as communication 'hacks' and 26 Moth Minors allocated glider tug duties.

1

Larger de Havilland types including the Dragon, Dragon Rapide, Dragonfly, Albatross and Express were also commandeered and used as transport aircraft as well as air ambulances.

The Miles family of aircraft were present in large numbers at pre-war airfields, with many examples impressed into military service. The Miles Hawk series was very similar to the RAF's Magister training aircraft and more than 20 were given military serials and allocated to Elementary Flying Training Schools. Meanwhile, eleven examples of the Miles Falcon and Monarch tourers were allocated to Station Flights to act as communication aircraft. More than 20 Miles Whitney Straights were also used in the liaison role.

Even archaic aircraft such as the Great War-vintage Avro 504 were returned to military service, with '504N variants used as glider tugs.

Geoffrey de Havilland's Moth family saw extensive service in various branches of the RAF

Maritime Patrol

With the cessation of airline operations Imperial Airways' fleet of pre-war flying boats were not exempt from military service, and these were found to be useful for maritime patrol work.

Four examples of the Short Empire served with 119 and 413 Sqns and three of the G-Class aircraft also served with 119 Sqn. Meanwhile, the sole Short Mercury found use with 320 Sqn.

While most airline flying stopped during the war, the British Overseas Airways Corporation (BOAC) was formed on November 24, 1939 by

1929

Fairey Fleetwing Designed as a two-seat carrier-borne spotter reconnaissance aircraft for the Fleet Air Arm the Fleetwing was stressed for catapulting and had a limited fighter capability. It lost out to the Hawker Osprey in the contest to win orders and only the prototype was built. Fitted with floats it was later used as a 'sea state investigator' aircraft by the RAF's High Speed Flight preparing for the Schneider Trophy races.

Gloster VI Gloster's entry into the 1929 Schneider Trophy was generally referred to as the 'Golden Arrow.' Unlike previous Gloster racers this was a monoplane but retained the same Napier Lion engine. Two were built but they suffered fuel supply problems when banking, which led to engine cut-outs and meant they were withdrawn from competition. However, one went on to establish a world speed record of 335.1mph.

Handley Page Hinaidi Developed from the Hyderabad [see p21] and named after the RAF Hinaidi air station in Iraq, the Hinaidi was used as a heavy night bomber. It benefited from Bristol Jupiter engines and an all-metal airframe, which meant it could carry a greater bombload at higher speeds. Ten Hyderabads were converted to Hinaidi Is (retaining the wooden airframe) and a further 26 Hinaidi IIs were produced from 1929.

Hawker Hornet The Hornet bridged the gap between the prototype Hawker F.20/27 and the Hawker Fury. The Hornet was a private aircraft that paired the F.20/27 airframe with the new Rolls-Royce F.XIS (later Kestrel) engine. After testing by the Air Ministry in comparative trials with the Westland Wizard and the Fairey Firefly II the Hornet was chosen as the victor and placed into production as the Hawker Fury [see page 20].

Hawker Tomtit The interwar RAF needed a new trainer to replace its elderly Avro 504Ns. The specification called for the all-metal aircraft to be powered by an Armstrong Siddeley Mongoose engine. Hawker's Sydney Camm developed the Tomtit and 24 were delivered to the RAF for evaluation in 1929. The Tomtit lost out to the Avro Tutor but the 'evaluation' aircraft remained in service until 1935. **SDB**

RAF Fast Fact

Even the rich and famous were not exempt from handing over their private aircraft and the Guinness family's Ford Trimotor saw extensive service with 271 Sqn.

1. de Havilland DH.87 Hornet Moth G-ADND was impressed into RAF service as a communications aircraft during World War Two and given the serial number W9385. It returned to its owners after the war and today it continues to fly as a tribute to the hundreds of civilian types commandeered by the Ministry. **SDB**
2. A camouflaged Boeing 314A Clipper being operated by BOAC during the war.

3. Three Foster Wikner Wicko aircraft were impressed into RAF service and generally referred to as the Warferry. Two survived the war and, of those, G-AFJB remains airworthy today.
4. One of the 21 Miles M.11 Whitney Straights that were impressed into the RAF.
5. The RAF also impressed four Messerschmitt Bf 108 Taifun aircraft into service at the outbreak of the war. The type was called the Aldon in British service and was the fastest light communications aircraft the service had at the time. A further 15 captured Taifuns flew in RAF colours during and after the war.

merging Imperial Airways and British Airways.

The two companies had already been working together since September 3 when their joint operations were evacuated from London to Bristol; but following the fall of France the new organisation would keep Britain connected with the Empire, the colonies and the rest of the Allied world.

BOAC inherited Imperial Airways' flying boat fleet alongside landplanes such as the ageing Handley Page HP.42 biplanes, but the fleet was boosted with impressed aircraft and new acquisitions including the de Havilland Albatross. In 1941, longer range Consolidated Catalinas, Boeing 314 Clippers and converted Short Sunderlands were introduced and many of the company's flights originated from Foynes in Ireland to reduce the chance of aircraft being intercepted by enemy fighters – or even shot down by friendly fire from Allied aircraft or ground-based gunners.

Converted bombers, such as the Consolidated Liberator, regularly flew transatlantic passenger routes and by the end of 1944 BOAC had made 1,000 crossings to the USA.

Overseas Operations

As the RAF's war expanded across the Empire and into far-flung lands, so it gained an eclectic fleet of ex-civilian aircraft as it went.

In India an Aeronca Chief and Zlin 212 were commandeered and former Imperial Airways examples of the Armstrong Whitworth Atlanta and Ensign were pressed into service with squadrons in India and Iraq. Airliners including Douglas DC-2s and DC-3 were handed over to the RAF and operated in the region, as well as in Burma.

Elsewhere in India. five Harlow PC5As were impressed and flown by the RAF. These were small, single-engined cabin monoplanes built locally by Hindustan Aircraft. They were allocated the RAF serials DR423-DR427 for their military service.

A civilian-owned Fairchild 91 amphibian was also used as an air-sea rescue aircraft in Egypt and the Middle East.

A number of overseas aircraft also flew in RAF hands. A Fokker F.XXXVI and a pair of Fokker XXIIs – all formerly in service with KLM Airlines in the Netherlands – were flown to Britain and saw service with 1 Air Observer Navigation School (AONS) at Prestwick.

A Danish Air Lines Focke-Wulf Fw 200 Condor was seized on British soil after the Germans invaded Denmark in 1940. The aircraft was briefly operated by BOAC but restrictions on flying German aircraft meant it was eventually handed over to the RAF. It crashed whilst being flown by the ATA in 1941.

During the latter days of the war a number of enemy aircraft were also impressed into the RAF, with liaison types such as the German Fieseler Storch proving to be a particular favourite 'run-around' with high ranking officers in Europe and North Africa. Like the majority of the ex-civilian aircraft that were commandeered by the RAF, the majority of these were scrapped shortly after the end of hostilities. A few private aircraft were returned to their rightful owners but even these were 'well used' and few would ever fly again. ■

1930

Supermarine S.6 Following the success of the Supermarine S.5 in the 1927 Schneider Trophy, designer R J Mitchell created the S.6 for the 1929 race. It was a refined S.5 and now used all-metal construction and the new 1,900hp Rolls Royce Type R engine. It had surface radiators built into the floats and wings, and airflow was actually routed through the wing's structure. Two were built and N247 won the race at 328.63mph.

Westland Interceptor A prototype fighter created for the daytime interceptor role. Emphasis was placed on high speed and rate of climb . The single example was powered by a Bristol Mercury and flew in early 1929, but the radical monoplane had what was described as "alarming handling." It was competing for orders against the DH.77, Vickers Jockey and Hawker Hornet; and therefore quickly lost out.

Avro Tutor Designed by Roy Chadwick as a replacement for the RAF's Avro 504 trainers. Power came from either a 155hp Armstrong Siddeley Mongoose or 180hp Armstrong Siddeley Lynx IV. In 1929, the RAF ordered 21 for evaluation alongside the Hawker Tomtit. In 1933, the Tutor was selected as the more successful aircraft and 381 Tutors and 15 float-equipped Sea Tutors eventually joined the RAF.

Blackburn Iris A tri-motor long-range reconnaissance flying boat. When the Iris entered RAF service it was the largest aircraft in its inventory. The first wooden hulled Iris I was later modified with a metal hull to become the Iris II. The four Iris IIIs had an all-metal superstructure and two were converted to Iris IV standard with 800hp Siddeley Leopard engines. Three were later updated as Iris Vs with 825hp Buzzard engines.

de Havilland DH.60T Gipsy Moth Compared to the earlier Moth, the DH.60T had an all-metal structure (covered in fabric) and a new 100hp DH Gipsy engine. The RAF eventually acquired 135 new DH.60Ts and other DH.60s were later impressed into service during World War Two. The type was primarily used as a basic trainer but also saw service in the communications role with Station Flights around the UK.

From Airliner to Bomber

When the Bristol 142 airliner proved to be faster than the RAF's latest fighter aircraft the service quickly paid attention. Soon, the airliner morphed into the Bristol Blenheim

In 1933, the Bristol Aircraft Company's chief designer, Frank Barnwell, suggested it would be possible for an eight-seat, twin-engined mini airliner to have a cruising speed of 217kts (250mph). This was a very bold proposition as the RAF's Hawker Fury fighter could only attain 194kts (223mph).

Undeterred, Barnwell put pen to paper and created a design that consisted of a low-winged, all-metal monocoque monoplane to be powered by a pair of 640hp Bristol Mercury engines.

2

Politically Motivated

Initially, with no orders on the horizon, the aircraft never left the drawing board. But that was all to change when newspaper mogul Lord Rothermere was made aware of the design.

Rothermere was a longstanding and outspoken critic of British aviation policy and, aware of the technological advancements being made overseas, he approached Bristol to order an example of Barnwell's airliner - which by now had gained official Bristol status as the Type 142.

His order for a 'personal aircraft' was undoubtedly placed to make a political point, but after consulting with the Air Ministry, Bristol agreed to provide him with an aircraft. He was charged £18,500 (around £1.3 million in today's money) for the privilege.

Even before the aircraft had been completed, Barnwell began working on a militarised version (the Type 142F) to meet interest from the Finnish government. This version would have interchangeable fuselage sections that would allow it to be used as a transport, attack aircraft, bomber or even an ambulance. It was at this point that the Air Ministry also began to show interest in a bomber version for the RAF.

The prototype Type 142 first took to the sky at Filton, Bristol on April 12, 1935. Its performance did not disappoint and Lord Rothermere donated it to the Air Ministry to help the bomber project – but not before he had named it *Britain First*.

Testing at the Aeroplane and Armament Experimental Establishment (AAEE) at Martlesham Heath, Suffolk pushed the aircraft to a top speed of 267kts (307mph).

Barnwell then set about creating a dedicated bomber variant by raising the wing to accommodate a bomb bay. He also fitted a dorsal turret featuring a .30 cal. Lewis gun and a machine gun was added in the port wing.

In August 1935, the Air Ministry ordered 150 Type 142Ms, which were to be powered by 840hp Mercuries and named the Blenheim.

Into Service

The first Blenheim Is entered service in March 1937 and as it became ever more likely that war was imminent the RAF began to replace older aircraft with Blenheims at a fast rate.

In addition to bombers, the air arm was also in need of a long range fighter. Some Blenheims were therefore modified with the addition of a belly-mounted gun pack featuring four machine guns. While this meant the aircraft was unable to use its bomb bay it created an effective fighter – referred to as the Blenheim IF.

However, all was not well with the Blenheim. The modifications needed to turn it from

RAF Fast Fact

On December 9, 1941, Sqn Ldr Arthur Scarf was flying Blenheim I L1134 (coded) FX-F in Malaya with 62 Sqn. He led a raid on Singora, but shortly after take off from RAF Butterworth a flight of Japanese aircraft destroyed the rest of the British machines. Undeterred, Scarf decided to fly on alone. He completed his bombing run but on the way home his aircraft was hit and he was severely wounded. His left arm was shattered, he had a large wound in his back and despite drifting in and out of consciousness he managed to crash-land the Blenheim without causing injury to his crew. He died two hours later – he was just 28 years old. Scarf was awarded the Victoria Cross for his bravery.

1930

Hawker Hart The Hart was the first in the spectacularly successful range of interwar Hawker biplanes [see also p20]. The family was also produced in more numbers than any other RAF aircraft of the period. Powered by the Kestrel V12 engine, 992 two-seat Hart day bombers were built and the aircraft spawned a myriad of variants. It remained in service until 1936 at 'home' and 1939 in the Far East.

Parnall Prawn An experimental single-engined flying boat powered by a 65hp water-cooled Ricardo-Burt engine. The Prawn's powerplant was fitted on a tilting mount, so that the propeller could be kept clear of the water on take off and landing. It also had a very small propeller in an attempt to keep it out of the water. Other than the engine, the aircraft was entirely conventional with a fabric covered parasol wing.

Vickers Jockey Created for the contest to be the RAF's new interceptor fighter, its rather angular looks were extenuated by the use of corrugated metal skinning. Power initially came from a 480hp Bristol Mercury IIA but this was later changed to a 530hp Jupiter VIIF. The aircraft lost out in the contest to the Hawker Hornet and the prototype was eventually lost in a flat spin in 1932, the pilot bailing out and surviving.

1931

Fairey Gordon Developed from the Fairey IIIF [see p24] and fitted with the new Armstrong Siddeley Panther engine. Around 80 IIIFs were converted to Gordons and 178 new-built aircraft were made for the RAF.
From the 154th aircraft the design was altered to include a larger fin and rudder; becoming the Gordon II. The Navy version of the Gordon was known as the Fairey Seal.

Handley Page Clive The troop-carrying variant of the Hinaidi bomber.
The Handley Page Clive I had wooden constriction whereas the Clive II was metal and had a longer nose. Two of the latter were built for the RAF and could carry up to 17 troops. Clives spent most of their flying careers operating with the RAF's Heavy Transport Flight in Lahore, India but the last example was finally retired by 1934.

2

3

4

1. The world's only airworthy Bristol Blenheim is this Mk I, restored and operated by The Aircraft Restoration Company at Duxford. It began life as L6739 and wears its original 23 Sqn markings from when it flew as a night fighter during the Battle of Britain. It was scrapped in December 1940 but the nose was saved and converted into an electric car! **SDB**
2. All-black night fighting Blenheim I K7159 / YX-N from 54 OTU at RAF Church Fenton in December 1940
3. Britain First was the sole Bristol Type 142. It began life as a civilian airliner but formed the basis for what would become the Blenheim.
4. Bristol Blenheim IVF V6083/FV-B of 13 OTU at RAF Bicester. This Operational Training Unit was established in April 1940 specifically to train Blenheim day bomber aircrew.

airliner to bomber had increased its weight considerably and the Mk I could therefore only reach around 226kts (260mph).

In an attempt to remedy the type's performance issues Bristol developed the Blenheim IV, which first flew on September 24, 1937. As well as the elongated nose to house a bomb aimer the new variant also boasted better defensive armament and greater fuel capacity. More importantly, it was fitted with more powerful 920hp Mercury XV engines. As with the earlier variant, the new aircraft could also be fitted with a gun pack, thus creating the Mk IVF.

Wartime Operations

By the time World War Two began in September 1939 the Blenheim I was in service with two British squadrons and eleven more units overseas in Aden, Egypt, India, Iraq and Singapore. More than 150 Blenheim IVs were also in squadron service and on the day that war was declared on Germany it was Blenheim IV N6215 (piloted by F/O Andrew McPherson) that was the first British aircraft to cross the German coast. The aircraft performed a high altitude reconnaissance mission in the vicinity of Wilhelmshaven and the following morning, 15 Blenheims set off on their first bombing missions to attack ships spotted by McPherson.

On March 11, 1940, Blenheim IV P4852 became the first RAF aircraft to sink a U-boat, having scored two direct hits on U-31.

Blenheims of the RAF Advanced Air Striking Force (AASF) also deployed to airfields in France at the start of the war in support of the British Expeditionary Force. AASF Blenheims played a role in the Battle of France but suffered heavy losses. Action by Blenheims of Bomber Command sustained a 25% aircraft loss rate and the depleted squadrons were soon withdrawn to Britain.

Despite being largely obsolete by late 1940 several Blenheim squadrons were also active during the Battle of Britain. They played an important role in bombing German-occupied airfields in France, often taking heavy casualties: some missions resulting in an almost 100% casualty rate.

The following year, Blenheims were used in an attempt to shut down the English Channel to all German shipping. By the end of 1941 almost 700 ships had been attacked; 41 of which had been sunk for the loss of 123 aircraft.

Even the Blenheim IF soon became obsolete and by June 1940 the remaining aircraft were relegated to night-fighter duties.

Overseas Action

The Blenheim played an extensive role in the war in Africa and the Mediterranean. Just hours after Italy joined the conflict on June 11, 1940, Blenheims were the first aircraft to attack Italian targets and continued to serve in the region for much of the war.

When war broke out in the Pacific some Blenheim units were re-tasked to the Far East to counter Japanese forces. These continued to fly in the region, particularly in Aden, the Dutch East Indies, India, Malaya and Singapore until late 1943 in bomber and fighter roles. The aircraft played a vital role in preventing India from falling and in recapturing Burma.

The final version was the Blenheim V Bisley, which first joined 139 Sqn in June 1942. The variant mostly saw service in the Middle East and Far East and equipped 13 units in both high altitude bombing and low altitude attack roles.

Although the Blenheim was retired from service in Britain in 1944 the type was retained by some squadrons in the Far East until the end of the war – all made possible thanks to the foresight of Lord Rothermere. ■

Hawker Audax A Hart variant designed for army cooperation duties in British Empire outposts. Modifications included a hook to pick up messages. Subvariants included the tropicalised Audax India, for service in India and the Audax Singapore for service there. The type saw limited wartime service in Africa on the Italian occupied Kenya-Abyssinia border and some even remained in operation as late as 1945.

Hawker Demon A fighter variant of the Hart light bomber, envisaged as an interim aircraft to serve until the RAF's new Fury fighters were available in larger numbers. An extra Vickers machine gun was added in the nose and many were fitted with a hydraulically-operated turret in the rear gunner's position. The RAF received 232 Demons and some would serve until 1938, when they were replaced by Blenheim Is. **SDB**

Hawker Fury The Hornet was renamed the Fury I by the time it entered service. It was the first operational RAF aircraft to exceed 200mph in level flight but its arrival into service coincided with the Great Depression, therefore austerity measures meant the Fury I only equipped three units. The Fury II entered service with six squadrons from 1936 and was 230mph faster. Nearly 50 remained in use as trainers during World War Two.

Short Rangoon Created to replace the Supermarine Southampton IIs of 203 Sqn based at RAF Basra, Iraq. The Rangoon was a military adaption of the civilian Short Calcutta with an enclosed cockpit and armament including three Lewis guns and underwing bomb racks. Six were purchased and used primarily for anti-smuggling patrols over the Persian Gulf. The type was retired at the end of 1935.

Supermarine S.6B The ultimate British racing seaplane. The S.6B [see also p22] was built for the 1931 Schneider Trophy and differed from the earlier S.5 and S.6 in having more powerful Rolls Royce R powerplant and redesigned floats that offered increased engine cooling. Two were built for the RAF's High Speed Flight; the type winning the trophy for Britain and increasing the world air speed record to 407.5 mph.

Landing by Moonlight

Although it was designed for army co-operation duties, the unconventional looking Westland Lysander found its true niche with the Special Operations Executive

Almost as soon as France fell to Nazi Germany in 1940, British Prime Minister Winston Churchill established the Special Operations Executive (SOE). The organisation was tasked with clandestine duties including espionage, sabotage and helping the French Resistance movement. Its existence was not revealed to the public until the war was won.

In order to fulfil its role, the SOE needed to be 'air dropped' into Occupied France or the Low Countries but as a standalone entity it did not have access to its own fleet of aircraft. An approach was therefore made to AVM Arthur 'Bomber' Harris to request the use of Bomber Command machines, but Harris initially refused to release aircraft and pilots "to carry ragamuffins to distant spots."

However, with Churchill as its main supporter, SOE's requests were soon met and over the next five years thousands of 'agents' were delivered to and picked up from Europe. Some were parachuted from bombers such as Armstrong Whitworth Whitleys, Handley Page Halifaxes or Short Stirlings; whilst others dropped from the Douglas Dakota transport aircraft, it was a much smaller aircraft that is most closely associated with the SOE.

1

Revolutionary Design

The Westland Lysander began life as an army co-operation aircraft, designed in 1934 to meet Air Ministry Specification A.39/34 for an aircraft to replace the Hawker Hector.

The competition was initially open to just Avro, Bristol and Hawker Aircraft but after lobbying the Ministry, Westland was invited to tender a proposal as well.

The Westland P.8 was created by Arthur Davenport under the leadership of William 'Teddy' Petter. The duo went to great lengths to interview RAF pilots to discover what they wanted from such an aircraft. The answers Petter received led him to believe low-speed handling, field of view and short field capabilities were the key attributes. However, the specification called for an aircraft capable of photographic reconnaissance and artillery observation up to 9 miles (14km) behind enemy lines.

Petter and Davenport did their best to combine these requirements and created a very unconventional aeroplane. The bulky fuselage housed a proven Bristol Mercury radial engine and the machine sat atop a high undercarriage with internally sprung wheels and large streamlined spats. The latter could be fitted with a Browning machine gun and small, removable 'stub' wings that could carry light bombs.

However, it was the high-mounted wing that was truly revolutionary. It had a reverse taper towards the root and was aerodynamically very advanced for its day. It also had fully automatic wing slots and slotted flaps which, coupled with a variable incidence tailplane, meant the aircraft would stall at just 56kts (65mph) but could reach 184kts (212mph) in a fast cruise.

'Lizzie'

Named the Lysander (although often referred to by the nickname 'Lizzie'), the new aircraft entered RAF service in June 1938 and were initially used for army co-operation duties including message dropping and artillery spotting for ground troops.

Five Lysander squadrons formed part of the British Expeditionary Force to France from late 1939 and following the German invasion of France and the Low Countries, Lysanders were put into action against ground targets. However, they made very easy prey for Luftwaffe fighters

1932

Blackburn Baffin Created to replace the Blackburn Ripon in the torpedo-bomber role. The prototype was a modified Ripon, with its elderly water-cooled Napier Lion engine replaced by a Bristol Pegasus radial engine. Orders were placed for 26 newly built aircraft and 38 conversions of Ripon airframes. A further 26 conversions were ordered in 1935. The Baffin was replaced by the Blackburn Shark and Fairey Swordfish by 1936.

de Havilland DH.82 Tiger Moth The DH.60T Gipsy Moth trainer [see p29] was modified into the Tiger Moth for the RAF. The key change was moving the top wing forwards to allow easier exit from the front cockpit in an emergency. To maintain the centre of gravity the wings were then swept back. An inverted Gipsy Major engine was also incorporated to improve visibility and the DH.82 would go on to serve the RAF until 1955.

Fairey Queen In 1932, the Air Ministry saw a need for a new gunnery target for anti-aircraft training. The first aircraft to be developed for the role was the Fairey Queen, which was essentially a radio-controlled pilotless version of the Fairey III biplane. Its wing had an increased angle of dihedral to improve its lateral stability for remote control. Only three were built and the first two crashed immediately after launch.

Handley Page Type 43 In 1928, Imperial Airways asked Handley Page to design a large four-engined biplane airliner and a smaller rimotor. The first led to the HP.42 but the second did not find favour. Later the RAF needed a bomber-transport to replace the Clive and Victoria, so HP submitted the HP.43. The prototype was found to handle badly, but it converted to monoplane configuration as the prototype Harrow.

Hawker Nimrod Intended to replace the Fairey Flycatcher in service. Developed from the radial-engined Hawker Hoopoe, with the same Kestrel engine used in the Fury. The prototype was called the Norn but renamed the Nimrod when an order was placed. It could operate as a floatplane or on wheels. An updated Nimrod II followed in September 1934 but the type had been replaced by the Sea Gladiator by May 1939. SDB

2

RAF Fast Fact

Almost 50 of the SOE agents in France were women; the most famous of which was Violette Szabo (illustrated). She was flown into and out of France by a Lysander in April 1944, then parachuted back in for her next mission. On June 10, she was captured after a gun battle in which she killed at least one German. Interrogated and executed, she was posthumously awarded the George Cross, Britain's highest civil decoration.

Another famous female SOE agent was Nancy Wake, who was codenamed "the White Mouse." The Gestapo placed a large bounty on her head but she continued to evade capture, helped countless downed aircrew to escape and led guerrilla fighters against German outposts. It is claimed she never travelled without her Chanel lipstick and famously said she "had not parachuted into France to fry eggs and bacon for the men." She survived the war and died at age of 98.

1. The Lysander's high-mounted wing had a reverse taper towards the root and was aerodynamically very advanced for its day. It also had fully automatic wing slots and slotted flaps which gave it a very short take off and landing run..**SDB**
2. Lysanders delivering members of the SOE operated from improvised airstrips as short as 150yds long. **SDB**
3. Later in the war it was found that an all-black aeroplane actually stood out well against low clouds so some aircraft were repainted with dark green and pale grey upper surfaces. This is a replica built for the 2016 film *Allied* starring Brad Pitt. **SDB**

3

and a staggering 118 of the 175 aircraft deployed to France were lost.

Following the Dunkirk evacuation, it became clear that the Lysander was unsuitable for coastal patrol and army co-operation roles. Feedback from pilots deemed it was too fast for artillery spotting but too slow to avoid the German fighters. It was also too heavy to operate from soft fields and too large to conceal on advanced landing grounds. It became evident that the Lysander had been developed by the RAF without asking the Army what it actually needed in an aircraft.

Army co-operation squadrons were soon re-equipped with camera-fitted Curtiss Tomahawk and North American Mustang fighters for reconnaissance operations, and the Taylorcraft Auster was used for artillery direction.

Special Duties

Some of the now-surplus Lysanders were used for coastal command duties and others were shipped to the Middle East and India. Meanwhile, it became obvious that the 'Lizzie' could actually fill the requirement for a dedicated SOE aircraft.

The first unit to use the type in this role was 419 Flight at RAF North Weald, Essex, which formed in August 1940 with a pair of Lysanders. The following month another example joined the Flight along with three Whitley bombers.

Its first clandestine mission was undertaken on September 3 when Wg Cdr Andrew Geddes flew an agent to a field near Tours, France in a Lysander. On the night of October 19, the first 'pick-up' sortie was flown when Flt Lt Farley liaised with Special Intelligence Service (SIS) agent Philip Schneidau. He had parachuted into France ten days prior, and used messenger pigeons to communicate with England and arrange his retrieval (small radio sets were not yet available).

1933

Hawker Osprey The carrier-borne version of the Hart flew in both the fighter and reconnaissance roles. Armament consisted of a .303in Vickers machine gun and a .303in Lewis gun. The first examples joined the FAA in 1932 and four years later Ospreys from 701 Sqn were deployed to RAF Kalafrana in Malta in the anti-submarine and anti-piracy role. Some remained in service as second-line training machines as late as 1944.

Short Sarafand A biplane flying boat designed by Oswald Short as a reconnaissance aircraft with transatlantic capability. It was an enlarged development of the Singapore II and when it flew in 1932 it was Britain's largest aeroplane. Although the six-engined Sarafand failed to win an order the prototype was used for experimental flying at the Marine Aircraft Experimental Establishment at Felixstowe until 1936.

Fairey Seal The shipborne version of the Fairey Gordon [see p30]. It differed from the land-based variant in being strengthened to allow it to be catapult launched. It had attachments allowing it to operate from floats. The Navy used it as a torpedo-bomber but the RAF also used the Fairey Seal as target tugs. In Ceylon, 273 Sqn used RAF Seals for coastal patrols against Japanese forces until 1942.

Handley Page Heyford Built as a heavy night bomber to replace the Vickers Virginia. A novel design feature saw the fuselage attached to the upper wing and the bomb bay built into the thickened centre section of the lower wing. The undercarriage was long to allow bombs to be reloaded while the two Kestrel engines were running. Heyfords entered service with 99 Sqn and eventually equipped nine units until 1939.

Saro Cloud An enlarged version of the Saunders Roe (Saro) Cutty Sark monoplane flying boat with room for two crew and eight passengers. Although conceived as a civilian aircraft the Air Ministry purchased 22 for use by the RAF as pilot and navigator training aircraft, with a classroom in the rear for six students. They were based at the Seaplane Training Squadron at RAF Calshot and served until 1939.

1 & 3. Although it was most famous for its operations in France the Lysanders of Special Duties squadrons also served in the Mediterranean where 148 (SD) Sqn picked up agents in Greece and Yugoslavia. Even further afield, 357 (SD) Sqn began operations in the Far East in 1944 supporting the SOE in Burma and resistance groups in Malaya. **SDB**
2. Gibraltar Farm Barn at RAF Tempsford was where agents were given their final instructions and equipment before boarding their Lysander flight to beyond enemy lines. **Andrew Kitney**

1

Upon hearing the inbound Lysander, Schneidau lit a three light flare path pattern to guide the aircraft on its landing in a small field.

The Lysander had been modified for the mission, with the rear cockpit glazing removed and a ladder welded to the side of the fuselage to help the agent quickly access the aircraft; thus minimising the time on the ground between landing and take off.

On the night of the planned meet-up the weather was atrocious, with high winds and heavy rain. The RAF abandoned all missions that evening but, knowing that Schneidau would be waiting for him, Farley convinced his commanding officer to let him fly.

The weather cleared over the field where Schneidau was hiding and Farley landed with ease. However, on departure a German soldier fired at the Lysander and a bullet entered the cockpit, passed between the pilot's legs and destroyed the compass.

Returning into the storm in the dark (with no compass) the heavy rain began entering the open rear cockpit and caused the wireless to stop working. They pressed on north, waiting for a gap in the clouds; not knowing if they would be over England or northern Germany. Six hours later they broke cloud and, running low on fuel, Farley attempted a landing. His aircraft hit anti-glider defences but the two survived.

Unable to understand the broad accent of the guardsmen who discovered them, the two restricted their answers to "name, rank and number." It was only some hours later that they realised they were in Oban in Scotland; 600 miles (966km) north of North Weald!

Squadron Status

In February 1941, the Flight had its designation changed to 1419 Flight to avoid confusion with the existing 419 Sqn.

It continued to expand and relocated to RAF Stapleford Tawney, Essex and then RAF Stradishall, Suffolk; when an extra five Whitleys were added in August 1941 it became 138 (Special Duties) Sqn.

For the remainder of the war the unit undertook the 'heavy lifting' of supplies and agents to France and other occupied countries, using ten Whitleys, three Halifaxes, a Martin Maryland and a pair of Lysanders. Pilots flew low and slow to deliver supplies accurately into the hands of resistance fighters.

Agents were parachuted from very low level – typically as low as 500ft (152m) – and a number were injured. When it came to extract them it was the Lysanders that returned to pick them up. The 'Lizzies' were painted matte black to help them merge into the night sky and operations almost always took place within a week of a full moon to aid navigation. They featured the same fixed ladder as fitted to Flt Lt Farley's aircraft, although they dispensed with the open rear cockpit. The Lysanders were also fitted with a 150 Imp Gal (682 lit) drop tank under the belly, which extended their range from 600 to 1,150 miles (966 to 1,851km).

The aircraft were also modified to carry two 'passengers' in the rear cockpit; although in several documented cases up to four agents were carried, albeit in extreme discomfort.

"The Barn"

The following February 138 (SD) Sqn was split, with its Lysanders and some of the bombers

2

combined with the King's Flight to form 161 Sqn at RAF Newmarket, Suffolk. The unit was commanded by Edward Fielden, an experienced pilot who had been the CO of the King's Flight [Ed: see page 76].

The unit moved to the Top Secret base at RAF Tempsford, Bedfordshire in April 1942. It would remain there until the end of the war. From this point 138 (SD) Sqn dropped the agents and 161 Sqn retrieved them. The latter also landed agents behind lines on occasion; normally if they lacked parachute experience or were unable to use one.

Tempsford was one of the most secret airfields in the country and to many onlookers it looked mostly like a farm. One of the most inauspicious looking buildings on the base was Gibraltar Farm Barn. Careful measures were taken to ensure it looked like a normal farm barn (to fool enemy aerial reconnaissance) but

1933

Vickers Viastra An all-metal 12-seat passenger high-wing monoplane airliner. It was built in one, two and three-engined versions; the first example flew in October 1930. A single Viastra X was converted to a VIP passenger version for the Prince of Wales. G-ACCC first flew in April 1933 and like most of his aircraft, was painted in the blue and red colours of the Brigade of Guards. It later passed to the RAF to test airborne wireless radios.

Vickers Vildebeest A land-based torpedo bomber that replaced the Horsley. The Vickers Vildebeest had a metal fuselage with fabric-covered wings and a Bristol Pegasus engine. The first 30 were two-seaters and the remaining 150 had a third crew place. Vildebeest IVs had a more powerful Perseus engine but this was prone to overheating so just 18 were built and these were unsuitable for overseas service.

Westland Wallace Created as a successor to the Wapiti [see p26] the Westlands Wallace had a longer fuselage and more powerful Pegasus engine. The first 68 were converted from Wapitis and 104 Wallace IIs were built afresh, some complete with an enclosed canopy. Most of the Wallaces were transferred directly to the Royal Auxiliary Air Force (RAuxAF) and the last one was not retired until mid-1943.

1934

Avro Rota The Cierva C.30A autogyro was built under licence by Avro from 1934. A dozen were constructed for the RAF and powered by the Armstrong Siddeley Genet Major IA. They originally served with the School of Army Co-operation at Old Sarum but from 1940 they moved to Duxford for radar calibration use. Many of the surviving civil aircraft were also impressed into RAF service between 1939 and 1940.

Blackburn Perth The magestic Perth began life as the Iris V but differed sufficiently to warrant a new name. The large patrol flying boat had Rolls Royce Buzzard engines and an enclosed cockpit for the pilots. Four were delivered to 209 Sqn and these could be fitted with a COW 37mm autocannon in the nose. They were retired in 1937 and were the largest biplane flying boat ever to serve with the RAF.

3

The Lysander had been developed by the RAF without asking the Army what it actually needed

it was actually where SOE agents were supplied with their equipment and readied to board the aircraft. Their supplies included cyanide pills, in case of capture.

Short Field Ops

Prior to their departure the BBC would broadcast coded messages to inform agents and Resistance leaders that the missions were going ahead. A memorable message from January 1943 stated that: *"Le castor foulera la neige deux fois" ("The beaver will tread the snow twice")*; notifying that two Lysanders rather than one would be making the pickup that night.

In order to boost their reach into occupied France the Lysanders initially stopped at RAF Tamgmere, Sussex – some 100 miles (161km) south of Tempsford – for fuel.

The aircraft then flew in darkness and radio silence to a pre-arranged location. Before the agents left Tempsford, they would have been taught how to stake out a flarepath with bicycle lamps to mark a landing site in the moonlight. As the Lysander approached, the agent flashed a pre-agreed letter in Morse code. When the pilot acknowledged the signal, the other lights were switched on.

The Lysander then landed on improvised airstrips as short as 150 yards (137m). Arriving agents then disembarked via the ladder and passengers waiting to be picked up ran onto the field and climbed aboard. Within three minutes the aircraft would be airborne and on its way backs to England.

This was some of the riskiest flying an pilot could be asked to undertake. Yet in the 279 sorties flown between 1940 and 1944 just 13 Lysanders and six pilots were lost.

By the end of the war the units had delivered more than 400 agents to Europe by Lysander and parachuted in a further 1,800. They also brought at least 250 home safely as well as 593 political activists, members of the French resistance and evading RAF or USAAF airmen.

The SOE was dissolved after the war and its assets transferred to the Special Operations Branch of the Secret Intelligence Service; MI6. The bravery of its men (and women) would never be forgotten. ■

Boulton Paul Overstrand The RAF's last twin-engine biplane medium bomber. The Boulton Paul Overstrand was a development of the earlier Sidestrand but had an enclosed cockpit. It was also the first RAF aircraft to have a power-operated turret. Four Sidestrands were converted and 24 Overstrands were built as new. Eleven remained in use at the start of World War Two, albeit solely in the gunnery training role.

Handley Page Type 47 Designed to replace the Vincent, the HP.47 was a low-wing monoplane powered by a Bristol Pegasus. The wing had large flaps as well as full span leading edge slats. Unusually, the tail fin moved as well as the rudder, albeit through smaller angles. The tailplane and single elevator were also coupled. The aircraft was criticised for its poor longitudinal stability and the contract was awarded to the Wellesley.

Vickers 253 Conceived as a multi-role aircraft capable of carrying out bombing, dive bombing, torpedo bombing, army co-operation, reconnaissance and casualty evacuation. The Type 253 was a Pegasus-powered biplane that used Barnes Wallis' geodetic construction method. The aircraft won a contract and 150 were ordered, but when Vickers flew the monoplane Wellesley in 1935 the order was changed to the newer type.

Vickers Valentia Based on the Napier Lion-powered Victoria transport aircraft but re-engined with more powerful Bristol Pegasus engines and a strengthened wing and undercarriage. The RAF ordered 28 Valentias and 54 Victorias were upgraded to the new standard. It entered service with 70 Sqn and was used extensively throughout the Middle East. Valentias were used for 'sky shouting' during air policing missions.

Vickers Vincent A development of the Vildebeest to replace the Wapiti and Fairey IIIF in the General Purpose role in the Middle East. The torpedo equipment was lost in favour of message pick-up and signalling gear. A total of 197 were delivered (although many of them were converted from Vildebeests) and 84 remained in service at the outbreak of the war. Some saw action against Italian forces in East Africa.

From Flop to Legend

While the Avro Manchester was plagued with problems it would lead to the legendary Lancaster as well as the Lincoln, York and Shackleton - the latter serving until 1992

History has not been kind to the Avro Manchester. It was underpowered, unreliable and generally unsatisfactory. However, it would form the basis for one of the most famous families of bomber aircraft.

Although the British aviation industry was desperately trying to produce as many fighter aircraft as possible in run-up to what would become known as the Battle of Britain, it became obvious that if the country was victorious it would need bombers to take the fight to the heart of the German heartland.

At the outbreak of World War Two, the RAF's frontline bomber fleet consisted mainly of Bristol Blenheim light bombers, even smaller single-engined Fairey Battles and the ageing Handley Page Harrow. They all lacked not just speed and manoeuvrability but also the range to reach deep into Europe. Furthermore, they carried woefully small bombloads and lacked both precision bombing equipment and effective defensive armament.

Even the RAF's larger and slightly more capable bombers, such as the Armstrong Whitworth Whitley, Handley Page Hampden and Vickers Wellington proved vulnerable to fighter attack and were only really suitable for night operations.

Manchester

The Avro Manchester was created in response to this need for a capable heavy bomber, which was set out in Air Ministry Spec P.13/36.

It was a twin-engined monoplane aeroplane, designed around the 24-cylinder Rolls-Royce Vulture 'X-block' engine. This was effectively two Rolls-Royce Peregrine 'V-12' powerplants mounted one on top of the other, with the bottom one inverted to give the 'X' shape.

The new engine showed great promise and could produce 1,760hp, but in practice it proved to be very unreliable and had to be de-rated to 1,480hp even before it had reached production. The technology behind the Vulture engine was just too ambitious for the time and the engine proved to be a huge disappointment.

Nevertheless, Avro pressed on with its new bomber and the prototype Manchester (L7246) took off from Manchester's Ringway Airport on its maiden flight on July 25, 1939.

Into Production

Testing revealed the aircraft lacked lateral stability so its twin-fin design was modified with the addition of a third, central tail fin.

1. The Lancaster would go on to become the best known of all RAF World War Two bombers. **SDB**
2. Avro Manchester I of 207 Sqn showing the variant's unusual triple fin configuration.
3. Lancasters typically flew at night where the cover of darkness offered them an extra degree of safety.
4. The four-engined Lancaster emerged from the twin-engined Manchester. The two troublesome Vulture powerplants were replaced by four Merlins and the wing and tail were increased in size and strength.

The first 20 production variants – dubbed the Mk I – flew with this unusual tail configuration but subsequent Mk IA aircraft reverted to twin tails using enlarged fins and rudders. A larger horizontal tailplane was fitted to the latter type.

Avro would go on to produce 177 Manchesters and Metropolitan-Vickers constructed a further 32 before construction was terminated in 1941.

The first Manchesters entered service with 207 Sqn in November 1940 and flew their first operational mission (to the French port of Brest) on the night of February 24-25, 1941.

However, all was not well and in April the type was temporarily grounded due to a higher than expected number of engine failures. Manchesters were eventually approved to return to flight but the problems persisted and the bombers were grounded again between June and August. Further issues soon manifested themselves including a propensity for the tailplane to flutter and the propellers failing to feather. These, combined with hydraulic failures and the general lack of performance and

1935

Avro Prefect The Prefect was almost identical to the Avro Tutor from which it was developed. Although it was aimed at the export market the RAF received seven for air navigation training. These initially served at the Air Navigation School at Andover but later moved to 48 Sqn at Manston. They survived into World War Two and while they were primarily used for communications some performed other miscellaneous duties.

de Havilland DH.82B Queen Bee Combining the engine, wings, undercarriage and tail of a Tiger Moth with the wooden fuselage of a Moth Major created the perfect RAF target drone. The Queen Bee [see also p25] was remotely flown by an operator using a control panel either in another aircraft or on the ground. It could fly from runways or be fired from a catapult. A total of 412 Queen Bees were constructed.

de Havilland DH.88 Comet Famous as the aircraft that won the 1934 MacRobertson Air Race from England to Australia, DH.88 G-ACSS was dismantled and shipped back to Britain after the race. It was then purchased by the Air Ministry and registered K5085. It was evaluated at RAF Martlesham Heath by the Aeroplane and Armament & Experimental Establishment before it was written off and sold.

Gloster Gauntlet A development of the Gloster SS.19B but powered by the Bristol Mercury VI. The RAF ordered 24, to be named Gauntlet, and this was followed by 204 Gauntlet IIs. The latter replaced the complicated welded structure with a tubular construction similar to the Hawker biplanes. The Gauntlet was 56mph faster than the Bulldog it replaced and remained the RAF's fastest aircraft until 1937.

Hawker Hardy Developed from the Hart, the Hardy was a General Purpose aircraft that replaced the Wapiti. The 47 aircraft had modified radiators, a message pick-up hook and a desert survival kit. It entered service with 30 Sqn in Mosul, Iraq and also served with 6 Sqn in Palestine and 237 Sqn in Kenya and Sudan. The Hardy saw limited wartime service in Africa and the Middle East but had been retired by May 1941.

unreliability across the fleet, led to production being halted in November 1941.

In total, Manchesters would be operated by eight bomber squadrons and two Coastal Command units. The type flew 1,269 combat sorties during the war, with the last being to Bremen, Germany on June 25, 1942.

From Manc' to Lanc'

Even before it entered active service, Avro was well aware of the Manchester's problems.

The company's chief designer, Roy Chadwick, felt that the airframe itself was sound and looked at replacing the troublesome Vulture with a more reliable and powerful engine. Thus, in late 1940, Avro engineers created the prototype Manchester III (BT308). As it was constructed from an uncompleted Mk I this retained the three fins but, most importantly, a wider wing was fitted and four Rolls-Royce Merlin engines mounted below it.

Shortly after its maiden flight from Ringway on January 9, 1941 the new aircraft was christened the Lancaster. It is noteworthy that this was more than a month before the Manchester had flown its first combat mission.

The second prototype Lancaster (DG595) discarded the central tail in favour of the two enlarged fins and rudders used on the Manchester IA. With its larger wings and four engines the Lancaster transformed a disappointing aircraft into one of the most capable bombers of the entire war.

Impressed by what it saw, the Air Ministry ordered the Lancaster into production and also decreed that partially-completed Manchesters remaining on the production line be converted into Lancasters prior to delivery.

RAF Fast Fact

More than 8,500 Avro Manchesters, Lancasters, Yorks, Lincolns and Shackletons served with the RAF between 1940 and 1992.

The first Lancaster I was delivered to 44 (Rhodesia) Sqn at RAF Waddington at the end of 1941 and the unit flew its first operation on March 3 of the following year.

Audacious Raids

In RAF service the Lancaster was famed for a number of brave and audacious missions. These included a daytime raid on the Schneider Works at Le Creusot, France by 90 Lancasters from 5 Group on October 17, 1942 and a series of round-the-clock raids on Hamburg in 1943.

Perhaps the most famous of all Lancaster exploits was Operation *Chastise*, flown on May 16-17, 1943 by 617 Sqn – the Dambusters.

Throughout July 1943, large numbers of Lancasters participated in the devastating round-the-clock raids on the city of Hamburg during Air Chief Marshal Harris' Operation *Gomorrah*. A particularly famous mission performed by the Lancaster was the mission flown 16–17 May 1943, codenamed Operation *Chastise*, to destroy the dams of the Ruhr Valley. The operation was carried out by modified Lancaster IIIs using special 'bouncing' bombs to destroy the dams of the Ruhr Valley.

The Dambusters also played an integral role in the sinking of the German battleship *Tirpitz* in late 1944. For this mission the Lancasters were loaded with 12,000lb *Tallboy* bombs. Later in the war some Lancasters were even modified to carry the 22,000lb *Grand Slam* bomb; the heaviest weapon used during the conflict.

Hawker Hind An improved version of the Hart bomber; purchased by the RAF as an interim aircraft to 'buy time' until modern monoplane bombers were fully developed. The Hind had a more powerful Kestrel V engine and the cut-down rear cockpit from the Demon. It would equip 20 squadrons and 613 Sqn retained the type in the army co-operation role until November 1939. Some were also used as advanced trainers.

Short Knuckleduster A twin-engined, gull-winged flying-boat designed to Air Ministry Spec R.24/31. The contract was awarded to the Stranraer and the Saro London but as the Knuckleduster was powered by experimental 720hp Rolls Royce Goshawk steam-cooled engines (complete with large condensers protruding from the nacelles) it conducted valuable research into steam-cooling of aero engines.

Short Singapore III The RAF's main long-range maritime patrol flying boat of the 1930s. Developed from the single twin-engined Singapore I and one-off four-engined Singapore II, the new type had an all-metal hull and four 675hp Kestrel IX engines mounted between the wings in a 'push-pull' configuration. It was obsolete by the time it entered service but 37 were built and the type soldiered on until October 1941.

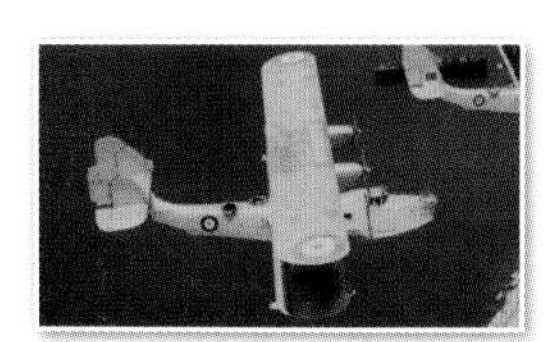

Supermarine Scapa Based on the Southampton – and originally referred to as the Southampton IV – the Scapa was a twin-engined flying boat created to use RJ Mitchell's new hydrodynamic hull design. Supermarine test pilot Joseph 'Mutt' Summers took the prototype aloft on July 8, 1932 and the RAF ordered 15. Soon the specification changed to include more powerful engines and the Stranraer was born.

Supermarine Walrus Developed in response to a 1929 Royal Australian Air Force requirement for an aircraft to be catapult-launched. The RAF ordered 12 aircraft – to be called the Walrus – and these were followed by orders for around 250 others. In RAF service the Walrus found fame with the specialist Air Sea Rescue Service squadrons. Over 1,000 downed aircrew were picked up by Walrus pilots.

Lancasters dropped 618,378 tonnes of bombs during the war

As the Allies liberated Europe in 1945 Lancasters dropped food into the occupied Netherlands during Operation *Manna*.

Between 1942 and 1945 Lancasters carried out a total of 156,000 sorties and dropped 618,378 tonnes of bombs. At the height of production, almost 60 Lancasters a week were being assembled at Avro's Woodford factory in Cheshire. However, it was still not enough and Lancaster production was also undertaken by other manufacturing companies including Austin Motors and Vickers Armstrong.

The type equipped around 50 squadrons but of the 7,377 Lancasters built, a staggering 3,249 failed to return from combat missions.

1

Postwar Operations

Lancasters were to have formed part of the RAF contribution to Operation *Downfall*; the planned invasion of Japan. Referred to as Tiger Force, the Lancasters were painted white with black undersides but Japan's surrender in August 1945 meant the war was over by the time the British bombers arrived in the region.

Nevertheless, the Lancaster would soldier on at the forefront of RAF Bomber Command for a few more years and examples also saw service with Coastal Command in reconnaissance and aerial mapping roles.

It would be December 1953 before the final Bomber Command Lancaster finally retired and another year before the type left RAF service completely; the final sortie being flown by an aerial mapping aircraft in Central Africa.

2

Transports

The Lancaster would spawn a pair of transport aircraft spin-offs. The Avro York flew as early as July 1942 but priority was not given to cargo and passenger aircraft until it looked more certain that Britain would be victorious in the war. As such it would be 1945 before the first examples entered service with 511 Sqn.

The York was a high-wing monoplane using the Lancaster's wing, engines and tail surfaces mated with a boxy fuselage that could accommodate 21 passengers.

Eventually, 208 Yorks would service with ten Transport Command squadrons and the type would play an important role in the Berlin Air Lift of 1948-49.

When the RAF retired its York fleet many were sold into civilian hands and other examples were built new for airlines.

The other transport derivative of the Lancaster was the Lancastrian. Pioneered by Canada's Victory Aircraft the programme saw war surplus Lancasters modified with streamlined noses and tails and fitted with long-range fuel tanks in the bomb bay. The armament was also removed and the Lancastrian could carry up to nine passengers across the Atlantic. British Overseas Airways Corporation (BOAC) took delivery of 30 Lancastrians in 1945 which it used for mail and cargo flights as well as VIP passenger transport.

Lincoln

The ultimate bomber derivative of the Manchester would be the Lincoln, which first flew on June 9, 1944 as the Lancaster V.

Designed to meet Air Ministry Specification B.14/43 for a post-war replacement for the RAF's four-engined heavy bomber fleet, the aircraft had an enlarged fuselage to accommodate more fuel and up to 11 tonnes of bombs. It also had a longer, stronger and more efficient wing and supercharged Merlin 85 engines. This gave it a ceiling of 35,000ft (10,668m) and a range of 4,450 miles (7,172km)

Soon renamed the Lincoln, the first production aircraft flew in February 1945 and joined 57 Sqn in August of the same year.

In the immediate post-war years almost

1936

Avro Anson I A modified version of the Avro 652 airliner acquired by the RAF for maritime reconnaissance missions. Ansons had a wooden wing and steel tube fuselage and were powered by two 350hp Armstrong Siddeley Cheetah engines. The Anson was the first RAF aeroplane to have retractable landing gear and it equipped 26 squadrons by 1939. The 'Annie's' true niche was training pilots to fly multi-engined aircraft.

Blackburn Shark A carrier-borne torpedo-spotter-reconnaissance biplane to replace the Fairey Seal. Although its FAA service was short (it was replaced by the Swordfish in 1937) more than 20 Sharks would be converted into target tugs for the RAF's British Air Observers' School . RAF Shark tugs at RAF Seletar, Singapore were also used for patrol missions and bombing raids against the Japanese in Malaya in January 1942.

Bristol 138 A high-altitude research aircraft that set nine separate world altitude records. At its peak the Bristol 138 [see also p19] reached 53,937ft. The aircraft was not pressurised but the pilot was provided with a special suit and a helmet containing breathing apparatus. Exhaled air travelled to a canister of carbon dioxide-absorbing chemicals prior to being oxygenated and re-circulated.

Fairey Hendon A night bomber created to replace the Vickers Virginia. The Hendon was a low-wing monoplane with a fabric covered tubular structure. Power came from a pair of 600hp Kestrel VIs. The RAF ordered 74 but the order was cancelled after just 14 had been delivered. By then the Armstrong Whitworth Whitley had flown and had much higher performance. The Hendons were phased out by 1938.

Fairey Swordfish A torpedo bomber affectionately nicknamed the 'Stringbag.' The big, single-engined, biplane replaced the Seal, Shark and Baffin in FAA service. The Swordfish was obsolete by the time war broke out in 1939 but it remained in service until 1945 and achieved spectacular and noteable successes. By the end of the war the Swordfish had sunk more Axis shipping than any other Allied aircraft.

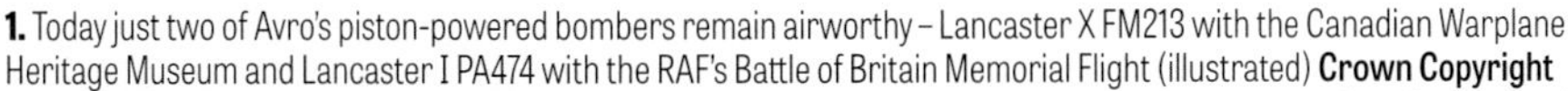

1. Today just two of Avro's piston-powered bombers remain airworthy – Lancaster X FM213 with the Canadian Warplane Heritage Museum and Lancaster I PA474 with the RAF's Battle of Britain Memorial Flight (illustrated) **Crown Copyright**
2. The Avro York transport was a high-wing monoplane that used the Lancaster's wing, engines and tail surfaces mated with a boxy fuselage that could accommodate 21 passengers.
3. The last Shackletons in RAF service with the fleet of 'stop-gap' AEW.2s, which were operated by 8 Sqn until 1992. WL757 is seen here in formation with an example of the Boeing E-3 Sentry which finally replaced the type in RAF service.
4. Avro Shackleton MR.1 WB847 was delivered to the RAF in 1951 and was later converted to T.4 standard..
5. Lancastrians were surplus Lancasters modified with streamlined noses and tails and long-range fuel tanks.
6. The Lincoln had an enlarged fuselage to accommodate more fuel and a longer, stronger and more efficient wing.

600 Lincolns were built for the RAF and the type would equip 29 squadrons. During the 1950s, RAF Lincolns flew missions in Kenya against Mau-Mau insurgents and also saw combat during the Malayan Emergency. In Malaya, Lincolns were used against communist insurgents and flew more than 3,000 missions from Changi and Tengah.The Lincoln would continue in service until the end of 1955.

Maritime Shackleton

The Lincoln itself formed the basis for the last piston-powered Avro aircraft in RAF service; the Shackleton.The type was developed as a long-range maritime patrol aircraft to counter the rapid expansion of the Soviet submarine force. Although it began life as the Lincoln ASR.3 the aircraft was renamed the Shackleton.

The new aircraft dispensed with the Merlin in favour of slower-revving Griffon engines that drove with 13ft (3.96m) diameter contra-rotating propellers. This helped counter the aircraft's higher weight and drag and also led to reduced fuel consumption.

'Shacks' entered RAF service with 120 Sqn in March 1951 and were initially used in the anti-submarine and maritime patrol roles. Soon this was developed to include SAR duties.

The first production model was the MR.1 – 29 of which were built before the MR.1A introduced more powerful engines. The existing airframes were modified to MR.1A standard and 47 new examples were also delivered.

The MR.2 entered service with 42 Sqn in 1953 and included a longer nose and a dorsal turret. The last ten MR.1s on the production line were completed as MR.2s and 80 new examples were ordered.

The most fundamental change with the MR.3 was the shift from conventional taildragger to a nose wheel configuration. The aircraft was also fitted with wingtip tanks to increase fuel capacity and the dorsal turret was deleted to increase internal space. The first of 34 aircraft entered service with 220 Sqn in August 1957. Later versions were fitted with a pair of Viper turbojets to help shorten the take off run.

Last of the Breed

From 1969, the jet powered Hawker Siddeley Nimrod began to replace the Shackleton in the maritime patrol role. However, plans to retire the fleet had to be put on hold when it became obvious that the RAF needed Airborne Early Warning (AEW) in the North Sea and North Atlantic. This had previously been undertaken by the FAA's Fairey Gannet but its retirement left the nation with a capability gap.

As such, the Gannet's AN/APS-20 radar was installed into 12 modified Shackleton MR.2s; thus creating the AEW.2.

The intention was for these to be merely a 'stop-gap' until they could be replaced by the new Nimrod AEW.3 - but the cancellation of that project in 1986 meant the last Shackletons would not be retired until the Boeing Sentry arrived in 1992.

When the last RAF Shackleton landed it marked the end of more than 50 years of continuous service by Avro piston-powered bombers; from the Manchester to Shackleton. ■

1937

Saro London Designed as 'General Purpose Open Sea Patrol Flying Boat' with an all-metal corrugated hull and a fabric-covered wing and tail. Only 31 were built and they served alongside the Stranraer. By the outbreak of war, Londons were still in service with 201 and 204 Sqns in Scotland and 202 Sqn in Gibraltar and these conducted patrols over the North Sea and Mediterranean until mid 1941.

Supermarine Stranraer Created as a coastal reconnaissance flying boat. However, despite high hopes just 17 Stranraers entered RAF service. They had a mostly duralumin structure with a sheet metal covered hull and fabric covered metal wings. The aircraft's marginal performance led to a number of very unkind nicknames: the 'Supermarine Strainer' being one of the more publish-able ones!

Airspeed Oxford Developed from the civilian Envoy and ordered in large numbers as a twin-engined trainer, the Oxford was also used for teaching nav, wireless and photography. Some were also used in communications, anti-submarine roles and as air ambulances in the Middle East. In Canada they formed part of the Empire Air Training Scheme (EATS) and British Commonwealth Air Training Plan (BCATP).

Armstrong Whitworth Whitley One of three twin-engined, medium bombers (alongside the Wellington and the Hampden) that were in RAF service at the outbreak of the war. As well as bombing, the Whitley flew in maritime reconnaissance, glider-tug, trainer and transport roles. Whitleys participated in the first RAF bombing raid on German territory; they flew 8,996 operations and dropped 9,845 tonnes of bombs.

Bristol Blenheim I Developed from the Bristol 142 airliner the Blenheim I light bomber [see also p30] was one of the first British aircraft with an all-metal stressed-skin, retractable undercarriage, a powered gun turret and variable-pitch propellers. The advances in fighters meant the Blenheim soon became vulnerable and they were re-tasked as night-fighters or moved to overseas theatres in Africa and the Mediterranean.

Spitfire – the Flying Legend

The Spitfire is surely one of the most famous aeroplanes to ever take flight and is certainly the most legendary of all RAF fighters. It remains as popular today as it always has been

Fresh from his success designing the Schneider Trophy-winning Rolls Royce Type R-powered Supermarine S.6B seaplane [Ed: see p24], Reginald J Mitchell set about creating a new fighter for the RAF.

The Type R would ultimately evolve into the Merlin engine and whereas the S.6 was not directly related to the Spitfire, it utilised a number of design elements from the air racer.

Mitchell's first attempt at a fighter came in response to a 1931 call from the RAF for a replacement for its Bristol Bulldog biplanes. The Supermarine Type 224 was an open cockpit monoplane with a low gull wing and fixed landing gear. Power came from a 600hp Rolls Royce Goshawk engine, but the contest was won by the Gloster Gladiator [Ed: see p28].

Undeterred, Mitchell developed the aircraft into the Type 300. It now had the elliptical wing that would become synonymous with the Spitfire but still retained the Goshawk engine. It was only after the airframe was married with the new Rolls Royce PV.12 powerplant (later renamed the Merlin) that the Air Ministry become interested.

On January 3, 1935, Supermarine was given a contract to produce a prototype and Specification F.37/34 was written around the new aircraft. Registered K5404, the machine was armed with eight .303 Browning machine guns and an all-metal stressed skin. It was a thoroughly modern aeroplane with the exception of its outdated two-bladed fixed-pitch wooden propeller. It was fitted with a 990hp Rolls Royce Merlin C.

Maiden Flight

On March 5, 1936, Vickers' chief test pilot Capt Joseph 'Mutt' Summers took K5404 into the skies from Eastleigh, Hampshire. He reportedly climbed down from the cockpit and said to Mitchell: "Don't touch a single thing."

The RAF was equally impressed with the new fighter, which Mitchell originally intended to call either the Supermarine Shrew or Scarab.

1

However, five days after the maiden flight the Air Ministry christened the aircraft the Spitfire. Mitchell is alleged to have said it was "just the sort of bloody silly name they would choose!"

On June 3, Supermarine received an order for 310 Spitfires, but just over a year later Mitchell would lose his battle with cancer. He was aged just 42.

Early Marks

After Mitchell's death, Joseph Smith, who had been the chief draughtsman on the project, took over as project lead. It was he who would evolve the Spitfire through 24 variants in just six years, ensuring it stayed at the forefront of the battle with Nazi Germany.

The first production Spitfire I was completed in June 1938 and in August the first examples entered service with 19 Sqn at RAF Duxford, Cambridgeshire where they replaced Gauntlets.

The Mk I was in constant development and

"Just the sort of bloody silly name they would choose!" - R J Mitchell

among the pre-war changes were the bulging of the canopy sides to help visibility, and the addition of armour plating and a bulletproof windscreen. From the 78th aircraft the fixed pitch two bladed wooden propeller was replaced by a de Havilland two speed, three bladed unit.

Production began slowly and by the outbreak of war on September 3, 1939, just 306 Spitfires had been delivered (and 36 of those had already been written off). As such, the RAF went into the war with only eight Spitfire squadrons.

Eventually, 1,566 Mk Is were built and by the end of the Dunkirk evacuations in early 1940 the RAF had 19 Spitfire squadrons. The

1937

de Havilland DH.86 Express Created for the Empire Air Mail Service from England to India, Malaya and Australia the DH.86 was a four-engined development of the de Havilland Dragon with tapered wings. Four were acquired by the Air Ministry from civil airlines and delivered to the RAF Wireless School to teach radio operators. Others were impressed into RAF service at the outbreak of war, serving in the communications role.

Fairey Battle A single-engined bomber designed as a monoplane successor to the Hart and Hind. It had the same Merlin engine as the fighters but carried a crew of three and a bombload, so it was slow and short ranged. It was vulnerable to enemy fighters and during the Battle of France 50% of Battles typically failed to return from missions. They were soon replaced but some operated coastal patrol missions as late as 1941.

Gloster Gladiator The RAF's last biplane fighter and the first with an enclosed cockpit. Developed from the Gauntlet, the Gladiator [see also p26] was obsolete by the time it entered service the RAF. However, it proved itself well in combat and was used by the RAF in France, the Battle of Britain, Norway, Greece, Malta, the Middle East, North Africa and the brief Anglo-Iraqi War. The RAF received 483 Gladiators.

Handley Page Harrow A high-wing bomber with a fixed undercarriage. The Harrow could carry 3,000lb of bombs and was fitted with powered nose and tail turrets. It was phased out of use as a bomber by late 1939 and re-tasked as a transport. Some were used to tow Long Aerial Mines (LAM) into the path of German bombers during the Blitz. The LAM had an explosive charge that was designed to explode on contact.

Hawker Hector A replacement for the Hawker Audax. Demand for Kestrel engines was high so a Napier Dagger III was used instead. The RAF received 165 to equip seven RAF army co-operation squadrons, but they began to be replaced by Lysanders from July 1938. Hectors of 613 Sqn dive bombed German positions during the Dunkirk evacuation and from 1940 survivors were used as target-tugs and for towing Hotspur gliders.

RAF Fast Fact

Early versions of the Spitfire's Merlin engine were fitted with an SU carburettor. When subjected to negative G force (such as pitching the nose hard), fuel was forced up to the top of the carburettor's float leading to loss of power or even the engine stopping. During the Battle of Britain, the fuel-injected German fighters could exploit this British weakness by pitching forward to escape.
The solution was created by Mrs Beatrice 'Tilly' Shilling, an engineer working at the Royal Aircraft Establishment (RAE), who came up with a flat washer which was placed into the carburettor. This allowed just enough fuel flow for maximum engine power and enabled a short period of inverted flight. The problem was not completely overcome until the introduction of the Bendix pressure carburettor in 1943 but the stopgap measure was popular with pilots, who affectionately named it 'Miss Shilling's Orifice' or 'Miss Tilly's Diaphragm'.

1.Spitfire IX MH434 spitting fire on start up at the Shuttleworth Collection. **SDB**
2.Shortly after arriving at RAF Duxford with 19 Sqn the RAF's first Spitfires flew to nearby Cambridge Airport for their first public appearance. **Marshall Aerospace Archive**
3.The prototype Spitfire was K5054. 'Mutt' Summers took it into the sky for its maiden flight on March 5, 1936.

Hurricane was still being produced quicker and outnumbered Spitfires during the Battle of Britain in the summer of 1940.

With the help of the newly developed radar stations the RAF's Spitfires and Hurricanes defeated the Luftwaffe's daytime offensive on Britain, but victory came at a cost. German Messerschmitt Bf 109 fighters shot down 219 Spitfires and 272 Hurricanes whereas the Spitfire shot down 180 Bf 109s, the Hurricane only 153. However, it must be remembered that Hurricanes were primarily tasked with shooting down bombers and – on the whole – they scored far more kills during the Battle than the Spitfire. Yet it was the Spitfire that captured the imagination of the public and even the Luftwaffe, whose pilots were said to suffer from "Spitfire snobbery" – nobody wanted to admit they'd been shot down by a Hurricane!

The later Spitfire II was very similar to the late model Mk Is but had a 1,150hp Merlin XII engine (a 120hp increase over the Mk I). Mk Is were built at Supermarine's factory at Eastleigh, Southampton whereas the Mk II was produced in a factory at Castle Bromwich near Birmingham. Production began in June 1940 and 611 Sqn at Digby, Lincolnshire was the first to receive the Mk II in August 1940.

A total of 1,567 Mk Is and 920 Mk IIs were built but most were phased out of service in 1941 to be replaced by the Spitfire V. The Spitfire III was the type's first major redesign and included a supercharged 1,240hp Merlin XX, clipped wings and a retractable tailwheel. Although initially ordered by the RAF, this was later cancelled as the Hurricane II had more urgent need of the Merlin XX. The Mk III was later abandoned in favour of the Mk V, although many of the improvements first seen in the Spitfire III were used in subsequent versions of the aircraft.

Even though it was designed as an 'interim' model, the Spitfire V - fitted with a 1,515hp Merlin 45 with a high altitude supercharger - was produced in greater numbers than any other single mark.

Several Mk I and II airframes were converted to Mk V standard on the production lines, enabling the new variant to start equipping fighter units from early 1941. Like its predecessors, the Spitfire V was constantly upgraded throughout its service with major changes including large oil coolers and the 'Malcolm' hood to improve visibility.

The Mk V was also the first Spitfire variant to see significant overseas use and in March 1942 a squadron's worth were delivered to RAF units in Malta to help defend the island. The type also deployed to the Far East to fly against the Japanese and saw extensive use in North Africa where its battle honours included El Alamein, flying top cover to protect ground attack aircraft from the Bf 109Fs of the German desert air force. For use in the desert the Mk V was fitted with a tropical 'Vokes' filter below the cowling to avoid sand ingestion into the engine.

The Mk VB variant was also the first production version of the Spitfire to use 'clipped' wingtips as an option; increasing

1938

Hawker Hurricane I The Hurricane I [see also p46] was essentially a monoplane version of the Fury. The new fighter had a retractable undercarriage and the new Merlin engine. The Mk I had fabric-covered wings and a wooden two-bladed, fixed-pitch propeller. Later Mk Is had a de Havilland or Rotol constant speed three-bladed, metal propeller and metal-covered wings. A total of 4,200 Hurricane Is were built.

Miles Magister Based on the civilian Miles Hawk Trainer, the Magister was an open-cockpit, low-wing wooden monoplane. Known as the 'Maggie' to the thousands who learned to fly on the type, it eventually equipped 16 Elementary Flying Training Schools. As part of British anti-invasion preparations some Magisters were fitted with bomb racks in 1940 with the intention of using them as light bombers in the event of an invasion.

Slingsby T.7 Cadet TX.1 & TX.2 Created by Slingsby for the civilian glider market as the T.7 Kirby Kadet. The aircraft was modified to meet an Air Ministry requirement for a training glider to form part of the Air Cadet scheme. It entered RAF service as the Cadet TX.1 and was later given a different wing and upgraded to T.8 Kirby Tutor/Cadet TX.2. The single-seat Cadets formed the basis of Air Training Corps flying until the 1970s.

Vickers Wellesley A single-engined medium bomber developed alongside the Vickers Type 253 biplane [see p35]. It used the same geodetic design but did not have the same multi-role capabilities. The performance was so improved that the RAF cancelled its order for Type 253 and replaced it with orders for 176 Wellesleys.It was obsolete by the start of the war and therefore mostly operated in the Africa and the Middle East theatres.

Airspeed Envoy A twin-engined development of the earlier Courier. Although the RAF ordered the Envoy into production as the Oxford [see p39] at least ten of the civilian variant were used by RAF crews. The RAF ordered seven examples as VIP transport aircraft and the King's Flight also took delivery of G-AEXX. The latter was later used by the RAF and at least two others were impressed at the outbreak of war.

Crews commented that they were 'clipped, cropped and clapped [out]

1. The Spitfire I entered RAF service in 1938. In recent years two very authentic Mk Is have been restored to appear at airshows, including N3200 which now belongs to the Imperial War Museum. **SDB**
2. The Spitfire V (foreground) met its match with the new Focke-Wulf Fw190 but modifications led to the superlative Mk IX (rear). Almost 6,000 were ultimately built for the RAF. **SDB**
3. The Spitfire VIII benefited from a retractable tail wheel and a broad-chord rudder. In Europe the Mk VIII saw most of its service during the invasion of Italy, but the type arrived in the Far East towards the end of 1943 and saw combat with the Japanese. **SDB**

the roll rate and airspeed at lower altitudes. Several airframes were modified with 'cropped' superchargers to boost performance but by the time these reached the squadrons the aircraft were often past their best. This led to crews commenting that they were "clipped, cropped and clapped [out]."

Superlative Mk IX

The arrival of the Luftwaffe's Focke-Wulf Fw190 in August 1941 meant the Spitfire was truly outclassed for the first in its history, although the Mk V remained the main RAF fighter until the summer of 1942 (and the low-level LF.V stayed in use into 1944). Losses were heavy but soon the new Mk IX would take on the Fw190 on a 'level playing field'.

Although the projected Spitfire VIII promised the performance to counter the new German fighter it involved a significant redesign and would therefore take time to produce in the numbers required.

As such, the single Mk III (N3297) was modified in September 1941 to take the Merlin 60/70 series engine, which had previously been earmarked for the Mk VIII. This aircraft would lead to the Mk VI, VII, VIII and IX.

Development of the Spitfire IX was given the greatest urgency and the prototype flew on February 26, 1942. Production began in June 1942 and a month later the first examples entered service with 64 Sqn at Hornchurch.

The Mk IX was 35kts (40mph) faster than the Mk V and the service ceiling rose from 36,200ft (11,034m) to 43,000ft (13,106m). Its first combat success came on July 30, 1942, when a Mk IX shot down a Fw190 – providing the RAF's answer to the Focke-Wulf scourge.

The RAF received 1,255 Mk IXs, 4,010 low-altitude LF.IXs and 410 high altitude optimised HF.IXs. A further 1,053 were built as Spitfire XVIs, these being identical to the Mk IX but fitted with a US-built Packard Merlin engine.

On October 5, 1944, Spitfire IXs of 401 Sqn became the first allied aircraft to shoot down a Messerschmitt Me 262 jet and Mk IXs remained in service until the end of the war.

The related Spitfire VI was a high altitude fighter, designed to deal with the threat posed by the very high flying Luftwaffe Junkers Ju 86. For this it had a pressurised canopy that had to be locked in place, making it very unpopular.

The Spitfire VII and VIII were intended to replace the Mk V but in reality the Mk IX did this job. The Mk VII was a pressurised fighter with a 1,700hp Merlin 71 and a strengthened and lengthened fuselage: 140 were built between 1942 and early 1944.

The related Mk VIII was unpressurised but benefited from a retractable tail wheel and a broad-chord (pointed-tip) rudder. A total of 1,657 were produced and with the success of the Mk IX at home the decision was made to deploy the Mk VIII overseas. In Europe the Mk VIII saw most of its service during the invasion of Italy, but arrived in the Far East in late 1943.

Photo Recce 'Spits'

In October 1939, two Spitfire Is were given to Sydney Cotton to develop as photo reconnaissance (PR) aircraft. These were the first of around 1,000 Spitfires to be either converted or built from scratch for the reconnaissance role to roam as far as Berlin, providing the RAF with vital aerial photography throughout the war.

Cotton removed the guns to reduce weight and sealed the gun ports improve speed. Two F.24 cameras were placed in the wings in place of the inner gun. On November 18, 1939 they flew their first PR mission over Aachen, Germany from bases in France.

The Spitfire PR.III was the first to be produced in significant numbers; all 40

1938

Blackburn Skua The first monoplane to see service in the FAA. Designed as a fighter and dive bomber, Skuas soon saw action in the early days of the war and on April 10, 1940 they sank the German cruiser Königsberg; the first major warship ever to be sunk by dive bombing. Skuas fared badly against fighters and were withdrawn from front line service in 1941. Some flew on as target tugs until March 1945.

Bristol 146 An eight-gun fighter designed to be powered by a Bristol Perseus sleeve valve radial engine, but this was not ready and the older, lower-horsepower Mercury IX was used instead. Tested against the Gloster F.5/34, Martin-Baker MB2 and Vickers Venom fighters it flew well but the RAF decided that fighters should be Merlin-engined. The sole prototype was damaged in a taxi accident and never repaired.

de Havilland DH.87B Hornet Moth A single-engined cabin biplane designed as a potential replacement for the Tiger Moth. There was no interest from the RAF so it was put into production for civilian owners. However, the RAF did acquire a small number as communications aircraft and a large number were subsequently impressed for military service during the war as liaison aircraft.

de Havilland DH.89 Dominie The militarised version of the Dragon Rapide airliner. It had been an unsuccessful entry into the competition that led to the Anson in 1936 but in late 1938 the first examples were acquired as VIP aircraft. Then, in 1939, the Dominie was ordered into produced as a wireless and navigation trainer. The RAF received 469 Dominies, many of which were flown straight into storage and never used.

de Havilland DH.93 Don A multi-role trainer intended to be used to teach pilots, radio operators, navigators and gunners. The latter involved the fitting of a dorsal gun turret but the aircraft was overweight so the turret was removed from production variants. The order for 250 Dons was reduced to 50; of which 20 were delivered engineless for ground training. The type was grounded in March 1939.

3

5

4. An oblique camera is loaded into the fuselage bay of an early PR Spitfire. As the recce variants evolved, so the performance improved and the amount of cameras they carried increased. The only Griffon-powered dedicated PR Spitfire was the PR.XIX. This combined the Mk XIV fuselage with PR.XI wings and had a top speed of 445mph.

4

6

5. A Spitfire VIII undergoes engine maintenance in the open in Italy in 1943.

6. The Mk XII was the first Griffon-powered Spitfire.

converted from fighters. However, it lacked range and was replaced by the PR.IV – which had a range of 2,000 miles (3,219km) – from October 1940. The RAF received 229, making it the most numerous of all PR Spitfire variants.

Later variants included the high-altitude PR.VI (15 built), the armed PR.VII (45 converted from Mk Vs) and the PR.X; the latter marrying the wings of a PR.XI with the fuselage from a Mk VII.

However, it was the PR.XI that was produced in greater numbers than any other PR variant, with over 470 manufactured in total. It had a Mk IX fuselage but contained extra fuel tanks and a universal camera installation, which allowed the cameras to be easily swapped.

Griffon Spitfires

By 1941, Rolls Royce had developed a higher performance version of the Type R racing engine and this became the Griffon.

The first Spitfire to fly with the new powerplant was Mk IV DP845, which took flight in November 1941. It was later re-designated as the prototype Mk XII and it was very fast at low levels, reaching a speed of 323kts (372mph). It was also faster than the Mk IX up to 20,000ft (6,096m), but only 100 were built, equipping 41 and 91 Sqns in early 1943.

Perhaps the most important of the Griffon Spitfires – and the only one to see significant wartime service – was the Mk XIV. The type was fitted with a 2,050hp supercharged Griffon 61 turning a five-bladed propeller, which required a larger tail to control the torque.

The Mk XIV was basically a Griffon-powered Mk VIII with a larger tail and the first six to fly were converted from Mk VIII airframes.

In total, 957 Mk XIVs were built; over 430 of which were fighter reconnaissance FR Mk XIV versions with vertical and horizontal cameras.

The Mk XIV was built in both 'high back' and 'low back' variants, the latter with a 'teardrop' canopy to improve rearward vision; as it was used mainly at low altitudes, most had clipped wingtips. From December 1944 the

Handley Page Hampden A twin-engine medium bomber that took part in most of the major bombing missions during the first part of the war including the first night raid on Berlin and the first 1,000-bomber raid on Cologne. A staggering 714 Hampdens (almost half of all built) were lost on operations, with 1,077 crew killed and 739 reported as missing. It was retired as a bomber by September 1942.

Martin Baker MB.2 A prototype fighter constructed of simple steel tubing. Power came from an 805hp Napier Dagger III 24-cylinder H-type engine that could be boosted to over 1,000hp for take off. A crash post was fitted, which automatically extended to protect the pilot in the event of a nose-over. Although the MB.2 was praised for its performance and ability to be quickly and cheaply built and repaired, it was not put into production.

Miles Nighthawk/Mentor The Nighthawk was developed from the Miles Falcon Six tourer and intended as a training and communications aircraft. Just five were built, one of which served the RAF as a VIP transport with 24 Sqn. The design was then modified to meet an Air Ministry spec and produced as the three-seat Mentor. The RAF received 45 for use by station flights and as day and night instrument and radio trainers.

North American Harvard I Developed from the NA-26 prototype the trainer went into production as the BC-1 for the USAAC and Harvard I for the RAF. Britain received 400 examples from December 1938, with the majority shipped to Canada and Southern Rhodesia for use by the Empire Air Training Scheme. The Harvard I was distinguishable from the later Mk II by its large tail fin and different wing shape.

Percival Q.6 Petrel The Q.6 was created by Edgar Percival as an airliner but was acquired by the RAF as a communications and liaison aircraft. It was Percival's first twin-engine aircraft and was of all-wood and fabric construction. The RAF received seven of the 27 built and named the type the Petrel. Most of the civil Q.6s in Britain were also impressed into RAF service at the start of the war.

1

type became the 2nd Tactical Air Force's main high altitude air superiority fighter in northern Europe, but by then it had already proved its worth at home by intercepting V-1 flying bombs. The Griffon's boost could be increased using 150 Octane fuel, allowing the Mk XIV to reach 348kts (400mph) at low altitude; enabling it to catch and shoot down the 'Doodlebugs'. West Malling, Kent-based 91 Sqn ended up with the best record against the flying bomb, shooting down 184 with its Mk XIVs.

The later Spitfire XVIII was very similar to late production Mk XIV although it was only built in 'low back' configuration. It used either a 2,035hp Griffon 65 or 2,340hp Griffon 67 and some examples saw postwar service in Malaya. In total 300 were produced, 200 of which were FR.XVIIIs, which sacrificed some fuel capacity in favour of cameras.

The only Griffon-powered dedicated PR Spitfire was the PR.XIX. This combined the Mk XIV fuselage with PR.XI wings and could carry a large drop tank to extend range. It had a top speed of 387kts (445mph) and a service ceiling of 42,600ft (12,984m), making it almost impossible for the Luftwaffe to catch. The RAF received 225 PR.XIXs and the first entered service in May 1944.

Ultimate Spitfire

The final Spitfire variant to see service in World War Two was the Mk.21. Although the fuselage was very reminiscent of earlier variants, the characteristic elliptical wing was changed from the Mk.21 to a more angular shape. The first Mk.21s were produced in September 1944 but they proved unstable in flight and it would be April 1945 before 91 Sqn received the first modified airframes. Only 120 were built before the order was cancelled but some remained in service until 1952.

The later Mk.22 was based on the Mk.21 but with the 'cut-down' fuselage and 'teardrop' canopy. However, this reintroduced the instability issues and an enormous tail (25% larger than the Mk.21) was fitted in an attempt to remedy the problem. This worked, but the war was over by the time the first of 260 examples were delivered.

The ultimate Spitfire was the Mk.24, which was similar to the Mk.22 but had increased fuel capacity and larger tail units as used on the Supermarine Spiteful. Introduced into service in 1946, a total of 81 Mk.24s were completed (27 converted from Mk.22s). The last Mk 24 to be built was delivered in February 1948 and the type was used by 80 Sqn until 1952.

2

The Mk.24 had a maximum speed of 395kts (454mph) – 78kts (90mph) faster than the Mk I. It was also twice as heavy and more than twice as powerful. Despite these changes, the Spitfire of 1945 was instantly recognisable as part of the same family as the prototype of 1936.

The Spitfire was also the only RAF fighter to be produced before, during and after World War Two and it legitimately lays claim to be the most famous aircraft in British history. ■

1938

Percival Vega Gull A development of Edgar Percival's earlier Gull with a fourth seat, dual controls and flaps. Used extensively for racing and record setting before the war, the type entered RAF service with 24 Sqn in 1938. Some 15 were acquired by the Air Ministry and used for communications duties and a further 21 were requisitioned at the start of hostilities and impressed into the RAF and FAA.

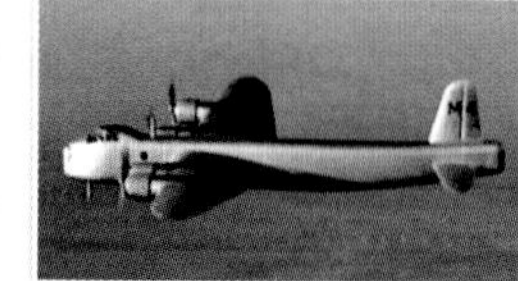

Short S.31 The Stirling would be the RAF's first four-engined heavy bomber, but before it took flight Short Bros flew a half-scale proof of concept version. The wooden S.31 was designed to prove the design's aerodynamic handling and was powered by four Pobjoy Niagara engines. It featured a retractable undercarriage and operable bomb bay doors and testing led to the eventual bomber having a taller undercarriage and a larger tailplane.

Short Scion Senior Created in 1935 as a nine-seat version of the Scion and sold as an airliner that could operate as a seaplane or landplane. None were ordered by the airlines but a handful were sold to survey companies. The last of six was acquired by the Air Ministry for testing flying boat hulls. A series of trials were undertaken by the Marine Aircraft Experimental Establishment but it was lost in March 1944.

Short Sunderland I-III A long-range patrol and reconnaissance flying boat. By the outbreak of war, Coastal Command was operating 40 Sunderland Is with a load of 2,000lb of bombs, depth charges or mines hung below the wing. The Germans nicknamed it the 'Flying Porcupine' due to its defensive firepower. Production shifted to the Mk II with larger engines and more armament and then the Mk III, which introduced a new hull.

Supermarine Spitfire I The first Spitfires entered service with 19 Sqn at Duxford in August 1938. The Mk Is were able to reach a maximum of 315kts at 18,500ft and were powered by the 1,030hp Merlin II engine driving a two-blade wooden fixed-pitch propeller. From the 78th airframe this was replaced by a three-bladed, two-position, metal propeller to improve take off run. In total, 1,567 were built.

3

4

5

6

1. Vokes filter equipped Spitfire Vs in North Africa in 1942.
2. Sqn Ldr E Bocock, the Officer Commanding 549 Sqn, poses in the cockpit of his Spitfire VIII with his beloved dog Sally. The unit was based in Australia from December 1943 until the end of the war.
3. Spitfire F.21 LA195 was delivered to the RAF in January 1946 and is seen here in service with 615 Sqn.
4. Spitfire F.22 VN315 was delivered in July 1946. The Mk.22 was based on the Mk.21 but with the 'cut-down' fuselage and 'teardrop' canopy. This caused instability issues and a very large tail had to be fitted in an attempt to remedy the problem.
5. Spitfire XIV G-SPIT was built as MV268 and following RAF service was transferred to the Indian Air Force. Today it is painted as MV293, the personal aircraft of 'Johnnie' Johnson, the highest scoring RAF pilot to survive the war. **SDB**
6. From the Spitfire I (illustrated) to the Spitfire F.24 the breed had doubled in weight and power output and was 90mph faster with an 80% better climb rate. **SDB**

1939

Vickers Wellington A long-range bomber constructed with a metal geodetic structure, covered with fabric. The Wellington equipped ten units at the outbreak of war and was used as a night bomber in the early years of the conflict. By 1943 it had been replaced by larger types but it continued in other roles, particularly on anti-submarine duties. The type also saw service in the Far East and North Africa.

Westland Lysander The Lysander [see also p34] was developed as an army co-operation aircraft but, despite being aerodynamically advanced, it was soon outmoded. Five squadrons saw service in France prior to the 1940 Dunkirk evacuation but by 1941 the type was replaced by P-40s and P-51s in reconnaissance role. The Lysander found its true niche flying with the Special Duties units.

Airspeed AS.5 Courier A six-seat single-engined light aircraft that saw limited use as a small airliner and air taxi. In 1933, the Courier was the first British aircraft with a retractable undercarriage to go into production. The aircraft came about via a request from Sir Alan Cobham for a machine to carry out a non-stop flight to India using airborne refuelling. At the outbreak of the war eleven were impressed into the RAF.

Avro Cadet A slightly smaller and cheaper to operate development of the Avro Tutor [see p29], created for civilian use. The type was also sold to the Irish Air Corps and Royal Australian Air Force but 32 privately owned examples were impressed into RAF service in 1939. These were mostly drawn from the larger flying schools and put into use as training aircraft with 3 ETFA at Hamble and Watchfield.

BA Swallow A British licence-built version of the German Klemm L.25 light aircraft. A large number of Swallows were impressed into the RAF in 1939. Ten of these were allocated to the RAF's Glider Training Squadron at RAF Ringway near Manchester. Their propellers were removed and tow hooks attached. The aircraft were towed (up to three at a time) by Whitley bombers before being released to glide down.

The Forgotten Hero?

One British fighter aircraft type shot down 55% of all Luftwaffe aircraft during the Battle of Britain. It wasn't the stallion-like Spitfire, it was the RAF's far less glamorous workhorse; the Hawker Hurricane

Ask a person to name a "fighter 'plane" and, almost without fail, they will answer "Spitfire."

RJ Mitchell's aeroplane was a propaganda dream in 1940 and that legacy lives on today. Yet in truth, the Hurricane was easier to build, easier to fly, easier to repair, easier to fight and had more successes during the Battle than its more glamorous cousin.

Even the Luftwaffe bought into the myth; downed Messerschmitt and Heinkel pilots would often lie about the aircraft that shot them from the skies – always claiming to have fallen to a Spitfire pilot's guns.

Monoplane Fury

The Hurricane was essentially an evolution of Sydney Camm's Hawker biplane family [Ed: see p22] and was created in response to a 1934 Air Ministry Specification (F.7/30) for a new generation of RAF fighter.

Camm came up with a new aircraft which he dubbed the 'Monoplane Fury'. It was a cantilever monoplane with a fixed undercarriage and a Rolls-Royce Goshawk engine. Armament was four machine guns: two in the wings and two in the fuselage, synchronised to fire through the propeller arc.

The design was rejected by the Ministry, so Camm refined it with a retractable undercarriage and replaced the problematic Goshawk with the Rolls Royce PV-12 (which would develop into the Merlin). Following preliminary wind tunnel testing of a one-tenth scale model, a prototype of the new aircraft was ordered as the 'Hawker Interceptor Fighter.'

The prototype (K5083) took off on its maiden flight from Hawker's Weybridge airfield (within the confines of the Brooklands motor racing circuit) on November 6, 1935 in the hands of Hawker's chief test pilot, George Bulman.

Engine problems prevailed and it would be March 1936 and four engines later before the aircraft achieved ten hours flying. It was then passed to the RAF for trials and met with an enthusiastic response. It could reach 15,000ft (4,572m) in just five and a half minutes, could reach 274kts (315mph) in level flight and stalled at just 49kts (57mph).

The only real snag was the aircraft's tendency for poor spin recovery, but the fitting of a ventral fairing below the rear fuselage solved this problem. As such, by July 1936, the RAF had ordered a batch of 600 of the new fighter, which it called the Hurricane.

1

Expansion Plan

The RAF's Expansion Plan F called for 600 Hurricanes to be delivered by March 1939 and although the first production Hurricane I flew on October 13, 1937, the deadline was missed by six months. By now war was imminent. The delay was mostly a result of teething problems with the Merlin and the 900hp example in the prototype was replaced by the 1,030 Merlin II. The first 435 had two-bladed, fixed pitch propellers but later examples were fitted with three bladed, two pitch units.

The early Hurricane Is had fabric covered wings but the revised Hurricane IA variants was introduced in mid-1940 with constant propellers, more powerful Merlin III engines and metal covered wings.

A total of 4,200 Hurricane I/IAs were built: 1,924 by Hawker, 1,850 by Gloster Aircraft Company and 426 by Canadian Car and Foundry; the latter were shipped to England to be fitted with engines and join the RAF.

By the start of World War Two in September 1939, Hawker had delivered 497 Hurricanes, enough to equip 18 squadrons.

Into Action

The Hurricane's rugged construction meant it was easy to maintain and/or repair in the field. As such it was chosen to be the RAF's main fighter in France during the so-called 'Phoney War.' Both 1 and 73 Sqns deployed as 67 Wing of the Advanced Air Striking Force, while 85 & 87 Sqns formed 60 Wing of the British Expeditionary Force's Air Component.

The Hurricane first saw combat on October

1939

Blackburn B-2 A development of the earlier Bluebird IV trainer with a new all-metal fuselage. Unusually, the instructor and student sat side by side. Although it was aimed at the military trainer market it failed to find favour with the RAF; but 31 of the 42 built equipped civilian flying schools teaching RAF students. These were impressed into the RAF in 1939 but retained their civilian registrations. **SDB**

Blackburn Roc Derived from the Skua [see p42] and fitted with a power-operated gun turret. It retained the wing-mounted dive brakes and bomb racks under each wing. Even before it entered service it became obvious that performance was too poor for a fighter and many were converted to target tugs while still on the production line. Some Rocs did see service as fighters but they only scored one victory.

Boeing PT-27 Kaydet Although it is most famous for its role as a basic training aircraft with the US Army Air Force and US Navy the PT-17 Stearman also served with the British Commonwealth Air Training Plan in Canada. Of the 10,626 built around 300 were delivered as part of the Lend-Lease scheme and operated as the PT-27 Kaydet, training thousands of members of RAF and commonwealth air crew. **SDB**

Boulton Paul Defiant Designed as a turret fighter, without any forward-firing guns, the Defiant was powered by the Merlin engine. It soon became obvious that the type proved vulnerable to attack by fighter aircraft. They were soon fitted with radar and relegated to night-fighter duties. Defiants were removed from combat duties in 1942 and used for training, target towing, electronic countermeasures and air-sea rescue.

Bristol Beaufort A torpedo bomber developed using experience gained with the Blenheim. Beauforts also flew with Coastal Command as conventional bombers and mine-layers, and saw extensive use in the Mediterranean. Those based in Egypt and Malta also flew missions against shipping in North Africa and some flew missions against the Japanese in the Pacific. By 1942 and was relegated to training and target tugging duties.

RAF Fast Fact

The RAF's leading Hurricane 'Ace' during the Battle of Britain was Czechoslovak-born Josef František. He flew with the Czech Air Force and then fled to Poland following German annexation of his native country, where he received the Cross of Valour four times. After the fall of Poland František joined the Free French Air Force, with some reports claiming he shot down eleven German aircraft before France capitulated. This time František fled to Britain and was assigned to 303 (Polish) Sqn flying Hurricanes. His first confirmed victory was shooting down a Messerschmitt Bf 109E on September 2, 1940, just days after the squadron joined the Battle. By the time he was killed on October 8 he was credited with shooting down 17 German aircraft and another probable. These included nine Bf 109s, six Heinkel He 111 bombers and a Junkers Ju 88. This made him one of the top scoring Allied fighter pilots of the Battle of Britain.
On October 8, František's Hurricane crashed in Surrey, while returning from a patrol. Nobody seems to know why; some claim it was battle fatigue or exhaustion but others think he was flying aerobatics to impress his girlfriend, who lived nearby.

1. The prototype Hurricane, K5083.
2. Pilots from 32 Sqn during a moment's respite during the Battle of Britain. They are, from left to right: P/O K R Gillman (shot down and killed 25/8/40), P/O John Proctor (finished the war with eleven victories and retired as a Wing Commander in 1957), Flt Lt Pete Brothers (finished the war with 16 'kills', and died in 2008, aged 91), P/O 'Grubby' Grice (shot down 10/8/40 and was badly burned. Became one of Dr Archibald McIndoe's 'Guinea Pigs' and after skin grafts he lived to almost 80), P/O P M Gardner (shot down 11/7/41 and became a POW).
3. The Hurricane was part canvas covered. It could therefore absorb a lot of damage and still fly home.

21, 1939, when aircraft from 46 Sqn (based at RAF North Coates, Lincolnshire) intercepted Heinkel He 115 floatplanes over the North Sea and quickly shot down five aircraft.

Back in France there was little action for the BEF but on October 30 a Hurricane shot down a Dornier Do 17P; the first RAF aircraft to down an enemy aircraft on the continent.

The Battle of France began in earnest on May 10, 1940. Hurricanes were immediately in action, soon joined by other squadrons. During the eleven days of combat, and over the Dunkirk evacuations later in May, Hurricane pilots claimed 499 kills and 123 'probables' (although postwar analysis of German losses reveal just 299 were lost during that period, alongside 65 heavily damaged).

In total, 452 Hurricanes were deployed to France but only 66 returned. Many were destroyed and more than 175 were abandoned as the Germans overran allied airfields.

Battle of Britain

On August 8, 1940, Hurricanes of 145 Sqn fired the first shots of the Battle of Britain. Over the coming months Spitfires would typically tackle the Luftwaffe's fighters leaving the Hurricane force to intercept the incoming German bombers. A total of 2,739 Luftwaffe aircraft were lost, with 55% falling to Hurricanes (compared to 42% to Spitfires and the remainder to other sundry types).

The Hurricane frequently demonstrated its resilience: several were badly damaged yet returned to base. In many cases, the enemy bullets and canon shells simply passed through the Hurricane's fabric and out the other side. In similar circumstances the stressed metal skin of a Spitfire would be far harder to repair.

However, the Hurricane's construction made it dangerous in the event of a fire, with the wood frame and fabric covering on the rear fuselage quickly catching alight. Worse still, the large fuel tank in front of the pilot was initially unprotected and prone to catching alight if damaged. Hawker later retrofitted the tanks with a self-expanding rubber coating called Linatex, which would expand when soaked with petrol.

Towards the end of the Battle in September 1940, the first examples of the Hurricane II began to enter service, albeit initially in only small numbers.

The new variant had a two stage supercharged Rolls Royce Merlin XX engine that increased the available power from 1,300hp in the Mk I to 1,460hp. The fuselage was also strengthened and increased by 7in (18cm). Later examples were given additional firepower: the Hurricane IIB had twelve .303 machine guns mounted in the wings and the IIC had four of the large 20mm Hispano cannons.

Overseas Operations

As early as 1939, thought had been given to the Hurricane operating overseas; in June 1940, a

Bristol Blenheim IV Developed from the Blenheim I [see p39] the Mk IV had increased fuel capacity and a lengthened nose that allowed room for a bomb aimer. The nose was 'scalloped' to improve visibility during take off and landing and the turret was fitted with a pair of .303 Brownings in place of the original single Vickers K gun. Blenheim IVs flew in all major theatres of the war and 3,307 were produced by June 1943.

Bristol Bombay Built as a bomber-transport aircraft to replace the Valentia fleet in the Middle East. Deliveries began in September 1939 with a few involved in the Dunkirk evacuation. In the Middle East, Bombays were used as night bombers with 250lb bombs mounted under the fuselage and others thrown out of the cargo door by hand! The type also evacuated thousands of casualties from Sicily.

Consolidated Catalina As with so many American military aircraft of the war, the 'Cat' gained its first combat experience in British hands. Although the first British example arrived in July 1939 it did not actually enter service until 1941. While some were operated from the UK (most notably Scotland), RAF Catalinas were more normally based in India, Sri Lanka and Africa on anti-submarine, convoy escort and air sea rescue missions.

de Havilland DH.80 Puss Moth Created in 1929 as a private aircraft. The aircraft had a steel tube fuselage and wooden wings as well as the new de Havilland Gipsy III inline engine. This was mound inverted so as to improve the view forwards from the cockpit. Between 1929 and 1933 de Havilland built 284 Puss Moths. In 1939, a total of 47 Puss Moths were impressed into RAF service to act as communication aircraft. **SDB**

de Havilland DH.84 Dragon A twin-engined six-seat airliner created for Hillman Airways in 1932. It proved to be one of the firstly truly economical airliners. Just over 200 were built before production switched the to the DH.89 Dragon Rapide. In 1939, 17 civilian Dragons were impressed into the RAF for communications duties. Some survived the war and were returned to the airlines. **SDB**

number were 'tropicalised' and sent to Egypt following Italy's entry into the war.

In Africa, Hurricanes of the Desert Air Force were often flown by British Commonwealth pilots; but while they faired quite well against Italy's Fiat CR.42 biplanes they found themselves quickly outclassed by the Messerschmitt Bf 109E & F. As such, they were replaced in the air superiority role from June 1941 by Curtiss Tomahawks acquired by Lend-Lease.

It was in the ground attack role that the Hurricane excelled in the desert, seeing extensive service in Libya and Tunisia in particular. During the second Battle of El Alamein, which began on October 23, 1942, six squadrons of RAF Hurricanes destroyed 39 tanks and more than 200 trucks and troop carriers. They also targeted fuel and ammunition dumps, flying 842 sorties with the loss of eleven pilots.

Elsewhere, Hurricanes played a vital role in the defence of Malta and the air defence of Russia. The type was the most numerous aircraft supplied to the Soviet Union via Lend-Lease [Ed: see p56] but before the first of 2,952 had been delivered, RAF Hurricanes played an important role defending the nation from German attack in 1941. Murmansk-based Hurricanes of 81 and 134 Sqns also helped protect British convoys delivering aid to Russia.

Further afield, the Hurricane provided valiant service in the Far East. The first to arrive in the area were 51 airframes that were originally destined for Iraq, but diverted to Singapore in January 1942 following the outbreak of war with Japan in the Pacific.

The aircraft were modified with large 'Vokes' dust filters under the nose and pressed into immediate service, mainly in the air defence role but also for ground attack and anti-shipping.

Later Variants

The Hurricane was progressively modified during the course of the war with a number of Mk IIs being fitted with drop-tanks and some altered to carry small bombs beneath the wings; thus earning the 'Hurri-Bomber' nickname.

The Hurricane III was essentially a Mk II powered by the American-built Packard Merlin, but by 1942 the Hurricane had largely been relegated from the fighter role and re-tasked as a ground attack aircraft. To optimise it for the job the Hurricane IIC was replaced by the IID from June onwards; which had two 40mm cannons and two .303 machine guns.

The ultimate ground attack version of the Hurricane was the Mk IV, which began life as the IIE but was sufficiently modified to justify an entirely new designation. This variant had a 'universal wing', which allowed a single airframe to be modified to fit whatever combat role was needed. It could fly as a fighter, be converted to a fighter-bomber or even a tank-killer. Weapons options included eight 60lb (27kg) unguided rockets or two 500lb (227kg) bombs.

A Hurricane V variant was proposed, using more powerful Merlin XXXII engines and four-bladed propellers, but by now the Hurricane had been pushed to its limits and only three airframes were produced.

Unlike the Spitfire, the Hurricane airframe did not lend itself to upgrades. Rather than continue to extend the line, Camm opted to develop a brand new aeroplane: the Typhoon [Ed: see p64].

The final RAF Hurricanes were retired in 1947 and for many years the type was almost extinct from British skies.

However, a recent resurgence in interest means there are now more than 15 airworthy examples in the world, nine of which were flying in the UK in early 2020. ■

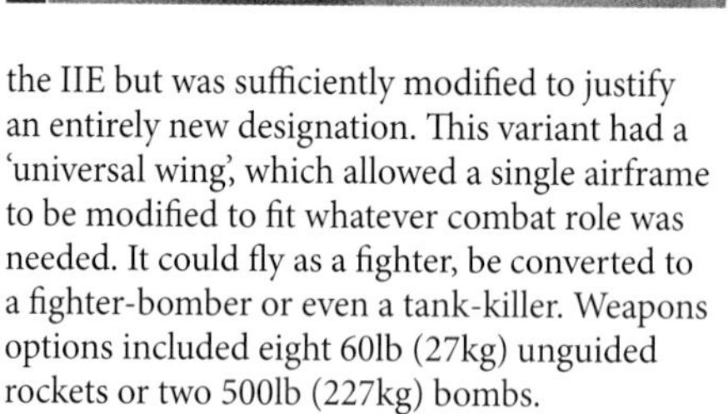

1. Hurricanes were used extensively by South East Asia Command, a fact remembered by the BBMF Hurricane IIC PZ865: seen here in the 34 Sqn SEAC markings, the personal aircraft of Flt Lt Jimmy Whalen DFC. **SDB**
2. Hurricane I P3395 in service with 1 Sqn at RAF Wittering in 1940. This was the personal aircraft of Sgt Arthur 'Darkie' Clowes, who finished the battle with eleven victories. He painted the wasp emblem on the nose himself.
3. Hurricane IVD KZ193 fitted with two 40mm Vickers guns and a Vokes tropical filter. This aircraft was temporarily converted to Mk V status for testing but then reverted to a Mk IV and was used by 164 Sqn RAF at Warmwell, Dorset for anti-shipping strikes.

1939

de Havilland DH.85 Leopard Moth A successor to the DH.80 Puss Moth. The Leopard Moth was similar in configuration but used an all-plywood structure that was lighter and improved range and load carrying capabilities. Like the Puss Moth, the pilot sat up front with two passengers behind. Between 1933 and 1936, de Havilland built 133; of which 44 were impressed into military service in 1939. **SDB**

de Havilland DH.90 Dragonfly An executive transport often described as the Learjet of its day. The Dragonfly was smaller than the Rapide with high aspect ratio swept wings. It also had a preformed plywood monocoque fuselage similar to that used by the DH.88 racer. Aimed at wealthy private owners the DH.90 seated four passengers in great luxury. Of the 67 built before the war, 23 were impressed into the RAF **SDB**

de Havilland DH.94 Moth Minor A monoplane created to replace the biplane DH.60 Moth series. It provided similar performance while using less power and was therefore cheaper to operate. Nearly 100 Moth Minors were completed by the time war broke out two years later and 26 were impressed into RAF service; mainly as glider tugs. Another 40 were produced in Australia for Royal Australian Air Force.

de Havilland DH.95 Flamingo Created as a 17-seat airliner but introduced just prior to the war. The Flamingo was the first all-metal stressed-skin aircraft built by de Havilland. The prototype was bought by the RAF and flown by 24 Sqn until it was lost in an accident in October 1940. The RAF ordered a further 40 as the Hertfordshire, but the order was cancelled as De Havilland was busy producing Tiger Moths.

Douglas DC-2 The forerunner of the famous DC-3/C-47 Dakota. Created in 1934 as a 14-seat airliner to compete with the Boeing 247, the DC-2 served with a number of airlines around the globe in the interwar period. A total of 198 were built before the war and nineteen of these were impressed into the RAF in 1939. These served exclusively with 31 Sqn in India, Iraq and Burma from 1941 to 1942.

In early 2020 there are 15 airworthy Hawker Hurricanes in the world, nine of which are based in the UK. Illustrated here are (from top to bottom): The Shuttleworth Collection's Sea Hurricane I G-BKTH, the Hangar 11 Collection Hurricane IIB G-HHII and Anglia Aircraft Restorations' Hurricane I G-ROBT. The middle aircraft has recently been sold and converted into a two-seat configuration by Hawker Restorations Ltd. **SDB**

The Wooden Wonder

Fast, agile and adaptable; the de Havilland Mosquito was one of the most important aircraft of World War Two

Although it was originally intended as a high-flying, unarmed bomber, the de Havilland Mosquito proved itself to be a true multi-role combat aircraft.

In 1938, the Air Ministry issued a request for a heavily-armed, multi-role aircraft but Geoffrey de Havilland tried to convince officials differently; suggesting that a powerful, twin-engined bomber would be so fast that it would not need defensive armament.

However, the 'men at the Ministry' failed to buy into the concept and instead ordered de Havilland Aircraft to act as sub-contractors, building wings for other companies' bombers.

Strategic Materials

As it happened, de Havilland persevered; after making a number of submissions, the Ministry really warmed to his vision when he suggested a 348kts (400mph) aircraft could actually be manufactured from wood.

Full-scale aircraft production was already underway to meet the RAF's need for new machinery to fight the imminent war, and this meant that metals and other strategic materials were in great demand. The use of wood as an alternative therefore intrigued the Ministry.

By this time, de Havilland already had a reputation for high-speed wooden aircraft with the DH.88 Comet winning long distance races and the 22-passenger DH.91 Albatross airliner capable of cruising at 182kts (210mph). The latter was built of a wooden 'sandwich' which not only saved weight but also reduced construction time.

The company settled on designing a new wooden aircraft that would be aerodynamically 'clean' and powered by the ubiquitous Merlin engines. The proposed de Havilland DH.98 would be faster than any foreseeable enemy fighter aircraft, enabling it to dispense with defensive armament, which would slow it down and make it more susceptible to interception.

Geoffrey de Havilland was so convinced of the design's success that he ordered three prototypes to be manufactured as 'private ventures' even before the government finally placed an order on March 1, 1940.

Mosquito

The initial order (under Specification B.1/40) was for 50 bomber-reconnaissance variants of the DH.98, which was officially named the 'Mosquito' by June 1940. Construction of the prototype began in secret in March 1940 at Salisbury Hall, Hertfordshire, but work was cancelled when the Minister of Aircraft Production (Lord Beaverbrook) decreed that there was no production capacity for an aircraft that was not expected to be in service until early 1942. Instead, he ordered that production should focus on five existing types: the Hurricane, Spitfire, Blenheim, Wellington and Whitley. At the same time he ordered de Havilland to concentrate on its primary work of producing Tiger Moths, licence building Airspeed Oxford trainers and repairing Hawker Hurricane fighters.

Only when de Havilland promised to provide 50 Mosquitos by the end of 1941 was permission granted to restart work on the project.

The airframe was built almost entirely from wood, with a monocoque shell fuselage made of sheets of Ecuadorean balsawood sandwiched between sheets of Canadian birch. The all-wooden wing was built as a one-piece structure and consisted of two main spars, spruce and plywood compression ribs, stringers, and a plywood covering. The entire airframe was then covered in woven cotton linen fabric and coated with a silver 'dope' before exterior camouflage markings were applied.

1

Operation Jericho destroyed the walls of Amiens prison to allow members of the French Resistance to escape

The prototype (W4050) was completed by November 1940 and the aircraft was transported by road from Salisbury Hall to de Havilland's airfield at Hatfield, Hertfordshire. On November 25, Geoffrey de Havilland Jr took the aircraft into the skies on its maiden flight.

Trials revealed W4050 could outpace a

1939

General Aircraft Monospar Swiss-born Helmuth Stieger was working for William Beardmore & Co when he came up with a new technique for creating strong and light cantilever wings. The wing needed only one spar and used internal bracing in the form of thin wires. Based on this design, the twin-engined low-wing Monospar ST-3 flew in 1932. This led to 45 aircraft of various configurations; 17 of which were impressed into the RAF.

Gloster F.9/37 A cannon-armed heavy fighter prototype. Two prototypes were built: one with Bristol Taurus engines and one with Rolls Royce Peregrine I inline powerplants. They performed well but the RAF felt it would become obsolete before it entered service. One was later converted into a turreted night-fighter called the Reaper, but this was also cancelled; allowing Gloster to concentrate on jet aircraft development.

Hawker Henley A two-seat target tug. The Henley was developed in response to a requirement for a light dive bomber and shared many components with the Hurricane. However, by the time it flew the RAF no longer needed a light bomber so the 200 production Henleys were relegated to target-towing duties before they had even left the factory. The type was plagued with engine problems and was retired by mid-1942.

Lockheed Hudson American-built light bomber and reconnaissance aircraft that was a conversion of the Super Electra airliner. The British Purchasing Commission ordered 200 aircraft and deliveries began in February 1939. Ultimately, almost 2,500 would fly with the RAF. On October 8, 1939, over Jutland, a Hudson became the first Allied aircraft operating from the British Isles to shoot down an enemy aircraft.

Messerschmitt Me 108 Aldon A four-seat sport aircraft was designed in 1934. Dubbed the Taifun (Typhoon) in Germany the aircraft was actively exported and in Britain it was sold by Harold Aldington's Frazer Nash cars. In 1939, the RAF impounded four Taifuns from the German Embassy and acquired one from the dealer. They were allocated to 24 Sqn and operated as the Aldon (a contraction of Aldington's surname).

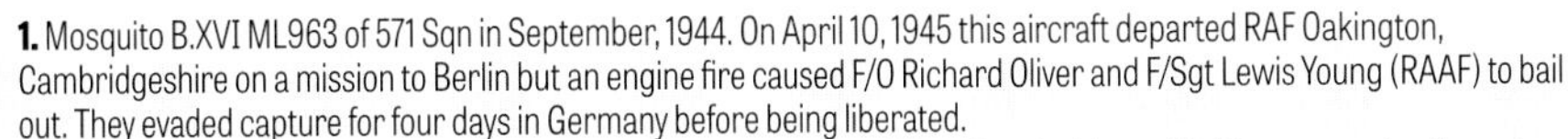

1. Mosquito B.XVI ML963 of 571 Sqn in September, 1944. On April 10, 1945 this aircraft departed RAF Oakington, Cambridgeshire on a mission to Berlin but an engine fire caused F/O Richard Oliver and F/Sgt Lewis Young (RAAF) to bail out. They evaded capture for four days in Germany before being liberated.
2. On June 9, 1944 Mosquito FB.IV DZ353 took off from RAF Woodhall Spa, Lincolnshire at 23:47hrs to attack railways to prevent German troop reinforcements reaching Normandy. Out of a total of 483 aircraft used on this mission only four were lost (three Lancasters and Mosquito DZ353). The aircraft in the background (DZ367) was lost during a daring raid on Berlin on January 30, 1943 to bomb rallies addressed by Nazi leaders. DZ367 was shot down by flack.
3. Mosquito PR.IX of 1409 (Meteorological) Flight, November 1944.

RAF Fast Fact

The largest gun mounted to a Mosquito was the U-Boat hunting 57mm Molins cannon. The Air Ministry doubted that the wooden structure could withstand the gun's recoil so de Havilland sawed the nose off a crashed Mosquito, mounted the 12ft long gun and test-fired it. The barrel recoiled 18in but the airframe was flexible enough to dampen the shock.

Spitfire at 6,000ft (1,829m) and tests by the Aeroplane and Armament Experimental Establishment (A&AEE) at Boscombe Down deemed it "pleasant" to fly.

Other prototypes followed, with W4052 optimised for the fighter role and W4051 being designated as the photo reconnaissance (PR) development aircraft.

Into Service

The Air Ministry authorised mass production for the Mosquito on June 21, 1941, ordering 19 PR models and 176 fighters. A month later, 50 bomber variants were ordered and by the end of 1942 contracts had been awarded for 1,378 Mosquitos of all variants.

In July 1941, W4051 was sent to No 1 Photographic Reconnaissance Unit (PRU) at RAF Benson, Oxfordshire and flew the type's first operational mission on September 19, 1941.

On November 15, the Mosquito B.IV entered service with 105 Sqn at RAF Swanton Morley, Norfolk, which used the aircraft on low level daylight strikes on infrastructure targets in occupied France, Norway and the Low Countries as well as the industrial areas in Northern and Western Germany.

The two-seat bomber variant of the Mosquito was able to carry a bigger bombload than the ten-man Boeing B-17, and fly it further.

However, the Mosquito remained 'Top Secret' and it was only after a high profile raid to Oslo, Norway on September 25, 1942 that the public was made aware of the new aircraft.

On January 30, 1943, the first daylight Mosquito raids were made on Berlin. These were timed to disrupt speeches by the Third Reich's Propaganda Minister Joseph Goebbels and Reichsmarschall Hermann Göring, the head of the Luftwaffe. The first attack saw three 105 Sqn Mosquitos attack the Berlin broadcasting station and the second involved 139 Sqn aircraft targeting Goebbels' speech at the nearby Berlin Sports Palace.

Pathfinders

Mosquito bombers from 109 Sqn were to play an important aircraft within Pathfinder Force (PFF) operations from December 1942. Using Oboe target marking technology the 'Mossies' would guide Lancasters to high profile locations such as power stations.

From early 1943 they became the main element of the Light Night Striking Force (LNSF) and were used for target marking. In the early stages of a raid the Mosquitos' precision-delivered pyrotechnics would clearly highlight the target, enabling the following larger bombers to hone their aim.

LNSF Mosquitos also took part in 'spoof' missions, dropping chaff to simulate large raids to draw Luftwaffe fighters away from real attacks. Other Mosquito squadrons joined the PFF later in the war.

Night Fighters

The first night fighter Mosquitos were introduced into service in mid-1942. The NF.II had four 20mm Hispano cannons in the belly and four .303in Browning machine-guns in the nose. It also carried Aircraft Interception (AI) radar or the Serrate radar detector; the latter allowing them to track down German aircraft by tracking their signal. The first kill occurred on May 30 and by the end of the war, Mosquito night fighters had claimed approximately 600 manned enemy aircraft and a similar number of

Miles Hawk Major A successor to the Miles Hawk with a larger de Havilland Gipsy III engine and trousered undercarriage. Created specifically for private owners and the air racing market, the prototype came second in the 1934 King's Cup. A total of 64 were built and the type led to the Miles Hawk Trainer, which became the Magister [see p41] in RAF service. Eleven Hawk Majors were also impressed in 1939 for training. **SDB**

Miles M.11 Whitney Straight Created by FG Miles in collaboration with Grand Prix driver Whitney Straight. Fifty were built between 1936 and 1937, offering private owners a sporting aircraft that had comfortable accommodation for two in an enclosed side-by-side cockpit. At the start of the war the RAF impressed 23 Whitney Straights into service as communications aircraft with units at home and in India and Egypt. **SDB**

Miles Master An advanced trainer to replace the poorly-performing DH Don. The first 900 Master Is were powered by the Rolls Royce Kestrel inline engine; this included 26 single-seat Master Fighters. When Kestrel production ceased the Bristol Mercury XX engine was fitted to 1,748 Master IIs. US-built P&W Twin Wasp Junior radial engines were fitted to 602 Master IIIs. Some airframes were delivered in glider-towing configuration.

Percival Proctor I-III A radio trainer and communications aircraft. Developed from the Vega Gull, the Proctor was longer and had larger cabin windows. The RAF received 147 Proctor Is as communications aircraft. and the Navy operated 100 as the IA. The Proctor II was optimised as a radio trainer (175 built including 112 IIA aircraft for the Navy) and 437 were built as Proctor IIIs to train Bomber Command radio operators.

Piper J-4 Cub Coupe While the Piper J-3 Cub served the USAAF as the L-4 Grasshopper, the RAF chose to use the Auster in the spotting role. However, 15 civilian examples of the J-4 Cub Coupe were impressed into RAF service. The Cub Coupe was a created in 1938 as a two place side-by-side version of the J-3. It was a much more modern aircraft but war meant just 1,251 were built – compared to nearly 20,000 J-3s.

pilotless V-1 flying bombs.

Night fighters also operated over Malta, Italy, Sicily and North Africa from late 1942 but by 1943, British heavy bombers were suffering heavy losses to Luftwaffe night fighters. Consequently, the decision was taken to set up 100 Group within Bomber Command. This comprised of 169 and 239 Sqns and was later supplemented by 141 Sqn and 85 Sqns. The Group used a number of Mosquito variants, including NF.XIX and NF.30 night fighters as well as Fighter and Fighter Bomber types to attack Luftwaffe fighters on the ground before they could take off. Mosquito PR.XVIs were also used for Electronic Intelligence (ELINT) operations, aiming to detect German radar and radio transmissions.

During the course of the war some 258 Luftwaffe night fighters were claimed by 100 Group, for the loss of some 70 Mosquitos.

Highball

Although Barnes Wallis' *Upkeep* is the most famous of his bouncing bomb designs, he also developed a smaller version to attack shipping. Dubbed *Highball*, these weapons were tailormade for the Mosquito and 618 Sqn was formed in April 1943 with priority given to attacking the German battleship *Tirpitz*.

With the bomb bay doors removed two 1,280lb (580kg) *Highballs* could be carried in each aircraft and these were dropped from a maximum altitude of 60ft (18m) at a speed of 313kts (360mph). As it happened, *Highball* was never used operationally because the *Tirpitz* was sunk by RAF Lancasters carrying *Tallboy* bombs during Operation *Catechism*.

Fighter-Bombers

Perhaps the most famous of all Mosquito operations were in the fighter-bomber role. The FB.VI first saw service in early 1943 and featured a strengthened wing for external weapons. In addition to its standard fighter armament it could carry two 250lb bombs in the bomb bay and two more under the wings, the latter of which could be swapped for eight 60lb wing-mounted rockets if needed. The FB.VI was the most numerous version of the Mosquito (2,292 were built).

Among the high-profile missions flown by the type was Operation *Jericho*, flown by 21 Sqn, 464 (RAAF) Sqn and 487 (NZ) Sqn in April 1944. This daring sortie destroyed the walls of Amiens prison to allow members of the French Resistance to escape.

1

The same month saw a request by Dutch resistance workers for an attack on the Kunstzaal Kleykamp Art Gallery in The Hague, Netherlands, which was being used by the Gestapo to store the Dutch Central Population Registry. Six Mosquitos of 613 Sqn made a pinpoint daylight attack at rooftop height, with the first two dropping high explosive bombs to open up the walls and the others dropping incendiary bombs to burn the records.

Photo Recce

Compared to the PR variants of the Spitfire the 'Mossie' proved to be a far better reconnaissance platform. It could carry more cameras, combined long range with high speed and had the security of two engines. Furthermore, having a crew of two meant the navigator could locate and identify targets whilst the pilot concentrated on the actual flying.

Production PR.I airframes joined 1 PRU at Benson in early 1942 and were soon flying missions as far afield as Poland and Murmansk.

The final wartime version of the Mosquito was the PR.34, designed for long range reconnaissance in the Pacific. To increase its range it had no armour and sported a bulged bomb bay to accommodate a larger fuel tank. It was flown to India in mid-1945 and arrived in the Pacific in time to conduct 38 sorties from the Cocos Islands before the Japanese surrender.

The 'Mossie' proved itself to be a genuine multi-role combat aircraft

Far East

Although it was famed for operations in the European Theatre, the RAF's Mosquitos did see limited service in the Far East with South East Asia Command.

The first examples arrived in April 1943 when 27 Sqn was allocated six airframes for evaluation. These passed to 681 (PR) Sqn in August and in October 47 Sqn received the first FB.VI variants in the region. Other fighter-bombers joined 45 Sqn in the Far East in early 1944 but soon the Mosquitos began falling from the skies. Analysis showed that the glue used to bind the wooden airframes together was breaking down in the heat and humidity and the aircraft was quickly grounded pending repairs.

The solution turned out to be two-part urea-formaldehyde glue. The urea glue was applied to one wooden surface and the formaldehyde catalyst brushed onto the other. When the two were clamped together they created a waterproof bond stronger than the wood itself.

By March 1945, both 82 and 110 Sqns would also be operational with Mosquitos in India

1939

Saunders Roe Lerwick An anti-submarine and convoy escort flying boat. However, the aircraft proved unstable and could not be flown 'hands off.' It also had a vicious stall and structural weakness meant floats kept breaking off. Furthermore, the Lerwick could not maintain height or heading if one engine failed. Of the 21 aircraft built, ten were lost in accidents before the Lerwick was replaced by the Catalina.

Saunders Roe Shrimp A half-size research aircraft designed to prove the concept of the Saunders-Roe S.38 four-engined patrol flying-boat. The S.38 was designed a replacement for the Sunderland but was cancelled in 1939. Undeterred, the Shrimp was completed as a private venture and used for trials work. The Ministry of Aircraft Production acquired it in 1944 for use in the Short Shetland project.

Slingsby Kirby Kite Created in the early 1930s as a high-performance glider that could be flown by inexperienced pilots. Based on the German Grunau Baby design it had longer gulled wings and a plywood skinned fuselage. British Kites were impressed into the RAF at the start of the war and used as training aircraft for assault glider pilots. Some were also used to assess the ability of radar systems to detect wooden aircraft. **SDB**

1940

Airspeed Queen Wasp Envisaged as a pilotless target aircraft to replace the Queen Bee. The aircraft was built by Airspeed and it was intended that the RAF would use a wheeled version while the FAA would receive a float equipped variant of the same type. The aircraft was found to be underpowered and had water handling difficulties.
Although 65 aircraft were ordered, just three were completed.

Avro Manchester A medium bomber that showed great promise but was let down by its unreliable Rolls Royce Vulture engines [see also p36]. The Manchester entered service with 207 Sqn in November 1940; however continuing engine troubles meant the type was soon grounded. Production was halted in November 1941, by which point eight squadrons were equipped with the type. It did, however, lead to the Lancaster.

2

3

4

1. Night fighter Mosquitos had four 20mm Hispano cannons in the belly and four .303in Browning machine-guns in the nose.
2. A 4,000lb 'Cookie' bomb is loaded into a Mosquito of the Light Night Strike Force. These aircraft would sometimes visit Berlin twice in one night carrying bombs, flown by two different crews. **3.** A member of the WAAF services a Mosquito Merlin engine between sorties.
4. Mosquito PR.XVI, NS502 of 544 Sqn based at RAF Benson.

and, along with 45 and 47 Sqns, these aircraft routinely made attacks on Japanese ground targets in Burma.

Post War

In Europe, the Mosquito flew its last wartime mission on May 21, 1945, when 143 and 248 Sqns searched for German submarines that might not have received the surrender signal.

Towards the end of the war in the Pacific some Mosquitos were withdrawn to prepare for the expected invasion of Malaya, but the Japanese surrender meant that this operation never happened. Mosquitoes of 110 Sqn dropped the final bombs of the war on August 20, 1945, against a group of Japanese 'hard liners' in Burma. In a serendipitous coincidence; six years earlier the same squadron had dropped the first bombs of the war.

In RAF service, the Mosquito would soldier on in limited numbers for some years. Although it was soon outclassed as a fighting machine, Mosquito T.3 trainers and TT.35 target tugs continued in operation at various bases. It would not be until May 1963 that the final TT.35 from No. 3 Civilian Anti-Aircraft Co-Operation Unit (CAACU) was finally retired.

The Mosquito had earned its 'Wooden Wonder' nickname and proved itself to be a genuine multi-role combat aircraft. A total of 33 different variants were built during the war to operate in the bomber, fighter-bomber, night-fighter, PR, high-speed courier, weather-recce, torpedo bomber, pathfinder, target marker, training and high speed target tug roles.

Many other aircraft types did many of these missions, but only the Mosquito did them all.

The Mosquito was finally replaced in RAF service by the English Electric Canberra, an unarmed bomber that was designed to fly fast and high enough to evade its pursuers. Notice the irony there? ■

Beech Traveller The military version of the 1932 Beech Staggerwing entered RAF service as the Traveller in mid-1940. The USAAC operated Staggerwings as the UC-43 in the liaison role and the RAF subsequently acquired 106 as the Traveller I via Lend-Lease. Beech also shipped a camouflaged UC-43 to Dutch Prince Bernhard, who was in exile in London. He used it for refugee work in and around London.

Blackburn B-20 An experimental aircraft that aimed to increase the performance of flying boats by using a retractable hull. It had a pontoon float that retracted upwards and the outer stabilising floats retracted to form the aircraft's wingtips. The aircraft lost out to the Lerwick but the Ministry was interested enough to order a prototype. On April 7, 1940 the B-20 crashed due to aileron flutter and the project was cancelled.

Blackburn Botha A four-seat spotter and torpedo bomber that was ordered alongside the Bristol Beaufort. The 850hp Bristol Perseus-powered Botha was underpowered and had poor lateral stability. Worse still, view to the side or rear was very poor, making it unsuitable for reconnaissance missions. Nonetheless, the RAF ordered 580 and they served mostly for convoy escort duties as well as target tugging.

Brewster Buffalo The US-built Buffalo was acquired by the British Purchasing Commission in 1940. The remaining 32 aircraft ordered by the Belgians, but not delivered by the time of the fall of France, were passed on to RAF and a further 171 were also ordered. Performance was too poor for the European theatre so RAF Buffalos were quickly shipped to Burma, Malaya and Singapore to fight the Japanese.

Bristol Beaufighter A multi-role aircraft conceived as a heavy fighter variant of the Beaufort. The Beaufighter proved to be an effective night fighter but it also found a niche as a rocket-armed ground attack and anti-shipping aircraft. Some were equipped with torpedoes and allocated to Coastal Command while others served in the Pacific. After the war 'Beaus' were converted to target tugs and some served until May 1960.

The Arsenal of Democracy

From 1941, the RAF received thousands of US-built aircraft under the so-called Lend-Lease scheme. Less well known is the role that 'Reverse Lend-Lease' played in the war

Although the USA was 'neutral in law' when World War Two broke out in Europe in September 1939, President Franklin D Roosevelt went to great lengths to assist nations engaged in the struggle against Nazi Germany.

Roosevelt wanted to help countries that lacked the supplies necessary to fight against the Germans and Britain was in particular need of assistance. The nation was not just short of money to pay for the armament it required from US manufacturers, but also food and other vital raw materials.

The Neutrality Act of 1939 allowed nations to purchase weapons from the US, but only on a 'cash and carry' basis. However, more pertinently, the Johnson Act of 1934 also prohibited the extension of credit to countries that had not repaid US loans made to them during the Great War – which included Britain.

While the majority of Americans favoured the British over Germany, public opinion still opposed getting involved in the war in Europe.

The US was just recovering from the Great Depression and Roosevelt knew that growth in manufacturing would help speed the growth of the economy. But while he wanted to help British and US fortunes, both American law and public fears that the USA would be drawn into the conflict stifled his plans. Furthermore, the US military opposed the supply of armaments to the UK; suggesting it might be better to bolster its own forces in readiness to defend the Western Hemisphere when Britain fell to a German invasion.He therefore had to devise a scheme that would satisfy the public, the military and the courts.

Tizard Mission

In September 1940, the British government sent the Tizard Mission to the USA: a technical and scientific group whose aim was to highlight British advances in technology and try to secure the industrial resources to exploit their full military potential.

1

In return for assistance, Britain was willing to share with the USA the cavity magnetron technology behind radar, details of Frank Whittle's jet engine and information about the feasibility of an atomic bomb. Other examples of British technologies shared with the Americans included the latest designs for superchargers, gyroscopic gunsights, plastic explosives and self-sealing fuel tanks.

Prime Minister Winston Churchill asked Roosevelt to provide more than 50 obsolete US destroyers as a gift, but the President knew that Congress would oppose such a deal. He therefore came up with a scheme where the ships would be provided in exchange for 99-year leases on land in Newfoundland and the Caribbean, which could be used as US air and naval bases.

The two leaders signed the deal the same month that the Tizard Mission landed in the USA, but by December it became obvious that

America would 'lend' the supplies and payment need not be in cash

the situation in Britain was intensifying and the nation was now unable to pay for most of its much needed supplies.

On December 17, Roosevelt proposed a new initiative that he called Lend-Lease. Under this scheme the USA would provide Britain with the supplies it needed to fight Germany, but would not request immediate payment. Rather, America would 'lend' the supplies and when payment did eventually take place, it need not be in cash.

In Roosevelt's words, the United States of America would become the world's 'Arsenal of Democracy'.

1940

Curtiss Cleveland The Curtiss SBC Helldiver was the last military biplane to join the US Navy but 50 were also exported to France in 1940. These were ex-Navy machines that were refurbished and fitted with French armament. They were shipped from Canada to France but only 44 would fit aboard the boat so five were transferred to the RAF. Shipped to England, they were never used and became ground trainers.

Curtiss Mohawk The P-36 Hawk was the predecessor of the P-40 Warhawk. The radial engined fighter was used by the RAF in the Far East as the Mohawk. Britain chose not to buy the Hawk but received 229 aircraft that were originally destined for the French. The armament was changed and conventional throttles fitted (in place of the French system where the pilot pushed forwards to decrease power).

Curtiss Tomahawk The P-36 Hawk had its radial engine replaced with an Allison V-1710 V-12 to create the P-40. As well as serving with the USAAC the aircraft was exported widely, with France ordering 230. However, the French surrendered before they were delivered, so they were transferred to the RAF as the Tomahawk I. These were the first P-40s to see combat when Desert Air Force aircraft took on Axis fighters in North Africa.

Douglas Boston After the fall of France, a large number of Douglas DB-7s were transferred to the RAF as the Boston. The French had planned to use them as attack aircraft, which meant the range was too short to attack German targets from Britain. They therefore replaced Blenheims in the Middle East and some were converted into night-fighters. A few had a searchlight fitted to illuminate enemy aircraft for other fighters.

Fairey Albacore A carrierborne torpedo bomber ordered as a replacement for the Swordfish; although it was outlived by the earlier machine! The Albacore was designed for reconnaissance as well as level, dive, and torpedo bombing. It eventually equipped 15 FAA squadrons (mostly in the Mediterranean) but the RAF also operated the type with 36 Sqn in Singapore and 119 Sqn at RAF Manston, Kent.

RAF Fast Fact

On December 17, 1940 President Franklin D Roosevelt announced the Lend-Lease scheme at a White House press conference by way of a modern parable.
"Suppose my neighbour's home catches fire," he said, "and I have a length of garden hose four or five hundred feet away. If he can take my garden hose and connect it up with his hydrant, I may help him to put out his fire. Now, what do I do? I don't say to him before that operation, 'Neighbour, my garden hose cost me $15; you have to pay me $15 for it.'
"What is the transaction that goes on? I don't want $15—I want my garden hose back after the fire is over. All right. If it goes through the fire all right, intact, without any damage to it, he gives it back to me and thanks me very much for the use of it.
"But suppose it gets smashed up - holes in it - during the fire. We don't have to have too much formality about it, but I say to him, 'I was glad to lend you that hose; I see I can't use it anymore, it's all smashed up.' He says, 'How many feet of it were there?' I tell him, 'There were 150ft of it.' He says, 'All right, I will replace it.' Now if I get a nice garden hose back, I am in pretty good shape."
Ohio Senator Robert Taft reportedly responded by saying: "Lending war equipment is a good deal like lending chewing gum—you certainly don't want the same gum back."

1. The RAF received 167 B-25C and B-25D Mitchell I bombers via Lend-Lease from August 1941. Later in the war it received 240 B-25Js, which entered service as Mitchell IIIs.
2. The RAF received 240 razorback P-47 Thunderbolts and 590 bubble-canopied examples. They specialised in ground attack missions and were used against the Japanese in Burma by 16 South East Asia Command squadrons.
3. The Boeing B-17C entered RAF service at the Boeing Fortress I in 1941. Twenty examples were acquired and these were later augmented 19 B-17Fs and 45 B-17Es.They were used for conventional bombing as well as anti-shipping duties.
4. The Brewster B-339 served the RAF as the Buffalo and 32 aircraft that had been ordered by the Belgians (but suspended following the fall of France) were joined by 170 purchased via Lend-Lease.
5. Although the RAF decided not to purchase the Curtiss Hawk it soon came in possession of 229 ex-French examples. Most were provided via Lend-Lease but some were flown to England by escaping French pilots. The aircraft were named Mohawks and had their throttles modified so that pushing them forward increased the power (the same as every other nation apart from the French system). RAF Mohawks saw extensive service in India and Burma.

Lend-Lease

After much negotiation, the USA and UK agreed that 'payment' would primarily consist of shared technology was well as joint action directed towards the creation of a liberalised international postwar economy.

Soon public opinion began to sway and a poll conducted in February 1941 revealed 54% of Americans were in favour of giving aid to the British people "without qualification", with only 22% of those surveyed vehemently against the President's proposal.

Roosevelt signed the Lend-Lease bill into law on March 11, 1941. This permitted him to "sell, transfer title to, exchange, lease, lend, or otherwise dispose of, to any such government whose defense the President deems vital to the defense of the United States any defense article."

Purchasing Commission

The UK Government established the British Purchasing Commission (BPC) in New York in January 1940 to arrange the production and purchase of armaments from US manufacturers.

The BPC was initially involved in purchasing via the 'Cash & Carry' scheme and paid for its purchases using Britain's gold reserves, but these resources were rapidly depleting.

Moving out of the Great Depression, the U.S. economy was rebounding and further growth in manufacturing would propel the economy forward. The mutually beneficial 'Cash and Carry' programme stimulated US manufacturing while allowing the Allied nations, particularly the United Kingdom, to purchase much needed military equipment.

The Commission was also responsible for fulfilling orders that had originally been placed by France, Belgium and Norway after their fall to German forces.

One of the BPC's largest expenditures was the acquisition of new aircraft for the RAF and Fleet Air Arm, especially vital as the British Expeditionary Force's evacuation from Dunkirk meant it had to abandon nearly all of its tanks, vehicles and equipment.

British manufacturers could not produce sufficient machines to meet demand so by the time the Lend-Lease scheme was signed the UK had already placed cash orders in excess of $1.2 billion ($22 billion today); these would see 500 aircraft per month delivered to the UK from mid 1941.

The scheme was extended to other nations and by the end of the war the USA had provided more than $50 billion (equivalent to approximately $715 billion) in assistance to more than 30 countries. Britain received $31.4 billion of that aid, $11.3 billion went to the Soviet Union, $3.2 billion to France, $1.6 billion to China, and the remaining $2.6 billion to the other Allies. Other nations received food and oil via the scheme.

Prior to Lend-Lease, all aircraft supplied to

Fokker T-8W A torpedo bomber and aerial reconnaissance floatplane designed and manufactured in the Netherlands for the Dutch Naval Aviation Service. Following the German invasion of the Netherlands in May 1940 nine aircraft were relocated to bases in France and then moved to the UK. These formed the nucleus of the RAF's 320 (Netherlands) Sqn, which performed convoy escort and anti-submarine patrols.

Folland Fo.108 Unkindly nicknamed the Folland Frightful, the Fo-108 was an engine testbed. It was a simple aircraft with fixed undercarriage and a large wing; it could house a pilot and two observers. Twelve were built and they were fitted with a variety of engines including the Hercules and Centaurus radials and Napier Sabre and Rolls Royce Griffon inline powerplants. Five of the aircraft were lost in crashes.

Handley Page Halifax Ordered as a back-up to the Avro Manchester, the Halifax was also originally to be powered by the woeful Vulture engine. It was, however, refitted with four Merlins or Bristol Hercules and quickly became a vital part of Bomber Command. The RAF received more than 6,000 examples, which flew a total of 82,773 missions. They were also used for troop transport and paradrop operations.

Hawker Hurricane II The Hurricane needed to be updated to keep pace with Luftwaffe developments. The Mk IIA was powered by a Merlin XX with a two-speed supercharger and would enter service in September 1940. From this the bomb rack-equipped Mk IIB and Hispano cannon-equipped Mk IIC were born along with the Mk IID. The latter had a 40 mm anti-tank autocannon below each wing.

Martin Maryland Although it lost out to the A-20 Havoc in the bid to win US orders the Maryland XA-22 found favour overseas. The French received 215 before it was overrun by Germany and the remaining 75 on order were delivered to the RAF as the Maryland. A further 150 were ordered directly by Britain. Based in Egypt and Malta, the RAF mainly used them for reconnaissance operations in North and East Africa.

Larger aircraft were flown directly across the Atlantic from Gander

the UK had to be transported across the border into Canada before being delivered to Britain; this was the only way of circumventing the US' neutrality laws which made it illegal to transport 'war materials' direct from US ports.

Aircraft were then shipped from Halifax, Nova Scotia on cargo ships. Upon arrival at Liverpool docks, the crated aircraft were then transported to RAF Speke where they were assembled and test flown. Larger aircraft were ferried directly across the Atlantic from RCAF Gander to RAF Prestwick.

Once Lend-Lease was operational, aircraft and other weapons could be supplied directly from the USA to the UK.

Hand-Me-Downs

While some aircraft provided to the RAF were ordered directly by the British, others were transferred to Britain when their original country of destination – be it Belgium, France, Netherlands or Norway - fell to the Germans.

By far the bulk of these 'second-hand' airframes came from orders placed by the French: they included the Consolidated LB-30 (120 of which were ordered for the Armée de l'air but not delivered), Curtiss SBC-4 (50 for the Aéronavale, the last five delivered to UK as the Curtiss Cleveland) and the Grumman F4F, which served with the Fleet Air Arm as the Grumman Martlet. A batch of Vought-Sikorsky 156 Vindicators was destined for the Aéronavale but these were also diverted to the Royal Navy, which flew them as the Chesapeake.

Not all of the 'hand-me-down' aircraft made it to the British, however. Sweden had ordered a batch of Vultee P-66s but following the invasion of Norway this order was cancelled and the aircraft transferred to the RAF. They were named the Vultee Vanguard, but before they could be delivered the US entered the war and all 144 aircraft were requisitioned by the US Army Air Corps.

Whereas most aircraft were unnamed by US forces the RAF had a policy of naming its machinery. Some of the names allocated by the RAF were subsequently adopted by the US; such as the Consolidated PBY flying boats, which became the Catalina in RAF service.

1

2

The terms of the Lend-Lease agreement decreed that the material was to be used until returned or destroyed. However, in practice very little equipment was returned except for a few transport ships. Some supplies that arrived after VJ Day were sold to Britain at a large discount.

Reverse Lend-Lease

In return for military and humanitarian aid, the USA was given leases on bases on British territory during the war; some of which were extended into the postwar period. It was also provided with various resources that it needed for its own war effort, from small items such as spark plugs to entire aircraft such as photo-reconnaissance Mosquitos. Rope and asbestos came from British Africa, rubber and tea were sourced in Ceylon, cocoa came from Nigeria and Australia and New Zealand provided food for US forces in the South Pacific.

It is estimated that more than 30% of the supplies used by the US Army in the Europe during the war was supplied by the British as Reverse Lend-Lease and most American soldiers stationed in England received supplemental food rations from British stocks.

1940

Miles M.20 Envisaged as a quick-to-build 'emergency' fighter, the M.20 would have boosted numbers if mainstream fighter factories were disrupted by German bombing. To aid production the M.20 was of all-wooden construction, lacked hydraulics and had fixed undercarriage. It was faster and carried twice the fuel and ammunition of the Hurricane. After the Battle of Britain the need passed and only two prototypes were built.

North American Harvard II The Harvard I [see p43] gave way to the Harvard II in October 1940, which was based on the USAAC's AT-6 variant. Compared to the earlier design the Harvard II had new wing panels with a swept-forward leading edge, and a triangular rudder. The RAF received more than 4,000 many of which served in Canada or Southern Rhodesia. The last examples retired in the 1950s. **SDB**

Northrop Nomad The Northrop Gamma 2F was an attack bomber derivative of the Gamma transport aircraft, with a revised tail, canopy and flaps. The USAAC ordered 239 as the A-17 and in June 1940, 93 were refurbished and sold to France. However, they were not delivered before the fall of France and 61 were taken over by the British Purchasing Commission for use by Commonwealth air forces as the Northrop Nomad I.

Short Stirling The RAF's first four-engined heavy bomber. The Air Ministry spec included strict requirements, including a maximum span of 100ft. The Stirling therefore used the same wing as the Sunderland; but cropped to meet the RAF edict. Eventually, this limited its ceiling and bomb carrying capabilities - so it was relegated to second line duties in late 1943. This included mine laying, glider towing and dropping supplies.

Supermarine Spitfire II The Spitfire II was built exclusively at the Supermarine 'shadow factory' at Castle Bromwich and differed from the Mk I in having an upgraded 1,175hp Merlin XII engine turning a wide-bladed Rotol propeller with a more rounded spinner. By April 1941, all Mk Is had been replaced by Mk IIs. The RAF received 921 Mk IIs, 50 of which were later used for air-sea rescue work. **SDB**

3

1 & 3. France ordered a variant of the Douglas A-20 as the DB-7. These were shipped to Casablanca for assembly and service in France and French North Africa and 64 examples saw service against the Germans. After the fall of France, there were still a substantial number of DB-7s which had not yet been delivered to the French and these were transferred to the RAF. Other examples were ordered direct and saw service with 24 squadrons as the Boston bomber and Havoc intruder/night fighter version.
2. The Bell Model P-400 was originally allocated RAF service name 'Caribou', but eventually entered service as the Airacobra. More than 800 were ordered but a combination of poor serviceability and distrust of its unusual configuration mean it only equipped one squadron and only flew a single operational mission before the remaining orders were cancelled. British Airacobras were then sent to the Soviet Air force.
4. The Martin Baltimore was originally ordered by the French in May 1940 as a follow-up to the earlier Martin Maryland. With the fall of France, the aircraft were diverted to the RAF and used almost exclusively in the Mediterranean and Middle East theatres.

4

A large amount of petroleum products were supplied from India. Crude oil from British oil fields in the Middle East was also refined at British plants in Iran and provided as gasoline and oil to the USAAF in China and India.

In total the USA received around $7.8 billion ($111 billion today) of 'reverse Lend-Lease' support during the war, 90% of which came from the British empire. The Soviet Union was able to provide a number of mineral resources needed by the US war effort, including manganese ore as well as platinum and wood.

The Soviets received more than 18,000 military aircraft from the USA during the war (around 30% of its air force) alongside 3,000 Hawker Hurricanes and 4,000 other aircraft from Britain. Other aid supplied to the beleaguered Soviets included more than 5,000 tanks and 15 million pairs of boots. In a speech made after the war, Soviet Premier Joseph Stalin spoke for many nations when he declared: "Without American machines the United Nations never could have won the war."

The Arsenal of Democracy had succeeded in keeping the Axis of Evil at bay, but it had come at a high cost. ■

American Aircraft Provided to Britain

US Designation	RAF Name
Bell Model 14/P-400	Bell Airacobra
Boeing B-17C	Boeing Fortress
Brewster B-339	Brewster Buffalo
Brewster B-340	Brewster Bermuda
Consolidated LB-30	Consolidated Liberator
Consolidated 28-5	Consolidated Catalina
Curtiss SBC-4	Curtiss Cleveland
Curtiss Model 75	Curtiss Mohawk
Curtiss Model 81A	Curtiss Tomahawk
Curtiss Model 87	Curtiss Kittyhawk
Douglas DB-7	Douglas Boston (bomber)
Douglas DB-19	Douglas Havoc (Intruder)
Grumman F4F	Grumman Martlet/Wildcat*
Lockheed Super Electra	Lockheed Hudson
Lockheed Ventura	Lockheed Ventura
Lockheed Model 322A	Lockheed Lightning
Martin B-26	Martin Maurauder
Martin Model 167	Martin Maryland
Martin Model 187	Martin Baltimore
North American NA-40	North American Mitchell
North American NA-57	North American Harvard
North American NA-73	North American Mustang
Northrop A-17	Northrop Nomad
Northrop N-3PB	Northrop N-3BP
Vought-Sikorsky 156	Vought-Sikorsky Chesapeake*
Republic P-47	Republic Thunderbolt
Vultee P-66	Vultee Vanguard
Vultee Model 72	Vultee Vengeance

*served with the Royal Navy rather than the RAF

1941

Supermarine Spitfire PR IV A few Spitfire Is were converted into photo-recce variants with armament replaced with cameras and extra fuel tanks. However, the first 'new-build' variant was the PR IV. Modifications allowed an extra 66 Imp Gal of fuel to be carried in each wing, while two vertically mounted F24 or F8 cameras were located in the rear fuselage. The RAF received a total of 229 PR IVs.

Westland Whirlwind A twin-engined, single-seat fighter with four 20mm autocannon in its nose. The Whirlwind first flew in 1938 but ongoing problems with its Rolls Royce Peregrine engines delayed its entry into service and it would be December 1940 before 263 Sqn flew the type's first operational missions. Engine unreliability meant only three squadrons would receive the type before they were retired in November 1943.

Bell Airacobra The P-39 had a tricycle undercarriage and the engine installed in the centre fuselage (behind the pilot) driving the propeller via a shaft. However, the absence of a turbo-supercharger limited its capabilities at high-altitude. Britain ordered 675 based on Bell's claimed performance figures but production versions proved to be inferior to the Hurricane. RAF Airacobras flew just one sortie before being rejected.

Boeing Fortress While waiting for indigenous four-engined bombers the RAF received 20 Boeing B-17Cs as the Fortress I from early 1941. By September, eight had been lost and they were transferred to Coastal Command as long-range maritime patrol aircraft, and were later joined by 19 Fortress IIs (B-17F) and 45 Fortress IIAs (B-17E).
RAF Fortresses sank eleven U-boats during the war.

Boulton Paul P.92/2 Designed as a two-seat, twin-engined, turret-armed fighter and ground attack aircraft. Following wind tunnel testing, Boulton Paul asked Heston Aircraft to build a half-scale piloted flying version named the P.92/2 and powered by two Gipsy Major engines. In May 1940, the P.92 programme was cancelled but the P.92/2 was completed and following testing was used by Boulton Paul as a 'runabout'.

Mustang - the American Legend

Although it was most famous for its wartime role with the United States Army Air Force the North American P-51 Mustang was actually created to meet a British requirement

With war in Europe underway the RAF was in desperate need for modern fighter aircraft. To boost the number of available aircraft the Air Ministry and the British Purchasing Commission (BPC) looked across the Atlantic for help in early 1940.

The BPC was headed up by Sir Henry Self, who was given overall responsibility for the production of RAF aircraft. Self was also involved in the British Air Council sub-committee on Supply, with particular responsibility for organising the manufacture and supply of American aircraft for the RAF.

However, in 1940 the choice was limited and no American aircraft met with the RAF's demanding specifications. Only the Curtiss P-40 Tomahawk came close, but the manufacturer was running at capacity and simply could not produce aircraft for the British.

The decision was therefore made to approach North American Aviation (NAA) to order a fleet of Tomahawks, which NAA would produce under licence from Curtiss.

1

All-New Design

However, the team at NAA had hopes to enter the fighter aircraft market themselves and – rather than build an old design from a rival company – NAA President 'Dutch' Kindelberger suggested to Self that his team could design and build an all-new and much more modern aircraft from scratch. He went as far as saying it could do this in the time it would take to set up the Tomahawk production line at the factory.

The company was already producing Harvard trainers for the RAF but had plenty of spare capacity so Self agreed, but with stipulations.

The new fighter would need to use the same 1,200hp Allison V-1710 engine and four .303in machine guns as the P-40. It would also need to have a unit cost of no more than $40,000 ($735,000 in today's money) and delivery of the first production aircraft had to be made by January 1941.

The Ministry of Aircraft Production placed an order for 320 aircraft in March 1940 and the contract was signed with NAA on April 24.

The NAA began work immediately on the fighter, which was dubbed the NA-73X and designed by a team led by Edgar Schmued. The aircraft was very modern for its day with a laminar flow wing, which had been developed jointly by NAA and the National Advisory Committee for Aeronautics (NACA) to generate low drag at high speeds.

Other radical features included a cooling system that reduced drag by having an aft positioned radiator which cooled both the water and oil. It was later discovered that this arrangement also created extra thrust as hot air left the radiator with a small amount of jet force – something now referred to as the Meredith Effect, but which was stumbled across purely by chance by NAA.

Armament was the required four .303in machine guns in the wings as well as two .50in machine guns. The latter were mounted under the engine and were synchronised to fire through the propeller arc.

The aircraft's semi-monocoque fuselage was constructed entirely of aluminium to save weight. The first prototype NA-73X was rolled out on September 9, 1940 and it performed its maiden flight, with test pilot Vance Breese at the controls, on October 26 – just 149 days since the contract was signed. By then, Britain had ordered 300 examples of the new fighter.

Lend-Lease

The United States Army Air Corps (USAAC) quickly became intrigued by the NA-73 and expressed interest in acquiring it for US use. Although the USA could block any sales it felt were against its own war interests, the NA-73 was considered to be an exception because of the British involvement in its development.

1941

Consolidated Liberator I Although best known for its USAAF use the B-24 Liberator also flew with the RAF. The first Liberator Is were ordered by the Anglo-French Purchasing Board in 1940 but transferred to the RAF after the fall of France. They were assigned to RAF Ferry Command and flew ferry pilots across the Atlantic. Some Liberator Is later joined Coastal Command on anti-submarine patrols.

de Havilland DH.98 Mosquito (PR) Originally conceived as an unarmed fast bomber, the Mosquito fulfilled many roles. The first examples to enter RAF service were in the photo recce role. Ten PR.Is were built and the first operational 'Mossie' sortie was made by a PR.1 on September 17, 1941. The RAF would go on to receive a large number of PR 'Mossies' including 30 PR.IVs, five PR.VIIIs, 90 PR.IXs, 435 PR.XVIs and 181 PR.34s.

Fairchild Argus Based on the civilian Fairchild 24 four-seater the type served the USAAC as the UC-61 and the RAF as the Argus. The majority of the 525 Warner Scarab radial engined Fairchild 24s went to the RAF under Lend-Lease as Argus I and Argus IIs, with some used by the Air Transport Auxiliary (ATA). A further 306 Argus IIIs (illustrated) were delivered to the RAF with in-line Ranger engines. **SDB**

General Aircraft Hotspur Conceived as a compact 'assault' glider capable of transporting eight troops into the battlefield. The wooden Hotspur fell foul to a change in requirements, which called for larger and less manoeuvrable gliders. As such, the 1,105 built were relegated to training duties and became the standard glider basic trainer. Hotspurs were towed by Hawker Hector or Audax as well as Miles Masters and Westland Lysanders.

Gloster E.28/39 Britain's first jet-engined aircraft, the Gloster E.28/39 [see also p68] was designed purely as a proof of concept aircraft. Created by the company's chief designer, George Carter, it was designed around Frank Whittle's Power Jets W.1 revolutionary turbojet engine. The E.28/39 also contributed greatly towards the development of the Gloster Meteor, the Allies first operational jet fighter.

RAF Fast Fact

On June 22, 1944, Sgt Tamowicz's Mustang III was seriously hit by flak and the 315 (Polish) Sqn pilot was forced to land in a marsh between the enemy and American lines near Normandy. Sqn Ldr Eugeniusz Horbaczewski – the squadron's Commanding Officer – landed at a nearby airfield, commandeered a Jeep and drove to find the downed aircraft. He waded through the marsh and discovered that Tamowicz had sustained leg injuries. The two drove back to the airfield and the injured pilot was placed into the cockpit of the Mustang. Sqn Ldr Horbaczewski took his place on the knees of his companion and although it was too cramped to close the canopy they set off for home. Upon landing back at their base at RAF Coolham, Tamowicz was quickly transferred to a hospital and treated. He survived the war but tragically Horbaczewski was killed on August 18, 1944 while leading his squadron on a mission over France. He was the third highest scoring Polish fighter ace, with 16.5 confirmed and one probable kill. He was awarded the Polish Cross of Valour four times, the Distinguished Flying Cross twice and the Distinguished Service Order.

1. An RAF Mustang I nearing completion at the NAA factory in California. Temporary wooden wheels have been fitted to help move the aircraft around the airfield. The elongated nose intake can be seen to good effect. **2.** Sqn Ldr Eugeniusz Horbaczewski and Sgt Tamowicz demonstrate how they shared a cockpit during an audacious rescue mission in June 1944 (see RAF Fast Fact for more details). **3.** Mustang IIIs of 19 Sqn based at Ford, Sussex in April 1944. The aircraft have the Malcolm Hood conversion which helped visibility below and behind.

However, in order to ensure an uninterrupted delivery schedule it was agreed to provide two the aircraft to the USAAC for evaluation.

The initial batch of machines were delivered to the RAF under the Lend-Lease scheme [Ed: see page 56]. For accounting purposes these fighters had to be on the books of the USAAC before they could be supplied to the British and the first 93 examples of the NA-73 – by now christened the Mustang by the RAF – were delivered in late 1941. These were referred to as the Mustang IA whereas the follow up batch of 50 P-51A equivalents were classed as Mustang Is.

RAF Service

British Mustang I and IAs began arriving in the UK in October 1941. This was considerably behind schedule and to make matters worse, 20 aircraft were lost at sea when the boat transporting them sank.

Mustangs entered RAF service with 26 Sqn at Gatwick in January 1942 and made their combat debut on May 10. These were powered by the Allison V-1710 engine and early tests showed it was around 26kts (30mph) faster than the contemporary Spitfire and had twice the range. However, there were problems. The nose intake caused induction issues at high angles of attack so NAA extended it right up to the spinner.

Worse, however, was the drop off in performance the V-1710 powerplant suffered at high altitude. It lacked a two-stage supercharger and early V-1710 powered aircraft such as the Bell P-39 Airacobra, Curtiss P-40 Tomahawk and the Mustang I/P-51A were generally limited to a combat ceiling of just 15,000ft (4,572m)

The engines did, however, prove to be robust and able to absorb a lot of battle damage. This, combined with the disappointing performance at altitude, meant the first RAF Mustangs were used for tactical reconnaissance and ground-attack by Army Co-Operation Command.

Four RAF Mustang squadrons saw action during the Dieppe Raid on the French coast in August 1942 and later in the war Mustang I and IIs were used to seek out V-1 flying bomb sites. On October 22, RAF Mustang Is made history when they escorted Wellington bombers on a daylight raid to Germany, thus becoming the first RAF single-seat fighters to fly over the country during the war.

Merlin Magic

However, this was at extremes of the aircraft's endurance and Fighter Command still needed an effective dogfighter and escort fighter that could fly at the same altitude as the bombers.

It was Rolls-Royce test pilot Ronald Harker who came up with the solution. With experience garnered on the successful Spitfire IX variant, Harker suggested taking the Rolls-Royce Merlin 61 engine from the Supermarine fighter and fitting it to the front of a Mustang. The engine had a two-speed, two-stage, intercooled supercharger that had been designed by Stanley

Hawker Typhoon The RAF's leading ground attack aircraft of the war, the Typhoon [see also p62] entered service in November 1941 but suffered teething troubles and was not used operationally until May 1942. It was the first RAF fighter with a maximum speed in level flight greater than 400mph and eventually proved to be robust and a stable gun platform. 'Tiffies' could also be fitted with rockets for ground attack missions.

Hillson Bi-Mono An unusual design, created to test the idea of 'slip-wings.' In theory the top wing could be used as an extra fuel tank and provided extra lift for take off; then jettisoned once at altitude. Hills and Son's Bi-Mono was flown successfully although tests showed the maximum speed of the biplane was slower than the stalling speed of the monoplane configuration so it lost hundreds of feet during 'transition.'

Lockheed Lodestar Developed from the 18-seat Lockheed 18 airliner (itself a development of the Lockheed 14 Super Electra) the Lodestar was created for the USAAC as a military transport aircraft. The aircraft also appealed to the RAF and the Air Ministry ordered ten Pratt & Whitney R-1690 Hornet-powered examples as the Lodestar IA. These were later augmented by Wright R-1820-powered Lodestar IIs.

Martin Baltimore A light attack bomber ordered by the French in May 1940 but diverted to the RAF after the fall of France. Developed from the earlier Martin Maryland it had a deeper fuselage and more powerful engines and more than 1,500 were delivered to the RAF. The Baltimore was only used in the Mediterranean and North Africa theatres and suffered massive losses in the low-level attack role.

North American Mitchell A medium bomber designed for the USAAC. Nearly 10,000 were built, including around 700 for the RAF. Britain received 23 B-25Bs as Mitchell Is from August 1941. These were used in the Bahamas ahead of the 167 B-25Cs and 371 B-25Ds (Mitchell IIs), which became operational in January 1943. The RAF was also allocated 316 B-25Js (Mitchell IIIs) but only about 240 actually reached Britain.

Hooker and increased the Mustang's horsepower from the 1,200hp to 1,620hp. In turn, this increased the top speed from 339kts (390mph) to 376kts (433mph) and boosted the service ceiling to in excess of 40,500 ft (12,340m).

The first of five Merlin-powered Mustang X development aircraft took to the skies from Rolls-Royce's airfield at Hucknall near Nottingham in October 1942.

Vice-Chief of the Air Staff Air Marshal Sir Wilfrid Freeman was greatly impressed and insisted that two of the aircraft be handed over to the USAAC for evaluation.

Impressed with what it saw, NAA put the modified type into production as the P-51B and P-51C variant (depending on which factory they were manufactured at); the first flying just a month after the British conversion. Compared to the Mustang X these had a tailor-made engine installation and a redesign of the radiator duct.

The Merlin was slightly heavier than the Allison engine and this resulted in the Mustang's centre-of-gravity (CofG) moving forward. NAA engineers therefore took the opportunity to include a large fuel tank behind the pilot; this both corrected the CofG and increased the fighter's range.In RAF service the P-51B/C variant was known as the Mustang III and the first examples entered service in late 1943. A total of 308 P-51Bs and 636 P-51Cs would ultimately be delivered to the British.

1. Mustang IVs were operated by 19 Sqn from April 1945 until October 1946. This restored P-51D wears the markings of 19 Sqn during the 1993 Fighter Meet Airshow. It now flies in the markings of KH774. **Neil Taylor**
2. The Mustang I first entered service with 26 Sqn at Gatwick. They were mostly used for tactical recce and ground-attack duties.

Malcolm Hoods and Bubbletops

Another downside of early Mustangs was the hinged and heavily framed cockpit canopy. This offered a poor field of vision and the RAF decided a modification was needed. The new canopy was a single, bulged, frameless Perspex unit that slid aft on rails. It offered more space in the cockpit alongside an improved view downwards and rearwards. As it was manufactured by R Malcolm & Co it became known simply as the 'Malcolm Hood.' These were fitted to most RAF Mustang IIIs and a number of US P-51B/Cs were also modified.

In search of an even better view, NAA modified a P-51B with ateardrop-shaped Plexiglass canopy to create the XP-51D.

The new variant entered production in early 1944 with examples built at the Inglewood, California factory referred to as the P-51D and those from the Dallas, Texas facility dubbed the P-51K. In RAF service these became the Mustang IV and IVA respectively.

The British received 284 IVs and 594 IVAs; the first being a pair of ex-USAAF examples (given the RAF registration TK586 and TK589) which were evaluated at Boscombe Down, Wiltshire. Mustang IV KH641 was the first to enter service with 122 Wing (19, 65 and 122 Sqns) in February 1944.

Whereas the Mustang Is were used in the armed reconnaissance role the Mustang III, IV and V were used as straightforward fighter aircraft. With some modifications the later Mustang could also be pushed to 362kts (417mph) at 2,000ft (610m) and this made them ideal for chasing the pulse-jet-powered V-1 flying bombs. After D-Day in June 1944, the majority of Mustang fighter squadrons moved to Europe where they performed ground attack and bomber escort duties.

At the end of the war just one unit (26 Sqn) was still using the Mustang I; having been re-equipped with the aircraft in October 1944 for low level reconnaissance missions over V-2 rocket sites. For these operations the early Mustang's combination of low level speed and long range was unequalled.

At the end of the war in Europe, the RAF took delivery of a large number of Mustang IVs for use against the Japanese. However, Japan surrendered before these could be put to use, and most were scrapped.

All bar the first few RAF Mustangs were delivered under the Lend-Lease scheme [Ed: see p56]. Those still on RAF charge at the end of the war were either scrapped by the RAF or returned to the US military.

What had started as a desperate plea for licence-produced out-of-date fighters turned out to be a genuine war winner. More than 15,000 were built, of which almost 2,000 served with the RAF. ■

1941

Northrop N-3PB Norway ordered 24 coastal reconnaissance versions of the N-3PB floatplane just prior to the German invasion of Norway in April 1940. The aircraft were delivered to the exiled Royal Norwegian Navy Air Service in Canada by March 1941 but later in the year they (and their crews) were transferred to the RAF to form 330 (Norwegian) Sqn based in Iceland. The aircraft were retired in favour of Sunderlands in 1943.

Percival Proctor IV Developed from the earlier Proctor as a dedicated four-seat radio trainer. The extra seat required an enlarged fuselage but all but one of the 258 built retained the same 210hp Gipsy Queen engine as the Proctor III. The aircraft was originally referred to as the Preceptor but was later renamed as the Proctor IV. One was fitted with a 250hp Gipsy Queen and used as a personal transport by AVM Sir Ralph Sorley.

Stinson Vigilant Designed in response to a USAAC requirement for a two-seat light observation aircraft. The Stinson Model 74 was fitted with high-lift slots and slats to boost low speed and high lift performance. It was capable of stopping in less than its own length and could fly at just 31mph. The RAF received 17 as the Vigilant I for spotting duties and 96 were designated Vigilant IIs for liaison flying. Of the latter only 54 were delivered.

Supermarine Spitfire V Developed as a stop-gap variant until the Mk IX was ready to enter service, the Spitfire V would become one of the most numerous versions of the fighter. The basic Mk V was a Mk I with the 1,440hp Merlin 45 engine and several Mk I were converted, in addition to 6,479 new-build airframes. These included a number of 'tropicalised' versions with Vokes engine filters for use in the deserts of North Africa.

Vultee Vanguard Vultee created four aircraft designs around a set of common wings and aft fuselages. These consisted of the V-48 fighter, BC-51 combat trainer, B-54 advanced trainer and BC-54D basic trainer. The BC-54D became the BT-13 Valiant and the V-48 became the P-66 Vanguard. The RAF received 100 for use as advanced trainers in Canada; but after trials they were shipped to China to equip the 3rd American Volunteer Group.

1. This is a P-51D painted to represent Mustang IV KH774 of 112 Sqn, which operated from Italy in 1945 on ground attack missions over the Balkans and along the Adriatic coast. It is seen here in the hands of Lars Ness. **SDB**
2. The Mustang X designation was given to the five airframes converted by Rolls-Royce to take the Merlin 61 engine. These formed the basis for the later P-51B/C and Mustang III variants.
3. In June 1944 TK586 and TK589 (illustrated) were the first Mustang IVs to join the RAF. These were taken from US stocks and TK589 had previously been 44-13332 with the USAAF.
4. Ground crew servicing a Mustang III in Italy in late 1944.

The Ultimate Fighter

Sydney Camm's Typhoon and Tempest were some of the most powerful and capable fighting aircraft of the war

Even before his Hawker Hurricane had entered squadron service, designer Sydney Camm was working on an aircraft that he felt would be a worthy successor.

Although he began drawing up the new aircraft in March 1937 it neatly fitted the 1938 Air Ministry Spec F.18/37 for a single-seat fighter-bomber.

Camm proposed two projects; one with an 'H-block' Napier Sabre engine (dubbed the Type N) and one fitted with an 'X-block' Rolls-Royce Vulture powerplant (the Type R). On paper, both fulfilled the specification's requirements for a top speed of 348kts (400mph) and a service ceiling of 35,000ft (10,668m).

Two prototypes of each were ordered with the Type N being dubbed the Tornado and the Type R becoming the Typhoon. However, production of the Vulture powerplant was curtailed in July 1941; partly due to problems it experienced in the Avro Manchester [Ed: see page 38], so only three Tornado prototypes would fly.

Postponed

The first of the Typhoon prototypes to fly was P5212, which took off from Langley near Slough on February 24, 1940 with Hawker Chief Test Pilot Philip Lucas at the controls.

It was a mix of traditional Hawker construction techniques (that could be traced back via the Hurricane to the Hart) and more modern methods including flush-riveting.

The wing had a deep section, which allowed ample room for fuel tanks and armament. It did, however, create a large amount of drag and limit the top speed.

During a test flight on May 4, 1940 the prototype suffered a mid-air structural failure and daylight could be seen between the forward and rear fuselage sections, just behind the pilot's seat. Instead of bailing out, Lucas landed the Typhoon and was later awarded the George Cross for his heroism.

By now, the War Office had decreed that valuable resources should be concentrated on the five major RAF aircraft. These were the Spitfire and Hurricane fighters as well as the Blenheim, Wellington and Whitley bombers. As such, the Typhoon project was postponed following Lucas' successful emergency landing.

It would therefore be May 3, 1941 before the second prototype flew. At this stage the cockpit featured an unusual 'car door' entry style and the rear fairing was solid metal. This was

1

subsequently found to offer poor rear visibility so this was soon changed to a bubble canopy, although the car door entry was retained.

Into Service

The first Typhoons were rushed into service with 56 and 609 Sqns in late 1941 to help counter the threat from the Luftwaffe's new Focke-Wulf Fw190.

The type suffered a number of teething problems with a modification needed to stop elevator flutter, alongside airframe strengthening to prevent structural breakup. The Sabre engine was also a source of problems in terms of reliability and performance.

It also became apparent that the Typhoon resembled a Fw190 from some angles, so airframes were soon painted with all-white noses and, later, with high visibility black and white stripes under the wings in an attempt to 'prevent friendly' fire incidents.

Tempest pilots would either use cannon fire or 'nudge' the V-1 to topple its directional gyros

A total of 109 production aircraft were completed as the Typhoon IA before a decision was taken to standardise on the cannon-equipped Typhoon IB variant.

Towards the end of 1942, Typhoons were moved to airfields near the south coasts of England to help counter Luftwaffe 'hit and run' raids. During this time, squadrons kept a pair of aircraft at readiness (ready to take off within two minutes) throughout daylight hours. In this role 486(NZ) Sqn claimed 23 aircraft downed between October 1942 and July 1943.

By this point the RAF was in need of a

1942

Airspeed Horsa A large troop-carrying glider capable of carrying up to 30 fully equipped paratroopers. Horsas were first used in November 1942 during an unsuccessful attack on a German Heavy Water Plant in Norway. The following year 27 Horsas were used during the Allied invasion of Sicily and in 1944 around 600 of the type were deployed during the D-Day landings in Normandy. More than 3,000 were built for the RAF.

Avro Lancaster Perhaps the most famous of all RAF bombers, the Lancaster [see also p36] was an evolution of the troublesome Manchester. Powered by four Merlin or Bristol Hercules engines, it was the mainstay of the RAF strategic bombing offensive over Europe. In 156,000 sorties Lancasters dropped more than 600,000 tonnes of bombs – making them the most heavily used of all RAF bombers.

Brewster Bermuda A single-engined bomber developed for the US Navy as the SB2A Buccaneer. The French ordered 250 examples and these were subsequently reallocated to the RAF and named Bermudas. Eventually, 192 were appropriated by the US after Pearl Harbor and the remaining 58 were delivered from July 1942. However, the RAF judged the type unsuitable for combat and they were used as target tugs.

Bristol Blenheim V (Bisley) The ultimate development of the Blenheim. The armoured ground attack Mk V was originally known as the Bisley. Compared to the Blenheim IV it had a strengthened airframe with armour for the pilot and an interchangeable nose with either a gun pack or a glazed bomb-aimer position. It also had a powered dorsal turret that could be traversed at high speed and served mostly in the Middle and Far East.

Consolidated Liberator II Derived from the Liberator I and also referred to as the LB-30 the Liberator IIs were the first combat ready version of the B-24 to join the RAF. They had a longer and deeper fuselage as well as self-sealing fuel tanks and armour. A total of 165 were built but 75 were retained by the US after it entered the war. In RAF service the type was operated by Coastal Command and Bomber Command.

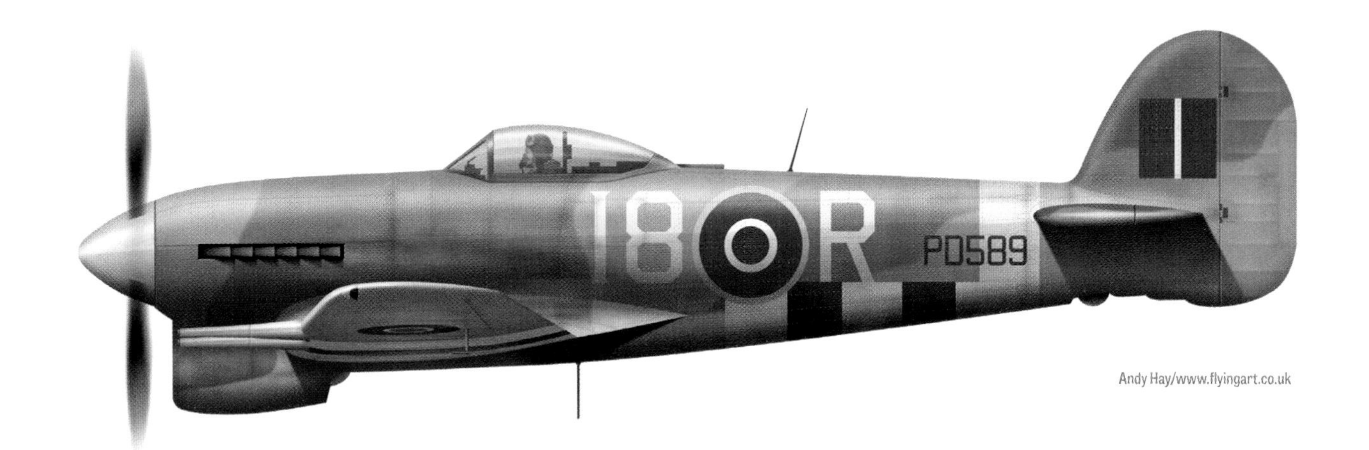

Andy Hay/www.flyingart.co.uk

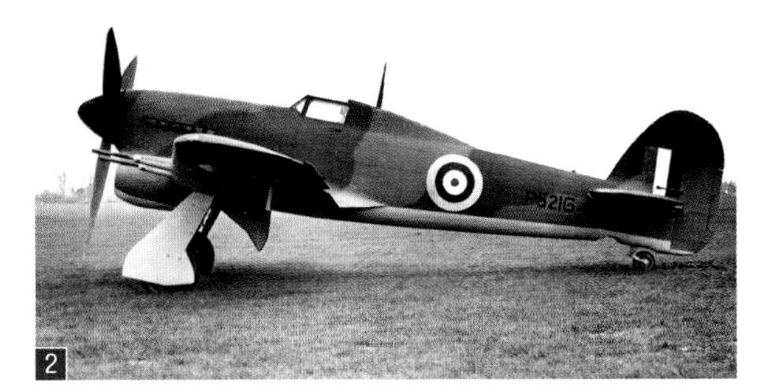

1. From September 1943 Typhoons were also armed with four RP-3 rockets under each wing.
2. The second prototype Typhoon I (P5216) at Langley in May 1941. At this stage the cockpit featured a solid metal rear fairing.
3. Hawker Typhoon of 56 Sqn with Eric Haabjoern showing the squadron's scoreboard.
4. The unusual 'car door' configuration was used in both the Typhoon and the Tempest V.
5. In an attempt to prevent friendly fire incidents, Typhoons were painted with stripes to differentiate them from the similar looking Fw190.
6. The sole example of the Tempest I was flown in February 1943.

ground-attack aircraft for missions in mainland Europe and the Typhoon was the obvious choice. Its powerful engine allowed it to carry a pair of 1,000lb bombs and the sturdy airframe was able to absorb large amounts of damage from ground based weaponry.

D-Day Tank Busters

The first 'Bombphoons' (as they became nicknamed) entered service with 181 Sqn in late 1942 and from September 1943 Typhoons were also armed with four RP-3 rockets under each wing. These were far from accurate weapons, but a single Typhoon's firepower was likened to "the equivalent to a destroyer's broadside" in contemporary propaganda.

By the end of the year a total of 18 rocket-equipped Typhoon squadrons formed the RAF's Second Tactical Air Force (2nd TAF), attacking targets in Europe ahead of D-Day.

During the Normandy landings in June 1944, the 2nd TAF was supplemented by nine Fighter Command Typhoon squadrons and proved to be an effective anti-tank strike force. The aircraft were used on raids against targets deep in North Western Europe ahead of the invasion and in support of the Allied ground forces.

The Typhoon force was also called upon for intelligence led operations, including a raid on Dordrecht on October 24, 1944. Aircraft from 146 Typhoon Wing attacked a building in which senior members of the German 15th Army staff were meeting; 17 staff officers and 36 other officers were killed. Later in the war large numbers of Typhoons were used to suppress German anti-aircraft guns during Operation *Varsity*, the Allied crossing of the Rhine.

Hawker developed a tactical reconnaissance version of the Typhoon in 1944; this being

Curtiss Kittyhawk RAF Tomahawks were superseded in North Africa by the more powerful Kittyhawk I from early 1942. The new variant served the USAAF as the P-40D and E. The RAF's Desert Air Force also received Merlin-engined P-40Fs as the Kityhawk II and Allison-powered P-40Ks and Ns as the Kittyhawk III and IV respectively. DAF began used them as fighter-bombers, leading to the 'Kittybomber' nickname.

de Havilland DH.98 Mosquito (Bomber) The unarmed, all-wooden Mosquito was a high-speed bomber designed to carry four 500lb bombs. The first bomber variant to enter service was the B IV, of which 273 were built from 1941 onwards. The B IV entered service in May 1942 and some were later modified to carry the 4,000lb 'Cookie' bomb. Other variants included the B IX, the B XVI and the B.35; the latter having a top speed of 366kts.

de Havilland DH.98 Mosquito (FB) Fighter-Bomber Mosquitos were used for anti-shipping, anti-tank and strike missions. The strengthened FB.VI was able to carry 250lb or 500lb bombs or eight rockets on rails below the wings – in addition to the fixed four 20mm cannon and four .303 machine guns. Two 500lb bombs could be carried in the bomb bay. The FB.XVIII carried a 57mm anti-tank gun for attacking shipping.

de Havilland DH.98 Mosquito (NF) The Ministry of Aircraft Production initially requested DH produce a turret-equipped Mosquito for night-fighter duties, but it soon became apparent that a turret was not needed. The first of 466 NF.IIs entered service in January 1942. It was similar to the F.II but was radar and antennae. The RAF also received various night-fighting Mossies; including 526 NF.30s with ECM equipment.

Douglas Dakota The C-47 was the workhorse of many air forces during and after the war; and the RAF was no exception. The Dakota I was the RAF designation for 53 C-47s received via Lend-Lease. The RAF also had nine Dakota IIs (C-53s), 962 Dakota IIIs (C-47As) and 896 Dakota IVs (C-47Bs). Eight civil DC-3s were also acquired. 'Daks' were used for cargo, passenger, gliding towing and paradrop duties.

referred to as the FR.IB and fitted with two vertical cameras in the rear fuselage and a forward-facing cine camera. Owing to the very poor picture quality, hampered by engine and airframe vibration, only 60 were built.

Some 246 Axis aircraft were claimed by Typhoon pilots during the war with the top-scoring Typhoon ace being Grp Capt Baldwin, who claimed 15 aircraft between 1942 and 1944.

Hawker Aircraft built 15 production examples of the Typhoon after which production was transferred to Gloster Aircraft at Hucclecote, who built the remaining 3,300.

Once the war in Europe was over Typhoons were quickly removed from front-line squadrons and by October 1945 the Typhoon had been phased out of operational use.

Tempest

In a bid to improve the type Camm developed the Typhoon II, but the differences between it and the Mk I were so significant that it was soon renamed the Hawker Tempest.

The new aircraft was created to be a low-level interceptor and used a new, thinner, laminar-flow wing. The wing was also a near elliptical planform but the tips were clipped. It contained four 20mm Hispano cannons and 800 rounds of ammunition as well as large fuel tanks. More unusually, the leading edge of the wing housed the radiators for cooling the engine; thus removing the distinctive 'chin' radiator used on the Typhoon and improved aerodynamics.

Camm and his team of 45 draughtsmen designed the new fighter around the new Napier Sabre IV engine but experience with the ill-fated Tornado programme led the Air Ministry to request six Tempest prototypes all using different engines.

These were a single Tempest I (HM599) powered by a Sabre IV, two Tempest IIs (LA602 and LA607) with the Bristol Centaurus IV, a Tempest III (LA610) with a Rolls-Royce Griffon IIB, a Tempest IV (LA614) with a Griffon 61, and a Tempest V (HM595) with the Sabre II.

Development problems with the Sabre IV meant it was the Tempest V that was the first to fly, on September 2, 1942. It retained the Typhoon's canopy and 'car door' style cockpit and had the same 'chin' radiator. It did, however, have a larger tail fin to improve stability.

A month before the maiden flight an order was placed for 400 Tempests – with the first 100 to be Tempest Vs and the rest to be Tempest Is with the leading-edge radiators.

The Tempest I prototype flew on February 24, 1943 and the lack of the chin radiator enabled the aircraft to reach 405kts (466mph). However, problems with the Sabre IV engine meant only one Tempest I was produced and all 400 aircraft were delivered as Mk Vs.

The Tempest V was as one of the most powerful fighters of World War Two and was the fastest single-engine propeller-driven aircraft of the war at low altitude.The first production aircraft, JN729, flew on June 21, 1943 and the type entered service with 3 Sqn and 486 (NZ) Sqn in April 1944.

By the end of the year, the aircraft was serving with five squadrons. Ahead of D-Day the aircraft would conduct sorties into Europe using a combination of cannons and bombs to attack airfields, radar units and the V-1 launch sites.

1

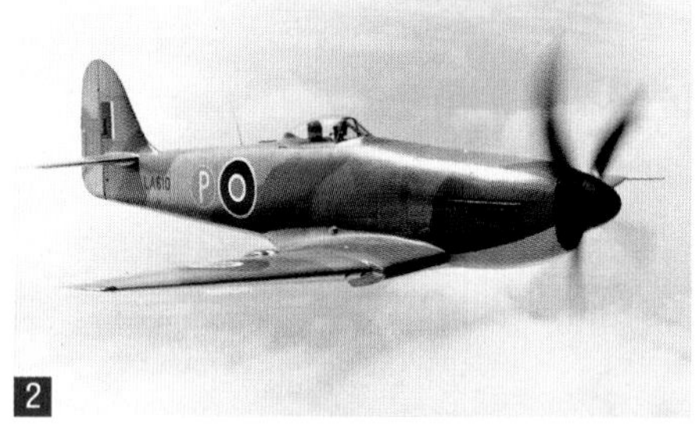

2

3

Doodlebugs

In June 1944, the first Doodlebug landed on London. The Tempest's excellent low-altitude performance made it an ideal tool to counter these fastmoving bombs and squadrons soon started knocking them out of the sky at an impressive rate. By the end of the war 638 of a total of 1,846 V-1s destroyed by aircraft fell to Tempests; which used external drop tanks to lurk off the south coast of England for nearly five hours waiting for the bombs to arrive.

Radar controllers would then guide the Tempests to their targets and pilots would either use cannon fire or 'nudge' the V-1 to topple its directional gyros.

In the latter months of the war, Tempests of the 2nd TAF were tasked with the destruction

1942

Fairey Fulmar A carrier-borne fighter-reconnaissance aircraft developed for the FAA. A development of the earlier Battle, the Fulmar proved to be a sturdy albeit underperforming aircraft that participated in the sinking of the German battleship Bismarck. It equipped 20 FAA squadrons but was also used by the RAF's 273 Sqn in Ceylon between April and August 1942. RAF Fulmars shot down several Japanese bombers.

General Aircraft Hamilcar A large glider designed to carry heavy cargo including a light tank or two Universal Carriers. A total of 344 Hamilcars were built but they were only used operationally on three occasions. Around 30 were used to carry anti-tank guns, vehicles and tanks into Normandy in June 1944. In March 1945, during Operation *Varsity*, they transported M22 Locust light tanks into Germany.

Lockheed Lightning The distinctive twin-boom P-38 saw extensive USAAF service in Britain. In March 1940, the Anglo-French Purchasing Committee also ordered 667 P-38Es but, unlike the counterrotating engines on USAAF P-38s, the RAF requested two right-hand-rotating Allisons. Following a poor review by a test pilot the order was cancelled. The RAF received three in 1942 for trials but they failed to find favour.

Lockheed Ventura Developed from the Lodestar [see p59] the Ventura had more powerful Pratt & Whitney Double Wasp engines and a stepped fuselage to accommodate a ventral turret. Although it was 40kts faster than the Hudson – and carried twice the bombload – it was was not popular with its crews. It entered service with 21 Sqn in May 1942 but was phased out in favour of Mosquitos by September 1942.

Martin Baker MB.3 A prototype fighter fitted with six 20mm cannon. Created by James Martin and Capt Valentine Baker, the MB.3 was powered by a 2,000hp Napier Sabre engine. On September 12, 1942, the engine failed and Baker crashed into a tree and was killed. The programme was cancelled but Martin, devastated by the loss of his best friend, devoted the remainder of his life to the development of the MB ejection seat.

4

1. Tempest V NV696 during a test flight on November, 25, 1944. The aircraft is piloted by William 'Bill' Humble, who did not normally wear a helmet. He was the grandfather of TV presenter Kate Humble.
2. Tempest III prototype LA610 was powered by the Rolls-Royce Griffon IIB engine.
3. Tempest II PR533 was one of the last examples of the breed to be produced.
4. Typhoon IBs of 56 Sqn, airborne from RAF Matlaske, Norfolk in April 1943.
5. Fury II prototype NX602. The type never entered RAF service but formed the basis for the Navy's Sea Fury.

5

of the German rail network and were also authorised to attack 'targets of opportunity'. In December 1944 alone they destroyed a total of 52 German fighters and 89 trains, for the loss of 20 Tempests. The aircraft proved particularly effective in the low-level interception role, including against the new generation of jet aircraft such as the Messerschmitt Me 262.

Tempest II

Although the Tempest III flew in November 1944 the Tempest III and IV programmes were cancelled as Griffon engines were needed for Spitfire XIVs.

The Tempest II was repeatedly delayed because of problems associated with its Centaurus powerplant. Orders for 500 were placed in September 1942, but as priority was given to building the Typhoon in 1943, the contract was allocated to the Bristol Aircraft Company instead.

This variant was powered by the Bristol Centaurus 18 cylinder radial engine that was closely cowled. The carburettor air intakes were located in the inner leading edges of the wings, and an oil cooler was positioned in the starboard wing.

The first Tempest II (LA602) flew on June 28, 1943 and the second (LA607) – with an enlarged dorsal fin - flew on September 18. These aircraft suffered from serious engine vibrations and the Centaurus was also found to be prone to overheating, had poor crankshaft lubrication and suffered reduction-gear seizures.

RAF Fast Fact

The Hawker Typhoon Preservation Group is overseeing the restoration of combat veteran Typhoon IB RB396 with the intention of returning the aircraft to flight powered by a Napier Sabre engine – something that hasn't been seen or heard for nearly 70 years. The project is run entirely by volunteers and has been funded exclusively by kind donations from the Supporters' Club and members of the public.

These delays meant the war in Europe was almost over by the time the Tempest II was ready for service. As such, the decision was made to 'tropicalise' the aircraft for service in South-East Asia Command (SEAC). This further delayed their delivery and the war in Japan had also ended by the time the RAF received its first Tempest IIs.

In the post war years, the type was mostly stationed with RAF overseas in Germany, India, Hong Kong and Malaysia. They saw combat use in the 1950s against guerrillas during the Malayan Emergency.

Some of the engineering changes from the Tempest II were incorporated into the Napier Sabre V powered Tempest VI. Just 142 examples were built before the type was superseded by jet propelled aircraft.

Furious Legacy

The ultimate incarnation of the Typhoon/ Tempest line was the Hawker Fury II, which began life as the 'Tempest Light Fighter' in January 1943.

It was designed to meet a specification calling for a fighter with a high rate of climb in excess of 4,500ft/min (23m/s) and a maximum speed of at least 391kts (450mph). The Admiralty also sought a 'navalised' version of the aircraft and six prototypes were ordered.

Orders were placed for the Fury and Sea Fury but the end of the war led to the RAF cancelling its order to concentrate on new jet aircraft. However, the Sea Fury would go on to operate with distinction in the Fleet Air Arm; becoming the fastest piston-powered aircraft ever to see British service.

The aircraft directly traced its history back through the Tempest and Typhoon to the Hurricane and, in turn, to Sydney Camm's Hart biplanes of the 1930s. Hawker Aircraft had created one of the most remarkable fighter families of all time. ■

Martin Marauder The Martin B-26 served with the USAAF but initially had a bad reputation as its small wing meant it was difficult to fly at low speed. Later versions had an increased wingspan and larger tail. The RAF received 52 of the original version as the Marauder I and 100 of the larger aircraft (Marauder II) under Len- Lease. These were based in the Mediterranean and Africa and used for bombing and anti-shipping missions.

Miles M.30 X-Minor The X-Minor was designed to explore the idea of blended fuselage and wing joins. Miles Aircraft began its X series of designs in 1938 as a 'scaleable' series of aircraft from small twin-engined machines to large eight-engined transatlantic transports. The M.30 was built to prove the concept and first flew in February 1942. A larger scale prototype of the X transport was planned but never built.

Miles M.35 Libellula A tandem wing prototype of a proposed carrier-based fighter. The idea was to sit the pilot at the very front to improve visibility during deck landing. The configuration also reduced wingspan and negated the need for folding wings for storage. Tests showed the M.35 would only take off if the throttle was rapidly closed whilst at speed! A change of centre of gravity helped but the Air Ministry rejected it as a fighter.

Miles Martinet The first British aircraft to be designed specifically as a target tug. Based upon the Miles Master II [see p51], the Martinet featured a longer nose, greater wingspan and higher cockpit. The airframe was also strengthened; target towing gear and a wind-powered winch were mounted in beneath the fuselage. A total of 1,724 were built including 69 Queen Martinets, a radio-controlled target drone version.

North American Mustang I & II Created in response to an RAF need for a new fighter, the first Allison V-1710-powered Mustang Is [see also p58] joined 26 Sqn in February 1942 and later became the first RAF single-seat fighters to fly over Germany. Britain also received 93 Mustang IAs and 50 Mustang IIs but the Allison engine lacked power above 15,000ft so production soon switched to the Merlin-powered variants.

The 'Rafwaffe'

At a time of war it is important to know your opponent's true capabilities. During World War Two, the RAF even set up a unit to specifically evaluate captured enemy aircraft

As long as man has used aircraft for combat it has been important to know how capable the enemy's machines really are.

During the Great War, a number of German aircraft were evaluated by British and American forces and after the Armistice a large number of Fokker D.VIIIs (deemed the most capable of Germany's fighters) were sent to Britain and the USA. The US Army and Navy alone evaluated 142 examples of the D.VIII and similar work was done in Britain.

Battle of Britain

When World War Two broke out the RAF soon found itself feeling the brunt of the Luftwaffe. During the Battle of Britain a number of enemy aircraft were downed over Britain and many of these damaged airframes were sent to Farnborough, Hampshire for examination and testing by the Royal Aircraft Establishment (RAE) Experimental Flying Department.

However, with the war in full motion the department soon found itself fully committed to the testing of new RAF types and it became obvious that a dedicated unit needed to be created to focus on these captured machines.

1

Duxford

On November 21, 1941 the RAF created 1426 (Enemy Aircraft) Flight at RAF Duxford, Cambridgeshire to both test and evaluate captured aircraft as well as demonstrate the machines to RAF (and later, United States Army Air Force) squadron pilots for familiarisation purposes. Unofficially dubbed the 'Rafwaffe', the unit was created in part to expose personnel to the performance, and even the sound of the latest enemy aircraft.

Duxford was already home to the Air Fighting Development Unit (AFDU), which developed operational tactics for the RAF and often used captured Luftwaffe and Italian aircraft in the process.

When it formed the new unit was manned by F/O Forbes, F/O Kinder, P/O Lewendon and Flt Sgt Gough, all of whom had been Maintenance Unit (MU) test pilots with 41 Group. Their first aircraft was a Heinkel He 111 bomber, which had been shot down over North Berwick the previous year and proved to be an invaluable research tool.

Soon the Heinkel was joined by a Messerschmitt Bf109E-3 that had been captured in France in late 1939 and a Junkers Ju-88A-5 that had landed at RAF Chivenor in error.

Quickly the fleet grew to include seven Messerschmitt Bf 109s, a Messerschmitt Me 110 and Me 410, four Focke-Wulf Fw190s, a Henschel 129, five Junkers Ju-88s and even an Italian Fiat CR42 Falco. The latter had force landed on the shingle beach at Orfordness, Suffolk on November 11, 1940 during one of only three recorded Italian air raids on Britain. The CR42 was moved by road to RAF Martlesham Heath for repair and then flown to RAE Farnborough where it was given RAF serial BT474 and roundels. It was later transferred to Duxford for further tests.

Make Do & Mend

The posting of maintenance personnel and groundcrew commenced on December 22 and Rafwaffe groundcrew faced an ongoing battle trying to return various aircraft to flight – let alone keep them airworthy without access to a store of parts. Engine and airframe components had to be scavenged from crashed and unserviceable aircraft and tools often had to be made from scratch.

Parts had to be scavenged from crashed and unserviceable aircraft

The first 'tour' of RAF stations began on February 11, 1942 with the captured aircraft visiting seven bases before returning to Duxford at the end of the month. In total, aircraft from the Flight conducted 12 such tours before the end of the war and individual aircraft were also deployed to stations for specific analysis and trials work whenever needed.

In the run-up to D-Day the entire unit deployed to RAF Station Thorney Island, Sussex for five weeks to provide recognition exercises flying over the Allied invasion fleet massing on the South Coast.

1942

Stinson Reliant Designed as a touring aircraft, the Stinson SR series was built in Michigan between 1933 and 1938. The V-77 military version flew in February 1942 and the type remained in production until late 1943 in several versions. The USAAF used it as the UC-81 utility aircraft whereas the RAF and FAA received around 500 as the Reliant. RAF Reliants were mostly used for navigation/radio training or communications.

Supermarine Spitfire VII A high altitude pressurised variant of the Spitfire with a two-stage supercharged Merlin. Extended pointed wingtips were fitted, increasing the wingspan and boosting high altitude performance. The canopy was double-glazed and used rubber tubing to create a pressure seal against the fuselage for pressurisation purposes, allowing it to operate at up to 45,000ft. A total of 140 were built.

Supermarine Spitfire IX When the Spitfire VB met its match in the Fw 190 the RAF needed a new fighter. The resulting Mk IX used the new supercharged Merlin 61 engine. It was envisaged as a temporary fix until the new aerodynamically improved and strengthened Mk VII and VIIIs could be readied for service; however it became the most produced variant with more than 5,600 eventually being completed.

Supermarine Spitfire Floatplane The concept of a float-equipped Spitfire that could fly from lakes was studied in 1942 following Japan's entry into the war. Spitfire V W3760 was fitted with a pair of floats and a fin extension under the tail to provide extra stability. It first flew on October 12, 1942 and was followed by three other examples. It was faster than a Hurricane but no role could be found for float equipped fighters.

Taylorcraft Auster I-IV Developed from the civilian Taylorcraft Plus D as an Air Observation Post (AOP) aircraft to direct artillery fire. Civilian Plus Ds were impressed into the RAF and others were purchased new as Austers. The Auster I had a Cirrus Minor I engine whereas the Auster III had a 130hp Gipsy Major engine. The later Auster IV which had a larger cabin to accommodate three seats and used the 130hp Lycoming O-290.

2

3

1. Messerschmitt Bf109E 'Black 12' was damaged by a Spitfire and belly-landed at RAF Manston in November 1940. Repaired and passed to 1426 (EA) Flight it was registered DG200. It is seen here flying without a canopy; such was the scarceness of parts at times. Today it can be seen at the RAF Museum, Hendon.
2. Heinkel He 111H-1 '1H+EN' of KG26 landed in a field near North Berwick on 9 February 1940 after being damaged by a Spitfire. Repaired and registered AW177 it served with various trials units and then became the founding aircraft of 1426 (EA) Flight.
3. A captured Focke-Wulf Fw190 is painted in RAF markings by German prisoners prior to test flying.
4. Messerschmitt Bf109G-2/Trop 'Black 6' found abandoned by 3 Sqn RAAF near Tobruk, Libya in November 1942. It joined 1426 (EA) Flight in late 1943 as RN228. It flew again as a civilian 'warbird' in 1991 and was a popular airshow aircraft until it was damaged in 1998. It is now displayed at the RAF Museum, Cosford.

4

Famous Focke-Wulf

One of the most famous aircraft evaluated by 1426 (EA) Flight was Focke-Wulf Fw190 Wrk Nr 313.

The Fw190 had been both admired and dreaded by RAF pilots ever since it made its combat debut in 1941. Its extensive capabilities were legendary and the British desperately needed an example to evaluate.

A number of outlandish schemes were put forward to 'obtain' an Fw190; including one put forward suggesting that a German-speaking RAF pilot (wearing a Luftwaffe uniform) flew one of 1426 (EA) Flight's Messersmitts to a German base in France. He would then swap his aircraft for an Fw190 and fly home!

Another proposal was Operation *Air Thief*, which called for Spitfire test pilot Jeffrey Quill to be smuggled into France to steal an Fw190 with assistance from members of the Resistance.

However, on June 23, 1942, these audacious plans would cease to be necessary. That evening Oberleutenant Armin Faber had been engaged in dogfights over the south of England. Disorientated and short on fuel he crossed a stretch of water – which he presumed to be the English Channel – and soon found an airfield upon which he could land.

As he shut off the engine and opened his canopy his heart must have sank when he saw an RAF officer running towards him with his service revolver drawn… Faber had landed in South Wales!

The water he had crossed had actually been the Bristol Channel and the airfield he assumed was in France was actually RAF Pembrey, the RAF's Air Gunnery School. The Fw190 was given the RAF serial number MP499 and extensively tested in comparative trials with Allied aircraft.

The Flight moved from Duxford to RAF Collyweston, Northamptonshire in March 1943 and the aircraft in the unit changed throughout the war as later marques came into the RAF's hands. Some were captured or crashed, others were gained during mistaken landings by lost German pilots and some defecting pilots even brought the latest examples of the Luftwaffe's hardware with them for analysis.

However, after D-Day the perceived need for the Flight declined and operations at Collyweston ceased on January 17, 1945. It briefly reformed at RAF Tangmere, Sussex (as the 'Enemy Aircraft Flight' of the Central Fighter Establishment) but finally disbanded on December 31, 1945. ■

RAF Fast Fact

In October and November 1945 the Royal Aircraft Establishment at Farnborough held a huge public open day and airshow to demonstrate many of the types captured from Germany during the war. Twenty five German machines were displayed alongside the most modern RAF aircraft, including jets from both nations.

1943

Vickers Type 432 A prototype high-altitude fighter resembling an enlarged Mosquito. Unlike the Mosquito, the Type 432 was all-metal and the elliptical wing featured a Barnes Wallis-designed stressed-skin structure for lightness. The aircraft suffered handling problems on the ground and in the air and the tail had to be altered to enable it to land safely. Engine issues meant the aircraft only flew 28 times.

Vultee Vengeance A dive bomber designed for the French but diverted to the British. The RAF had little use for dive bombers in Europe so based the aircraft in Burma to carry out close support bombing of the jungles. They were replaced by fighter bombers after the Japanese were defeated but the RAF continued to receive large numbers of Lend -Lease Vengeances. Some were used for spraying malarial mosquitoes.

Armstrong Whitworth Albemarle Plans to use the Albemarle as a bomber were dropped before it entered service as it was inferior to aircraft already in use. The aircraft was used as a transport but also proved ideal for paratrooping and glider towing. Albemarles were used in most British airborne operations from the invasion of Sicily to the D-Day landings and Operation *Market Garden* at Arnham.

Avro York Avro saw a need for a four-engined transport aircraft and paired a box section fuselage with the wings, tail, undercarriage and Merlin engines from the Lancaster. The York was designed in 1942 but due to the importance of Lancaster production it would not enter large scale service until 1945. However, in 1943 York LV633 was delivered to 24 Sqn and finished as a 'flying boardroom' for use by the Prime Minister.

Beechcraft Expeditor The Beechcraft Model 18 was continuously produced from 1937 to 1969 with more than 9,000 built. During the war, over 5,024 were built for military service as light transports and aircrew trainers. Of those, 236 served under the Expeditor name with the RAF and a total of 67 flew with the FAA. The majority of the RAF's examples served with South East Asia Command.

Jet Age Pioneer

Gutless and flawed; the Gloster E.28/39 was nonetheless the first of a new generation of RAF jet-powered fighter

As early as the 1920s, British pilot and inventor Frank Whittle was contemplating the technology behind the turbojet engine.

Expanding on the ideas published in AA Griffith's seminal 1926 paper *An Aerodynamic Theory of Turbine Design,* Whittle patented the centrifugal-flow turbojet in 1930. However, as the RAF pilot could not afford the £5 fee (approximately £350 today) to renew the patent five years later, the Air Ministry refused to pay it on his behalf; referring to the design as being "impracticable."

Meanwhile, German engineer Hans von Ohain had been independently studying a concept for "an engine that did not require a propeller" and by 1936 had earned a patent for his version of the jet engine.

Undeterred, Frank Whittle had secured limited funding to create Power Jets Ltd in 1936 and the WU (Whittle Unit) engine ran successfully on April 12, 1937; just a month after von Ohain's but with a fraction of the budget and no official backing.

First to Fly

The von Ohain engine was soon developed into the flight-worthy HeS 3b version and on August 27, 1939, test pilot Erich Warsitz eased the HeS 3b-powered Heinkel He 178 into the sky for the first time at Rostock, Germany. The world had entered the jet age.

Meanwhile, back in Britain Frank Whittle's Power Jets team had been enduring mixed fortunes. The project was still being conducted on a shoestring budget and it would be March 1938 before limited funds were made available by the Air Ministry. This, however, was a double-edged sword as the funds came with the condition that the team signed the Official Secrets Act – something that made obtaining further outside investment almost impossible.

Luckily, the next time the Air Ministry came to visit, the WU ran for 20 minutes without a snag and the delegation went home convinced of the engine's importance. It issued a contract for Power Jets to start work on the 'Whittle Supercharger Type W1' engine: in September 1939 the Gloster Aircraft Company was awarded the job of designing a simple flight test aircraft to evaluate the engine.

Gloster E.28/39

Gloster's chief designer, George Carter, was given the highly confidential job of creating Britain's first jet aeroplane. He had already been instrumental in the development of the Gauntlet and Gladiator [Ed: see p28] and had created a number of innovative designs that eventually led to the Hawker Typhoon [see p62].

2

The Air Ministry subsequently issued Gloster with a formal specification, on February 13, 1940. This called for an aircraft capable of 330kts (380mph) that could easily be converted from trials machine to fighter and could carry four Browning machine guns.

The contract was for two aircraft (later serials W4041 and W4046) and £18,500 (around £1.2 million today) was allocated per aircraft. The Air Ministry also agreed to the construction of two sets of wings; a 'high lift' wing for initial testing and a 'high speed' wing for later trials.

To avoid prying eyes the design work was mostly completed on a farm near Cheltenham and construction then began amid high levels of secrecy at Gloster's Brockworth plant. However, fears of the factory's susceptibility to German bombing saw the project moved to the nearby Regent Motors garage in Cheltenham, Gloucestershire. Once completed, the airframe was moved back to Brockworth airfield and the powerplant fitted. Engine runs began on April 6, 1941 with the aircraft in the hangar yet only its jet pipe protruding through the open doors.

"One of the most exciting aircraft I ever flew"

Jet Flight

Taxi trials began the following evening with test pilot Gerry Sayer praising controllability but

1943

Consolidated Coronado A large flying boat patrol bomber designed for both anti-submarine and transport roles. The PB2Y served the US Navy in large numbers in the Pacific and found a niche as flying hospitals. The RAF received ten under Lend-Lease as the Coronado I but found them inferior to the Sunderland in the patrol bomber role. As such, they were used as transatlantic transports delivering equipment and cargo.

Consolidated Liberator III & V The B-24D was the first mass-produced variant and served the RAF as the Liberator III. British versions differed from USAAF aircraft by having a single .303in Browning machine gun in the nose, two in each waist position, and four more in a tail turret. The Liberator V was similar but had extra fuel capacity. Most of the 322 aircraft delivered via Lend-Lease served with Coastal Command.

Consolidated Liberator VI & VIII The RAF operated the B-24H and B-24J as the Liberator VI and VIII respectively. The Mk VI was the first to house a nose turret to help defend the aircraft from head-on attack. The Mk VIII was almost identical but built at the Willow Run factory. The RAF received 1,568 Liberator VI and VIII airframes. They were used as heavy bombers in the Middle and Far East as well as serving Coastal Command.

Fairchild Cornell Derived from the USAAC's PT-19 basic trainer and supplied to the British Commonwealth Air Training Plan in Canada, the PT-26 was delivered in three versions. The PT-26 Cornell I was the same as the PT-19A but with an enclosed cockpit; the PT-26A Cornell II was built under licence by Fleet Aircraft and PT-26B Cornell III had minor changes. In total 1,727 were delivered; all of which served in Canada.

Fairey Barracuda A carrier-borne torpedo and dive bomber that was the FAA's first all metal aircraft. The first Barracudas entered operational service with 827 Sqn FAA on January 10, 1943 and would eventually a equip 24 front-line FAA units. The RAF also operated Barracudas in the target tug role, with the first joining 567 (anti-aircraft co-operation) Sqn in 1943. The type also served with 667, 679 and 691 Sqn in a similar role.

RAF Fast Fact

The E.28/39 ultimately paved the way for Britain's first successful jet fighter, the twin-engined Gloster Meteor [Ed: see p70]. However, it also led to a little-known single-engined jet-powered interceptor: the Gloster E.1/44 Ace.

With an eye towards ever-improving turbojet technology Gloster created the aircraft in 1944 to meet Specification E.1/44 and proposed a fighter capable of reaching a ceiling 48,000ft (14,630m) and 487kts (560mph).

Three prototypes were ordered and the aircraft officially named the Gloster Ace. However, the Air Ministry constantly 'tinkered' with the requirements and, as such, development was slow. It would be July 1947 before the first Ace (SM809) finally appeared.

In preparation for its first flight, SM809 was dispatched by road to Boscombe Down, Hampshire, but during the journey the trailer jack-knifed and the Ace was written off.

On March 9, 1948 Ace TX145 was ready to fly and Gloster's test pilot, Sqn Ldr William 'Bill' Waterton took it into the sky. Waterton was famed for his acerbic reviews of aircraft and he took an instant dislike to the Ace, later assessing it as "lethargic" and dubbing it the "Gloster Gormless".

The 'Gormless' Ace was beset with problems during testing and all orders for the type were soon cancelled. Those prototypes that had been built were dispatched to the Proof and Experimental Establishment (P&EE) at Shoeburyness in Essex, where they were subsequently destroyed by gunfire.

1. The Air Ministry agreed to fund the construction of two sets of wings for the Gloster E.28/39, which enabled the initial tests to be made with a 'high lift' wing and later ones with a 'high speed' one.
2. The unpainted Gloster E.28/39 W4041 is photographed on the ground at Brockworth shortly after completion.
3. In December 1942 the aircraft was transferred to RAE Farnborough and was subsequently returned to Brockworth for further work. End-plate fins were fitted to the tailplane to improve stability and a W2/500 engine was installed.

criticising the lack of acceleration. As the grass runway at Brockworth was deemed too short and bumpy for flight testing, the aeroplane was taken by road to RAF Cranwell, Lincolnshire for further evaluation while the team waited for a weather window.

Then, at 5.40pm on May 14, 1941, the rain and cloud had improved enough for Sayer to attempt a flight. With the canopy left open he ran the engine run up to 16,500rpm before releasing the brakes. Seconds later, Britain's first jet aircraft was airborne.

After 17 minutes the aeroplane landed successfully and Britain had entered the jet age – almost two years after the Heinkel He 178 had flown in Germany.

Some 17 flights were conducted before the aeroplane was trucked back to Gloucester and ensconced in Crabtree's Garage in Cheltenham, where engineers replaced the 'high lift' wing with the 'high speed' one and fitted a newly arrived W1A engine.

On February 16, 1942, W4041 was ready to fly again and the second E.28/39 (W4046) joined the fleet in March 1943. However, this new addition did not enjoy a long career as it was lost in July when its ailerons jammed, forcing Sqn Ldr Douglas Davie to bail out. The second aeroplane had made 134 flights in just five months – compared to W4041 that would make just 110 flights in its entire four-year career as a trials aircraft.

Legendary test pilot Eric 'Winkle' Brown was at the controls for some of those test flights. He joined the test programme in April 1944 and later recalled the E.28/39 as "one of the most exciting aircraft I ever flew."

W4041 continued flying until late 1944, by which time more advanced turbojet-powered aircraft were available. The Gloster E.28/39 was uncomplicated, simple and pleasant to fly and provided the perfect platform for proving Whittle's theories. ■

Grumman Goose The amphibious Grumman G-21 was Grumman's first monoplane, first twin-engined aircraft, and its first aircraft to enter airline service. Although marketed as a 'flying yacht' for well-heeled businessmen the G-21 also found military favour and served the USAAC as the OA-9 and US Navy as the JRF. The RAF received 44 under Lend -Lease as the Goose IA; using the type for observer training in Trinidad.

Handley Page HP.75 Manx Experimental flying wing with twin pusher engines. The Manx had a swept wing with twin vertical stabilisers in lieu of a tailplane. The wing had elevons for pitch and roll control and while the main gear was retractable the nose gear was fixed. The Manx was completed in 1939 but had to be rede-signed as it was too heavy. It would be June 1943 before it took flight but it only flew 17 hours before it was grounded.

Hawker Hurricane IV The ultimate development of the Hurricane; the Mk IV introduced a 'universal wing' that could carry either two 250lb or 500lb bombs, two 40mm Vickers S guns, eight RP-3 rockets or two drop tanks. The aircraft had a Merlin XX engine with a larger and armoured radiator. The engine also benefited from armour plating within the cowling. A total of 524 were built and the first joined 6 Sqn in Italy in 1943.

Martin Mariner Designed to operate alongside the Catalina and Coronado flying boats. The Mariner had a myriad of gun emplacements and carried its bomb load within the engine nacelles. The type entered US Navy service as the PBM-1 in September 1940 and sunk ten U boats during the war. The RAF acquired 32 PBM-3Bs as the Mariner I but never used the type operationally and some were returned to the US Navy 'unused'.

Miles M.39B Libellula Derived from the M.35 [see p65] the M.39B Libellula was a tandem wing experimental aircraft designed to give the pilot an improved view during carrier landing. The M.39 was designed as a high speed bomber to be powered by three Power Jets turbojet engines but to prove the concept Miles constructed the 5/8th scale M.39B. The aircraft flew well but was scrapped when the bomber project was cancelled.

First Generation Jets

The Gloster Meteor was the RAF's first operational jet fighter, followed by the de Havilland Vampire; athough it could easily have been the other way around

With the Gloster E.28/39 [Ed: see p68] proving the viability of the jet fighter concept, Gloster began concentrating on 'militarising' the aircraft.

The low power output from the Whittle W2B engines made it virtually impossible for the E.28/39 to carry weapons, so the manufacturer decided to use two powerplants and create a brand new twin-engined fighter.

In spite of its unusual engines the resulting Meteor was a very conventional aircraft, lacking the aerodynamical advances being pioneered by German designs such as the swept wing Messerschmitt Me262.

Powerplant Delays

It soon became clear that the F.9/40 Meteor prototype's airframe would be ready before its powerplants, which had been sub-contracted out to companies that had little or no experience of aircraft engine manufacture.

The first engines – produced by Rover Motors – were delivered in July 1942 but they only produced 1,000lb/thrust instead of the expected 1,800lb/thrust. They were fitted to prototype DG202/G (the 'G' suffix indicating the need for the aircraft to be under armed guard at all times) but were only suitable for taxying trials.

Luckily, other companies were also working on jet engines and both de Havilland and Metropolitan-Vickers were encouraged to progress their Halford H.1 and Metrovik F.2 units to provide insurance against further problems with the W.2B engine.

Gloster was therefore tasked with preparing prototypes to be take the alternative engines. The W2B-powered prototype would be the Meteor I and the Halford-engined example would be the Meteor II.

The first two H.1 engines were ready by January 1943 and, fitted to the Meteor DG206, the aircraft performed the type's maiden flight on March 5 of the same year. The machine flew well but test pilot Michael Daunt complained about the directional instability; something that was to plague all early Meteors.

1

By January 1944 the first production Meteor Is were ready to fly. By now, Rolls Royce had taken over development of the W2B and renamed it the Welland, succeeding in coaxing 1,700lb/thrust from the engine.

Into Combat

The first Meteors joined 616 Sqn, based at RAF Culmhead, Scotland in July 1944. By the end of the month the squadron had seven Meteors and had re-located to RAF Manston, Kent to help defend against German V-1 flying bombs.

However, the Meteor's relatively low level of armament meant shooting down a V-1 was difficult and the first 'kill' only came on August 4 after F/O Dean realised that by flying alongside his quarry he could use his wingtip to nudge the flying bomb, toppling its gyro and sending it spinning from the sky. The unit would go on to claim 14 of the bombs before the end of the war.

By Christmas, 616 Sqn had received its first Meteor IIIs, which were fitted with a more developed version of the W2B known as the Derwent. They also had increased fuel capacity and a strengthened airframe. 18 RAF units operated the Meteor I and III but the type never saw combat against a Luftwaffe jet. In fact, the Meteor never downed another aircraft in combat during World War Two; but it was credited with destroying 42 enemy aircraft during ground attack missions.

Postwar Use

The Meteor would form the backbone of the postwar RAF, with the Derwent 5-powered F.4 the first into service. By 1946, a total of 16

1943

Miles Messenger Designed to meet an Army requirement for a slow speed air observation post and liaison aircraft. The Messenger had large flaps and triple fins and rudders to help maintain controllability down to as slow as just 22kts! It lost out to the Auster in the AOP role but 23 were ordered as VIP transport aircraft. In this guise it became the personal transport of Field Marshal Montgomery during the D-Day landings.

North American Mustang III Replacing the Mustang's Allison engine with a Merlin transformed the fighter. It raised the service ceiling by 10,000ft and the top speed by 43kts. The USAAF operated the new variant as the P-51B (manufactured at Inglewood, California) and the P-51C (produced in Dallas) but the type was christened Mustang Mk III by the RAF. A total of 308 P-51Bs and 636 P-51Cs were delivered to Britain [see p58].

Slingsby Hengist Named after the Jute invader Hengist, the 15-seat troop carrying glider was designed by John 'Jack' Frost. The prototype flew in January 1942 – towed aloft by an Armstrong Whitworth Whitley – and 14 production aircraft were delivered between February 1943 and March 1944. Production halted when Lend-Lease Waco Hadrian gliders became available and all but two never left storage.

Stinson Sentinel The Stinson L-5 was unusual in that it was a purpose-built military liaison aircraft; whereas most of its contemporaries were converted civilian aircraft. It was capable of operating from short airstrips and proved ideal for jungle operations. The RAF received 40 L-5s under Lend-Lease as the Sentinel I and 60 L-5Bs as the Sentinel II. The latter had a hatch in the rear fuselage to allow loading of a stretcher or cargo.

Supermarine Sea Otter The last biplane to enter RAF service. The Sea Otter was a modernised version of the Walrus with longer range. The main difference between the two was that the Walrus had a rear-facing engine and the Sea Otter's engine faced forward with a tractor propeller. The prototype flew in 1938 but didn't enter service until 1943. The Sea Otter was used for air-sea rescue and patrol roles.

RAF Fast Fact

The Meteor was a difficult aircraft to fly and in total 890 were lost between 1944 and 1986: of those 436 were fatal accidents. The RAF lost 150 Meteors in 1952 alone. The aircraft was particularly troublesome in the event of an engine failure, when the leg forces required to keep the rudder depressed to counter the asymmetric forces of the single remaining engine have been described as "knee trembling". At one time the RAF routinely practiced simulated asymmetric flying but it eventually became apparent that more pilots were being killed during practice than by actual engine failures.
The Meteor T.7 was also notorious for the 'Phantom Dive'; a phenomenon that occurred when a pilot lowered the undercarriage while the air brakes were deployed. One landing gear leg came down, causing the aircraft to yaw and blank the airflow over one wing. This would cause the aircraft to roll over and – at low altitude – there was usually insufficient time to recover. The absence of an ejector seat meant almost all instances were fatal.

1. The prototype Meteor is preserved for posterity and on display at the RAF Museum, Cosford, Shropshire. **SDB**
2. Gloster Meteor Is of 616 Sqn at RAF Manston in January 1945.
3. The definitive day fighter Meteor was the F.8. VZ865 (illustrated) was the last to fly with the RAF and now resides in Australia. **SDB**

squadrons had equipped with the type and the RAF would receive 535 examples of the type, most of which had 'clipped' wings.

However, the design was still far from perfected. Gloster improved on the F.4 by stretching the fuselage, modifying the tail, changing the framed canopy for a 'blown' unit, further increasing fuel capacity and power output from the Derwent and – finally – fitting an ejection seat.

The resulting Meteor F.8 was built in greater numbers than any other Meteor variant (nearly 40% of total production) but it was never to fire its guns in anger during its RAF service.

The first F.8s entered service with 245 Sqn in June 1950 and the RAF would go on to receive 1,090 of what would become the ultimate day fighter variant of the Meteor.

The F.8 was also modified into the armed low-level reconnaissance FR.9 variant, which first flew in March 1950. It was 8in (20cm) longer with a new nose incorporating a remote controlled camera and window. Developed alongside the FR.9, the PR.10 was a high altitude reconnaissance Meteor. Based on the F.4, it had the cannons removed and a single camera placed in the nose along with two more in the rear fuselage. A total of 56 were delivered to the RAF but it was phased out from 1956 when improvements in surface-to-air missiles rendered the aircraft vulnerable.

Two-Seaters

Scores of pilots now found themselves either converting from propeller-driven fighters or learning to fly jets from scratch. As many of these pilots were to discover at their peril, jet aircraft had quite different handling characteristics to their piston-powered forebears. With an escalating accident rate it became obvious that something quickly needed to be done.

In December 1946 the Air Ministry issued Operational Requirement OR/238, which called for a "two seat, dual-control version" of the Meteor F.4.

The specification called for an unarmed aircraft but a gun-camera was required for the front cockpit. Interestingly, the Air Staff stipulated that ejection systems were "desirable but not essential." As such, one was not fitted.

The resulting Meteor T.7 was 30in (76cm) longer – to allow a tandem cockpit to be fitted – and the prototype first flew on March 19, 1948. The removal of the single-seater's armament more than made up for the addition of a second seat, so much so that that the T.7 was almost 1,000lb lighter than the F.4. This gave it sprightly performance and a particularly short take off roll, and at their heyday, T.7s equipped nine RAF flying schools.

The fourth production T.7 was modified into a prototype night fighter and made its maiden flight in NF.11 guise in May 1950. Alongside a pressurised fuselage, which was extended by 5ft (1.52m), it featured the longer-span wings of the earlier single-seaters and the later F.8-style tail unit. An elongated nose housed the AI.10 radar, which displaced the 20mm guns to the wings. The majority were built under licence by Armstrong Whitworth.

There were three further night fighter variants incorporating aerodynamic and equipment refinements, but more Vampire

Supermarine Spitfire VIII Apart from the lack of cabin pressurisation and deletion of the extended wingtips the Spitfire VIII differed very little from the Mk VII [see p66]. It was intended to become the main RAF fighter variant but when the 'interim' Mk IX proved so successful in Europe the Mk VIII almost exclusively served overseas; notably in the Mediterranean, South East Asia, North Africa and the South Pacific.

Supermarine Spitfire XI The dedicated photo reconnaissance Spitfire PR.XI combined the best parts of the Mks VII, VIII and IX. It was the first PR variant to use two vertically mounted F52 cameras behind the cockpit. Those used for tactical reconnaissance used a vertically pointing camera in a fairing under each wing. The aircraft had a deeper cowling housing a larger oil tank. If required the 471 PR.XIs could operate at 44,000ft.

Supermarine Spitfire XII The first Griffon-powered Spitfire to enter service. The first 55 were based on Mk VC airframes and had a single fuel tank resulting in a range of just 380 miles. The final 45 were based on Mk VIII airframes with two wing fuel tanks and retractable tailwheels. The single-stage Griffon and clipped wings gave incredible low level performance and this meant they were ideal for downing V-1 flying bombs.

Taylorcraft Auster IV & V While the Auster III [see p66] addressed the earlier variant's lack of power it still didn't improve manoeuvrability or visibility. As such, Taylorcraft created the Auster IV with an altered rear cockpit, flaps and a Lycoming O-290. A total of 254 would ultimately be produced from December 1943. The later Auster V introduced improved flaps and a blind flying panel to enable it to fly in adverse weather. **SDB**

Vickers Warwick The largest British twin-engined aircraft to see use during the war. More than just a scaled up Wellington, the Warwick was designed in 1938 but delays in producing higher-powered engines meant it would not enter service until 1943 – by which time it was vulnerable to modern fighters. Of the 856 built only 16 were used as bombers; the rest utilised by Transport Command and Coastal Command.

1. Gloster Meteor T.7 WA591 is the oldest airworthy British jet aeroplane. It is currently based in the USA but available for sale. **SDB**
2. The last Vampires to serve with the RAF were two-seat T.11s like WZ507. This aircraft is still airworthy as G-VTII but is currently for sale. **SDB**
3. The Vampire and Venom (illustrated) used a Coffman start system that involved an explosive cartridge. When the aircraft's ignition is turned on and the cartridge is fired, high-velocity, high-pressure gas forced the turbine to spin. **SDB**

1

NF.11s were built for the RAF (311) than the others combined.

The 100 NF.12 had a longer nose to house an American AN/APS-21 radar, the 40 NF.13s were 'tropicalised' versions of the NF.11 for use in Cyprus, Egypt and Malta; and the 101 NF.14s had an all-glass canopy to replace the heavy-framed version on earlier airframes. These also had a longer nose, giving an overall length of 51ft 4in (15.66m). The RAF's last Meteor NF.14 (WS848) was delivered in May 1955: it was also the last ever Meteor to be built.

Twin Boomers

The RAF's second operational jet fighter, the de Havilland DH.100 Vampire, had a more unconventional layout. The poor performance of early jet engines meant that the jet pipe needed to be kept as short as possible to minimise power loss. The DH.100 achieved this by having a short fuselage with the tail mounted on twin booms.

Work on the design began in 1941 and both the aircraft and de Havilland's Halford H.1 engine were almost ready to take to the air when the Air Ministry decreed that the flightworthy H.1 should be 'donated' to the Meteor programme.

As such, the prototype DH.100 – which was originally to be called the Spider Crab – did not fly until September 20, 1943 and the first production examples did not join RAF squadrons until early 1946.

Nevertheless, the Vampire quickly proved to be an effective aircraft and was adopted as a replacement for many wartime piston-engined fighter aircraft. During its early service, it was recognised for accomplishing several aviation firsts and various records, including the first jet aircraft to traverse the Atlantic Ocean.

Like the Meteor, the Vampire was modified into training and night-fighter variants and the last examples (T.11 trainers) were not withdrawn from RAF service until 1966.

2

3

In 1948, de Havilland proposed a replacement for their Vampire. With a more powerful engine and thinner wings enabling better high speed and high altitude performance, the DH.112 Venom served in large numbers with the RAF. The type saw combat in Malaya, the Suez Crisis and against rebels in Aden, Africa and Oman: however, Venoms had a relatively short life and the last RAF example was retired in July 1962 in favour of the Hawker Hunter FGA.9.

It would be the Meteor that soldiered on as the longest serving of all the first generation jets. The RAF did jot retire its last target-tug variants until 1977 and even today, British ejection seat manufacturer Martin-Baker still uses a pair of highly modified T.7/F.8s hybrids as flying test beds. These regularly conduct live ejection trials.

As such, Britain's first jet would become one of its most useful. ■

1943

Vickers Windsor Designed as a pressurised four-engined replacement for the Wellington with remote controlled turrets in barbettes in the rear of the engine nacelles. The elliptical wing housed four Merlin engines and had a hollow geodetic tube running from tip to tip (in place of a spar). In order to spread the weight evenly there were four undercarriage legs - one in each nacelle. Only three were built before it was cancelled.

Waco Hadrian The Waco CG-4A glider was constructed of fabric-covered wood and could carry 13 fully equipped troops, or a Jeep or 75mm howitzer. Between 1942 and 1945 almost 14,000 were built. The RAF received CG-4As under Lend Lease as the Hadrian; the first being aero-towed across the Atlantic by a Dakota. RAF Hadrians were used solely in the invasion of Sicily as British-built gliders offered greater capacity.

1944

Bristol Buckingham The Air Ministry preferred to source medium bombers from the US but allowed Bristol to adapt an original design (but not create a brand new one). The Buckingham was based on the Beaufighter with a new centre and front fuselage, a mid-upper turret, twin tail fins and a larger wing (essentially a brand new design!). It handled badly but 119 were ordered for use overseas in the courier role.

Consolidated Liberator II Mod Soon after delivery Liberator II AL504 was given a VIP interior and – named *Commando* – was used by Winston Churchill. It originally retained the regular Liberator nose and tail but in 1944 it was converted to have a covered nose and also the same single tail fin used on the PB4Y-2 Privateer. In May 1945 it disappeared without trace over the Atlantic.

Douglas Skymaster The first example of the Douglas C-54 cargo-lifter to join the RAF was EW999. This was C-54B presented by President Roosevelt for the personal use of Winston Churchill. It was fitted with a conference table, sleeping accommodation for six and a stateroom. It entered service in November 1944 and was later joined by ten C-54D Skymaster Is for use by Transport Command on routes to the Far East.

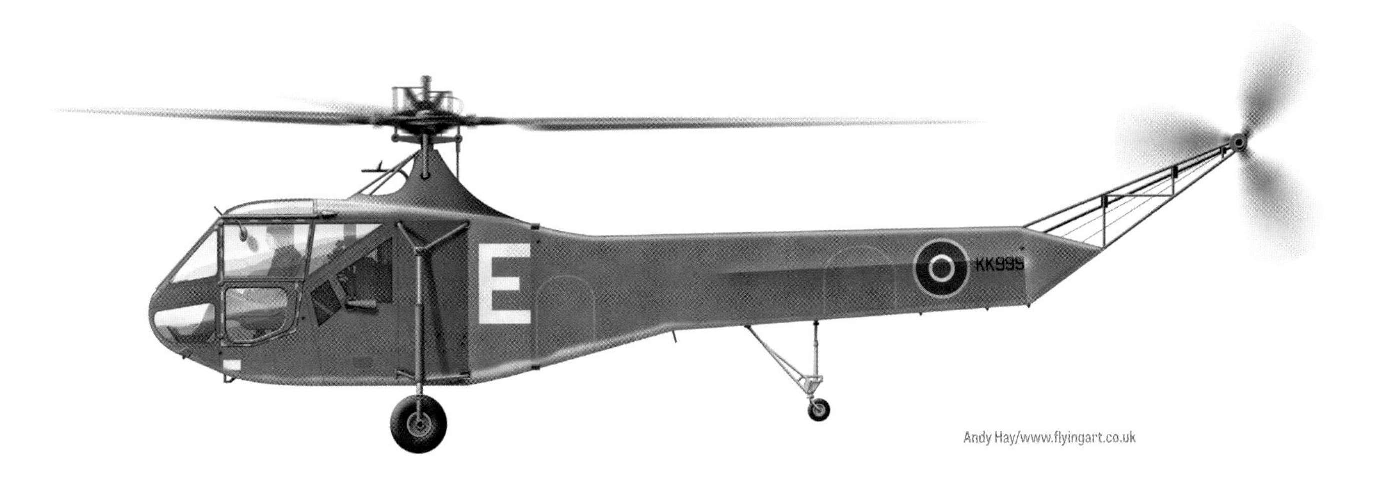

Andy Hay/www.flyingart.co.uk

Hoverfly

The helicopter has long been a key part of the RAF arsenal, playing a vital role in combat and humanitarian operations around the globe. The first was the diminutive Hoverfly

The Sikorsky R-4 was the first mass-produced helicopter in the world and also the first to be used by the RAF and Royal Navy as well as the USAAF, US Navy and Coast Guard.

It is directly descended from Igor Sikorsky's VS-300 helicopter, which was demonstrated in 1940 and – while not initially given priority status by the military – was adopted by the USAAF in 1942.

The prototype XR-4 first flew on January 14, 1942 and immediately began setting rotary winged records. It could attain 78kts (90mph) in forward flight and established an altitude record of 12,000ft (3,658m).

The British Air Ministry instantly saw the potential of this new type of aircraft and upon request were allocated two of the first eight for evaluation. It would go on to order 240 of the R-4B variant as the Hoverfly I for the RAF and Royal Navy, but only 52 were delivered as the end of World War Two in August 1945 deemed them unnecessary.

While some US examples saw limited use in the war – notably in the casualty evacuation role in the China-Burma-India theatre – the RAF examples arrived too late for active service.

The RAF established the Helicopter Training School at RAF Andover, Hampshire in January 1945 to conduct both flying training and operational research. Nine Hoverfly Is were attached the unit, which was initially commanded by Sqn Ldr B H Arkell.

Although it was the first hypothetically practical allied helicopter, the Hoverfly I had an inadequate load carrying capability and was used by the RAF mainly to prove the potential of rotary wing operations. As such, one was also used for Radar Calibration by 529 Sqn and one was used by Fairey Aviation to develop rotor systems for its Gyrodyne helicopter.

Whilst relatively underpowered it could do all the basic tasks carried out as a matter of course by modern helicopters, paving the way for the first truly capable Allied machines.

Although RAF Andover was operated by the RAF, the base was primarily used to train members of the Army in the Air Observation Post (AOP) role and in February 1947 the resident C Flight of 657 Squadron was renamed 1901 Flight and re-equipped with six Sikorsky R-6A Hoverfly II helicopters.

Compared to earlier examples, the new helicopters had completely new streamlined fuselages as the tail booms were lengthened and straightened. The new aircraft could attain 87kts (100 mph). The British originally intended to receive 150 R-6 Hoverfly IIs but production delays meant only 27 were delivered to the RAF before the type was superseded by more modern designs.

1. Hoverfly II KN839 at Middle Wallop in 1948. This aircraft was built as 43-45422 and delivered to the RAF in July 1945. It was struck off charge on May 9, 1951 and scrapped.

Of these, 15 were passed on to the Royal Navy's Fleet Air Arm for training and liaison duties with 705 and 771 Sqns.

Their performance may not have been sparkling, but the RAF Hoverfly fleet paved the way for today's military helicopters. ■

General Aircraft GAL.56 The 'Tailless Aircraft Advisory Committee' was created in to investigate tailless and tail-first aircraft. General Aircraft were asked to produce three unpowered proof-of-concept GAL 56 aircraft. They proved incredibly difficult to fly and after a fatal accident the programme was terminated. The legendary test pilot Eric 'Winkle' Brown later described the GAL.56 as the most difficult aircraft he had ever flown!

Gloster Meteor I The RAF's first jet fighter. The first production Meteor Is joined 616 Sqn at RAF Culmhead, Somerset on July 12, 1944. The unit quickly moved to Manston, Kent where the new jets were used to counter the V-1 flying bomb threat from July 27. In total, Meteors downed 14 'Doodlebugs'. Originally 300 Meteor Is were ordered, but just 20 were delivered before more modern versions arrived.

Gloster Meteor III By mid December 1944, the Meteor III had replaced the earlier variant with 616 Sqn. The first batch of 15 differed in having a sliding canopy and increased fuel capacity but later airframes had Derwent engines in place of the original Wellands. The last batch of 195 also had longer nacelles that added 65kts to the top speed. In January 1945 they moved to Europe to fly recce and ground attack operations.

Hawker Fury II Designed as a successor to the Tempest, the Fury II began life as the 'Tempest Light Fighter'. The wing was shortened in span and the fuselage was a fully monocoque structure. The RAF expressed interest in the type as the Fury II and the FAA ordered it as the Sea Fury. Six prototypes were built from 1944 (with different powerplants) but the end of the war in 1945 led to the cancellation of the RAF order.

Hawker Tempest II Developed in parallel with the Tempest V the first Tempest II flew in June 1943 and was powered by a 2,520hp Bristol Centaurus IV engine. With the end of the war in sight the order for 1,800 Tempest IIs was cut to just 402 – 100 of which were fighters and 302 were fighter-bombers. The war ended before they could be deployed but Tempest IIs saw combat during the early stages of the Malayan Emergency.

Royal Flying

The British monarchy has had its own Royal Flight since 1936, although in recent years increasing amounts of royal travel has been conducted with private operators

Ever since the dawn of flight, the British monarchy has been staunch supporters of aviation and patrons of organisations associated with the aircraft industry.

The first recorded flight by a member of the British royal family occurred on July 17, 1917, when the then Prince of Wales (who would go on to be King Edward VIII) was flown over northern France as a passenger in a Bristol F.2B. He would fly several times before the end of the conflict, including a trip over Italy with Victoria Cross winning pilot Maj William 'Bill' Barker.

However, when he learned of this, King Edward VII forbade any further flying by his son. It would be the late '20s before he relented and the Prince of Wales began flying again.

The Royal Flight

The Prince's first two acquisitions were Westland Wapitis, which arrived with 24 Sqn at RAF Northolt in 1928 and were flown in the VIP transport role. In 1929 Prince Edward was allowed to learn to fly and he bought de Havilland DH.60 Moth G-AALG, which his younger brothers, the Dukes of Gloucester and Kent, also used to qualify for their pilots' wings.

By the time he ascended to the throne in 1936 the Prince would buy a further eleven aircraft including two de Havilland Puss Moth (G-ABNN & G-ABFV), Fox Moth G-ACDD, Dragon G-ACGG, several Dragon Rapides and a specially commissioned Vickers Viastra X (G-ACCC). It was lavishly fitted out as a 'Royal Barge' and was painted in the blue and red colours of the Brigade of Guards. Most of his aircraft would also gain similar paint schemes.

The Prince employed Flt Lt Edward 'Mouse' Fielden as a full-time pilot, who accompanied him on all flights other than his single-seat Comper Swift air racer. Most of the aircraft were based at Hendon, where they were unofficially referred to as 'The Royal Flight'.

The King's Flight

When he ascended to the throne in 1936 as King Edward VIII, one of his first decisions was to create an official King's Flight; the world's first head of state aircraft unit.

The basis for the Flight was 24 Sqn at RAF Northolt, London – which had been operating the aforementioned Wapitis as part of its Communications Flight since 1928. 'Mouse' Fielden was promoted to Captain and retained as the head of the Flight; a post he was to hold until 1961, retiring as AVM Sir Edward Fielden.

1

The King abdicated in December 1936 and was succeeded by his brother. The new King Edward VI continued the Flight and in May 1937 an Airspeed Envoy III (G-AEXX) joined the unit. It was equipped with luxurious seats for four passengers plus a pilot, wireless operator and steward.

Postwar Flying

With the outbreak of World War Two it was deemed prudent to replace the Envoy with an armed Lockheed Hudson; a de Havilland Flamingo (R2766) was also added to the King's Flight in September 1940.

The unit disbanded in 1942, with 161 Sqn taking over the role of transporting the royals and other VIPs until May 1946 when the King's Flight reformed at RAF Benson, Oxfordshire

The King forbade any further flying by the Prince of Wales

with a Dragon Rapide and, later, four Vickers Vikings and several Avro Yorks.

Her Majesty Queen Elizabeth succeeded her father as monarch in 1952 and over the coming years the now-called Queen's Flight continued to go from strength to strength.

The Vikings and Yorks were soon supplemented by twin-engined de Havilland DH.104 Devons and four-engined DH.114 Herons. Later Beagle Bassets and turboprop-powered Hawker SiddeleyAndover aircraft would join the unit.

1944

Hawker Tempest V Originally known as the Typhoon II, the Tempest [see also p62] was created to offer a better high altitude performance by fitting a thinner laminar flow wing. The first Tempest V entered service in April 1944. Fitted with a 2,010hp Napier Sabre IIB it was the highest performing RAF fighter of the war. In total 801 were produced and after the war some were converted into target tugs.

Martin Baker MB.5 Considered by many to be 'the greatest fighter the RAF never had' the MB.5 was the ultimate piston-powered fighter. Power came from a 2,340hp Griffon 83 driving two three-bladed contra-rotating propellers. Despite its performance the MB.5 was snubbed by the RAF, which was focused on the new jet-powered fighters, and it would never enter production. It is a true 'what if' of aviation history.

Miles Monitor Created in response to a very unusual specification that called for a high speed, twin engine target tug capable of 300mph and could also be dismantled and fitted into standard packing crates. After the prototype had flown in April 1944 the RAF decided it no longer needed the aircraft so the order for 600 Monitors was taken over by the FAA. By the end of the war only 20 had been built and the rest were cancelled.

North American Mustang IV Combat experience showed the Mustang had poor visibility to the rear so the 'bubble' canopied P-51D variant was created in 1944. Some 280 of the 8,102 built were allocated go the RAF as the Mustang IV. The RAF also received 594 of the 1,500 P-51K variant (as the Mustang IVA); these being equipped with an Aeroproducts propeller in place of the Hamilton Standard unit. **SDB**

Republic Thunderbolt One of the biggest and heaviest single-seat fighters of the war. The P-47 served the USAAF in the thousands but the RAF also received 240 'razorback' P-47Ds (Thunderbolt Is) and 590 'bubbletop' P-47D-25s (Thunderbolt IIs) from 1944. There was no need for another high altitude fighter so the RAF adapted the aircraft for ground attack; they were used by 16 squadrons in South East Asia Command.

RAF Fast Fact

When Prince William left the RAF in 2008 he began work as a civilian Air Ambulance helicopter pilot. He was awarded a salary of almost £50,000: all of which he donated to charity.

1. AgustaWestland A109E of 32 (The Royal) Sqn overhead Buckingham Palace. **Crown Copyright**
2. Edward, Prince of Wales in the rear cockpit of a Bristol F.2B Fighter in Italy in 1918. He gained his pilot's licence in 1929. **Crown Copyright**
3. The first aircraft specifically ordered for Royal use was this Vickers Viastra delivered in May 1933 at a cost of £4250. It was painted in the red and blue colours of the Brigade of Guards. **Crown Copyright**

Helicopters

By the 1950s and 60s, the increasing reliability and safety of helicopters made them ideal platforms for the Queen's Flight, enabling the royals to land close to official engagements within the British Isles. Landing at a nearby sports field reduced the logistics and security concerns of transporting VIPs by road or rail.

The Queen Mother was the first member of the Family to fly in a helicopter (a Westland Dragonfly in the mid-1950s) and soon they became a favoured mode of royal transport.

In 1959, the Flight took delivery of its own Westland Whirlwind helicopters (XN127 & XN126) and these served with distinction until they were replaced by the Westland Wessex – a pair of which joined the Flight in 1969.

Prince Charles, Princess Anne and the Queen Mother were regular passengers and Prince Philip even piloted the aircraft himself for many years. However, it would be 1977 before Queen Elizabeth herself finally took a seat on board.

32 (The Royal) Sqn

In 1969, the Metropolitan Communications Squadron was renamed as 32 Sqn and took on the role of VIP transport alongside the Queen's Flight. In 1971, the squadron acquired four Hawker Siddeley HS.125 Dominie CC.1 business jets to transport the royals and other VIPs. Two years later these were replaced by a pair of improved CC.2 versions and in 1982 the first of six C.3s were delivered.

4. HRH the Prince of Wales seen climbing aboard one of his Westland Wapitis. **Crown Copyright**
5. This Avro York was delivered to the Duke and Duchess of Gloucester in 1945 for use in Australia. It was fitted out with a luxurious interior complete with bathroom and a kitchen that even included an electric potato peeling machine!

Aérospatiale Gazelle helicopters started service in 1976 and these were used by the royals for 20 years until they were replaced by Aérospatiale Twin Squirrels.

Meanwhile, the RAF acquired a pair of British Aerospace BAe 146 airliners in 1986 for use by the Queen's Flight - and a third was delivered in 1990. Compared to the Andovers they replaced the new type provided a 60%

1945

Supermarine Spitfire XIV Rolls Royce developed the Griffon 65 with a two-stage supercharger to boost power output at altitude. Based on the Mk VIII, the Spitfire XIV had the new Griffon turning a five bladed propeller. Mk XIVs were built in both high back and 'bubble' canopy versions; the longer nose and the increased slipstream necessitated a taller and broader tail unit. In total, 957 were built.

Supermarine Spitfire XVI The Spitfire XVI was almost identical to the Mk IX in every way apart from its Merlin 266 engine. This was a Merlin 66 built under licence by the Packard Motor Company in the USA. A total of 1,054 were built; all of which were low-altitude fighters with clipped wings and engines optimised for the thicker air found at low altitude. Many Mk XVIs also featured cut-down rear fuselages with bubble canopies.

Supermarine Spitfire XIX The PR XIX combined the PR XI equipment with the engine and airframe of the Mk XIV. In all 225 were built and they served on the front line until 1954. On April 1, 1954, PS888 performed the RAF's last operational Spitfire sortie, flying from RAF Seletar in Singapore. On June 9, 1957, the RAF's last 'non-operational' Spitfire flight was made by a PR XIX from the Temperature and Humidity Flight.

Westland Welkin Designed to fight Junkers Ju 86P aircraft at extremely high altitudes, the Welkin was proposed in 1940 but construction did not begin until 1942. The concern that the Luftwaffe might bomb from the stratosphere led to Westland creating a pressurised twin-engined fighter with a 70ft span high aspect ratio wing. The complex design meant it would be 1944 before it entered service, by which time the threat had passed.

Auster AOP.6 Designed as a successor to the Auster V, with a strengthened fuselage, increased lifting capabilities and a 145hp Gipsy Major. It had lengthened landing gear and large aerofoil flaps that protruded from the rear of the wing. The type entered RAF service in 1945 and almost 700 were built for the service with AOP units. A dual-control training version (the Auster T.7) was produced and 77 were delivered to the RAF.

1

increase in range and a much larger capacity for passengers. The aircraft have specially designed 'Royal Suite' cabins, which can seat up to 26 passengers in comfort (compared to 70-94 in a standard BAe 146).

On occasions when the Queen's Flight aircraft lacked the range to conduct overseas trips other RAF or civilian aircraft have been used. These most often involved the RAF's Vickers VC10 fleet but the Queen has also been a regular passenger with British Airways.

2

3

Current Fleet

On April 1, 1995, the decision was made to merge 32 Sqn with the Queen's Flight; thus creating 32 (The Royal) Sqn. The Queen's Flight's Wessex HCC.4 helicopters and BAe 146s relocated from Benson to Northolt.

Although it is often (erroneously) referred to in the media as the 'Royal Flight', the new squadron's duties are wide ranging. Its aircraft were used as military transports during the Gulf War as well as in Afghanistan and Iraq and regulations mean they can only be used for VIP flights when they are not needed for military duties. In 2004, the decision was made to repaint the '146 fleet to dispense with the distinctive livery they had worn with the Queen's Flight. The familiar red flying surfaces were felt to add to the aircraft's vulnerability to terrorist attack and the aircraft were repainted white to resemble 'normal' airliners.

The following year, the Twin Squirrels were replaced by three AgustaWestland AW109 helicopters. The final Dominie was retired in March 2015, but by this time two additional BAe 146s had been acquired (from TNT Airways) and allocated to the squadron for tactical freight and VIP transport use.

Today, the unit is split into A Flight and B Flight; the former operating two BAe 146-100 CC.2s and two BAe 146-200 C.3s. A single AgustaWestland AW109SP equips B Flight.

Today, the airborne transportation of the

1945

Avro Lancastrian A modified Lancaster without armament and with the gun turrets faired over. A fast, long range transport capable of carrying a heavy load of cargo in the converted bomb bay. Lancastrians were used to carry petrol during the Berlin Airlift and the RAF also used them to test jet engines; it could operate on just two Merlin engines if required and could easily accept various powerplants below the wings.

Avro Lincoln The last and ultimate bomber development of the Lancaster. The Lincoln entered service in August 1945 and was initially assigned Tiger Force units in the Far East for missions against Japan. The war ended before they saw action but during the 1950s RAF Lincolns were used during the Malayan Emergency and against guerrilla fighters during the Mau Mau Uprising in Kenya. The last examples retired in March 1963.

Bristol Buckmaster Advanced trainer created to bridge the gap between the antiquated Anson and the latest combat aircraft. Some 65 Buckinghams [see p72] remained unfinished on the production line and were finished as Buckmasters. This involved mating the Buckingham wing with a new fuselage that seated a trainee and instructor side by side with a wireless operator behind. Another 47 were constructed from scratch.

Cierva W.9 An experimental helicopter which dispensed with the tail rotor in favour of hot jet exhaust gases discharged from the side of the fuselage. It was created to be a safer and more efficient helicopter than the Sikorsky Hoverfly and flight testing began in 1945. The prototype (PX203) was flown at the 1946 SBAC Airshow at Radlett but crashed later that year during testing and the project was abandoned.

de Havilland DH.98 Mosquito (TT) The last Mosquito variant to enter service and the last version to serve with the RAF was the TT.35 target tug. A number of B.35 bombers were converted to TT.35 standard from 1945 for towing the targets that allowed aircrew to practice their shooting skills. The last in service were with 3 Civilian Anti-Aircraft Cooperation Unit (CAAC) at RAF Exeter in Devon, which were retired in 1963.

4

Royal Aviators

When Edward, Prince of Wales learned to fly in 1929 he set a precedent for countless future members of the British royal family.
HRH Prince Philip, Duke of Edinburgh gained his RAF Wings in 1953, his helicopter wings with the Royal Navy in 1956 and his Private Pilots Licence in 1959. He gave up flying in August 1997 after accumulating 5,986 hours as a pilot in 59 types of aircraft in 44 years. The Duke was the first member of the royal family to fly out of Buckingham Palace garden by helicopter and he remains involved with a great many aviation organisations; in particular the Honourable Company of Air Pilots (HCAP) for which he is Patron.
HRH Prince Andrew, Duke of York learned to fly helicopters with the Royal Navy in 1979 and saw active service flying the Westland Wasp during the Falklands War.
HRH Prince Charles, Prince of Wales, served in the RAF and Navy. He learned to fly on a Chipmunk, then flew the Jet Provost and a Beagle Basset multi-engine trainer. The Prince regularly flew the Hawker Siddeley Andover, Westland Wessex and BAe 146 aircraft of the Queen's Flight but gave up flying after crashing a BAe 146 in the Hebrides in 1994.
From 2003 to 2013 HRH Prince William, Duke of Cambridge, flew as a Sea King Search and Rescue helicopter pilot with the RAF. He then gained his Air Transport Pilots Licence in order to fly as a civilian pilot with the East Anglian Air Ambulance at Cambridge Airport from 2014 to 2017. He described the job as a "huge privilege."
Prince William's brother, HRH Prince Harry Duke of Sussex, also followed his father into a military flying career. In December 2008, Prince Harry began training to become an Army Air Corps pilot and spent ten years flying the Apache helicopter gunship.
He undertook two operational tours of Afghanistan, one as a Forward Air Controller in 2007/08 and one as an Apache Pilot between September 2012 and January 2013.

5

1. Vickers Vikings of the King's Flight glimmer in the sunshine during a 1947 royal tour of South Africa.
2. In 2004, the BAe 146s were repainted to make them look more like conventional airliners. It was hoped this would make them less vulnerable to terrorist attack. **Crown Copyright**
3. Andover XS790 was delivered to the RAF in 1964 and served with the Queen's Flight until it was transferred to the Defence Research Agency in 1992. **Crown Copyright**
4. A BAe 146 and a pair of HS 125 Dominies show their characteristic colour scheme during the Queen's Birthday Flypast over London. **Crown Copyright**
5. Her Majesty the Queen leaving HS Andover XS790 in 1964 **Crown Copyright**

royal family and members of Her Majesties Government depends on circumstances and can be undertaken by a mixture of military and civilian operators. In addition to 32 (The Royal) Sqn the royals and other VIPs can call upon the RAF's Airbus Voyager for long-haul flights and one airframe (ZZ336) has been specially fitted with a VIP interior. The aircraft has also been outfitted with a secure satellite communications suite and missile detection system.

The Queen's Helicopter Flight, which forms part of the Royal Household rather than being an RAF entity, was formed in 1997. The Flight is tasked by the Royal Travel Office at Buckingham Palace and operates the Sikorsky S-76C+ twin-engined helicopter in a striking maroon scheme. The first example was delivered in 1998 and registered G-XXEA in honour of G-AEXX, the Airspeed Envoy that the Queen's uncle, the Prince of Wales first flew in the King's Flight.

'EA was flown until 2009 when it was replaced by a new Sikorsky S-76C++ helicopter registered G-XXEB.

With Prince William already an enormous advocate of aviation the future of royal flying is hopefully secure for another generation. ■

General Aviation Hamilcar X A powered variant of the Hamilcar glider, produced in an attempt to extend the range so it could serve in the Pacific. A pair of Bristol Mercury engines were fitted. The first of ten examples flew in February 1945. A Hamilcar X could be towed by a Halifax to boost its range, but if it took off under its own power it could not maintain height if fully loaded. Luckily the war was over before the aircraft was needed.

Gloster Trent Meteor The world's first turboprop-powered aircraft. Meteor I EE227 was provided to Rolls Royce for experiments into turboprop propulsion. The Trent was a simple turboprop, which used a jet turbine to drive a propeller. EE227 had undercarriage to give ground clearance for the 7ft 7in diameter airscrews and first flew in September 1945. The programme provided valuable insight into the new technology.

Hawker Tempest VI The final variant of the Tempest – and therefore the final piston-powered Hawker fighter. The Tempest VI was powered by a 2,340hp Napier Sabre V engine but although 250 were ordered the end of the war meant just 142 were built. When West Germany-based Tempest VIs were replaced by Vampires in 1949 they became the last frontline piston-engined fighters in operational RAF service.

Percival Proctor V With the Percival Proctor IV proving such a success with the RAF, Edgar Percival created a civilian version for use by private pilots and charter companies. The Proctor 5 had to compete with the large number of surplus ex-RAF aircraft being sold at the end of the war but 150 were produced, including four acquired by the RAF (as the Proctor V) for use by air attachés around the world. **SDB**

Reid & Sigrist R.S.3 Desford A development of the civilian pre-war R.S.1 Snargasher, the R.S.3 Desford was created as a twin-engined, three-seat advanced trainer for postwar use. The prototype flew in July 1945 but although the aircraft was found to have good handling it was not chosen for service as the RAF had a myriad of war surplus aircraft to use as trainers. It was later modified into the R.S.4 Bobsleigh [see p91].

The Next Generation

The Air Training Corps organisation has introduced young people to the RAF way of life for generations. Today it remains a vital part of RAF recruiting

Since its inception the Air Cadet movement has inspired generations of young people into a life of 'airmindedness'.

The original idea came from Air Commodore Sir John Chamier, a former Great War pilot. He served in both the RFC and the RAF and retired in 1929 to become Secretary General of the Air League. The organisation had been established to increase public awareness of the importance of aviation and Chamier felt that the best way to do this was to target young people when they were at their most eager to learn.

Air Defence Cadet Corps

As was often the case, it was impending conflict that drove progress and in 1938, with war clouds forming over Europe, Chamier's plan came to fruition.

His Air Defence Cadet Corps (ADCC) was created to attract and train boys and young men who had an interest in aviation. His plan was to set up squadrons of cadets in towns the length and breadth of the country and recruit local volunteers to run them.

The objective was to imitate and practice the work carried out by RAF squadrons and, where possible, gliding should be included to give the youngsters air experience flights.

Boys between 14 and 18 were allowed to join and in the immediate pre-war years the Air Commodore's scheme soon gained momentum with cadets signing up in their thousands, each paying a weekly subscription of 3d (around 49p in today's money).

Each squadron consisted of 100 boys, divided into flights of 25, and the first squadron was formed at Leicester in July 1938. By the end of 1938 some 41 squadrons had been formed and during 1939 more than 16,800 boys and 700 officers were members of the ADCC.

The squadron's activities were tailored towards preparing cadets for service in the RAF and therefore included marching drill, discipline, and how to behave on RAF stations.

1

Physical training and athletics, especially cross-country running, were popular activities as were camping, shooting and, of course, flying.

Wartime Activities

At the outbreak of World War Two many ADCC instructors and officers were called up into regular service. A large number of older cadets were also sent to work on RAF stations, where they initially undertook general admin duties and worked as messengers. As the war progressed some cadets were put to work loading ammunitions or pushing aircraft.

The War Cabinet soon asked the ADCC to help train young men who were waiting to be called up into the RAF; effectively preparing them for the start of basic training.

In late 1940, the government took over the running of the ADCC and renamed it as the Air Training Corps (ATC). The new organisation was formally established on February 5, 1941

The aircraft conducted very short 'hops', launched via a V-shaped bungee!

and soon had almost 20,000 cadets.

Throughout the war years the ATC became provided an important service; providing the RAF with recruits who were 'airminded' when they enlisted.

Post War Gliding

The cessation in conflict did not spell the end of the ATC but there was a need to change the training offered to cadets. In 1947, the Royal Warrant was altered to include training in Citizenship, the promotion of sport and adventure activities within the ATC's aims.

1945

Short Sunderland V Over its career the Sunderland had become heavy – particularly with the addition of radar equipment – and the Pegasus engines proved inadequate. The Mk V therefore introduced 1,200hp US-built P&W R-1830 Twin Wasp engines, which also enabled the flying boat to stay aloft on two engines. A total of 155 were built and another 33 Mk IIIs re-engined. They remained in service with the RAF in Singapore until 1959.

Sikorsky Hoverfly I The RAF's first operational helicopter. The Hoverfly [see also p73] was developed from Igor Sikorsky's 1940 VS-300 and the British received two of the first eight airframes produced for trials. Although the USAAF's Hoverflies saw wartime action, the RAF's 52 examples were issued to the Helicopter Training School in January 1945 and were not flown operationally. Many were later transferred to the Royal Navy.

Supermarine Spitfire F.21 & F.22 The F.21 was the last fighter variant to enter wartime service. The main difference was the new wing, which was 47% stronger but lost the type's classic curve. The first of 120 entered service in January 1945. The F.22 was a 'bubble' canopied development of the F.21 with a much larger tail to improve stability. Production began in March 1945 but the variant was too late to see active service.

1946

Bristol Brigand Designed as a replacement for the Beaufighter in the anti-shipping and ground-attack roles. The Brigand used the wings, tail and undercarriage of the Buckingham with a new fuselage housing a pilot, navigator/bomb aimer and radio-operator/gunner. The first eleven of the 147 were built as torpedo bombers; the rest as bombers. The RAF used them in Kenya and Malaya and the last was not retired until 1958.

de Havilland DH.100 Vampire I The low power of early jets meant the jet pipe needed to be short. DH used this to its advantage by creating a twin-boom design with a fuselage 'pod'. The DH.100 used a mixture of wood and metal construction and first flew in September 1943, but pressures to supply Mosquitos and the availability of engines meant the first of 244 production Vampire Is did not join 247 Sqn until April 1946.

2

4

RAF Fast Fact

Legend has it that the prototype Slingsby T.45 Swallow got its name when the prototype crashed and ended up hanging from some telephone wires "just like all the other swallows."

1. A Slingsby Sedbergh glider returns from a flight. **SDB**
2. Air cadets are taught the basics of flight in 1944.
3. A generation of cadets had their first flight in the venerable Chipmunk. **SDB**
4. The one millionth air cadet to have a Chipmunk air experience flight was Flt Sgt Cadet Terry Jones, who flew in WP896 from RAF Woodvale on October 2, 1983. His flight was witnessed by Malcolm Edwards, who had been the first cadet to do so back in 1958.

3

The following year also saw the introduction of dedicated ATC gliding facilities. Gliding had officially been part of the syllabus since 1943 but now the ATC was put in control of 87 volunteer-led gliding schools.

The first gliders in use with cadet squadrons were the very basic, single-seat Slingsby T.7 Kirby Cadets, which first flew in 1935 and were dubbed the Cadet TX.1 in RAF use. It was based on the civilian Kirby Kadet.

These were followed in 1944 by the two-seat T.8 Tutor (Cadet TX.2 in RAF service). More than 60 were acquired and a number of TX.1s were also fitted with two-seat fuselages. Cadet TX.2s would remain in Air Training Corps use until the 1970s.

The Elliots of Newbury (EoN) Primary was an even more basic glider; consisting of just a fabric covered wing and tail mounted to an open-truss framework. The cadet didn't sit 'in' a Primary, they sat 'on' it!

The aircraft was a copy of the German SG 38 Schulgleiter and several were adopted by the ATC in 1948 as the Eton TX.1.The aircraft only conducted very short 'hops' and was generally launched via a V-shaped bungee rope that was pulled by an eager team of cadets.

Some Etons were modified to use the same, more efficient, wing as the Cadet TX.1 and 115 of these were delivered to the ATC in 1952. Incredibly, the last examples remained in use until the late 1980s.

The two-seat Slingsby T-21 glider first flew in 1944 and traced its roots back to the German Grunau Baby, which Slingsby had built under licence between the wars. It was designed for the ATC but was initially rejected by them and it would be 1947 before the slightly modified T-21B variant was finally accepted for service as the Sedbergh TX.1 (named after the public school of that name).

It was the first tandem-seat, dual-control glider available to cadets and vastly sped up the flight training syllabus. The RAF would go on to receive 95 Sedberghs, some of which flew well into the 1980s.

The single-seat T.30 Prefect TX.1 also had its origins in the Grunau Baby and 15 served with the ATC from the late 1940s.

By then gliding had become such a vital part of cadet life that in addition to air experience sorties 250 lucky cadets were selected each year for a full scholarship. These would be trained to Private Pilot Licence standard.

The ultimate development of the Slingsby Cadet family was the TX.3; the first of which arrived with Gliding Schools in 1951. Also known as the Tandem Tutor, the new aircraft used the same wings and tail as the earlier machines but had a longer and wider fuselage. The RAF took delivery of 126 TX.3s between 1951 and 1959. The force also operated five examples of single-seat Slingsby T.45 Swallow.

An experiment in the early 1960s saw the RAF order a small fleet of metal Slingsby T.53

de Havilland DH.103 Hornet Although it looked like a Mosquito the Hornet was a brand new design. Fuselage construction was identical to the balsa-ply-built Mosquito, but the laminar flow wings had stressed Alclad skins. The Merlin engines rotated in opposite directions to cancel out torque and the Hornet set a British speed record of 435.871mph. They saw combat during the Malayan Emergency but were retired by May 1955.

de Havilland DH.108 Swallow An experimental aircraft featuring a tailless, swept wing with a single vertical stabiliser. Initially created to evaluate swept wing handling characteristics at low speeds – as part of the plan to create the Comet airliner. However, when the Comet design evolved to include a conventional tail the three Swallow prototypes were used to investigate handling up to supersonic speeds.

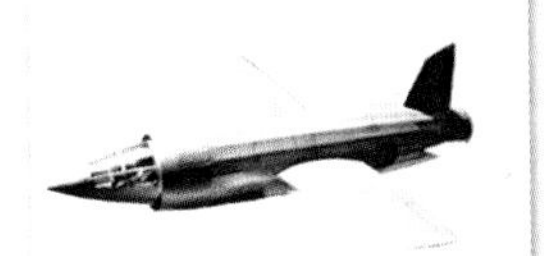

Miles M.52 A research project aimed at producing an aircraft capable of 1,000mph. Cutting-edge aerodynamic research was employed under great secrecy but the project was terminated by the new Labour government . After a public outcry the programme was revived as an unmanned 30% scale model that later reached Mach 1.38. The research was shared with US-based Bell Aircraft, which created the supersonic Bell X-1.

Short Seaford A long-range patrol bomber developed from the Sunderland for use in the Pacific. A new 'planing' hull was fitted and four Bristol Hercules. Better defensive armament was provided by a myriad of turrets and gun emplacements. Testing revealed the extra power required a larger fin and tailplane but the changes meant the war was over by the time it was ready to enter service. As such, just six Seafords were delivered.

Sikorsky Hoverfly II Developed from the Hoverfly I. The new Hoverfly II had a streamlined fuselage and the boom carrying the tail rotor was lengthened and straightened. Although the same main rotor and transmission system were retained, the new version increased the top speed from 82mph to 100mph. The RAF received 26 airframes in 1946 although 15 were passed to the Navy. RAF examples served with 657 (AOP) Sqn.

1 & 2. Up until 2018 VGS organisations flew the Grob Vigilant motorglider. Today, Air Experience Flightsand University Air Squadrons use Grob Tutor aircraft. **Both Crown Copyright**

3. The ATC operated five examples of single-seat Slingsby T.45 Swallow TX.1s. **SDB**

gliders. Following evaluation the order was cancelled but not before Leading Cadet Stitt became the first cadet to solo the new type, on August 15, 1968.

Although they were initially established as Gliding Schools, these were re-designated as Volunteer Gliding Schools (VGSs) in 1978. In 2005, they were renamed Volunteer Gliding Squadrons, thus keeping their VGS abbreviation.

In 1984, the decision was made to replace the now ageing wood and fabric Cadet family with new glassfibre gliders and the Grob G103 Twin II entered service that October as the Viking T.1. Over the course of the next year the ATC would receive 100 of the new gliders.

It would also receive ten Schleicher ASK 21 Vanguard, five Schleicher ASW 19 Valiant and two Schempp-Hirth Janus C (Kestrel TX.1) gliders for competition flying.

These would ultimately be sold in 2000 when budget restrictions led to the disbandment of the competition fleet; bringing to an end many successful years of competing and world record distance setting.

Air Experience

In 1970, the ATC began trials with self-launching motorgliders. The Slingsby Venture T.1 could take off under the power of its 45hp powerplant and cadets could then turn the engine off at altitude and fly it as a glider. It was a licence-built version of the Scheibe Motor Falke and 40 would ultimately serve with the VGS organisations until 1991 when they were replaced with the Grob Vigilant T.1s that remain in service today.

Although gliders offered cadets an excellent taster to flying – and continue to do so – it was felt that for more intensive training the ATC should have its own fleet of powered aircraft. Therefore, the first of a fleet of 50 de Havilland Canada DHC-1 Chipmunks was delivered in 1957. These were manufactuered in Britain and allocated to 13 Air Experience Flights (AEFs) located at existing University Air Squadrons (UAS). An entire generation had their first taste of flight in an air cadet operated Chipmunk. At the same time, there were 27 ATC Gliding Schools in existence and in the ten years from 1951 to 1961 more than 58,000 ATC trained cadets entered the RAF.

In the 1970s, the AEF began replacing its Chipmunk fleet with Scottish Aviation Bulldogs and these served until 2001 when they in turn were replaced by Grob Tutors.

21st Century Cadets

In 2020, the ATC remains a popular organisation which offers challenges, excitement and adventure to young people – both boys and girls – aged 13 or above.

Frequent activities include camping and survival training as well as adventure training. The latter includes rock climbing, abseiling, high-level hill walking, mountain-biking, canoeing and even sailing.

A key part of being a cadet is training and the current syllabus includes specialist technical training, lectures and hands-on projects. For those that show leadership potential the ATC runs a physically demanding seven-day summer cadet leadership course.

Of course, flying is still central to cadet life and members are promised plenty of opportunities to take to the air. Today's ATC comprises of Viking T.1 gliders whereas UAS Tutors are used by the AEF units.

If you or somebody you know is a fan of aviation, action and adventure there are more than 1,000 ATC squadrons across the UK to choose from. ■

1946

Supermarine Spiteful The Spitfire's famous wing was ironically its limiting factor. As airspeed increased the aeroelasticity of the lightweight wing meant it would flex. The Spiteful mated a Spitfire XIV fuselage with a new straight-tapered laminar flow wing. It also had a wider undercarriarge to help ground handling. Although 150 were ordered the growing belief in jet fighters meant just 19 Spitefuls were built.

Vickers Viking The Viking was designed as an interim civil airliner and was initially known as the 'Wellington Transport Aircraft' as it used the wings, engine nacelles and under-carriage of the bomber. The aircraft was a sales success with 163 built for airlines around the world. The RAF ordered the type as the Valetta [see p84] but 12 Vikings were ordered for VIP transports to be used by the Kings Flight.

1947

Armstrong Whitworth AW.52 An experimental aircraft for research into a proposed flying wing bomber and jetliner. The aircraft had swept wings with a straight trailing edge and small fins and rudders at the tips. Trials were disappointing, with lower than expected speeds and long take off runs. The first prototype crashed on May 30, 1949; the pilot becoming the first RAF member to eject from a stricken aircraft.

de Havilland DH.100 Vampire F.3 Compared to the earlier F.1 the Vampire F.3 had much greater fuel capacity and could also carry drop tanks. It also featured a redesigned tailplane with a lowered stabiliser and more rounded fins and rudders. The first of 182 entered service in 1947 and some Royal Auxiliary Air Force (RAuxAF) units retained their F.3s until 1952. Vampire F.3s of 54 Sqn became the first jets to cross the Atlantic.

EoN Olympia Elliotts of Newbury (EoN) built the Olympia from 1947 to 1957. Around 150 of the single-seat gliders were built, including two acquired by the Empire Test Pilots School (ETPS). All test pilot trainees were expected to fly five hours in gliders and VV400 and VV401 were popular steeds. In 1951 one was flown by Bill Bedford to break the British distance record by flying 413km from Farnborough to Newcastle.

Multi Role Canberra

The English Electric Canberra was a pioneering jet bomber but also found fame in a variety of roles in the RAF

In the latter years of World War Two it became obvious that the jet era was progressing rapidly and soon the world's air forces would be competing for the latest in turbojet powered fighters and bombers.

Great Britain was at the forefront of this technology and it is therefore unsurprising that work on a jet powered bomber began as early as 1944. The British Ministry of Aircraft Procurement (MAP) issued a specification calling for design concepts for a fast, high-altitude, jet-powered medium bomber to replace aircraft such as the Mosquito.

At this time William 'Teddy' Petter was working as chief designer and technical director at Westland Aircraft and already devising a twin engined fighter bomber dubbed the P.1056. Powered by a pair of fuselage-mounted Metrovick F.2/4 Beryl engines the project went no further than the drawing board but when Petter left to join English Electric Aircraft at Preston, Lancashire in December 1944, he was encouraged to adapt the design to suit the MAP specification.

Simple Design

The Canberra was initially envisaged as a single engined, straight winged bomber with a circular cross-section (to help pressurise the aircraft), but this was changed to increase the space available for fuel and bombs.

The original fuselage-mounted engine configuration had aerodynamic advantages but when the new Rolls-Royce Avon engines became available the slim diameter made it possible to mount them on the wings, thus increasing fuselage capacity further still.

The aircraft bore a strong resemblance to a scaled-up Gloster Meteor with the low-aspect ratio wings broken only by the tubular engine nacelles. Rather than devote space and weight to defensive armament the Canberra was designed to fly fast and high to avoid air-to-air combat; a factor that made it a true descendent of the Mosquito [Ed: see p50].

The aircraft was mostly built of metal but the forward portion of the tail fin was of wooden construction and covered with layers of plywood.

The fuselage had a semi-monocoque construction with a pressurised nose containing Martin-Baker ejection seats for both crew members. The fuselage also contained a bomb bay with conventional clam-shell doors.

Maiden Flight

Construction of the prototype, registered VN799, began in 1948 and an order for 90 airframes was placed before the aircraft had even flown.

Interestingly the all-blue prototype looked almost identical to the production aircraft except for a rounded tip to the fin and a long tail-fin strake along the top of the fuselage: such was the soundness of the design that very few modifications were needed throughout its life.

Test pilot Roland Beamont was at the controls of VN799 when taxi trials began on May 8, 1949 – just five years after the end of the war in Europe. He took the aeroplane into the sky for the first time on Friday May 13. The aircraft proved to have vice-free handling and the only major modification was the addition of a glazed nose to accommodate a bomb aimer (as the hoped-for H2S bombing radar was not ready for production). The engines were also uprated and distinctive teardrop-shaped fuel tanks were fitted to the wingtips to create the Canberra B.2, which first flew on April 21, 1950.

1. The prototype Canberra (VN799) first flew on May 13, 1949 with Roland Beamont at the controls. To celebrate the type's fiftieth anniversary, Canberra T.4 WJ874 (illustrated) was repainted to represent VN799 in 1999. **Crown Copyright**

Into Service

The B.2 entered squadron service with 101 Sqn in May 1951 and although the jet proved easy to fly, it was felt necessary to create a dual-control variant to ease transition to the type. The resulting Canberra T.4 first flew on June 12, 1951 and entered service with 231 OCU in early 1954.

Gloster Meteor F.4 Although it flew in May 1945, the end of the war meant there was less urgency to re-equip fighter units and the Meteor F.4 did not enter service until early 1947. The new Derwent V engines offered a 50% power increase and, as such, the F.4 could reach 570mph at 10,000ft and would twice create new World Air Speed Records. A shorter wingspan also improved the roll rate. F.4s served 27 RAF squadrons until 1952.

Hawker P.1040 The natural evolution of the high-performance Typhoon and Tempest was for Hawker to enter the jet age. The P.1040 was a Rolls Royce Nene-powered fighter marketed to the RAF and FAA, and was unusual in having two bifurcated exhausts in the trailing edge of the wing root. The prototype first flew on September 2, 1947, but the postwar RAF decided to focus on other projects and didn't order the P.1040.

Percival Prentice A basic trainer designed around the concept that a student and instructor could sit in the front seats on a lesson while another could sit in the rear to receive 'air experience.' The Prentice was the first all-metal aircraft to be produced by Percival but with just 251hp to carry a 4,200lb aircraft it was woefully underpowered. Nevertheless, over 370 were delivered to the RAF between 1947 and 1949. The last was retired in 1956.

Saunders Roe SR.A/1 A prototype flying boat fighter that was the world's first jet-propelled aircraft to take off and land on water. The concept was conceived in reaction to Japan's use of floatplane fighters. The Air Ministry ordered a prototype in 1944 but the war was over by the time it was completed. It eventually flew in July 1947 but when it was evaluated the RAF decided it was incapable of matching the performance of land-based fighters.

Supermarine Spitfire XVIII Spitfire XVIIIs was very similar to the bubble canopied Mk XIVs but had extra fuel capacity. Some 300 were built, including 200 Fighter-Reconnaissance FR.XVIIIs. Mk XVIIIs were built from 1945 to 1946 but were initially delivered straight into storage. It would be January 1947 before the first examples joined 60 Sqn in Singapore. The type saw limited action in Malaya and Palestine.

The final RAF Canberras were retired 57 years after its first flight

The Canberra proved to be a very adaptable airframe and it would go on to be used in a variety of roles, including strategic reconnaissance, replacing the de Havilland Mosquito. To meet the photo recce requirement the B.2 design was modified by adding a bay in the front fuselage to house seven cameras alongside an additional fuel tank in the bomb bay. The prototype PR.3 variant first flew on March 19, 1950 and the first of 35 aircraft entered service in December 1952.

Development

Canberra production was accelerated as a result of the outbreak of the Korean War and the aircraft was designated as a 'super priority.' Five squadrons were equipped by the end of 1952 and as the design evolved, the Canberra was modified in ever-increasing ways.

The improved Canberra B.6, with more powerful Avon 109 engines and more fuel, started to equip UK based squadrons from June 1954. This freed up older airframes to join squadrons forming overseas in Germany, Cyprus and the Far East.

The B.6 was later modified significantly to form the 'third generation' Canberra. Designated the B(I).8, the airframe was fitted with a new forward fuselage with a teardrop canopy for the pilot on the port side. The first airframe was converted from the sole B.5 and made its maiden flight on July 23, 1954. The B(I).8 was introduced as a night-intruder bomber/interdictor aircraft to fly low-level missions in the European theatre. It was fitted with a Boulton Paul gun-pack containing four 20mm Aden guns in the rear of the bomb bay. Special bomb bay doors allowed the B(I).8 to carry flares to illuminate night targets. The aircraft could also carry a 500lb bomb or two 250lb bombs on each underwing pylon.

Into Combat

The Canberra first saw active service during the Malayan Emergency from July 1950 to July 1960 when aircraft for the RAF, RAAF and RNZAF were deployed against Communist guerrillas.

During the 1956 Suez Crisis the RAF deployed around 100 Canberras to fly bombing and reconnaissance missions from airfields in Malta and Cyprus. A total of 278 Canberra sorties were flown, dropping 1,439 1,000lb bombs. The only Canberra shot down during the Suez campaign was a PR.7 targeted by a Syrian Gloster Meteor fighter on 6 November 1956, the last day of the war.

The RAAF also deployed a squadron of Canberras to take part in the Vietnam War alongside US B-57s. They were mostly used in the low-level bombing role and two RAAF aircraft were lost before the type was withdrawn from the theatre in 1971.

The Canberra also saw extensive military action whilst in service with the Indian Air Force, beginning in 1962 when they were employed during a UN campaign against the breakaway African Republic of Katanga. Both Rhodesia and South Africa also utilised Canberras in their respective Bush Wars and Ethiopian Canberras were used against Eritrea and Somalia during the 1970s.

RAF Bomber Command retired the last of its Canberras in September 1961, but squadrons based in Cyprus, Germany and Singapore continued to fly the type in the nuclear strike role. The Cyprus-based squadrons and one of the RAF Germany squadrons disbanded in

1. The Canberra eventually equipped 62 RAF squadrons.
2. The Canberra B(I).8 had a new forward fuselage with teardrop canopy. It was designed as a night-intruder bomber/interdictor aircraft to fly low-level missions. WT329 was a development aircraft and in 1956 it set the World Speed Record between London and Cairo. It was later sold to the RNZAF (as NZ6101) but crashed on November 2, 1960.
3. The last version of the Canberra to fly with the RAF was the PR.9 photo-reconnaissance variant. A total of were 23 built by Short Brothers & Harland with Avon 206 engines that produced with 10,030lb/thrust each. **Crown Copyright**

1948

Avro Anson C.19 – T.22 Towards the end of the war the Brabazon Committee was created to help the British aircraft industry convert from military to civil aircraft production. One suggestion was a civilian Anson. This had a raised roofline, an all-metal wing and saw limited commercial success. The RAF ordered 264 as Anson C.19 transports and these were joined by 59 T.20 trainers, 252 T.21 nav trainers and 54 T.22 radio trainers.

Avro Tudor 8 A piston-engined airliner loosely based on the Lincoln bomber. It was Britain's first pressurised airliner but with its antiquated tailwheel undercarriage it failed to sell and less than 40 were built. The RAF received a single Tudor 8 variant in September 1948 to evaluate new turbine engines. The aircraft (VX195) was fitted with four Rolls Royce Nene 4 turbojets in under-wing paired nacelles and was used for high-altitude tests.

de Havilland DH.100 Vampire FB.5 Optimised for the fighter-bomber role, the FB.5 retained the same powerplant as the F.3 but had additional armour plating around the engine and clipped wings. It also had longer undercarriage to allow it to carry larger underwing weaponry. At its peak the FB.5 flew with 19 units in Germany, the Middle East and the Far East and saw combat in Malaya against insurgents in remote jungle areas.

de Havilland DH.104 Devon The Brabazon Committee identified a need for an all-metal short-haul feeder airliner to be a monoplane successor to the Dragon Rapide biplane. The DH.104 Dove was selected and 544 aircraft were built including 140 military derivatives named the Devon. These included 40 delivered to the RAF and flown by 32 and 207 Sqn in the VIP and light transport role; the last example being retired in 1984.

EoN Eton TX.1 The EoN Primary was based on the German SG 38 Schulgleiter. The glider was adopted by the ATC in 1948 under the name Eton TX.1 and consisted of a high-mounted fabric covered wooden wing above an open-truss framework. In 1952, Slingsby created the Grasshopper TX.1 by combining the 'fuselage' with the wing from the Kirby Cadet. Almost 200 Etons and Grasshoppers were delivered to the ATC. **SDB**

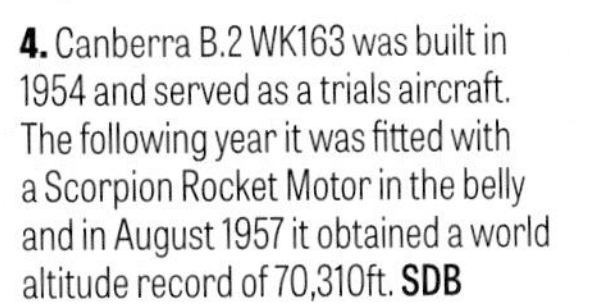

4. Canberra B.2 WK163 was built in 1954 and served as a trials aircraft. The following year it was fitted with a Scorpion Rocket Motor in the belly and in August 1957 it obtained a world altitude record of 70,310ft. **SDB**
5. Nearly 1,352 Canberras were produced around the world and the type remained in service for more than fifty years. Canberra PR.9 XH134 was the last example to fly in the UK. **SDB**
6. Canberra B.2 WJ731 cruises at high altitude in 1993 offering good view of the Canberra's large wing area. This aircraft was delivered in December 1953 and was finally scrapped at RAF Wyton in April 1994. **Crown Copyright**

1969, with the Singapore-based unit following in 1970. The three remaining RAF Germany units remained operational until 1972, when the last RAF Canberra bombers were retired.

Recce Canberras

Early on in the aircraft's development it became obvious that the Canberra made an ideal reconnaissance platform as it was stable and had copious space for cameras and sensors.

The Canberra PR.3 first flew on March 19, 1950 and boasted a 14in (36cm) extension to the fuselage to house the camera bay and additional fuel. These were followed into service by 74 Canberra PR.7s, which were based on the B.6 complete with the uprated Avon 109 engines. The PR.7's longer wings accommodated extra fuel tanks, enabling them to be flown deep into Soviet territory on spy flights.

The ultimate incarnation of the Canberra was the PR.9 photo-reconnaissance version based on B(I).8 but with its fuselage and wings stretched. The powerplants were also changed to Avon 206 engines that produced with 10,030lbs/thrust each. A total of were 23 built by Short Brothers and these would see extended service with the RAF into the new millennium. Based primarily at RAF Wyton, Cambridgeshire and RAF Luqa in Malta, the PR9s were fitted with special LOROP (Long-Range Optical Photography) cameras enabling targets deep into Eastern Europe to be photographed while flying along the inner German border. The aircraft were also fitted with infrared linescan cameras for low level night reconnaissance.

In 1972, RAF PR Canberras were used to search for hidden arms dumps in Northern Ireland during Operation *Motorman* and during the 1982 Falklands War there was a plan to supply two PR.9s to the Chilean Air Force. The idea was to secretly operate them with RAF crews over Argentina but the operation was abandoned for political reasons. The aircraft got as far as Belize before the cancellation.

The aircraft were also employed in the humanitarian role, searching for refugees in Uganda and locating mass graves in Kosovo during the Bosnian War in the 1990s.

In more recent years, the few remaining PR.9s were flown exclusively by 39 Sqn at RAF Marham, Norfolk and were involved in the war in the Balkans, the invasion of Iraq in 2003 and the war in Afghanistan in 2006; both in the strategic reconnaissance and photographic mapping roles.

The final three example of the PR.9 returned to Marham in July 2006 and the last RAF Canberra was finally retired; 57 years after the type's first flight. ■

Gloster E.1/44 Ace. While the Meteor used two jet engines there was concern that limited supply might restrict production. As such, in 1942, Gloster set about creating a single-engined fighter. By the time it was ready to fly in 1948 the engine shortages had been resolved so when testing revealed unpromising performance the project was cancelled. But not before test pilot Bill Waterton had unkindly nicknamed it the 'Gormless'!

Handley Page Hastings A four-engined troop-carrier and freighter that was the largest cargo aircraft ever designed for the RAF when it entered service. HP chose to use the Halifax as the basis for the Hastings, with Halifax wings mated to a pressurised circular fuselage. The type was rushed into service in September 1948 so it could assist in the Berlin Airlift and the RAF received 141 examples, some of which flew on until 1977.

Hawker P.1052 A development of the P.1040 [see p81] using swept wings. The tailplane had adjustable incidence to allow changes in trim at the high speeds. The first of three prototypes flew in November 1948 and the aircraft performed vital research into swept wing flight. As such, the P.1052 was part of a transition from the centrifugally powered, straight-winged Sea Hawk to the axially powered, swept-wing Hunter.

Slingsby Prefect TX.1 The Prefect was developed from the 1932 Grunau Baby as a semi-aerobatic glider. It was an open cockpit, single-seat, fabric-covered wooden airframe fitted with air brakes. Although designed for the civilian market the Prefect was ordered by the Royal Air Force Gliding & Soaring Association (RAFGSA) and to the Air Training Corps (ATC) as the Prefect TX.1. They would serve from 1948 to 1984. **SDB**

Slingsby Sedbergh TX.1 A side-by-side two-seat glider with an open cockpit that first flew in 1944 as the Type 21. It was designed for the ATC but rejected and put into store until the end of the war. A slightly modified T.21B version was eventually ordered by ATC in 1947 and the first of 95 entered service as the Sedbergh TX.1 in 1948. It was the first two-seat glider available to cadets and was retained until 1984. **SDB**

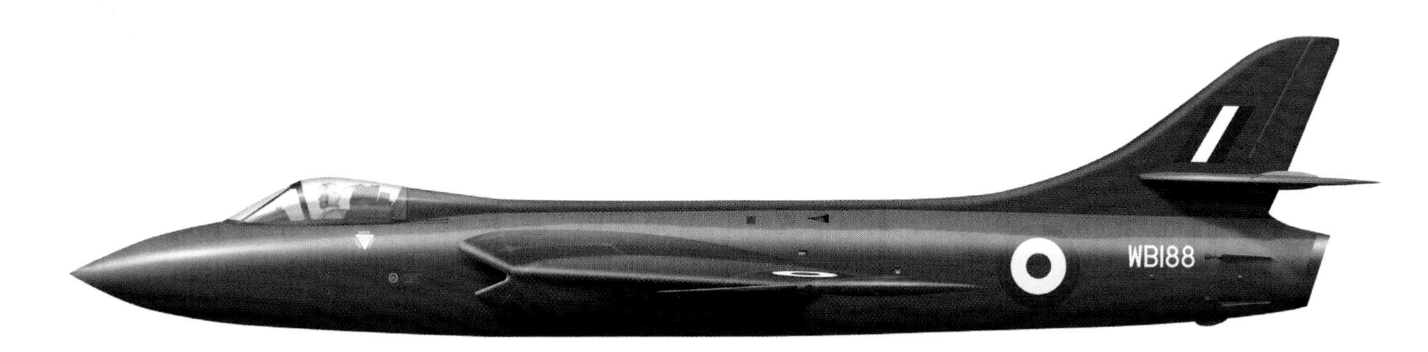

Andy Hay/www.flyingart.co.uk

Record Breakers

In the immediate postwar years the RAF and its American counterparts engaged in friendly rivalry over who could fly highest or furthest... but the quest to be the fastest in the world was the most keenly fought battle

On April 26, 1939, with the world on the brink of war, Fritz Wendel pushed his Messerschmitt Me 209V1 up to 469.220mph to gain the World Speed Record in a publicity coup for Nazi Germany.

Although the constant stream of new aircraft that emerged over the next six years would be progressively faster and more capable, the quest to regain the record would have to wait until the return to peace in mid-1945. And so it was that a group of skilled British pilots found themselves at Herne Bay, Kent in November 1945 with the mission of bringing the record back to 'Blighty.'

Herne Bay - 1945

By late 1945 Britain had a distinct lead over the USA when it came to jet engine development and the Gloster Meteor was making a name for itself in frontline RAF squadrons. This was an obvious chance to steal a lead on the Americans and post a fast speed that would take some time to surpass.

Gloster provided a pair of specially honed Meteor IVs, EE454 and EE455, which had been fitted with the latest Rolls-Royce Derwent engines. These were to be flown by Gloster's chief test pilot Eric Greenwood and Grp Capt Hugh J 'Willy' Wilson from the RAF.

The weather in Kent in November is rarely conducive for flying small aircraft, let alone the low level high speed flying needed for a record attempt. However, with the clock ticking the team needed to set a record as soon as possible and preparations were made for a number of flights off the coast at Herne Bay.

The Fédération Aéronautique Internationale (FAI) stipulated record attempts must make two runs, in opposite directions, over a 1.9 mile (3km) course at a maximum altitude of 200ft (61m) – something that would take as little as 110 seconds each way at 600mph.

Day after day the poor weather stopped flying – even though Flt Lt 'Nobby' Clarke took a Meteor 'hack' aloft at regular intervals to check the conditions. However, this did give time for EE454 to be christened *Britannia* and for both jets to be painted a lurid canary yellow scheme.

Finally, on November 7, 1945 the weather lifted. Nobby in the 'Met Check' Meteor declared the conditions safe and both Greenwood and Wilson launched in succession and took their turn on the course. Hours later, shortly after 10.00pm, the call came from the timing crew: "Greenwood 603mph... Wilson 606mph!" Britain had the speed record and Wilson's Meteor had averaged 606.38mph.

High Speed Flight

On June 14, 1946 the RAF re-formed the High Speed Flight [Ed: see p24] to try to push the record even higher. Whispers abounded that the USA was preparing a Lockheed P-80 Shooting Star to reclaim the honours, but the general consensus was that they would only 'just' reach 615mph and raise the speed by the 1% the FAI demanded for a new record.

1948

Supermarine 510 Effectively a Supermarine Attacker naval jet fighter that had been fitted with a swept wing and tailplane. The Supermarine 510 was designed to explore the high subsonic speed range and retained the same tailwheel undercarriage of the Attacker. It was a handful to fly and even worse on the ground but led to the Type 528 and the Type 535 – the latter becoming the prototype Swift [see p99].

Supermarine Spitfire F.24 The final Spitfire variant, the F.24, was similar to the F.22 but had increased fuel capacity. Spitfire F.24s were also fitted with fittings to carry rocket projectiles under the wings. The type could attain 454mph and reach 30,000ft in just eight minutes. A total of 81 F.24s were built, including 27 converted from F.22s. The first entered service in Germany in 1948 and would serve until December 1951.

Vickers Nene Viking The Vickers Viking [see p88] was chosen by the Air Ministry and Rolls Royce as a testbed for the Nene jet engines. Viking G-AJPH was reregistered VX856 and fitted with two Nenes; flying the first time on April 6, 1948 and becoming the first British transport aircraft to fly under turbojet power. It was used as a test aircraft until 1954 when it was converted back to propeller power and sold for use as an airliner.

Vickers Valetta A military transport version of the Viking airliner [see p88]. The Valetta had more powerful Hercules engines, a strengthened floor and large loading doors. The first of 262 aircraft entered RAF service in 1948, replacing Dakotas in Transport Command as well as joining squadrons in the Far East. Valettas saw active service in Aden and the Malayan Emergency and also carried out parachute drops during the Suez Crisis.

Youngman-Baynes High Lift An experimental monoplane with a fixed tailwheel undercarriage. The High Lift was created in 1947 to test the newly created slotted flaps designed by RT Youngman. It was designed by Mr L Baynes using parts of a war surplus Percival Proctor and built by the Heston Aircraft Company. Registered VT789, the aircraft flew on February 5, 1948 and was later passed to the College of Aeronautics at Cranfield.

2

1

1. 'Teddy' Donaldson streaks for the finish line in Meteor F.4 EE550 on September 7, 1946.
2. For the 1945 record the Meteors were painted bright yellow and EE454 was christened Britannia.
3-6. Left to Right: Grp Capt Hugh J 'Willy' Wilson (606.40mph), Grp Capt Edward 'Teddy' Donaldson (615.78mph), Sqn Ldr Neville Duke (727.60mph) & Lt Cdr Mike Lithgow (735.70mph).

Grp Capt Edward 'Teddy' Donaldson was chosen to lead the High Speed Flight. He had commanded the RAF's first Meteor squadron so was well acquainted with the type. He was joined by test pilots Neville Duke and Bill Waterton, and the Flight equipped with a pair of Meteor IVs (EE549 and EE550). Unlike the aircraft used in 1945, these newer jets benefitted from more powerful engines fitted with turbine blades made from a new substance called Nimonic. Scientific support declared that if the air temperature exceeded 21 degrees C, the new engines would power the Meteor to 623mph.

Problems during testing meant August soon gave way to a chilly September and the chance of a temperature advantage was ebbing away. Finally, a weather window emerged on September 7 and Donaldson and Waterton both made runs across the course off the coast of Littlehampton.

Waterton suffered trim problems in EE549 and at just under 600mph he suffered a temporary loss of control, forcing him to hold hard left aileron to maintain level flight. In his acidic autobiography, *The Quick and the Dead,* he wrote: "At 605mph the agony was indescribable. It seemed as though every bone from the tip of my elbow to the palm of my hand was in the grip of a giant, remorseless nutcracker."

He continued the run and landed back safely to await the results. Shortly after midnight the news arrived: Waterton had pushed the Meteor to 614mph but Donaldson has secured the record with a speed of 615.78mph.

The team tried to better their speeds over the coming weeks, but the colder and worsening weather defeated their plans. The Americans finally regained the speed record the following June when Col Albert Boyd reached 623.74mph in a modified P-80.

US Dominance

For speed watchers, 1953 was a busy year with the title swapping between the UK and USA on a regular basis.

The year began with the title held by American pilot J Slade Nash. He had flown his North American F-86D Sabre to 698.5mph on November 18 of the previous year and America was adamant that it was going to retain the glory of being the fastest country on (or at least over) the world. Accordingly, fellow US pilot William Barnes, using another F-86D, pushed the record up to 715.75mph early in the new year.

All looked promising for the Americans until word came that two teams in the UK were making significant progress with modern fighters destined for the RAF: both intended to stake their claim in the record books by pushing their aircraft through the speed record.

Sydney Camm's Hawker Hunter first flew on July 20, 1951 and was already showing much promise. With such a potent machine it was perhaps inevitable that Hawkers would make an attempt on the speed record, vying with the perceived leading runners in the competition – rival manufacturers, Supermarine.

The Supermarine Swift had proved to be a very fast aircraft at low level and plans to use the prototype Swift F.4 (WK198) for a record attempt were well known. However, much to Supermarine's dismay, Hawker made rapid progress with its own plans.

1949

Auster T.7 The dual control training version of the Auster AOP.6 [see p75]. The RAF received 77 Auster T.7s, which were allocated to AOP squadrons and operated alongside AOP.6s. The aircraft were equipped for simulated instrument and night flying and were used for conversion, continuation and currency flights. In 1956, a pair of T.7s were fitted with skies and larger tail surfaces to take part in the Trans-Antarctic Expedition. **SDB**

Avro 707 A proof of concept aircraft to explore delta wing technology. The aircraft was fitted with no tailplane and control came from elevators and ailerons on the trailing edge of the wings (not elevons as on later deltas). All five 707s were powered by a single Rolls Royce Derwent jet engine and the first (VX784) flew on September 4, 1949. The 707 programme provided valuable insights into the Vulcan's flight characteristics.

Gloster Meteor T.7 Early jets proved tricky to fly; not to least to pilots more used to the instant power provided by a propeller driven fighter. The jet engines responded slowly, but when they were up to speed things happened very quickly. It was obvious that a dual-control jet trainer was needed and Gloster obliged by modifying a Meteor F.4 into the prototype T.7. The RAF received around 500 T.7s from August 1949 until mid 1954. **SDB**

1950

Avro 707B The second of the Avro 707s to fly was 707B VX790. Compared to the original Avro 707 [see Left] this had a longer nose and different cockpit canopy as well as a longer nosewheel leg to help maintain the incidence required for landing and take off. The 707B first flew on September 6, 1950 and was used alongside the 707 to test low speed characteristics. In September 1956, it was damaged on landing and scrapped.

Avro Ashton The Avro Tudor 9 was developed from the jet-powered Tudor 8 [see p82] but was eventually renamed the Ashton. The RAF used six as research aircraft. Compared to the Tudor they had larger tail fins and tricycle landing gear. At least one was fitted with streamlined underwing bomb containers for trials work. One was later fittedwith two Olympus engines to test the engine ahead of its use on the Vulcan.

1. Neville Duke demonstrates the scarlet Hunter to the crowds at the SBAC Airshow at Farnborough in 1953, just prior to making his successful speed record flight. **2.** Supermarine Swift WK198 breaks the World Speed Record in Libya in September 1953. To help the timing team the Swift had black bands applied to its nose and tail over its pale blue finish.

The Scarlett Hunter

With development of the RAF's Hunter F.1 well underway, Hawker opted to modify the original prototype for its speed record attempt. WB188 was fitted with an afterburning version of the familiar Rolls-Royce Avon turbojet that developed 9,600lb thrust as opposed to the 6,500lb thrust produced by the original engine.

Its airbrakes were removed to minimise drag and the aircraft gained a pointed nose as well as a shallower raked canopy to minimise aerodynamic drag. Finally, and perhaps most noticeably, it shed its duck egg green paint in favour of a vibrant scarlet scheme that was highly polished to make the aeroplane was as streamlined as possible.

Flight testing showed the prototype had immense potential and Hawker chief test pilot Sqn Ldr Neville Duke felt ready to push the aircraft to its limits on September 7, 1953.

It was decided that the flight should originate from the RAF Tangmere, Sussex (the former base of the RAF High Speed Flight) by virtue of its proximity to the coastal resort of Littlehampton, over whose sandy beaches the speed record would be made.

At this time all record attempts were required to take place at an altitude lower than 328ft (100m) so Sqn Ldr Duke transited to the coast, descending and opening up the throttle for his crucial runs between the timing points. All seemed well from within the cockpit and signs were equally positive once Duke had landed at Tangmere. Word came through from the invigilators: WB188 had well and truly broken the record at a stunning 727.63mph, some 12mph faster than the American F-86D Sabre.

Sqn Ldr Duke and WB188 had secured their place in the record books.

Short Lived

However, WB188's triumph was a moment of fleeting glory. Across the Atlantic the Americans were ready to unleash two of their new jets at the record attempt, namely the Douglas F-4D Skyray and North American F-100 Super Sabre. Simultaneously, pressure started to mount as Supermarine's window of opportunity for the Swift record began to narrow.

After much deliberation it was decided to make the attempt in Libya, which offered the hot and dry conditions ideal for high-speed flight.

Test pilot Mike Lithgow flew Swift F.4 WK198 down to Castel Idris el Awal and on September 26 he achieved 735.7mph, less than three weeks after Duke had claimed the previous record.

Lithgow's flight had been flown along the main road between Azizia and Bur El Gnem, 50 miles (80km) from Tripoli. It cut a dead straight line through the featureless desert for 10 miles.

Writing after the record he described how he noticed a line of cars near the road and several goats scattering in all directions, while the camels never even looked up!

Reporting the Swift's record, aviation journal *Flight* noted: "In all fairness to the Hunter (and bearing in mind that several American speed records have been made in high temperatures and over a dry lake-bed below sea level) it must be pointed out that the speed of sound increases as air temperature goes up, at a rate of 7mph per 10°F. Thus, as the Hunter's designer Sir Sydney Camm has pointed out, Duke's record of 727mph might well have been 745mph had the prevailing temperature been 105°F, even allowing for the loss of engine thrust due to the increase in temperature. In fact, the Hunter's speed was achieved in far from ideal conditions and with an air temperature of only 74°F."

It was suggested that Duke's Hunter be taken to Libya to make a further attempt at the record but it all became academic two weeks later.

On October 3, US Navy pilot James B Verdin pushed his F-4D Skyray to 752.90mph to regain the record for the USA; Mike Lithgow was the fastest man in the world for just a week!

Later in the month USAF pilot Frank K Everest upped the record to 755.1mph in his Super Sabre – bringing the number of new record claimants to five for 1953 alone. ■

RAF Fast Fact

The Royal Air Force has held the World Air Speed Record on eight occasions:

September 10, 1929 336.30mph	**George Stainforth** Gloster VI
September 12, 1929 357.70mph	**Augustus Orlebar** Supermarine S.6
September 13, 1931 407.50mph	**George Stainforth** Supermarine S.6B
November 7, 1945 606.40mph	**Hugh 'Willy' Wilson** Gloster Meteor F.4
September 7, 1946 615.78mph	**Edward Donaldson** Gloster Meteor F.4
September 7, 1953 727.60mph	**Neville Duke** Hawker Hunter F.3
September 26, 1953 735.70mph	**Mike Lithgow** Supermarine Swift F4
March 10, 1956 1,132.00mph	**Peter Twiss** Fairey Delta 2

1950

Avro Athena Designed to meet Spec T.7/45 for a turboprop-powered trainer. However, the spec was later reissued with the requirement to use a Rolls Royce Merlin 35 piston engine (of which it had large stocks in store). Avro built two Athenas – one with the Armstrong Siddeley Mamba turboprop and one with the Merlin. The latter was evaluated against the Boulton Paul Balliol and while 15 were ordered the Balliol was preferred.

Boeing Washington By 1950 the RAF's long range bomber fleet was limited to just a few squadrons of Lincolns but postwar financial pressures meant the V Bombers were some years away from readiness. As such, the RAF received 88 retired USAF B-29 Superfortresses from June 1950 under the American military aid programme. They served as the Washington B.1 until replaced by Canberras in 1954.

Boulton Paul Balliol Developed to replace the Harvard. The Mamba turboprop-powered prototype aircraft first flew on May 17, 1948. In doing so it became the world's first single-engined turboprop aircraft to fly. The Merlin equipped Balliol was chosen over the Athena. The RAF received 145 before a change in policy meant all-jet training was preferred; as such the Balliol saw limited service and were retired in 1957.

Boulton Paul P.111 Designed to explore the concept of tailless delta wings. The P.111 was created with wings that could be flown as 'cropped' or with one of two pairs of extensions, thus allowing the aerodynamic effects of different tip shapes to be evaluated. Unlike the Avro 707, roll and pitch were controlled by elevons. The P.111 was difficult to fly and following a landing accident was rebuilt with airbrakes to lower landing speeds.

de Havilland Canada DHC-1 Chipmunk A single-engined trainer developed to replace the Tiger Moth. The Chipmunk was the first postwar aircraft designed by de Havilland Canada. Britain was impressed by the Chipmunk and having secured a deal for the type to be built under licence in the UK, the RAF received 735 from 1950. 'Chippies' served with the University Air Squadrons, the ATC and Air Experience Flights until 1996.

BUY NOW
Order today by visiting our website
www.militaria.ma/specialedition
or by calling 01778 392027
WIN A RIDE IN A LANCASTER
100 YEARS OF THE
RAF
1918-2018
ICONIC AIRCRAFT
Sopwith Camel, Hurricane, Spitfire, Mosquito, Lancaster,

Women of the Royal Air Force

Women have served as members of the RAF since 1918, conducting support roles to free up men to fly and fight. Today, women are serving permanently in their own right

Over the last century the attitudes towards women and their role in society has changed dramatically. Conflict is a powerful catalyst for change and during both World Wars women serving with the armed forces contributed significantly to the war effort. Perhaps more importantly, these women also successfully broke down gender stereotypes.

1

Great War Girls

During the 1914-1918 Great War women worked in all manner of roles – from nursing to engineering – and the Women's Royal Air Force (WRAF) was formed on the same date as the RAF (April 1, 1918). More than 80,000 women enlisted during the war and served in a variety of non-combatant roles in many organisations. The majority were assigned to the Queen Alexandra's Imperial Military Nursing Service (QAIMNS), the First Aid Nursing Yeomanry (FANY), and the Queen Mary's Women's Army Auxiliary Corps (WAAC).

The latter was formed by Helen Gwynne-Vaughan and Mrs Chalmers-Watson and was divided into four sections: cookery, mechanical, clerical and miscellaneous. It would form the basis of the WRAF and in September 1918 Gwynne-Vaughan was given the powers of a Brigadier and tasked with organising the service.

The WRAF was disbanded in 1920 but the Princess Mary's Royal Air Force Nursing Service was established in 1923.

Women of World War Two

In 1938, the Auxiliary Territorial Service (ATS) was created as the women's branch of the British Army and its 48 'Companies' were absorbed into the newly formed Women's Auxiliary Air Force (WAAF) the following year.

Helen Gwynne-Vaughan was appointed Director of the ATS; a position which she held until her retirement in 1941.

Although they did not participate in combat, members of the WAAF were active in parachute packing and the crewing of barrage balloons. Others were employed in aircraft maintenance, catering, meteorology, radar, transport and communications. Some were trained to specialise in codes and ciphers or the analysis of reconnaissance photographs. Women were also vital members of the operations and plotting rooms; directing fighter aircraft to intercept Luftwaffe raids. Women were paid two-thirds of the salary of male counterparts in RAF ranks.

From 1941, women aged between 20 and 30 were conscripted into the war effort and given the choice of joining the auxiliary services or undertaking factory work.

Speaking after the war Air Vice Marshall Sir William Sefton Brancker commented that "The WRAF was the best disciplined and best turned-out women's organisation in the country. This remarkable achievement was due to Dame Helen Gwynne-Vaughan".

Women were paid two-thirds of the salary of male counterparts in RAF ranks

Ferry Pilots

Women did not serve as aircrew during World War Two and the use of female pilots was limited to the civilian-run Air Transport Auxiliary (ATA).

The ATA was set up to ferry new, repaired and damaged military aircraft from factories, assembly plants and maintenance units to active squadrons. It also flew personnel that needed to be urgently moved around the country and, on occasion, flew air ambulance flights.

Notably, from 1943 female members of the ATA received equal pay to their male co-workers; a first for the British government.

1950

Gloster Meteor F.8 The Meteor F.8 flew in October 1948 but testing showed the aircraft was aerodynamically unstable in some areas of flight so the tail from the E.1/44 was fitted, giving the F.8 a much taller appearance than earlier versions. It was also 30in longer than the F.4 and fitted with a teardrop canopy to improve vision. Later models had ejection seats. Between 1950 and 1955, the F.8 was the mainstay of Fighter Command.

Gloster Meteor FR.9 The RAF's need to replace the Spitfire and Mosquito in the armed fighter recce role led to the Meteor F.8 being modified into the FR.9. The new aircraft was 8in longer and had a new nose featuring a camera window. The camera could be controlled by the pilot to shoot straight ahead or obliquely. The four 20mm guns were retained. The first of 126 FR.9s entered service with 208 Sqn in Egypt.

Gloster Meteor PR.10 Whereas the Meteor FR.9 was optimised for low-level tactical reconnaissance the PR.10 was developed for high altitude missions. It had the earlier F.4-style tail and the longer span wings to help it perform at altitude; specifically to replace the Spitfire PR.XIX. The armament was removed and a single camera placed in the nose along with two more in the rear fuselage. The RAF operated 59 PR.10s.

Handley Page HPR.2 Basic Trainer A low winged monoplane with a fixed tailwheel undercarriage and an AS Cheetah radial engine, created to replace the Prentice. Designed in response to Air Ministry Spec T16/48 the HPR.2 first flew in May 1950. Tests showed that the canopy created significant turbulence and this was replaced. Test pilots felt it was less forgiving to fly than the rival Provost so no orders were placed.

Hawker P.1072 Snarler A development of the P.1040 [see p81] that acted as a test bed for the Snarler rocket booster engine. The liquid-fuelled rocket motor was mounted in the tail and produced 2,000lb/thrust in addition to the Nene engine's 5,180lb/thrust. It flew six times before a small explosion damaged the aircraft. Before it could return to flight the RAF had decided that turbojets with reheat would be used instead of rockets.

1. The first WAAF nursing orderlies selected to fly on air-ambulance duties in France after D-Day. From left to right: Leading Aircraftwoman Myra Roberts of Oswestry, Corporal Lydia Alford of Eastleigh and Leading Aircraftwoman Edna Birbeck of Wellingborough.
2. Female RAF air mechanics working on the fuselage of an Avro 504 in 1918.
3. Flt Lt Michelle Goodman was the first woman to be awarded the Distinguished Flying Cross.

Post War

Over 250,000 women served in the WAAF, of which 183,317 were volunteers. The majority were aged between 18 and 40 and they came from all walks of life – even Winston Churchill's daughter, Sarah, served as a WAAF. By 1943, some 48 nationalities were represented in the force and they served in over 110 trades.

After the end of the war, most women returned to civilian life and membership of the WAAF dropped to just a few hundred. These continued to serve and, conscious of the contribution made by women during the war, the government proposed retaining a permanent female peacetime force.

The passing of the Army and Air Force (Women's Service) Act in 1948 created the opportunity for women to join the RAF as a permanent career and as a result the Women's Royal Air Force was re-formed in February1949.

This time, the WRAF was established to be as closely integrated into the RAF as possible. All new entrants were therefore commissioned or enlisted, taking the same oath as the men, and subject to the same conditions of service and discipline. Around 80% of trades were open to women including driving, ground signalling, clerical work and catering.The only restriction placed on the WRAF was that they should not undertake combat duties.

Despite this, members of the WRAF found themselves at the heart of conflicts in places such as Malaya and Kenya.

Aircrew at Last

As time went by ever more career opportunities were opened to women including 'technical' trades such as Air Traffic Control. In 1959, the new trade of Air Quartermaster was opened to female applicants and three years later these became the first females to be recognised as aircrew. In 1968, female officers adopted the same rank titles of their RAF counterparts and in 1970 the first female entrants were admitted into the RAF College, Cranwell.

However, it would be another twenty years before women would be accepted for flying duties. The first of these was Flt Lt Julie Gibson, who graduated in 1990 as a Hercules pilot. She was the RAF's first operational female pilot.

In 1994, the WRAF was formally merged with the RAF. The same year, Flt Lt Jo Salter became the first operational RAF fast jet pilot; flying Tornados with 617 'Dambusters' Sqn. Since then, female RAF pilots have flown operationally in warzones around the world, including Afghanistan and Iraq. In 2009, Flt Lt Kirsty Moore became the first female member of the Red Arrows and two years later Flt Lt Juliette (Jules) Flemming was awarded the job of the RAF's solo Hawk display pilot.

Perhaps the ultimate embodiment of how far women have come in the RAF occurred on June 1, 2007 when Flt Lt Michelle Goodman was awarded the Distinguished Flying Cross (DFC).

Flying a Merlin helicopter, Flt Lt Goodman and her crew were alerted that there was a serious casualty following a mortar attack on the centre of Basra, Iraq.

Landing an aircraft at the location was assessed to be very high risk and intelligence reports indicated a large, 'spectacular' attack would occur somewhere in Basra, with a helicopter being a possible target. Flt Lt Goodman was fully aware of the elevated threat level but pressed on under heavy fire. Her DFC Citation said that without the rescue, "the casualty would have died within 15 minutes. Despite extreme pressure, whilst in the face of the enemy, Flt Lt Goodman made the right decision. This was a bold and daring sortie which undoubtedly saved life."

As the RAF enters its second century contribution by women continues to grow and the lines between the sexes become increasingly blurred. Even pregnancy, once considered grounds for discharge, is no longer a barrier for employment within the service. ■

1951

Vickers Tay Viscount The last of the experimental jetliners built in the immediate postwar years. The V.633 Tay Viscount began life as G-AHRG but was acquired by the Ministry of Supply in March 1950 and reregistered as VX217. Its Dart turboprops were replaced with a pair of Tay turbojets in pods below the wing and the interior was fitted out with test instrumentation to test the powered control system for the Vickers Valiant.

Westland Dragonfly Westland Aircraft and Sikorsky signed an agreement in 1946 that allowed the S-51 helicopter to be produced under licence in Britain. Powered by the 500hp Alvis Leonides radial engine, the Westland Dragonfly entered service with the RAF and Royal Navy in 1950 in the air-sea rescue and casualty evacuation roles. The RAF had two Dragonfly HC.2s and 12 HC.4s; the latter having all-metal rotor blades.

Armstrong Whitworth Meteor NF.11 The RAF urgently needed to replace the Mosquito in the night fighter role and, pending the arrival of a new design, the Meteor was adapted as a stopgap. Based on the T.7, the NF.11 also used the tail of the F.8 and the longer wings of the F.3. The radar was housed in an extended nose, which meant the cannon were moved into the wings. The first examples joined 29 Sqn in August 1951.

Avro 707A The third variant of the Type 707 was the single Avro 707A (WD280), which was built for higher speed testing. Whereas the earlier 707 and 707B had a dorsal air intake for the engine this was found to suffer from turbulence at higher speeds (caused by the cockpit canopy) so the 707A had its air intakes moved to the wing roots. A second airframe (WZ736) flew in 1953 to help speed up the Vulcan development programme.

Avro Shackleton MR.1 Developed from the Lincoln, the Shackleton was created as a maritime patrol aircraft to counter the rapid expansion of the Soviet Navy's submarine force. Powered by four Griffon engines the first Shackleton MR.1s entered service with 120 Sqn in March 1951 but by this time it had already become outdated and a newer version was to follow in 1953. The RAF received 29 MR.1s and 47 MR.1As.

If it looks right...

One of Britain's most successful fighter jets, the Hawker Hunter was as impressive to fly as it was to look at

There's a well-used adage in the aviation world: "If it looks right, it probably flies right" and in the case of the Hawker Hunter, it certainly holds true: the jet has sportscar styling and handling to match.

Hawker already had experience building jets, with the straight-winged Sea Hawk and the experimental P.1052 of 1948 gave the company its first taste of swept-wing technology. The P.1052 later morphed into the P.1081 with a swept tailplane and revised fuselage. Although the prototype was lost in a crash in 1951, the lessons learned were employed in Hawker's entry into the competition for the Air Ministry's Specification F.43/46 for a daytime jet-powered interceptor fighter.

The spec called for a swept-winged fighter powered by the Avon turbojet and was later updated to include a requirement to reach 550kts (633mph) at 45,000ft (13,716m).

1

P.1067

Dubbed the Hawker P.1067, the new fighter would be the first single-seat jet in the world to carry four cannons; these being mounted in a single unit (complete with ammunition) to enable the aircraft to be quickly re-armed by simply winching the pack down and replacing it with another.

However, there remained doubt over the availability and reliability of the new Avon engine. The Air Ministry therefore requested three prototypes be constructed to evaluate two different engines. The first two examples, WB188 and WB195, were to be powered by the Avon whereas the third example (WB202) would use the Metrovick F.9 (later known as the Armstrong-Siddeley Sapphire).

In March 1950, the Air Ministry placed an initial order for 20 examples, by now christened the Hunter F.1. On July 20, 1951, test pilot Neville Duke took the duck-egg blue prototype (WB188) aloft for its maiden flight. The following April he took the aircraft through the sound barrier for the first time.

A month later he performed the maiden flight of WB195, upgraded from the first aeroplane with a reheated Avon 7 engine and full military equipment including cannon and radar. WB202, the first Sapphire-powered Hunter, followed the first two aircraft into the air in November 1952.

The first production F.1 (WT555) flew on May 16, 1953 but problems quickly became apparent. Using the flaps as airbrakes caused severe nose-down pitching at high speeds so a simple hinged airbrake needed to be fitted beneath the fuselage. Nevertheless, the problems continued in some flight regimes; firing the cannons at low altitudes could cause the engine to fail. This was when it ingested the cordite gases exhausted from the guns, and spent ammunition links were damaging the underside of the lower fuselage.

Speed Record

In September 1953, Duke established the world speed record in WB188 [Ed: see p84] but Hawker also had more pressing engagements to concentrate upon: producing and delivering the RAF's first Hunters.

A further 119 F.1s were ordered and the first of these entered service in July 1954, replacing 43 Sqn's Meteor F.8s.

The first Hunter F.2 (the Sapphire-engined variant which first flew on October 14, 1953) entered service in November 1954 with 257 Sqn, this version not afflicted by the gun-induced engine surges.

However, both the F.1 and F.2 were woefully

Firing the cannon at low altitudes could cause the engine to fail

short of fuel capacity and were of little use as operational fighters so work soon began on the improved F.4.

The aircraft benefited from additional bag-type fuel tanks in the wings and provision was made for under-wing tankage to further improve the jet's range. The F.4 also gained bulges beneath the nose to catch the spent ammunition links and reduce damage to the fuselage. It also had an all-moving tail to improve handling. The first F.4 made its first flight on October 20, 1954, just a day after the Sapphire 101-powered F.5.

Ultimately 349 Avon-engined F.4s were produced at both Kingston-upon-Thames and Blackpool, whereas 105 Hunter F.5s were built under licence by Armstrong Whitworth at Coventry's Baginton airfield.

1951

de Havilland DH.110 Created in response to a joint RAF/Royal Navy spec for a new night fighter. The DH.110 was supersonic in a shallow dive and the RAF ordered nine prototypes (along with four of the rival Gloster Javelin). The first crashed at Farnborough in 1952 killing 31 people and by the time the programme had returned to flight the RAF had ordered the Javelin. However, the DH.110 would go on to serve the FAA as the Sea Vixen.

de Havilland DH.113 Vampire NF.10 The night fighter variant of the Vampire used the same wings and tail booms as the earlier aircraft but the fuselage was changed to accommodate two crew side-by-side. The nose was also lengthened to house the AI.10 radar but unlike the Meteor NF.11 Vampire retained its guns in the lower fuselage. A total of 78 Vampire NF.10s served three RAF units (23, 25 & 151 Sqns) from 1951 until 1954.

English Electric Canberra B.2 The RAF's first jet bomber. The Canberra was designed as an unarmed, high speed bomber in the same vein as the Mosquito had been a decade earlier. In 1951, it became the first jet to make a non-stop transatlantic flight and in January of that year the first Canberra B.2s joined 101 Sqn. Canberras replaced Mosquitos, Lincolns and Washingtons as front line bombers. In total, 410 B.2s were built.

Fairey Delta I Originally intended as a ramp-launched vertical take off fighter, the FD.1 was reclassified as a research aircraft to explore delta wing technology. The prototype flew in March 1951 but suffered from poor handling and stability. As such the remaining two aircraft were cancelled. One of the key problems was caused by the large flying surfaces, which made the aircraft very 'twitchy' – but it had an incredible roll rate.

Folland Midge A concept demonstrator for the Gnat light fighter. Designer W.E.W 'Teddy' Petter felt that instead of building ever larger and more expensive fighters the RAF should buy smaller, simpler and cheaper fighters in larger numbers. Unable to follow his passion at English Electric he left and joined Folland, where he was allowed to create the Fo-139 Midge. It was destroyed in a crash but had demonstrated Petter's concept.

RAF Fast Fact

In April 1969, Flt Lt Al Pollock was displeased that more had not been scheduled to mark the RAF's 50th anniversary. On April 5, he was flying a Hunter FGA.9 when he decided to divert and circle the Houses of Parliament. To avoid overflying built-up areas Al flew via the Thames and in 2011 he recalled to the editor what happened next... "I was so intoxicated with the views that it was literally just before my wings crossed London Bridge that I looked ahead and saw Tower Bridge! There, standing like some proud, strong sentinel across the Thames, this famous matronly structure blocked my low level path to the east. It was easy enough to fly over it, but the idea of flying through the spans suddenly struck me. I had a long six seconds before the bridge, grappling with the seductive proposition few ground attack pilots could have resisted." Al was discharged from the RAF on medical grounds. This avoided a court martial and the embarrassment to the government of him explaining the reason for his flight.

1. Wearing the markings of the famous 111 Sqn Black Arrows, Hunter T.7A WV318 flew as a jet warbird for many years as G-FFOX. It was restored by Delta Jets and was later sold to the Hunter Flight Academy. 'Firefox' was sold to Canada in 2018. **SDB**
2. This distinctively marked former Swiss AF Hunter F.58 is operated by Hawker Hunter Aviation at RAF Scampton, Lincolnshire.
3. Hunter FGA.9 XJ687 flew with the RAF and was then sold to the Chilean Air Force. Today it is preserved at Chile's Museo Nacional Aeronáutico y del Espacio.

Interceptor

The first flight of the prototype Hunter F.6 (XF833) actually took place in January 1954, before the F.4 and F.5 had taken to the skies. However, this variant was a very different aeroplane; being optimised for the interceptor role but also having a ground-attack capability.

The F.6 was fitted with a 10,150lb/thrust Avon 203 engine and also benefited from an improved all-moving tail to improve pitch response at high speed. These modifications were joined by a revised wing with a leading edge 'dogtooth' and four hardpoints.

By mid-1956 more than 100 F.6s had been built and an eventual total of 384 would be created for the RAF, replacing the Sabre, Vampire and Venom in service. By 1957 some 19 squadrons operated the Hunter and the variant would serve as the primary day-fighter for ten years until it was replaced by the Lightning in 1963.

Many F.6s were then converted to FGA.9 standard and used in the close air support and ground attack roles. These gained a strengthened wing, as well as a weight in the pitch control circuit to increase stick forces during ground attack manoeuvres. In total, some 128 were converted and the variant entered service with 8 Sqn in January 1960, soon seeing action in Aden and against Indonesian terrorists in Borneo.

Early in the Hunter programme it became evident that a two-seat variant would be both useful and profitable in the export market.

Apart from a new nose section with side-by-side seating and the removal of the gun pack (replaced by a single 30mm cannon fitted to the starboard side), the subsequent T.7 aircraft remained essentially unchanged. The RAF also used the Hunter FR.10 variant in the photo reconnaissance role. These jets were rebuilt from F.6 airframes and housed three F95 cameras in a modified nose section.

By 1970 the RAF's Hunter FGA.9s and FR.10s were leaving service, but this wasn't the end of the type's use in the UK. The RAF retained some T.7s for Buccaneer training until 1994 and even today the type plays an important military role.

In an environment where governments have to balance ever-spiralling defence costs with budgetary constraints, privately-owned Hawker Hunter Aviation (HHA) operates a fleet of former Swiss Air Force Hunter F.58s on the military register for MoD contract work including 'Aerial Threat Simulation & Mission Support Training'. Even though the airframes are 60 years old, their use in the 21st century just goes to prove that you need to go a long way to find a better aircraft than a Hawker Hunter! ■

Handley Page Marathon Designed by Miles Aircraft as a 20-seat airliner. However, Miles went bankrupt before production could begin so Handley Page took over. The Marathon did not perform as advertised and a number of airlines returned their aircraft or cancelled their orders. Most were diverted to the RAF for use as navigation trainers. They were plagued with unreliability so were hastily retired in 1959.

Handley Page Type 88 A research aircraft built to test the aerodynamics of the Victor's crescent wing design. The fuselage from the Supermarine 510 was fitted with a one third scale equivalent of the Victor's and a T-tail. However, as the Victor design was refined, the HP.88 was no longer representative of the eventual bomber. Testing revealed the aircraft was prone to pitch oscillations and it broke up in flight on its 26th sortie.

Hawker P.1067 The ultimate development of the P.1040 was the swept wing P.1067; which was created by Hawker in response to Air Ministry Spec (F.3/48) calling for a fighter capable of 629mph at 45,000ft. The outbreak of the Korean War led to added urgency and the RAF ordered the P.1067 'off the drawing board' in 1950. The prototype P.1067 (WB188) first flew on July 20, 1951 and would soon evolve into the Hawker Hunter.

Reid & Sigrist R.S.4 Bobsleigh When the RAF began to explore 'prone position' technology (which involved the pilot lying face down to fly the aircraft – in an attempt to increase G tolerance) a trials aircraft was needed. The R.S.3 Desford [see p77] was modified to explore slow speed handling and the resulting R.S.4 Bobsleigh (VZ728) had a transparent nosecone. It first flew in June 1951 and tests continued until 1956.

Short SB.1 A tailless research glider designed to test the concept of the aero-isoclinic wing; which maintained a constant angle of incidence regardless of flexing. This was to prevent the tip st[illegible] characteristics of conventional s[illegible] wings and their tendency for [illegible] to reverse at high speed [illegible] written off on its third [illegible] the development of the je[illegible] SB.4 Sherpa.

1

Smoke on, Go!

The Red Arrows has impressed crowds for five decades, but it is just the latest in a long line of RAF aerobatic teams

Unlike the Army and Royal Navy, at the end of the Great War on November 11, 1918, the recently created RAF had no charitable fund upon which injured servicemen and their dependents could call upon for help when needed.

As such, the Royal Air Force Memorial Fund (later renamed as the Royal Air Force Benevolent Fund) was created in 1919 and, keen to raise donations, organised the first Aerial Pageant at RAF Hendon on the outskirts of London a year later.

A staggering 60,000 members of the public came to watch the flying and raised £6,700 (around £250,000 today) for the new fund. The airshow itself included demonstrations by the most modern RAF aircraft (and some captured German aircraft) as well as parachuting and air racing. But it was the formation displays that really captured the public's imagination, as demonstrated by Flt Lt Arthur Coningham and Capt Gerald Gibbs – both instructors at the Central Flying School (CFS) – who flew a spirited routine in a pair of Sopwith Snipes.

Annual Pageant

The Pageant became an annual fixture and in 1921, CFS fielded a team of five Snipes. The following year, 24 Sqn wowed the crowds with a nine-ship formation of Bristol F2B Fighters but 1927 was the real watershed year as CFS introduced formation aerobatics to the display. Using five de Havilland Genet Moths, led by Flt Lt D'Arcy Greig, the team began its display with a formation loop at 2,000ft (610m), followed by a bunt (an inverted half loop) and a half roll. The routine went on for a further six minutes and concluded with a formation spin, with all five aircraft spinning vertically downwards whilst still maintaining formation. In doing so, the CFS team effectively became the first Royal Air Force aerobatic team (RAFAT).

Other CFS teams included five red and white painted Avro Tutors, which demonstrated inverted formation flying in 1933, but as time went by the teams at the annual Pageants

1951

Short Sperrin The SA.4 Sperrin was a 'failsafe' option in case the more technologically advanced V bombers experienced delays. It was a conventional design, powered by four Avon engines, but by the time it was ready to fly the first Valiant was only six months behind it. The project was cancelled but the two prototypes flew as research aircraft and proved useful as engine testbeds and for trials relating to bomb shapes.

Slingsby Kirby Cadet TX.3 The need for a dual control glider for use with ATC Cadet units led to a two seat development of the Cadet TX.2. The new aircraft – dubbed the Kirby Cadet TX.3 by the RAF and T.31B Tandem Tutor in civilian hands – took the fuselage of the T.29 Motor Tutor and increased in length and width. The wings and tail were unchanged. The RAF ordered 126 TX.3s between 1951 and 1959 and they remained in service until 1986.

Vickers Varsity Created as a twin-engined training aircraft to replace the Valetta [see p84]. The key difference was the introduction of a new tricycle undercarriage but the aircraft also had a longer fuselage and greater wingspan. A ventral pannier was also fitted to allow trainee bomb aimers to lie in a prone position and aim the 25 smoke bombs carried within the bomb bay. Varsities flew with the RAF from 1951 until 1976.

1952

Boulton Paul P.120 Developed from the P.111 [see p86] the P.120 had a swept fin and rudder with horizontal tail surfaces high on the fin to improve stability. Unlike the P.111 the wingtips of the P.120 were not removable. It reportedly had pleasant flying characteristics but after just eleven hours of flying it suffered severe flutter, which led to the loss of one of the elevons. The pilot ejected safely, making the first ejection from a delta winged aircraft.

Bristol Sycamore The first British designed helicopter to serve with the RAF. Although it was created as a transport helicopter – for both cargo and/or passengers – the Sycamore was normally used in the search and rescue (SAR) and casualty evacuation roles. Sycamores proved invaluable in the inhospitable terrain of the Malayan and Aden Emergencies and the last SAR examples were finally retired in Singapore in 1964.

2

3

4

1. The modern-day Red Arrows display is split to include large formation sections and more dynamic 'synchro pair' routines. **SDB**
2. In 1933 CFS displayed a team of five red and white painted Avro Tutors at Hendon. **SDB**
3. Gloster Gladiators from 87 Sqn fly in close formation while practicing for the 1937 Hendon Air Pageant. Note the wingtips are tied together!
4. The first RAF jet display teams used the de Havilland Vampire F.1 and F.3.
5. The Black Arrows Hunter team was the first RAF jet team to adopt a special colour scheme; in this case an all-black gloss finish.

5

moved from training aircraft to fighters such as the Bristol Bulldog, Hawker Fury and Gloster Gamecock and Gladiator.

These became regular fixtures at the Pageant and the Empire Air Days held across the country, but the imminent outbreak of war effectively brought 'flying for fun' to a halt in 1938. The last team to appear was a three-ship of Gladiators from 87 Sqn, which was so bold as to tie their aircraft together for their formation aerobatic routines!

The Jet Age

The advancements in technology between 1938 and the return to peace in 1945 took the RAF from biplanes such as the Gladiator to the first generation of jet fighters.

It was therefore this new breed of aircraft that was chosen in 1947 to form the first postwar display team. The job fell to 54 Sqn, which was by then flying the de Havilland Vampire F.1 at RAF Odiham, Hampshire, and three of the jets were displayed by W/O Bill Wood and Flt Lt Colin Colquhoun, led by Sqn Ldr Mike Lyne. Later in the year a fourth jet, flown by Flt Lt John Stacey, joined the team.

After just eleven practice flights the team was signed off to display. Although it had a successful season, including displays in Belgium, the team was disbanded at the end of the year.

For 1948, a joint display team was created by members of 54, 72 and 247 Sqns (all of which were based at Odiham) flying six of the newly delivered Vampire F.3s. During the course of the

de Havilland DH.100 Vampire FB.9 Operating the Vampire in tropical climates was not easy or pleasant. As such, the FB.9 was introduced with air conditioning systems for the pilot and more power to help offset the loss in performance experienced in hot conditions. FB.9s were deployed to Africa where they were used against Mau Mau insurgents in Kenya. A total of 326 were built but they were replaced by Venoms from 1954.

de Havilland DH.112 Venom FB.1 A fighter-bomber developed from the Vampire. The Venom's wing had a swept leading edge and the FB.1 was powered by the Ghost 103 turbojet. It was an interim fighter, bridging the gap from straight wing fighters with centrifugal flow engines and swept-wing aircraft with axial flow engines. The RAF received 375 FB.1s, many of which served in West Germany as well as the Middle East.

de Havilland DH.115 Vampire T.11 The need for a two-seat trainer variant of the Vampire led to the DH.115 programme. This drew upon the design of the Vampire NF.10 and was effectively a night fighter with dual controls fitted and the radar and armament removed. An uprated engine was also fitted. The RAF received 538 Vampire T.11s from October 1952 onwards and more than 3,000 pilots earned their wings on the type.

English Electric Canberra PR.3 & 7 A jet powered replacement for the photo recce Mosquito. The Canberra PR.3 was based on the B.2 but had a 14in bay added behind the cockpit to house seven cameras. It also had an additional fuel tank capacity. The first of 35 production variants was delivered in December 1952. The PR.3 was succeeded by the improved PR.7 variant with greater fuel capacity and more powerful Avon engines.

GAF Jindivik A radio-controlled target drone produced by the Government Aircraft Factories (GAF) in Australia. The Jindivik (named after an Aboriginal word meaning "the hunted one") was powered by an Armstrong Siddeley Viper engine. The RAF received 502 between 1952 and 1986 and the production line was re-opened in 1997 to build another 15. Most British flights took place from RAF Llanbedr in North Wales.

The Blue Diamonds split into two formations of seven and nine aircraft mid display

year, the team crossed the Atlantic to appear in Canada and the USA: the first ever jet-powered crossing of the ocean.

The Vampire remained the chosen display aircraft in 1949 and 1950, with 72 and 54 Sqns both fielding teams; the latter introducing smoke to their routine for the first time.

Meteorites

Meanwhile, both 64 Sqn and 600 Sqn created aerobatic teams flying the Gloster Meteor, but it was the Meteor T.7s of the CFS team that became the first RAFAT to be named. Under the command of Flt Lt Caryl Gordon the 'Meteorites' flew in the 1952 and 1953 seasons, the second year being particularly busy as it coincided with the Queen's coronation. Although the aircraft retained their standard silver colours, they gained high visibility yellow anti-collision training markings towards the end of their first season.

The RAF's new Hawker Hunter began to equip a number of unofficial squadron teams from 1955 onwards, with 54 Sqn the first to fly the type at air displays. The team consisted of four Hunter F.1s and were named the 'Black Knights' for the 1956 season.

That year, 43 Sqn also created a Hunter F.1 team called 'The Fighting Cocks' (a reference to their squadron emblem) but the official RAFAT for the season was deemed to be the Hunters F.6s of 111 ('Treble One') Sqn.

Black & Blue

The Treble One team was the first RAF jet team to adopt a special colour scheme, in this case an all-black gloss finish. Although it was initially unnamed, the team, which was led by Sqn Ldr Roger Topp, were referred to as "Les Fleches Noires" while displaying in France and from then on the 'Black Arrows' name was always associated with the unit.

Although it normally flew five aircraft, the team was famed for its large formation loops and this peaked at the 1958 Farnborough Airshow when it looped and barrel rolled a world record 22 Hunters in formation.

1

2

3

The Black Arrows continued as the RAF's official team until 1961 when it was replaced by the 'Blue Diamonds', which flew 16 blue Hunters belonging to 92 Sqn. Under the leadership of Sqn Ldr Brian Mercer (an ex-Black Arrows pilot) the Blue Diamonds split into two formations of seven and nine aircraft mid display and also flew as four formations of four Hunters. A highlight of the routine was a loop, beginning as four sections of four aircraft that combined into one huge diamond at the top of the manoeuvre, while inverted.

Lightning Force

The English Electric Lightning entered service with 74 Sqn in 1960 and the following year the unit formed a display team using nine of the fighter jets. Named the 'Tigers', it was the first team to fly Mach 2-capable jets and on occasion joined forces with the Blue Diamonds for joint display appearances.

From 1962, the Tigers became the official RAFAT and the powerful aircraft proved to be a crowd favourite, even if it was quite a handful for the pilots to fly in close formation.

In 1963, the mantle of being the RAF's official team was passed to RAF Wattisham-based 56 Sqn, which flew nine red and silver Lightning F.1As in a team called the 'Firebirds.' The team displayed extensively throughout the UK and Europe during the season but it was soon becoming apparent that the Lightning was not

1952

Lockheed Neptune A maritime patrol and anti-submarine warfare aircraft developed for the US Navy to replace the Lockheed PV-1 Ventura. The RAF's 210 Sqn received the first of 52 Neptune Is in January 1952. The Neptune was a stopgap aircraft, pending the arrival of Shackletons, and were used for maritime patrol and Airborne Early Warning (AEW) duties. They were returned to the USA in 1957.

North American RB-45 Tornado Although the B-45 Tornado bomber was quickly superseded the RB-45 recce version flew with the USAF from 1950 until 1959. However, as the USAF was forbidden by the US President from overflying the USSR four RB-45Cs were allocated to the 35 and 115 Sqns at RAF Sculthorpe as part of Operation *Jiu Jitsu*. Painted in RAF markings the aircraft were operated from 1952 until 1955.

Short SB.5 Created to aid the design of the English Electric Lightning. There was dispute over how well a highly swept wing would handle at low speed and whether the tailplane should be mounted below the fuselage or atop the fin. The SB.5 was built to investigate the low speed handling of the various configurations. The plywood wing's sweep could be adjusted and the rear fuselage was detachable to enable the two different tails to be fitted.

1953

Armstrong Whitworth Meteor NF.12 The Meteor NF.11 used fairly antiquated radar equipment but as technology developed, a new night-fighter was developed to use the improved US-built APS-21 system. The resulting NF.12 was 17in longer to accommodate the radar set and the aircraft also had a larger fin to help compensate for the effect of the swinging radar. The type equipped seven squadrons.

Armstrong Whitworth Meteor NF.13 A 'tropicalised' version of the NF.11 for use the Middle East. Developed to replace the Mosquito NF.36 in service with 39 Sqn in Malta and Cyprus and 219 Sqn based in Egypt. Some of the 40 aircraft delivered saw operational service during the Suez Crisis but the type was plagued with problems and were soon retired. Former Royal Air Force aircraft were later sold to Egypt, France, Israel (illustrated).

1. The first English Electric Lightning team was 74 Sqn's Tigers but in 1963 the Firebirds (illustrated) were formed by 56 Sqn. However, the Lightning was a large aircraft to fly in formation and expensive to operate, so soon teams of big fighters were dropped in favour of training aircraft.
2. The first of the RAF's Jet Provost teams was the T.1-equipped CFS Jet Aerobatic Team.
3. In 1961 the Black Arrows were replaced by the Blue Diamonds, which flew 16 blue Hunters belonging to 92 Sqn.
4. The Red Arrows was formed in 1965 and was initially equipped with seven Folland Gnat T.1s.**SDB**

RAF Fast Fact

The Red Arrows is not the only RAF aerial display team. The RAF Falcons parachute display team performs at venues nationwide and is famous for its 'canopy stack' routine.
Based at RAF Brize Norton, Oxfordshire as part of No. 1 Parachute Training School, the team traces its history back to 1961 when the school's instructors formed a team nicknamed 'Big Six'. This soon doubled in size and in 1965 was adopted by the RAF as their official parachute display team, named The Falcons. The Falcons is the only centrally funded, military parachute display team in the UK. It has performed many times for the Royal Family and heads of state, and holds a number of world records.

only unwieldy to display but also expensive to operate. As such, it disbanded in 1964 and holds the distinction of being the final RAFAT to be equipped with fighter aircraft.

Jet Provost

Training aircraft were far more affordable and capable display mounts and CFS had operated the Percival Provost in 1957 and 1958 as the 'Sparrows.' The team formed using four aircraft but in mid 1958 it was re-equipped with the new Hunting Percival Jet Provost T.1. The Sparrows only operated until the end of the season but paved the way for a whole generation of RAF Jet Provost (JP) teams.

For the 1959 season, two of the Sparrows aircraft appeared as a duo; displaying as the 'Redskins' team. Smoke canisters were fitted under each wing and used during synchronised aerobatics. Increased to four JP T.3s in 1960, the team performed for two seasons under the 'CFS Jet Aerobatic Team' moniker. In 1962, the team became the first to operate the JP T.4; with five aircraft and a new name: the 'Red Pelicans'.

A further increase to six aircraft, painted in all-over day-glo red, occurred in 1963 and the Red Pelicans were declared the RAF's official aerobatic team for the 1964 season.

Although it briefly reverted to the CFS Jet Aerobatic Team name for 1965, the Red Pelicans returned in 1966 and continued to appear at displays until 1973; having progressed to the JP T.5 in 1970.

Other Jet Provost teams included the 'Macaws', 'Viper Red', 'Linton Gins', 'Linton Blades', 'Gemini Pair', the 'Swords' and the 'Poachers'. The Poachers' final display was at Waterbeach on September 5, 1976 and it marked not only the demise of the team but also the end, after nearly 20 years, of RAF JP display teams.

From Yellow to Red

Although the official 1964 RAFAT was the Red Pelicans, flying six JP T.4s, several other unofficial teams existed. In fact, by now, almost every RAF flying training school had a display team of one sort or another. Among them, was 4 Flying Training School (4 FTS), which formed a team using the newly-delivered Folland Gnat T.1. Under the command of Flt Lt Lee Jones the jets were painted yellow and took their name from Jones' 'Yellowjack' callsign.

At the 1964 SBAC Display at Farnborough the Red Pelicans joined forces with the Yellowjacks for a combined display, but it was obvious to onlookers that they were witnessing a changing of the guard.

At the end of the 1964 season, all the RAF display teams were amalgamated, as it was feared pilots were spending too much time practising formation aerobatics rather than operational training.

The Gnat seemed the perfect blend of fighter and trainer qualities, so the 4FTS team was selected to represent the RAF in 1965. However, the yellow colour had proved difficult to see in the air (both from a spectator and piloting point

Avro 707C The final Avro 707 variant to fly was the side-by-side two-seat 707C. The RAF had originally ordered four to be used as orientation trainers but the order was subsequently cut to just one (WZ744). The version first flew on July 1, 1953 and played little part in the development of the Vulcan. However, in 1956 it joined the Royal Aircraft Establishment and was fitted with one of the world's first fly-by-wire control systems.

Avro Shackleton MR.2 The MR.2 differed from the MR.1 by having a longer nose and the radome was moved to a ventral position. The aircraft also gained a lookout position in tail and a dorsal turret. The last ten MR.1s on the production line were completed as MR.2s and 59 examples were built as new. MR.2s participated in the 1958 Jebel Akhdar War in Oman and the Malaya; scanning the seas for arms smuggling vessels.

Canadair Sabre 4 In 1948, the RCAF began to re-equip with the North American F-86E Sabre and Canadair was contracted to produce them under licence. The company also produced the type for export and the Sabre 4 was chosen by the RAF as an 'interim' fighter, pending the arrival of the Hunter. Some 438 were provided from January 1953; many under the mutual aid programme. They equipped eleven RAF squadrons.

de Havilland DH.113 Venom NF.2 The Venom NF.2 was developed as a replacement for the Vampire NF.10 and had a modified fuselage to accommodate a two-man crew in side-by-side configuration. The airborne interception radar was installed in an extended nose. The Venom NF.2 entered service in 1953 and was later replaced by the NF.3, which featured enhanced radar and other improvements.

Hawker Hunter Mk 3 Although the first production Hunter F.1 flew in March 1953 delays meant the type would not enter service until 1954 and the sole Mk 3 beat it into service. The F.3 was the modified first prototype (WB188) fitted with an afterburning Avon and aerodynamic modifications. On September 7, 1953, Neville Duke broke the world air speed record in WB188, reaching a speed of 727.63mph [see also p84].

1. In 1980 the Red Arrows swapped its Gnats for Hawks and it has retained them ever since. **RAFAT Archives**
2. The 1965 Red Arrows air and ground crew pose for the camera at RAF Wattisham. **RAFAT Archives**

of view) so the jets were repainted in Post Office red. In tribute to the famed Red Pelicans and Black Arrows, the new RAFAT was christened the 'Red Arrows'.

Red Arrows

With seven Gnats forming the new team, the nucleus of the Yellowjacks' display routine remained in place but a paired synchro element was now added.

Besides Jones, ex-Yellowjacks' pilots Flt Lts Gerry Ranscombe and Henry Prince, plus F/O Peter Hay, were also part of the first Red Arrows line-up. To these were added Flt Lts Ray Hanna, Bill Loverseed and Bryan Nice.

The press got its initial taste of a Red Arrows display when, on May 6, 1965 a special launch event was held at RAF Little Rissington, Gloucestershire. Then, within the same week, Clermont-Ferrand's French National Air Meeting saw the team perform before public eyes for the very first time.

On May 15, the team made its British debut at the Biggin Hill Air Fair and by the end of the 1965 season the Red Arrows had performed more than 60 displays.

Unexpectedly, there was a brief Lightning aerobatics resurgence in 1965 when 111 Sqn's short-lived 'Black Diamonds' displayed at the Paris Air Salon immediately before the Red Arrows. The two teams joined up for two brief passes; neatly transitioning the RAFAT history from the jet fighter era to the jet trainer age.

In 1968, Red Arrows leader Ray Hanna expanded the team from seven to nine jets, as he wanted to expand the permutations of formation patterns. The 'Diamond Nine' pattern was formed and it has remained the team's trademark pattern ever since.

Although the Red Arrows were supposed to be the only RAF display team, others have made brief appearances over the years; including the 'Skylarks' which flew four de Havilland Canada Chipmunk trainers from 1967 to 1971 under the leadership of Flt Lt J F Merry.

Gnat to Hawk

With the BAe Hawk replacing the Gnat in RAF service from the late 1970s the decision was made to transition the 'Reds' to the new aircraft.

1

2

As such, on September 15, 1979 the team flew its 1,292nd and final public Gnat display.

Initially, the team operated to the same limits as in the Gnat but Sqn Ldr Steve Johnson's collision with a boat mast during a Synchro Pair crossing manoeuvre at Brighton on May 17, 1980 resulted in new regulations.

Since 1983, the Red Arrows has been based at RAF Scampton, Lincolnshire and in its fifty plus year history the team has displayed in more than 50 countries as far afield as the USA, Russia, Australia and Asia and is rapidly approaching its 5,000th public display.

Today, the Red Arrows have become a household name and there can surely be almost nobody in the UK that does not know who or what they are. In light of this, the team remains an effective way for the RAF to recruit new members, promote its work and proudly wave the flag for British engineering. ■

1953

Hunting Percival Pembroke The P.66 was a military development of the Percival Prince airliner with a longer wing to help it carry an increased load. The first of 44 entered RAF service in 1953 as the Pembroke C.1 in 1953 to replace the Anson in the communication and transport roles. Six were later built to C(PR).1 photo recce aircraft that saw clandestine service during the Malayan Emergency and in Berlin. **SDB**

Hunting Percival Provost The P.56 Provost beat the Handley Page HPR.2 [see p88] in the bid to become the RAF's replacement for the Prentice trainer. An initial order for 200 aircraft was placed in 1951 and by the time production ended in 1961 some 461 had been built, 388 of which served the RAF. The Provost entered service with CFS in 1953 and students would learn basic flying skills on it before progressing to the Vampire T.11.

Rolls Royce Thrust Measuring Rig The Thrust Measuring Rig (TMR), was better known as the *Flying Bedstead* and was the world's first vertical take off and landing jet. It lacked any lifting surfaces; instead, lift was generated purely by the thrust generated by the Nene engines. The TMR first flew on August 19, 1953 and was initially tethered to a gantry during flights. The programme was of huge value to future VTOL aircraft.

Scottish Aviation Pioneer II A short take off & landing (STOL) communications aircraft. Based on the underpowered A.4/45 Pioneer, but with the 240hp Gipsy Queen replaced with a 520hp Alvis Leonides, the Pioneer II demonstrated incredible STOL performance and was ordered by the RAF as the Pioneer CC.1. It was operated in the casevac role in Aden and Cyprus as well as during the Malayan Emergency.

Short SB.4 Sherpa An experimental jet aircraft to test the aero-isoclinic wing. The SB.4 was based upon (and used some components of) the Short SB.1 glider [see p91] but was powered by two tiny Turbomeca Palas engines. The wing was fitted with rotating tips that acted like elevons and proved to fly well. The name Sherpa was an acronym of Short & Harland Experimental Research Prototype Aircraft.

The RAF Aerobatic Team has used the BAe Hawk T.1 since 1980. In 2019, the Red Arrows went on major tour of Canada and the USA waving the flag for British industry and trade. **Crown Copyright**

Teddy's Supersonic Rocket Ship

Created by Edward 'Teddy' Petter, the English Electric Lightning was the first RAF's first Mach 2 fighter aircraft and the first to be able to climb supersonically from take off

When English Electric set about designing a 1,000mph fighter in the late 1940s its engineers could not have dreamed that their product would be in service for nearly three decades.

The English Electric Lightning came about following the cancellation of the Air Ministry's 1942 E.24/43 supersonic research aircraft specification - which had resulted in the Miles M.52 programme.

English Electric designer William 'Teddy' Petter was a keen early proponent of Britain's need to develop a supersonic fighter aircraft and, after it was proven that the RAF's Gloster Meteor F.4 would be entirely unable to intercept a bomber travelling at 50,000ft (15,240m) and Mach 0.85, he approached the Ministry of Supply (MoS) in 1947 with a proposal to remedy the situation.

Working in response to the new Specification ER.103, which called for a single research aircraft capable of flight at Mach 1.5 and 50,000ft (15,240m), Petter came up with the English Electric P.1.

1

Swept Wing

Petter set about producing a new aircraft with heavily swept wings, a configuration chosen to delay the effects of compressibility which used technology that originated in wartime Germany and had since been adopted by the US (with the F-86). Regardless of wing configuration, two engines would be needed to give the jet any chance of breaching Mach 1. Petter's ingenious design placed these two engines atop each other – rather than side by side – with both being fed air from a single oval intake in the nose.

The MoS issued a design study contract for the production and development of a single aircraft – dubbed the P.1 by English Electric.

In the spring of 1948, English Electric's test pilot, Wg Cdr Roland 'Bee' Beamont was given the chance to fly the XP-86 in California, and in doing so he became the first British pilot to break the sound barrier (in a dive). On his return he relayed his experiences to English Electric and immediately became part of the P.1 design team; the first time a pilot had been allowed to be so intimately involved.

Meanwhile, as Petter's design team set to work on the prototype there was much discussion regarding angle of wing sweep and the positioning of the tail.

Short Brothers were contracted to produce an 'airborne test vehicle' [the SB.5] with the unique ability to carry a selection of wing and tail layouts. Testing of wing sweep at 50, 60 and 69 degrees was undertaken, as was the 'T-tail' and low tail configurations.After several months of trials a wing sweep of 60 degrees and a low set tailplane was found to be the best layout; the swept wing blanked out the effectiveness of the T-tail at high angles of attack.

By May 1949 a formal contract was issued for a 'Design Study For A Fighter With Transonic Performance', but in January 1950 Petter resigned from English Electric and, taking several of his design team with him, moved to Folland Aircraft where he went on to mastermind the Midge and the Gnat.

The company's Chief Stress Analyst, Freddie W Page (later Sir Freddie Page and Chairman of British Aerospace) become the project manager for the P.1 and in April the company received the all-important contract for the design and manufacture of three prototype aircraft.

Engine Choice

From the outset Petter had designed the P.1 to be powered by the Rolls-Royce Avon engine but, after development delays and with production prioritised to the Canberra, none would be available for the proposed first flight date. It was therefore proposed that the non-reheated 7,500lb/thrust Armstrong Siddeley Sapphire S would be used as a temporary replacement.

1954

Armstrong Whitworth Meteor NF.14 The final Meteor night fighter, which was based on the NF.12 but with an even longer nose to accommodate new radar equipment. The biggest improvement over the earlier designs was the introduction of a large bubble canopy to replace the framed version that dated back to the T.7. The first of 100 entered service in 1954 but the type began being replaced by the Javelin within two years.

English Electric Canberra B.6 The second-generation Canberra bomber had two Avon RA.7 engines and extra fuel tanks in the wings. The fuselage was also stretched . In June 1954, the first of 84 B.6s began replacing B.2s with 101 Sqn and this was quickly followed by other units. In turn, this freed up older B.2s to be allocated to overseas units in West Germany and in Cyprus. The last B.6 left Bomber Command service in 1961.

English Electric Canberra T.4 A dual-control training variant of the Canberra based on the B.2. The T.4 introduced side-by-side seating for the pilot and the instructor and the glazed nose was also replaced with a solid unit. The variant entered service with 231 OCU in early 1954. In total the RAF received 68 T.4s and all B.2 equipped bomber squadrons received at least one T.4 for training purposes.

English Electric P.1A In 1948, designer W.E.W 'Teddy' Petter approached the Ministry of Supply with a proposal to build a fighter capable of Mach 2 and 50,000ft. Following Petter's resignation F. W. 'Freddie' Page took over and in 1950 an order was placed for two P.1 prototypes. Power was to come from two reheated Avon engines but these were delayed and the P.1 was powered by Sapphires when it flew in August 1954.

Fairey Delta 2 A delta-winged supersonic research aircraft powered by an afterburning Avon. The long nose (which would normally have obscured the pilot's forward vision during landing) had an innovative drooping mechanism similar to that later used on Concorde. It was the first aircraft to exceed 1,000mph in level flight and in March 1956 it set a world speed record of 1,132mph. It was later modified to BAC 221 standard.

RAF Fast Fact

Lightning F.1 XM135 flew with 74 Sqn as part of the Tigers aerobatic team but is most famous for a single flight that occurred in 1966.
RAF engineer Wg Cdr Walter 'Taff' Holden was carrying out a ground test when he inadvertently activated the aircraft's afterburners and was forced to take off. He was able to land it safely. He later recalled: "I needed to do one more test. On opening the throttles for that final test, I obviously pushed them too far, misinterpreting the thrust...and they got locked into reheat... I had gained flying speed... and I had no runway left. I did not need to heave it off the runway, the previous test pilot had trimmed it exactly for take-off and with only a slight backward touch of the stick I was gathering height and speed... Once airborne, with adrenaline running rather high, I found myself in a rather unenviable position. No canopy, no radio, an unusable ejector seat, no jet flying experience, Comets and Britannias somewhere around me and speed building up...'
Today, XM135 can be seen on display at the Imperial War Museum at Duxford, Cambridgeshire.

1. In August 1955 the MoS issued a contract for the production of three P.1Bs. The first, XA847, performed its maiden flight on April 4, 1957. Although these were only the second version of the aircraft the design would change very little between the P.1B and the Lightning..
2. The father of the breed – English Electric P.1A WG760 first flew in 1954 and paved the way for one of the most charismatic and spectacular aircraft to ever fly with the RAF.
3. Perhaps the most famous of all Lightning photographs was taken by professional photographer Jim Meads. It shows test pilot George Aird ejecting from XG332 at Hatfield on September 19, 1962. There had been a fire in the aircraft's tail when unburnt fuel in the rear fuselage was ignited by a small crack in the jet pipe. This weakened the tailplane actuator anchorage, which broke at 100ft while the jet was landing. Aird landed on a greenhouse and fell through the roof, breaking both legs. The water from the sprinkler system for the tomatoes woke him and he is reported to have said that his first thought was that he must be in heaven.
4. RAF Lightnings could carry either the *Red Top* or *Firestreak* air-to-air missiles.

However - the engine's poor acceleration, coupled with the P.1's lack of fuel capacity, would make supersonic flight very difficult to achieve.

Flying with 'Q'

Traditional cable-operated flight control systems were known to jam at high speeds so irreversible hydraulic screw-jacks were fitted to the P.1. However, these had the disadvantage of removing 'feel' from the pilot, so English Electric introduced a 'Q' unit consisting of a collection of cams and cogs to introduce artificial feel.

With an approach and landing speed estimated to be around 160kts (184mph) it was expected that the first landings would be carried out at speeds approaching 200kts (230mph) – and thus the 1,700m (5,577ft) runway at English Electric's Warton, Lancashire plant was deemed too short and the P.1 was shipped to Boscombe Down for its early 'shake-down' flights.

The first airframe, P.1A WG760, was built at Samlesbury, Lancashire under complete secrecy and it was not until the publication of the 1954 Defence White Paper that the existence of the project was revealed to the public.

The aircraft was ready for its first taxi trials at Boscombe Down on July 24, 1954 and, on at least one occasion, Beamont exceeded 125kts (144mph) - very briefly lifting WG760 from the runway during these 'ground' trials.

Maiden Flight

Having already familiarised himself with the SB.5, Beamont was ready for the maiden flight. It had been hoped to take the jet into the sky on August 3, but as Beamont entered the cockpit, he accidently set off the engine-bay fire extinguishers. It took a day to clear up the mess and it would be 09.58 the following day before the aircraft was airborne. Speed was restricted to just 450kts (518mph) during the first flight and an altitude of 17,000ft (5,182m) was reached, but the aircraft flew much as expected. Despite the flight only lasting 33 minutes, Britain could finally boast its own supersonic fighter. It was the start of three decades of Lightning flying.

Gloster Meteor Prone Pilot A much modified Meteor F.8 created to evaluate the effects of G Force on a pilot flying in a prone position. The jet was used along with the Bobsleigh [see p91] to test the concept. A standard fighter cockpit was retained and it was never flown solo from the prone cockpit. Following 99 test flights, the results showed that the difficulties in rearward visibility and ejection outweighed any advantages.

Hawker Hunter F.1 The first production Hunter F.1 flew in March 1953 but the need to include a ventral air brake delayed the entry into service until July 1954. The first unit to receive the new fighter was 43 Sqn at Leuchars and the only others to receive the F.1 were 54, 222 and 247 Sqns. It was soon discovered that the F.1 could not fire its 30mm Aden guns above 30,000ft without the exhaust gasses causing the engine to flame out.

Hawker Hunter F.2 As an insurance against development problems with the Avon engine, Hawker fitted the third prototype with the AS Sapphire 101 back in 1952. The decision was made to put the engine/airframe combination into production as the Hunter F.2 and 45 joined the RAF. The F.2 did not suffer from the engine flame outs that beset the F.1, but ejected cannon ammunition links did damage the underside of the fuselage.

Supermarine Swift F.1, 2 & 3 A swept wing fighter.. Development problems delayed the F.1's entry into service until 1954 and, even then, the type was hit by a spate of accidents that resulted in it being grounded for a time. The 20 F.1s served with 56 Sqn and the 16 F.2 – which introduced an extra two cannons and a cranked leading edge – joined just days later. The 25 F.3s had a reheated Avon engine but never entered service.

Westland Whirlwind The Sikorsky S.55 built under licence in the UK by Westland. The RAF received its first of 33 HAR.2 variants in 1954 and later that year it was joined by the first of 24 'tropicalised' HAR.4s; these being more suitable to hot and high conditions. A lack of power led to the turbine-powered HAR.10, 68 of which were built and continued in SAR service until 1981. The Royal Flight also operated four Whirlwinds.

The Lightning could accelerate to Mach 2 in under 3½ minutes

Supersonic

On August 11, Beamont flew WG760 for the third time and with throttles pushed to maximum, the airspeed indicator settled at Mach 0.98 at 30,000ft (9,144m). With fuel low, he took the opportunity to carry out a maximum speed turn and landed safely. The following day he would learn that that the Airspeed Indicator (ASI) was calibrated incorrectly and that he had actually become the first British pilot to break the sound barrier in level flight.

On July 18, 1955 the second P.1A, WG763, joined the programme – this benefiting from a removable 2,000 Imp Gal (909lit) ventral fuel tank. A pair of 30mm Aden cannon were also fitted in the upper nose.

Work was soon underway on the next incarnation of the P.1 and in August 1955 the MoS issued a contract for the production of three P.1Bs, soon followed by a further 20 development aircraft.

The first P.1B, XA847, performed its maiden flight on April 4, 1957. Compared to earlier examples, the most notable difference was the replacement of the oval intake with a circular one: this contained a 'bullet' fairing housing an AI.23 radar. The cockpit canopy was raised to increase visibility and a HUD (Head Up Display) was also fitted.

The P.1B was also the first of the family to be fitted with a pair of 11,250lb/thrust Rolls Royce Avon engines.

Although these were only the second version of the aircraft the design would change very little between the P.1B and the Lightning that would enter service. The major difference was the development of a larger fin to improve directional control; this being introduced by the time the first of the development batch aircraft, XG307, flew on April 3, 1958.

Lightning

On October 23, 1958 during the annual SBAC Airshow at Farnborough, XA847 was officially named the 'Lightning' – the same aircraft going on to exceed Mach 2 just a month later.

Soon pre-service trials were underway at Boscombe Down; the first order for 20 Lightning F.1s having been placed by the Air Ministry back in November 1956. The F.1 was powered by a pair of 14,430lb/thrust Avon 200Rs; its armaments consisted of a pair of 30mm Aden cannons in the nose and two *Firestreak* missiles. In June 1960, 74 'Tiger' Sqn became the RAF's first supersonic squadron when it relinquished its Hunters for Lightnings.

With a top speed of over Mach 2 and a ceiling around the 60,000ft (18,288m) mark, the Lightning could reach its operational altitude approximately two and a half minutes after take off. The jet could accelerate to Mach 2 in under three and a half minutes and Mach 1 could be breached without selecting reheat. The aeroplane was also the first RAF single-seater to introduce an integrated weapon system.

1. Avro Vulcan B.2 XH561 of the Waddington Wing is escorted by four Lightning F.6s of 5 Sqn on April 30, 1968 to mark the formation of RAF Strike Command by amalgamating Bomber and Fighter Commands. **Crown Copyright**

Order Book

The F.1 was supplemented by 28 advanced F.1As versions, the first of which (XM169) flew on August 16, 1960. Changes included a refuelling probe under the port wing, a windscreen rain dispersal system and a new UHF radio. The new variant entered service with 56 Sqn at Wattisham in December 1960, followed by 111 Sqn the following April.

The vast majority of F.1s and F.1As were passed onto the operational conversion units by the mid 1960s.

Fifty F.2 variants were ordered in December 1959 (later reduced to 44), this version having a revised cockpit with an Integrated Flight System, an autopilot and a liquid oxygen breathing system. The F.2 entered service with 19 Sqn at Leconfield in December 1962 – the unit moving to West Germany in 1965 to become the first

1955

Auster AOP.9 A successor to the Auster AOP.6 with a much larger wing area and more powerful 180hp Blackburn Cirrus engine. It could take off and land in even tighter spaces than the AOP.6 and could operate from ploughed fields using low pressure tyres. Deliveries to Air Observation Post squadrons began in 1955 but following the formation of the Army Air Corps in 1957 the Austers passed to the Army.

de Havilland DH.112 Venom FB.4 The definitive RAF Venom had a Ghost 103 turbojet and was the first of the family to be fitted with an ejector seat. The tail was also redesigned to prevent yaw problems and the wing with hydraulically-powered ailerons and underwing fuel tanks. The RAF received 250 FB.4s and they saw action during the Suez crisis. Aden-based FB.4s also saw action during the 1957 Omani rebellion. **SDB**

de Havilland DH.114 Heron A small propeller-driven four-engined airliner that was developed from the earlier Dove/Devon [see p82]. The fuselage was longer than the Dove and four 250hp Gipsy Queen engines meant it could carry 14 passengers. The RAF received a single Heron C.2, two Heron C.3s and a Heron C.4 for use by the Queen's Flight at RAF Benson, Oxfordshire. The Herons were fitted with luxurious VIP interiors.

Folland Gnat F.1 A slightly larger version of Petter's Midge [see p90]; the Folland Gnat F.1 was a single-seat fighter armed with a 30mm Aden cannon. Power came from a Bristol Orpheus, which needed larger air intakes than the Midge. Six aircraft were ordered by the Ministry of Supply for evaluation purposes. The RAF did not order the fighter version, but did see the type's potential as a trainer [see p110].

Gloster Meteor U.15 & U.16 In 1955, Flight Refuelling Ltd was contracted to convert 92 Meteor F.4 airframes into unmanned targets to help develop new ground and air-launched missiles. These were called U.15s (U standing for unmanned) and flew from RAF Llanbedr in North Wales. Later, 108 Meteor F.8s were similarly converted into U.16s with the remote control equipment in a 30in nose extension.

2. Lightning F.6 XR760 demonstrates the Lightning's swept wing to good effect as it banks away from the camera. The aircraft first flew in February 1965 and served the RAF until July 15, 1986 when it was lost over the North Sea. The aircraft had just been refuelled from a Victor tanker when a fire started in the jet pipe area and the control column seized. The pilot - Flt Lt R G Bees - ejected and the aircraft crashed seven miles off Whitby, Yorkshire.
3. This is what the Lightning was designed to do; intercepting a Soviet Tupolev Tu-95 Bear bomber at high altitude.

Lightning to serve overseas.

The aircraft were later modified as F.2As with a new fin and the ability to carry either a 610 Imp Gal (2,773 lit) ventral fuel tank or a mixed fuel/Aden-gun pack – something that would remain standard on all subsequent variants. However, the major change to the airframe from the F.2A was a cranked and cambered wing.

F.3 & T-Birds

The Lightning F.3 raised the bar to another level and was the most prolific of the variants. It introduced the more powerful 16,360lb/thrust Avon 301R as well as the larger square cut fin. It had no cannons but could be fitted with either *Firestreak* or *Red Top* missiles and also had the provision of over-wing ferry tanks. XP695 became the first of the breed to enter RAF service on January 1, 1964 at Binbrook.

The need for a two-seat Lightning was evident from the start and the first example, developed from the F.1, entered service in 1962. Dubbed the T.4 the aircraft were eventually replaced by the T.5 (based on the F.3) which also gave the student the added benefit of being able to carry, and fire, missiles.

Ultimate Lightning

The final mark of the Lightning saw the best parts of the F.2A and F.3 rolled into one and was initially designated the 'F.3A Interim' before being redesignated as the F.6.

The aircraft was essentially an F.3 with the cambered wing and enlarged ventral fuel tank from the F.2A. The first example (XP697) flew on April 17, 1964 and the type entered service with 5 Sqn at Binbrook in December 1965. By August 1967 the last of 278 Lightnings had been delivered to the RAF.

Throughout the 1970s the Lightning was the backbone of the UK air defence network, but the arrival of the McDonnell Douglas F-4J Phantom and the later Panavia Tornado F.3 would see the gradual retirement of the fleet.

However, thanks to a variety of avionics upgrades and some careful maintenance, the last Lightning F.6s and T.5s would fly on until 1988, almost three decades after the type initially entered squadron service – not bad for an aircraft that was supposed to have a 'shelf-life' of no more than a decade. ■

4. From front to rear, Lightnings from 29, 56, 111 and 72 Sqns line up neatly for the camera. The 29 and 72 Sqn machines have the taller fins of the F.1 and F.2 whereas the 56 and 111 Sqn aircraft have the square cut fin introduced from the F.3 onwards
5. Lightning F.6 XR773 wears one of the camouflage schemes given to the type in their latter years of service. XR773 joined the RAF in 1966 and following retirement was given the civilian registration G-OPIB. It never flew in the UK but was exported to South Africa where it was operated as ZU-BEW for many years.

1956

Hawker Hunter F.4 & F.5 The F.4 introduced a modified wing featuring 'bag' type fuel tanks in the leading edge and hardpoints designed to carry drop tanks. The F.4 also had bulges below the fuselage to catch spent ammunition cases. These were dubbed 'Sabrinas' after a movie star Norma 'Sabrina' Sykes. The RAF received 349 Avon-powered F.4s and 105 of the almost identical F.5, which was fitted by the Sapphire 101 engine.

Hunting Percival Jet Provost T.1 The RAF's first purpose-designed jet trainer. The Jet Provost (JP) was developed from the Provost [see p96] and used many of the same parts. In the case of the first 12 examples this included the same long, spindly undercarriage legs. The RAF ordered ten of these as JP T.1s for trials in 1955; these paving the way for a family of JP trainers that served the RAF until the 1990s. **SDB**

Supermarine Swift F.4 The F.4 introduced a variable incidence tailplane to correct handling problems that had plagued earlier Swifts. It also had an afterburner but testing showed this would not ignite at high altitude. The F.4 would be the last Swift variant designed for the interceptor role but performance was so bad that half of the airframes built were converted to FR.5 standard while still at the factory.

Vickers Valiant The Valiant was used in early atomic tests and had the dubious distinction of being the only V bomber to drop live nuclear weapons. The first Valiants joined 138 Sqn, but advances in missile technology meant the fleet was switched to the low-level strike and tanking roles. Valiants were used for conventional bombing during the Suez Crisis but in 1965 premature fatigue was found and Valiants were retired.

Blackburn Beverley Developed from the General Aircraft GAL.60 Universal Freighter, the Beverley was powered by four 2,850hp Centaurus engines. Even fully loaded it could take off in 787 yards and land in 283 yards. The first of 47 was delivered in March 1956 and they were used for cargo and troop carriers, accommodating 94 troops in the main cabin and 36 more in the tail boom. They flew until 1967.

Mutual Assured Destruction

The V Force was designed to protect Britain from nuclear attack and – if necessary – retaliate. Thankfully they never needed to undertake the role for which they were created

In the postwar years, there was an urgent need for Britain to develop a bomber capable of dropping a thermonuclear weapon on cities within the Soviet Bloc. The intention was never to drop such a bomb; it was hoped that merely having the capability would act as a deterrent to the USSR. This was the Mutual Assured Destruction (MAD) concept and worked on the "if you bomb us, we'll bomb you" principle.

The requirement for a nuclear-capable long-range jet bomber was noted as early as July 3, 1945 when a Joint Technical Warfare Committee report examined the future potential of nuclear weapons. The following year the Air Ministry issued requirements for the development of turbojet-powered heavy bombers capable of carrying thermonuclear weapons at high altitude and high speed. The new aircraft would have no need for defensive armament.

In January 1947 the requirements were formulated into Specification B.35/46. This called for a four-engined, swept-wing bomber with a cruising speed of 500kts (575mph) and a ceiling of at least 55,000ft (16,764m). It needed to be capable of carrying one 10,000lb bomb to a target 1,500 miles (2,414km) from its base.

From the organisations who applied, the Ministry shortlisted three manufacturers to submit advanced designs - AV Roe, Handley-Page and Vickers-Armstrong - and it was decided to award contracts to each company as a form of insurance in case one design failed.

1

Valiant

Vickers' Type 660 was ordered in April 1948 (against Specification B.9/48 which had been written around the design) and in February 1949 two prototypes of the aircraft were ordered.

The aircraft had a shoulder-mounted wing with a 'compound sweep.' This gave the wing a 37-degree angle of sweepback across the inner third of its span, reducing to 21 degrees at the tips to postpone the effect of buffeting and drag at high speed.

The entire airframe was built from a complex zinc/magnesium/copper aluminium alloy called DTD683 and the cockpit section was pressurised, allowing the pilot, co-pilot, two navigators and an electronics operator an element of comfort – although only the pilot and co-pilot had ejection seats.

The first prototype (WB210), wearing a gleaming natural-metal finish, took to the air on May 18, 1951 – just 27 months since the contract had been placed – and a month after its maiden flight the aircraft was given the official name of 'Valiant'; the name selected by a survey of Vickers employees.

The first production Valiant B.1 flew in December 1953 with four 9,500lb/thrust Avon 201 engines. It featured bomb bay doors that retracted up into the fuselage to facilitate bomb loading and the nosewheel could be extended to provide additional ground clearance. By the time production ended in August 1957, some 107 Valiants had been produced.

The RAF roundels were repainted in a faded pink-white-baby-blue

Anti-Flash

Valiants, as well as other V bombers, were originally finished in silver but once equipped with nuclear weapons they were painted in 'anti-flash' white to reflect the glare of a nuclear blast. Initially the RAF roundels were left in solid red-white-blue but as it was later realised the insignia might be permanently burned into an aircraft by a nuclear blast, they were repainted in a faded pink-white-baby-blue.

1956

de Havilland DH.106 Comet 2 Developed from the Comet 1 (which suffered high profile accidents in the early 1950s) the Mk 2 was modified with thicker skin and rounded windows. Although 12 were built as airliners for BOAC eight joined the RAF, becoming the first jet transports in military service. The RAF eventually operated 15 C/2s in the transport, flying hospital, signals intelligence (SIGINT) and electronic intelligence (ELINT) roles.

English Electric Canberra B(I).6 &8 Low-level strike and ground attack 'interdictor' variant of the Canberra. The B(I).6 was a B.6 converted to carry four 20mm cannon in the bomb bay and had underwing pylons for bombs and rockets. The first of 22 joined the RAF in March 1956 but was beaten into service (by two months) by the new-build B(I).8, which had a new forward fuselage and offset teardrop canopy.

Gloster Javelin FAW.1 & 2 A night and all-weather interceptor. Although the Javelin [see also p108] first flew in 1951, delays to its weapons system meant it would be 1956 before it entered service. The FAW.1 had Sapphire Sa.6 engines, British-built AI.17 radar and an electrically operated all moving tailplane. After 40 had been built production switched to the 30 FAW.2s, with US-made AN/APQ-43 radar and a hydraulically operated tail.

Gloster Meteor T.7 ½ Meteor T.7 WA638 became an ejector seat trials aircraft in 1949. During a major service in December 1956 the aircraft was fitted with the tail from a Meteor F.8 to confer greater stability than the original rounded unit. This led to it being designated as a 'Meteor 7 ½'. Since then the aircraft, and sistership WL419, have conducted hundreds of live ejections. In 2015 the aircraft were given civilian registrations.

Hawker Hunter F.6 The F.6 mated an Avon 203 with a new wing that had a distinctive 'dogtooth' leading edge notch to improve pitch response at high speed. The F.6 joined 19 and 66 Sqns in October 1956, but of the 515 ordered by the RAF only 379 would be supplied (the rest cancelled in the 1957 Defence White Paper). The last F.6s were replaced in the day fighter role by English Electric Lightnings by 1963.

2

RAF Fast Fact

A 1953 report estimated that an attack on the UK by the USSR with 132 nuclear fission weapons would generate 2 million casualties. In the event that hydrogen bombs were used it was estimated that as few as ten could reduce the entire UK to radioactive ruin. There was no defence against these weapons, other than the threat of Mutual Assured Destruction; in other words "if you bomb us, we'll bomb you back." In 1957, the Air Ministry drew up a list of 44 Soviet cities with crucial administrative centres. It was estimated that their destruction would kill around 30% of the population of the Soviet Union, about 38 million people. V bombers relied on the concept of dispersal to escape the effects of an enemy attack on their ten main bases. In times of heightened tension the force, already loaded with their nuclear weapons, could be flown to the 26 dispersal bases where they could be kept at a few minutes readiness.

3

1. The V Bomber trinity: Vulcan, Victor and Valiant. **Crown Copyright**
2. The second prototype Vickers Valiant (WB215) had larger air intakes and a stronger tail than the first aircraft.
3. A line-up of eight Valiant B.1s shortly after delivery. The aircraft shed their silver schemes in favour of anti-flash white when they took on the nuclear bombing role.

The Valiant B.1 flew with eight squadrons at its peak (7, 49, 90, 138, 148, 207, 214 and 543) and served with distinction in the Suez Crisis in late 1956, dropping conventional bombs on Egyptian targets.

The Valiant also played a vital role in nuclear testing and, as such, was the only V bomber to ever drop live nuclear weapons.

Once the other V bombers were in full service (by 1962) the Valiant force was retasked as a Tactical Bomber Force, operating at low level to deal with ever-improving Soviet defences. Some were converted to tankers but corrosion and fatigue cracking led to the fleet being grounded and eventually retired in 1965.

The Valiant had played its role in the V Force; it had provided the RAF with a perfectly capable bomber while the more radical and advanced Victor and Vulcan were being developed.

The 'Mighty Delta'

Perhaps the most famous of all the V bombers was the Avro 698 Vulcan – the radical delta-winged leviathan that captured the imagination of generations.

The type would be the second V bomber to fly and although the unusual design met favour with the Air Ministry, it was considered risky enough to warrant a series of scaled-down flight-test demonstrators. These small delta-winged jets (christened the Avro 707s) would evaluate the handling characteristics of the wing concept and, by all accounts, showed much promise. As such, Avro proceeded with a pair of full-scale prototypes even before the 707 programme had concluded.

The Avro 698 would carry a crew of five (pilot, co-pilot, navigator/radar, navigator plotter and air electronics officer) who were accommodated on two levels within the pressurised cabin.

The planned Bristol Olympus turbojets were not ready in time for the maiden flight so the prototype (VX770) was powered by four 6,500lb/thrust Rolls-Royce Avons when it first flew on August 30, 1952, with test pilot 'Roly' Falk at the controls.

Two landing gear door fairings fell off during the flight, but inspection by a chase aircraft revealed the aircraft was safe to land.

The original plan had called for the aircraft to be named 'Ottawa' (in line with the RAF tradition of naming bombers after cities) but by October 1952 the name 'Vulcan' had been settled upon.

The first Vulcan B.1 version flew on February 4, 1955: the type entered service with 230 OCU in early 1957 and was declared squadron-ready in July when 83 Sqn received its first example. A total of 45 B.1s were built before April 1959 and equipped 44, 50, 83, 101 and 617 Sqns, initially in silver but later clad in 'anti-flash' white paint.

1957

Saunders Roe Skeeter A training helicopter based on the Cierva W.14. The Skeeter had a 215hp Gipsy Major engine and three bladed rotors. The Army ordered 64 Skeeter AOP.12s, the first of which entered service in 1956. When the Army Air Corps was formed in 1957 the Skeeters transferred to it from RAF operation. However, the RAF operated three Skeeter T.13s at the CFS Helicopter Wing until 1964. **RuthAS/WikiCommons**

Supermarine Swift FR.5 & 7 By the time the Swift programme was scrapped it had cost £20 million (around £490 million in 2020!). It did, however, lead to 94 fighter-recce Swift FR.5s, which replaced the Meteor FR.9 in RAF Germany from 1956. It had a lengthened nose and a new wing featuring a 'saw tooth' leading edge. The follow-on Swift F.7 was to be fitted with guided missiles, but only 14 were built and none ever serviced with the RAF.

Avro Shackleton MR.3 A major redesign of the earlier Shackleton with a tricycle undercarriage. The MR.3 also had wingtip fuel tanks to extend the endurance and soundproofing for the crew. The type entered service with 220 Sqn in August 1957 and had a normal endurance of 18 hours; although some reportedly stayed aloft for more than 24 hours. Later versions had two Viper jet engines to improve take off performance.

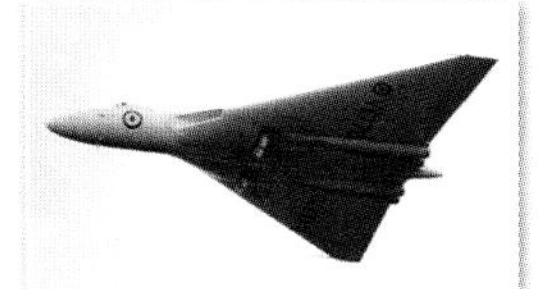

Avro Vulcan B.1 The second V bomber to enter service. B.1s originally had a wing with a straight leading edge but these were later retrofitted with 'kinked' wings. A total of 45 B.1s were delivered, 28 of which were later upgraded to B.1A standard with ECM and in-flight refuelling receiving equipment. Unlike the B.2, the B.1As did not undergo wing strengthening for low level operations, and were retired by 1967.

English Electric P.1B A second phase of prototypes aimed at pushing the Lightning to Mach 2. Compared to the P.1A the three P.1B prototypes looked very similar to the eventual production aircraft and had the conical inlet cone. They also had variable reheat and AI.23 radar. The first example exceeded Mach 1 on its maiden flight in May 1957 and on November 25 it became the first British aircraft to reach Mach 2.

'Kinked'

The two prototypes were fitted with a simple delta wing with a 52-degree sweepback but this suffered from buffeting at high speed. The Royal Aircraft Establishment therefore proposed a 'kinked' wing, with the sweep reduced to 42 degrees at one-third span and returned to 52 degrees at two-thirds span.

Although the first five B.1s were delivered with straight wings (in order to meet delivery schedules) they were refitted with the kinked wings while in service.

The aircraft could carry a total bomb load in excess of 21,000lbs (9,525kg) and was designed to accommodate the 40-kiloton *Blue Danube* fission bomb and the *Green Cheese* anti-ship weapon – although the latter was later cancelled.

An ARI 18074 *Green Palm* voice channel jammer was the B.1's only defensive countermeasures system. This was increased for the 28 B.1A variants which were retrofitted with a *Blue Diver* low-band jammer, *Red Shrimp* high-band jammer, *Blue Saga* radar warning receiver and chaff dispensers as well as a *Red Steer* tail-warning radar derived from the system used on Meteor night fighters.

However, Avro was already working on the B.2 variant of the Vulcan. This would include the aforementioned countermeasures and retained the 'kinked' wing. The separate elevator and aileron control surfaces were also modified to act as combined 'elevons'.

The first Vulcan B.2 flew for the first time on August 31, 1957 and the type entered service in July 1960. This variant would eventually fly with 9, 12, 27, 35, 44, 50, 101 and 617 Sqns and the last of 89 B.2s were delivered in January 1965.

The Vulcan B.2 formed the backbone of British nuclear strike capability in the 1960s and remained in the role through the 1970s.

It was originally equipped with the *Yellow Sun* Mk 2 thermonuclear weapon but by 1963 was retrofitted to carry the *Blue Steel* rocket-powered stand-off weapon that could be launched long distances from its target and cruise at Mach 2.3.

However, the adoption of Polaris-equipped submarines as the UK's nuclear deterrent symbolised the end of the road for the V-Force. The bombers were camouflaged, fitted with terrain-following radar and relegated to low-level flying duties, penetrating enemy lines at just 50ft (15.24m).

1

2

'Black Buck'

The entire Vulcan fleet was slated to retire in 1982 as the Tornado GR.1 was entering service in the low-level attack role. However, the Vulcan had time for one final 'hurrah' as it was called into combat for the first and last time.

In the type's eleventh hour, it was considered to be the only aircraft capable of dropping conventional bombs onto the runway at Port Stanley on the Falkland Islands, which had been invaded by hostile forces belonging to Argentina's military. [Ed: see p116]

Five Vulcan B.2s were selected to fly with 101 Sqn during *Black Buck* missions conducted as part of Operation *Corporate*. Operating from Wideawake airfield on Ascension Island in the mid-Atlantic, the Vulcans would fly the longest bombing missions ever (at the time). Using eleven Victor tankers for support, the Vulcans set out on the night of April 30, 1982 with a full load of 21 x 1,000lb bombs. The 7,500-mile round trip took 16 hours and *Black Buck 1* was a success – the Vulcan had finally been blooded.

It was in the refuelling role that the Victor really made its name

The final mission, *Black Buck 7*, took place on the night of June 11and by December 1982 the last Vulcan bomber was retired.

A small number of K.2 tanker conversions continued to operate until 1984 but in March of that year the Vulcan was withdrawn from service completely.

The RAF bowed to public pressure and kept two examples (XL426 and later XH558) as display aircraft until the end of 1992 but on March 23 of the following year, XH558 made the final flight by an RAF V bomber.

1957

Gloster Javelin FAW.4 & 5 The FAW.4 was similar to the FAW.1 but included an all-moving tailplane. The 50 FAW.4 also included vortex generators on wings to improve the stall characteristics. The first joined 141 Sqn in February 1957. The 64 FAW.5s was very similar to the FAW.4 but had additional fuel tanks within the wings. The 33 later FAW.6s (based on the FAW.5) had US-built radar in place of the British AI.17 unit.

Gloster Javelin T.3 The Javelin's handling proved to be sufficiently 'different' to warrant the development of a dual-control training variant. The first of 21 Javelin T.3s entered service in October 1957. The T.3 lost the fighter's radar but retained the cannons for gunnery training. It also had a bulged canopy to improve instructor visibility and a lengthened fuselage to compensate for altered centre of gravity.

Handley Page Victor B.1 The most futuristic-looking of all V bombers, the Victor had a highly swept T-tail and a crescent-shaped wing. Weapons included a single 10,000lb nuclear bomb or 48 x 1,000lb bombs. The first of 50 B.1s were delivered in late 1957; 24 of which were later converted to B.1As with ECM equipment. When the V-Force was relegated to low-level operations, 21 B.1As were converted to refuelling tankers.

Hawker Hunter T.7 The two-seat Hunter was created as an advance trainer for the RAF. Apart from a new nose section with side-by-side seating, the 'dogtooth' wing from the F.6 and the removal of the gun pack the T.7 was essentially unchanged from the F.4. In fact six examples rebuilt from damaged or retired F.4s and 65 airframes built as two-seaters from new. Some were later converted to T.7A standard with Buccaneer instruments.

Miles M.100 Student Created as a private venture by FG and George Miles as a lightweight trainer for the RAF. The Miles M.100 Student was an all-metal, side-by-side, two seater powered by a single 882lb/thrust Turbomeca Marbore jet engine. The prototype flew for the first time on May 15, 1957 as G-APLK and was registered XS941 for testing by the RAF. The Student lost out to the Jet Provost in the contest.

1. Some members of the Valiant fleet were modified to BK.1 tanker configuration, as demonstrated by WZ376.
2. Valiants prepare to perform a simulated scramble at the 1960 SBAC Airshow at Farnborough.
3. The earliest Vulcans had a straight leading edge, whereas later examples had a 'kinked' wing.
4. VX770 was the first Vulcan to fly, taking off from Woodford, Cheshire on August 30, 1952, with 'Roly' Falk at the controls.
5. Three Avro Vulcan B.1As of the Waddington Wing in flight sometime in 1957. **Crown Copyright**
6. The two prototype Vulcans (VX770 & VX777) join forces with the four Avro 707s at the 1953 Farnborough Airshow.
7. The prototype Handley Page HP.80 aloft in early 1953. It was later painted black and silver with a red cheatline for its appearance at that year's SBAC Airshow at Farnborough.
8. Victor B.1 XA918 lands at the 1957 SBAC Airshow at Farnborough with Vulcan prototype VX777 in the background.

1958

Saunders Roe SR.53 A prototype mixed-power interceptor fitted with a Viper jet and Spectre rocket. It would use the rocket to climb towards bombers and then return to base using the jet. The SR.53 first flew in May 1957; just a month after the 1957 Defence White Paper was published outlining Britain's policy to abandon piloted aircraft. Nevertheless, the SR.53 flew 56 times before the programme was cancelled in July 1960.

Short SC.1 The first British fixed-wing vertical take-off and landing jet aircraft and the first VTOL-capable aircraft with fly-by-wire. The SC.1 was designed specifically for exploring the transition between vertical and horizontal flight and was powered by five RB108 turbojets; four for vertical flight and one for conventional horizontal flight. It flew for over ten years and provided data for concepts such as the 'puffer jet' controls on the Harrier.

Gloster Javelin FAW.7 The first Javelin capable of carrying the *Firestreak* - Britain's first infrared homing air-to-air missile. It also had uprated Sapphire 7 engines and could carry four drop tanks. The FAW.7 entered service in June 1958 and it became the most prolific model with 142 being produced. However, due to the quick introduction of the FAW.8, around 80 FAW.7s never saw service and were placed directly into storage.

Hunting Percival Jet Provost T.3 The RAF was impressed with the JP T.1 [see p101] but requested some changes. These included a dorsal fillet, a more powerful Armstrong Siddeley Viper engine and - most notably - a shortened and strengthened undercarriage. The RAF ordered a total of 201 of the resulting T.3, which were delivered between 1958 and 1962 and many remained in service until 1993.

Scottish Aviation Twin Pioneer A STOL aircraft designed for both civil and military operators. Powered by two Alvis Leonides engines and fitted with three tail fins to help maintain control at very low speeds, the 'Twin Pin' could also carry bombs under the stub wings. The RAF received 39 examples and these were mostly operated in Aden. It saw extensive use in the Malayan Emergency and in later conflicts in Borneo.

Victor

Handley-Page answered Specification B.35/46 with its HP.80 design – an aircraft that was perhaps the most unconventional of all three bombers and one that still looks 'space-age' to this day.

The aircraft was intended to operate at high speed and above the ceiling of its contemporary fighters. To achieve this it featured a revolutionary 'crescent' wing, with the sweep decreasing in three steps from 48.5 degrees to 37.5 degrees and finally to 26.75 degrees from the root to the tip. The chord similarly decreased to ensure a constant limiting Mach number across the entire wing and guarantee a high cruise speed.

In 1952 the prototype HP.80 (WB771) was hauled by road from the Handley-Page factory to Boscombe Down for flight trials. To disguise the aircraft from prying eyes, it was shrouded in wooden frames and wrapped in tarpaulins. 'Geleypandhy/ Southampton' was written on the side, as if it were a boat being transported to harbour ('Geleypandhy' was supposed to be an anagram of 'Handley Page', but it actually decoded as 'Handley-Pyge'!).

The HP.80 was a striking aircraft. It had four Sapphire turbojet engines buried in the thick wing roots and a highly swept T-tail with considerable dihedral. The nose bulged to accommodate the cockpit and targeting radar. The original specification called for the entire nose to detach as an escape pod but this was later abandoned.

The aircraft would accommodate a five-man crew, but as with the other V bombers, only the pilots were provided with ejector seats; the others relying on 'explosive cushions' inflated by a CO2 bottle that would help them from their seats and towards the door to bail out!

1

Into service

WB771 took to the skies on Christmas Eve 1952 with Sqn Ldr Hedley Hazelden at the controls. Flight testing revealed some deficiencies and on July 14, 1954 WB771 was lost when the tail unit sheered off at low level. The crew were all killed.

The second prototype (WB775) already featured a reinforced tail and performed its initial flight on September 11, 1954; the first sortie including a triumphant flypast at that year's SBAC airshow.

The first production variant emerged on February 1, 1956 – by which time the aircraft had been officially named the Victor B.1. Just over a year later, test pilot Johnny Allam 'accidentally' broke the sound barrier during a test flight; the Victor becoming the largest aircraft to exceed Mach 1 at the time.

The aircraft entered RAF service in November 1957, with the first machines joining 232 OCU. The first operational unit (10 Sqn) began receiving its jets in April 1958.

A total of 50 B.1s were built, equipping 15, 55 and 57 Sqns. The last was delivered in February 1961 by which time production switched to the Victor B.2. This featured the *Red Steer, Blue Saga, Green Palm, Blue Diver* and *Red Shrimp* and also had 17,250lb/thrust Rolls-Royce Conway 103 turbojets alongside larger air inlets to provide greater airflow. The first of 34 B.2s flew on February 20, 1959 and joined 139 Sqn in February 1962. It would also equip 100 Sqn.

Soon the introduction of Soviet surface-to-air missiles made the V Force's high-altitude tactics obsolete and in common with the other V bombers, the Victors were re-tasked as low-level bombers. For this they received updated navigation radar and rolling map displays and were camouflaged from 1964.

The Valiant was the only V bomber to ever drop live nuclear weapons

Tanking & Spying

The Victor never fired a shot in anger; the closest it got was a deployment to Singapore in response to Indonesian hostility towards Malaysia but its services were never needed.

In the mid-1960s, eight Victors were converted to B(SR).2 strategic reconnaissance configuration, the first flying on February 23, 1965. This version accommodated up to 15 film cameras in the bomb bay and was mostly used for maritime reconnaissance missions.

The introduction of the B.2 quickly made the early B.1/1A variants obsolete. Rather than retiring the aircraft, they were converted to tanker configuration, becoming the B.1A(K2P) variant from February 1966.

Like the Valiant, the Victor was not cut out

1958 **1959** 

Slingsby Swallow TX.1 A fabric covered wooden glider with a 13.05m wingspan. The first T.45 Swallow flew in October 1957 and while most of the 115 built were sold to private owners and clubs, 14 were operated by the RAF as the Swallow TX.1. The Air Training Corps received five examples and nine others were operated by branches of the Royal Air Force Gliding and Soaring Association. The Royal Navy Gliding Association also had four. **SDB**

Bristol Britannia A medium-range turboprop civil airliner that was known as the 'The Whispering Giant' for its quiet Proteus engines. When the RAF's Vickers V.1000 programme was cancelled in 1955 the decision was made to order Britannias. The RAF ultimately received 23 of the type; 20 Britannia C.1s and three C.2s. The C.1 could accommodate 115 troops or cargo whereas the C.2 was a pure transporter with a heavy duty floor.

English Electric Lightning F.1 An order for the full production version of the Lightning F.1 was received in November 1956 and the first of 19 airframes made its maiden flight on October 3, 1959. The new fighter entered service with the Central Fighter Establishment in December 1959. The F.1 had a pair of 14,430lb/thrust Avon 200R engines and was fitted with a VHF radio, a pair of 30mm Aden cannons and two *Firestreak* missiles.

Gloster Javelin FAW.8 The FAW.8 benefited from reheated Sapphire Sa.7R/204 engines; however, problems with the fuel pumps meant reheat could only be engaged above 20,000ft. The Javelin FAW.8 was also fitted with an autopilot and drooping outer leading edges on the wing. The 48th Javelin FAW.8 (XJ615) was the last Javelin to be produced and also the last aircraft to be manufactured by Gloster.

Avro Vulcan B.2 Fitted with a larger and thinner wing than the B.1 and more powerful Olympus engines. The first of 89 B.2s (XH558) was delivered to the RAF in July 1960. Later, B.2s later had their wings strengthened to give additional fatigue life to enable them to fly at low level and nine were modified for a maritime radar reconnaissance role. Six also became airborne tankers. The type was finally retired in 1984.

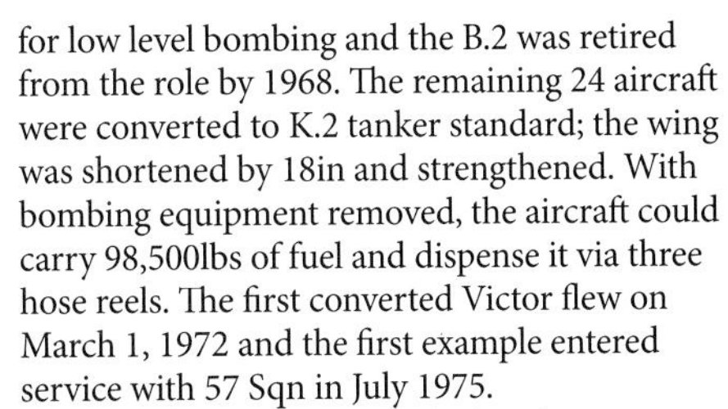

for low level bombing and the B.2 was retired from the role by 1968. The remaining 24 aircraft were converted to K.2 tanker standard; the wing was shortened by 18in and strengthened. With bombing equipment removed, the aircraft could carry 98,500lbs of fuel and dispense it via three hose reels. The first converted Victor flew on March 1, 1972 and the first example entered service with 57 Sqn in July 1975.

It was in the refuelling role that the Victor really made its name. In 1982 the aircraft played a vital part in Operation *Corporate*, refuelling aircraft en route to the Falkland Islands – including the Avro Vulcans of the famous *Black Buck* missions.

Operation *Corporate* involved more than 600 Victor sorties and decimated the tanker fleet's airframe life. Just 15 aircraft flew on after the campaign but eight of would return to war one final time following Iraq's invasion of Kuwait.

As part of Operation *Granby*, Victors provided tanker services to RAF and US aircraft, flying 229 sorties supporting air patrols over Iraq into 1993.

Almost immediately after their return to the UK, 55 Sqn (the last Victor unit and the last squadron to operate a V 'bomber') disbanded in October 1993. The V-Force had finally had its day. In 2007, Avro Vulcan B.2 XH558 returned to the air as a civlian-owned airshow machine. 'Vulcan 558' was a crowd favourite until it was finally grounded at Doncaster Airport in October 2015 when the last remnants of its fatigue life were expended. ■

1. Although it first took flight in 1952 the Handley Page Victor still looks 'space age' today. The bulged nose accommodated a pressurised area for the flight crew .
2. The Victor found its post-nuclear niche as an aerial refueller. This Victor K.1 is re fuelling Lightning F.6s.
3. When it was relegated to low-level bombing, the V Bomber fleet was camouflaged.
4. Victor K.2s wait on the ground at Ascension Island in the North Atlantic pending their next tanking mission during Operation *Corporate* in 1982. In the foreground are Nimrods and Harrier GR.3s.
5. The Victor's swansong came in 1991 when examples of the K.2 variant were despatched to the Gulf to refuel allied aircraft during Operation *Granby*.
6. Ely Cathedral provides the backdrop for a flypast of two aircraft from RAF Wyton on August 28, 1959. Victor B.1 XA935 leads Valiant B(PR).1 WZ391 of 543 Sqn. **Crown Copyright**

English Electric Canberra PR.9 The final version of the Canberra had powerful Avon 206 engines. A total of 23 were built by Short Brothers & Harland and fitted with special LOROP (Long-Range Optical Photography) cameras as well as infra-red linescan cameras; the latter used to search for arms dumps in Northern Ireland. The PR.9 was used in the Kosovo War, Iraq and Afghanistan. The last PR.9 was not retired until 2006. **SDB**

English Electric Lightning F.1A The F.1A saw the Lightning's capability increase with the fitting of a long refuelling probe under the port wing as well as a wind-screen rain dispersal system and a UHF radio. The first of 28 examples, XM169, made its maiden flight on August 16, 1960 and the type entered service with 56 Sqn at Wattisham in December 1960. Like the F.1, the F.1A was limited to Mach 1.7 and was soon replaced by the F.2.

English Electric Lightning T.4 The first two-seat variant of the Lightning, which was developed from the F.1 and had a widened cockpit to accommodate an instructor and pupil in a side-by-side layout. The cannons were removed but the sights and radar displays retained to allow weapons training. Although 30 examples were ordered just 21 were completed and deliveries began (to the Lightning Conversion Squadron) in 1960.

Gloster Javelin FAW.9 The ultimate version of the Javelin was the FAW.9, all of which were converted from FAW.7s. Gloster began by modifying the 76 unused FAW.7s that were in storage; these gained FAW.8 leading edges, autopilot and reheated engines. Around 40 examples also gained refuelling probes to become FAW.9Rs. Other FAW.7s were returned from squadrons for conversion and in total some 118 FAW.9s were produced.

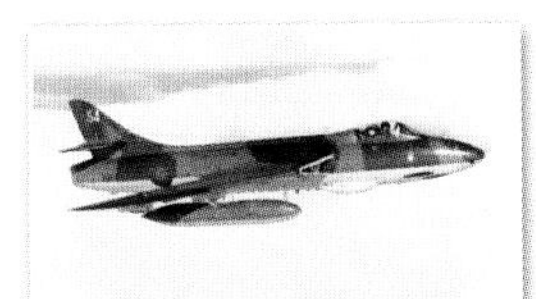

Hawker Hunter FGA.9 With the Hunter F.6 being retired from its day fighter role (being replaced by the Lightning) many surplus airframes were returned to Hawker and converted to FGA.9s for close air support missions. The woeful performance of the Swift left the RAF in need of a ground attack aircraft and 128 airframes gained strengthened wings, large drop tanks, a braking 'chute and modifications to increase stick forces.

The Flying Flat Iron

The Gloster Javelin heralded a new generation of jet-powered all-weather RAF interceptor

During World War Two both the Allies and Axis nations honed the technology and skillset necessary to fight aerial battles at night. However, the advent of jet technology would have a major effect on the next generation of night-fighter.

The first postwar RAF aircraft to carry out these duties were the de Havilland Vampire and Gloster Meteor but in 1948 Air Ministry Specification F.4/48 (OR.227) was issued calling for a two-seat, twin engined night/all-weather fighter. Both de Havilland and Gloster reached the final stages of the contest with very technologically advanced aircraft.

In the end, de Havilland's DH.110 was considered best suited to the Royal Navy (and would become the Sea Vixen) and the RAF opted for the Gloster GA.5.

In late 1948 the Air Ministry ordered the construction of the first three GA.5 prototypes – the aircraft being based around a large delta wing with a tall T-tail and a wide fuselage housing a pair of 8,000lb/thrust Bristol Siddeley Sapphire Sa.6 engines. Armament would come in the form of four 30mm Aden cannons and a number of missiles were being developed in conjunction with the airframe.

The large delta wing and tailplane soon led to Javelins being nicknamed the 'Flying Flat Iron'.

Lucky Escape

On November 26, 1951, the prototype Gloster GA.5 (WD804) became the world's first twin-engined delta-wing fighter to fly when Gloster's chief test pilot Sqn Ldr W A 'Bill' Waterton took it aloft from Moreton Valance, Gloucestershire.

Although it was unarmed and relatively light, flight testing revealed the aircraft had a propensity for buffet and 'flutter' at high speeds. This reached a critical point on June 29, 1952 when the elevators were ripped off and Waterton managed to force-land the crippled jet just as it was catching fire. Despite the inferno, he managed to remove the flight data recorder – an act that earned him the George Medal.

The second prototype (WD808) took to the air on August 20, 1952 but it flew very little over the next year as engineers struggled to find solutions to the 'flutter' issues. It was eventually fitted with a redesigned wing, as was third prototype, which also the first example to be fitted with Aden guns and radar. By now the aircraft had officially been dubbed the Javelin.

The project was struck a huge blow on June 11, 1953 when WD808 was lost after the aircraft entered a 'deep stall', a problem that would remain with Javelin throughout its life. In such a situation the wing acts as an airbrake and kills forward motion, also blanking the airflow over the stabiliser; meaning the elevators cannot be used to remedy the situation.

Above. Javelin FAW.7 XH794 of 64 Sqn. This aircraft was written off on September 9, 1962 when it overshot on landing at Wildenrath, West Germany due to hydraulic failure. It struck a telegraph pole, then ran through the boundary fence. The pilot ejected moments before it came to rest inverted. The navigator did not eject and was trapped for several hours before being released with serious injuries. **Andy Hay/www.flyingart.co.uk**

Into Service

The Ministry of Supply ordered 40 Javelins in 1952 and the first production Javelin FAW.1 entered service with 46 Sqn at RAF Odiham, Hampshire in February 1956. The FAW.1 was fitted with four 30mm Aden cannons and a British-built AI.17 radar but the latter was the cause of much consternation with crews and engineers. The unit simply proved 'un-useable' in the early days and the 30 Javelin FAW.2 variants would see this replaced by the American Westinghouse AN/APQ-43 radar – dubbed the AI.22 by the RAF.

The type soon evolved into the FAW.4, which reverted to the original AI.17 radar but,

1960

Hawker Hunter FR.10 Like the FGA.9, the 33 fighter reconnaissance Hunter FR.10s were developed from surplus F.6s. The FR.10 was created as a replacement for the Swift FR.5 in the 2nd Tactical Air Force and fitted with three cameras in the nose. The type saw service in Aden, alongside FGA.9s, during the Radfan campaign against insurgents attempting to overthrow the Federation of South Arabia.

Hawker P.1127 The forerunner of the Harrier [see also p112] conducted its initial tethered flights in October 1960. Powered by an early version of the Pegasus, the P.1127 had to be stripped of all unnecessary weight in order to hover. Conventional flying followed in February 1961 and the first transition took place in the June. Six were built, proving the VTOL fighter concept and paving the way for the subsequent Kestrel [see p111].

1961

Armstrong Whitworth Argosy A troop transport and cargo aircraft with four Dart turboprops and a distinctive twin boom design. Known by many nicknames, including 'The Whistling Wheelbarrow', the first of 56 entered RAF service in November 1961 and Argosies replaced the Valetta and Hastings in the transport role. It could carry 69 troops, 48 stretcher cases or 29,000lb of freight. The last cargo variant retired in 1975.

Bristol Belvedere Developed in conjunction with a Navy version (that was later cancelled) the Belvedere gained some naval design features. Notably, the front undercarriage was taller than the rear to give clearance for loading torpedoes. This, however, hampered troop transportation as the main door was 4ft above the ground. The RAF received 26 Belvederes, which saw combat in the Aden Emergency and in Borneo.

Handley Page HP.115 A research aircraft built test the low-speed handling characteristics of slender delta wings. The HP.115 featured a very low aspect ratio delta with fixed undercarriage 'borrowed' from a Jet Provost. A Viper turbojet was mounted over the wing at the base of the fin. Testing showed the aircraft could fly safely at speeds as slow as 60kts and over 13 years of testing it provided valuable research data.

1. The Javelin FAW.1 entered service with 46 Sqn at RAF Odiham, Hampshire in February 1956. The FAW.1 was fitted with four 30mm Aden cannons and AI.17 radar.
2. Javelin FAW.8 XH976 shows its Firestreak missiles as it banks away . This variant had reheated Sapphire Sa.7R/204 engines that could each produce 12,390lb thrust – however, problems with the fuel pumps meant reheat could only be engaged above 20,000ft.
3. The ultimate version of the Javelin was the FAW.9, seen here in Singapore..

more importantly, benefited from a number of modifications to overcome the 'deep stall' phenomenon. Most significantly, the aircraft gained a hydraulic all-moving tailplane to give more elevator control (the original elevators were retained as trim control) but vortex generators were fitted on the upper surface of the large wing to help prevent the early onset of a stall.

The FAW.4 entered service with 141 Sqn at RAF Horsham St Faith, Norfolk in February 1957 and the FAW.5 (which introduced a new wing capable of carrying an additional 250 Imp Gal of fuel) joined 151 Sqn at RAF Leuchars, Fife in May of the same year.

In total, some 50 FAW.4s and 64 FAW.5s were produced and these were supplemented from October 1957 by 33 FAW.6s – which were based on the FAW.5 but fitted with the American AI.22 radar.

Firestreak & Reheat

The next major development of the Javelin saw the introduction of the *Firestreak* missile – Britain's first infrared homing air-to-air missile.

The FAW.7 was the first Javelin capable of carrying the *Firestreak* and the new variant also benefited from uprated 11,000lb/thrust Sapphire 7 engines. The FAW.7 could also carry four drop tanks and from a pilot's perspective, the variant was the most pleasant of all Javelins to fly – primarily because of its yaw stabilisation system.

The FAW.7 entered service with 33 Sqn at RAF Leeming in June 1958 and it became the most prolific model with 142 being produced by both Gloster Armstrong Whitworth.

However, due to the quick introduction of the FAW.8, around 80 FAW.7s never saw service and were placed directly into storage.

The much-modified FAW.8 benefited from reheated Sapphire Sa.7R/204 engines that could each produce 12,390lb thrust; however, problems with the fuel pumps meant reheat could only be engaged above 20,000ft (6,096m). This Javelin variant was also fitted with an autopilot and drooping outer leading edges on the wing. The 48th Javelin FAW.8 (XJ615) was the last Javelin to be produced when it left the Moreton Valance factory in August 1960. It was also the last aircraft to be built by Gloster.

The large delta wing and tailplane led to the nickname the 'Flying Flat Iron'

Upgraded

With the last Javelin manufactured in 1960, Gloster set about a major modification programme that would convert 76 of the FAW.7s in storage to FAW.9 standard.

The aircraft gained the FAW.8's leading edges, autopilot and reheated engines; 40 examples also gained 20ft-long refuelling probes to become FAW.9Rs. Other FAW.7s were returned from squadrons for conversion and in total some 118 FAW.9s were produced for the RAF.

At its peak, the Javelin served with 14 units in the UK, Europe and the Far East but the closest that the RAF's Javelins came to combat was during the Malaysian Confrontation (1963-65) when 60 and 64 Sqn aircraft from RAF Tengah in Singapore flew combat patrols over the jungles of Malaysia.

Javelins were also deployed to Zambia during the early stages of Rhodesia's Unilateral Declaration of Independence in 1965 and 60 Sqn deployed to Kai Tak in Hong Kong in 1967 because of unrest during China's Great Proletarian Cultural Revolution.

In June 1967, a flypast at RAF Tengah, Singapore marked the end of eleven years of Javelin operations. ■

1962

Handley Page Victor B.2 In order to boost the altitude of the Victor it was fitted with Conway turbofans. The resulting Victor B.2 also had extended wingtips and the first of 32 joined the RAF in October 1961. Later, 21 were modified to B.2R standard with 20,600lb/thrust Conways and the ability to to carry a *Blue Steel* nuclear missile. When they switched to low level the Victors were camouflaged and flew at less than 1,000ft.

Hunting Percival Jet Provost T.4 Hunting Percival looked into ways of improving the JP T.3 design further. The airframe was found to be 'sound' but instructors requested a boost in performance. The T.4 replaced the 1,750lb/thrust Viper 8 with a more powerful 2,500lb/thrust Viper 11 engine. Apart from the engine change the T.4 was indistinguishable to the T.3. The first of 198 was delivered in November 1961.

Bristol 188 A supersonic research aircraft nicknamed the 'Flaming Pencil'. Created to assess the kinetic 'heat soak' effects of flying at Mach 2 for extended periods of time, the Bristol 188 was made of 'puddle welded' stainless steel. Power came from two Gyron Junior turbojets but these thirsty engines combined with the limited fuel capacity in the slender fuselage meant endurance was just 25 minutes. Neither could it reach Mach 2.

de Havilland DH.106 Comet 4 The most successful of the Comet jetliner series was the Mk 4. It had the stretched fuselage from the one-off Comet 3 with greater fuel capacity and was powered by four Avon engines. In airline service it could seat up to 119 passengers but in RAF use the Comet 4 accommodated 94 troops. Just five were delivered to the RAF; the first arriving in February 1962. The final Comet C.4s retired in 1975.

English Electric Lightning F.2 & F.2A Compared to the Flightning F.1 the 44 F.2s gained a liquid oxygen breathing system and an autopilot. Later, 30 F.2s were returned to the Warton factory for conversion to F.2A standard. These aircraft gained a new tail fin and could house either an enlarged ventral fuel tank or a mixed fuel/Aden-gun pack setup in the belly. It also boasted a cranked and cambered wing.

Naval Leftovers

The RAF didn't initially want the Blackburn Buccaneer, but when it received surplus Royal Navy examples it put them to good use. The type eventually went to war in 1991

1

The Soviet Navy's Sverdlov Class cruisers, which were introduced in the early 1950s, represented a significant threat to NATO as they were far superior to anything hitherto available.

The Royal Navy suggested employing carrier-borne aircraft as the most cost-effective solution but, contrary to the prevailing practice, these would be required to fly at very low-level and high-speed to avoid detection: most likely whilst delivering a tactical nuclear weapon.

The Admiralty issued a specification in June 1952 as Requirement NA.39, calling for a two-seat bomber that could fly at Mach 0.85 at 200ft (61m) over a range of 400 miles (644km) while carrying all weaponry internally. For the early 1950s, such a specification would require considerable advances in design and manufacturing techniques: some advised the government that such an undertaking was beyond the abilities and expertise of the day.

Initial plans required the aircraft to carry a new Fairey Aviation anti-shipping nuclear missile, known as *Green Cheese*; but when this was scrapped in the mid-1950s, the primary weapon became the *Red Beard* freefall nuclear bomb. Other weapons were to include rockets, bombs and missiles; while secondary roles included reconnaissance and performing in-flight refuelling.

Blackburn had a long association with providing aircraft for the Fleet Air Arm (FAA), but this had ended in the late 1940s. As such, the company had very little experience of the complexities of modern jet design and certainly nothing to match the enormity of the project they were bidding for. Blackburn was, in many respects, the surprise winner, but would prove any doubters wrong with its outstanding low-level strike aircraft.

Boundary Layer Control

Critical issues included creating an airframe robust enough to withstand the constant stresses of carrier take offs and landings, and low-level flying. Also key were the slow-speed handling characteristics of the aircraft, particularly the ability to maintain sufficient lift during approach and landing.

Wind tunnel tests on Blackburn's initial design revealed problematic airflow issues across several areas of the airframe. This was solved by applying recently discovered US transonic research known as the 'Whitcomb Area Rule': bulging the rear of the aircraft and narrowing the front slightly. It gave the NA.39 a very distinctive 'Coke bottle' appearance, but minimised drag and improved range.

In order to reduce approach speeds Blackburn considered deflecting the engine exhausts, but instead adopted Boundary Layer Control (BLC). This required the jet exhaust to be diverted from the engine and blown via a series of slots along the leading edge of the wing, and near the flaps and ailerons. Research indicated that take off and landing speeds could be reduced while the amount of lift generated by the wing would almost double, allowing a smaller wing to be employed.

Construction of the first prototype (XK486) commenced in 1957 and the still-unnamed Blackburn NA.39 prototype completed its maiden flight on April 30, 1958. Blackburn was taken over by Hawker Siddeley in 1960, by which time the NA.39 had been christened the Buccaneer S.1.

64 aircraft transferred from the FAA to the RAF

The original de Havilland Gyron Junior engines proved insufficiently powerful so a decision was taken to re-engine the aircraft with Rolls Royce Speys before the S.1 had even entered service, leading to the Buccaneer S.2.

The 'Bucc' (as it was commonly known) entered FAA service in 1961 and 801 Naval Air Squadron (NAS) became the first operational Buccaneer unit in July 1962.

However, the Buccaneer's time with the Navy was to be limited as a change to defence policy in the mid-1960s resulted in large reductions to the Britih armed forces. Among the casualties was the FAA, with three of its frontline Buccaneer squadrons (736, 800 and 803 NAS) soon being disbanded.

1962 — 1963 — 1964

Folland Gnat T.1 Although the RAF failed to order the Gnat F.1 [see p100], Folland modified it into a two-seater. It was ordered as an advanced trainer to transition pilots between the Vampire T.11 and operational fighters. The last of 105 was in service by May 1965. The primary user was 4 FTSl but they also served with the Yellowjacks display team in 1964 and the Red Arrows from 1965 to 1979. The last 4 FTS examples were retired in 1978. **SDB**

Hunting H.126 A trails aircraft to evaluate blown flaps. These routed exhaust gasses through ducts and blew it across the flying controls; thus simulating a higher speed than the aircraft was actually flying. This meant the aircraft could fly extremely slowly. Jet nozzles in the tail controlled pitch and yaw while wingtip nozzles controlled roll. Full span flaperons with air blown across them meant the take off speed was just 32mph!

BAC 221 One of the Fairey Delta 2s [see p98] was later modified with a new ogival delta wing and used as a test aircraft for the Concorde programme. The fuselage was extended by 6ft and a much taller landing gear was fitted (to simulate that used on Concorde). The engine intakes were also moved under the wing and extra fuel tanks fitted. Fitted with an Avon RA.28, the aircraft flew on May 1, 1964 and would eventually reach Mach 1.6.

BAC TSR.2 A tactical strike and reconnaissance aircraft developed to be used at high speed and low level by the RAF. The prototype flew in September 1964 but the project was cancelled due to escalating costs and military/political infighting. Hawker's Sir Sydney Camm famously said: "All modern aircraft have four dimensions: span, length, height and politics. TSR-2 simply got the first three right."

English Electric Lightning F.3 & F.3A The F.3 was the most prolific mark of Lightning. It introduced the more powerful Avon 301R but retained the original straight edged wing. F.3s also had a square cut fin and provision for over-wing tanks. The F.3 had upgraded radar that could control *Firestreak* or *Red Top* missiles. The first of 70 entered service on January 1, 1964. The 16 F.3As had extended range ventral tanks.

RAF Fast Fact

For much of its development the Buccaneer was referred to as the Blackburn Advanced Naval Aircraft or BANA. This led to a nickname that lasted – the 'Banana Bomber'.

1. Although operated by the RAF the Buccaneer retained the folding wings that were designed for use aboard carriers. **SDB**
2. RAF Buccaneers served alongside Tornados and Jaguars during the first Gulf War. **SDB**
3. Pre-production Buccaneer S.1 XK534 was one of four that attended the 1961 SBAC Airshow at Farnborough and flew an aerobatic display.

RAF Service

Meanwhile, the defence cuts also spelled the end for the RAF's BAC TSR.2 attack aircraft and later for its planned replacement (the General Dynamics F-111K). With a limited number of options available to replace the Canberra fleet, the Buccaneer was shoehorned into service with the RAF, and the irony was palpable.

Blackburn had originally suggested a version of the Buccaneer for the contract that was ultimately awarded to the TSR.2. Meanwhile, the RAF had spent a decade ignoring and refusing to contemplate the Buccaneer while the Navy had campaigned tirelessly against the TSR.2. In a twist of fate, the Navy was now being downsized and its Buccaneers passed to the RAF!

In July 1968 the RAF ordered 26 Buccaneers and a further 17 bolstered numbers in 1974. Upon inheriting the 64 aircraft from the FAA the RAF also took on the maritime strike role.

In 1972, the final FAA unit (809 NAS) moved to RAF Honington, Suffolk. It operated alongside the RAF until it disbanded in December 1978, bringing Naval Buccaneer operations to an end.

The RAF received two versions of the Buccaneer, the S.2A and S.2B, the latter being capable of carrying the Martel anti-radiation missile. The first unit to receive them was 12 Sqn (in October 1969) followed by 15 Sqn, 16 Sqn, 208 Sqn, 216 Sqn and 237 OCU (Operational Conversation Unit). While 12 and 216 Sqns were assigned to anti-shipping duties, the others performed overland interdiction and strike missions, with 15 and 16 Sqns based at RAFG Laarbruch in Germany.

The 1980s saw 12 Sqn move from Honington to RAF Lossiemouth in Scotland and absorb 216 Sqn. They were soon followed by 208 Sqn and 237 OCU with the Buccaneer fleet in Scotland focusing on anti-shipping applications.

The aircraft would continue in this capacity with the RAF into the 1990s. However, the Buccaneers in the overland strike role with 15 and 16 Sqns were replaced in 1984 as the new Tornado GR.1 came into service.

Middle East Missions

Both the FAA and RAF Buccaneers saw operational service.

FAA examples were deployed to trouble spots to provide air cover, such as in 1966 when 800 NAS aboard HMS *Eagle* helped enforce the Rhodesian oil embargo.

Later, RAF Buccaneers deployed to RAF Akrotiri, Cyprus in September 1983 for six months in support of British peace-keeping troops involved in the civil war in Lebanon. This included very low-level flights flown over Beirut to demonstrate what was described as "British intent and capability".

However, the single event that really brought the Buccaneer to wider public attention was the Gulf War and Operation *Granby* in 1991. It was decided that the RAF Tornado strike force would bomb from medium level with Buccaneers despatched from the UK to support them in the target laser designation role with the ANQ-23E *Pave Spike* pod.

The first mission supporting the Tornados was on February 2, but once air superiority was achieved they swapped self-defence missiles in favour of laser-guided *Paveway* bombs, the first being dropped by a Buccaneer on February 21. During the conflict 12 Buccaneers and 18 crews were deployed, flying 226 sorties with no losses.

However, by now the Buccaneer was already past its projected retirement date and the final RAF examples performed their last landings in March 1994. After nearly 32 years of operational service the Buccaneer was finally grounded as a front-line military aircraft. ■

1965

Hawker Siddeley Kestrel The Ministry of Aviation obtained the budget to produce nine production standard P.1127 aircraft [see p108] to be operated by the Tri-partite Evaluation Squadron (TES) in collaboration with the US and West Germany. The resulting Kestrel FGA.1 was a P.1127 with swept wings, a larger tail and a 15,000lb/thrust Pegasus 5 engine. The TES proved the aircraft's suitability for operations and led to the Harrier.

Westland Wessex A heavy lift helicopter based on the Sikorsky H-34 built under licence in Britain. One of the main changes was the replacement of the piston-engine with a pair of de Havilland Gnome turboshafts. The RAF used Wessexes for SAR duties as well as a battlefield transport. The Queen's Flight also had the type and both Princes Philip and Charles flew them. The last RAF Wessex was not retired until 2003.

Beagle Basset A twin-engined light transport designed for civilian operators. The RAF ordered 20 Bassets as high speed aircraft to transport fully equipped V-Bomber crews to dispersal airfields in the event of war. However, the weight of the crew was so high that on landing the undercarriage would depress and the propellers would touch the ground! In reality, two Bassets were required: one for the crew and one for their equipment.

English Electric Canberra T.17 The 'wart-nosed' Canberra provided a unique service to the RAF. Fitted with electronic countermeasures (ECM) it was used to provide a realistic 'opposition' during exercises. Equipment could simulate Soviet equipment and even broadcast 'spoof' radio calls. The RAF received 24 T.17s (all converted from B.2s), some of which were upgraded to T.17As with more powerful ECM 'gadgets'.

English Electric Lightning F.6 Initially designated the 'F.3A Interim' the final RAF single-seater Lightning saw the best parts of the F.2A and F.3 rolled into one. The 55 F.6s had the cambered wing and enlarged ventral fuel tank from the F.2A. The first new F.6 entered service with 5 Sqn at Binbrook in December 1965 and would continue in RAF service until 1988; when it was finally replaced by the Tornado F.3.

Harrier – A Vertical Reality

The Harrier 'jump jet' was the most innovative aircraft ever to serve the RAF. Designed to operate from forward bases during the Cold War it saw combat around the globe

The idea of a jet fighter that was capable of high sub-sonic speeds but could stop in flight and land vertically in the middle of forest clearings or even a supermarket carpark might have seemed like 'pie in the sky' in the 1950s, but that was exactly what the 'boffins' at Hawker Siddeley were trying to make a reality.

However, in a typically British trait, the technology behind this revolutionary machine was initially largely ignored by the UK government. Had it not been for US funding the Harrier might never have left the drawing board.

Research into Vertical Take Off & Landing (VTOL) fixed wing flight really began in France in the 1950s. Michel Wibault submitted a proposal to the French Air Ministry for a VTOL fighter aircraft called the Gyroptére. Although the aircraft was too heavy and complicated, the engine – which directed its exhaust out of centrifugal blowers – showed potential.

However, the French government refused to fund further research and Wibault was advised to approach the US for financial support through the Mutual Weapons Development Program (MWDP). This had been set up in the postwar period to help finance the development of weapons of interest to NATO, but which were not being supported by their own governments.

The MWDP approached the British government for help but the response was lukewarm at best. However, the MWDP knew that Bristol Aero Engines was interested in VTOL projects and arranged for Wibault to meet the company.

Bristol's Brainchild

Bristol took Wibault's concept and both lightened and simplified it. It then fitted an Orpheus turbojet with a second drive shaft and a turbine driving the first two stages of an Olympus compressor. The Olympus exhausted via two nozzles (which could be rotated from aft to vertically downwards) and the Orpheus exhausted rearwards in a conventional jet pipe.

1

Soon, engineers realised that splitting the Orpheus' jet pipe and fitting two more nozzles would permit all of the engine thrust to be vectored. In order to control the aircraft in the hover – when the flying surfaces would be ineffective as no air was passing over them – the decision was made to vent some of the exhaust to small 'puffers' on the nose and wingtips.

The new engine, named the Pegasus, was marketed to Hawker Aircraft Ltd (later Hawker Siddeley Aviation), which was already working on a lightweight Short Take Off & Landing (STOL) aircraft referred to as the P.1127.

US Funding

Design work on the P.1127 was conducted by Sir Sydney Camm and Ralph Hooper of Hawker Aircraft and Stanley Hooker of Bristol Aero Engines. The aircraft showed great potential but, again, the UK government failed to show any meaningful support of the project. Luckily, the MWDP had more vision and in June 1958 it agreed to provide 75% of the funding for a small number of Pegasus engines.

The following year the British Ministry of Supply (MoS) published a requirement for a Hawker Hunter ground attack and reconnaissance replacement.

The aircraft's dimensions and configuration were dictated by the unusual layout of the Pegasus engine. It needed to have a high or shoulder mounted wing to accommodate the nozzles and this meant a conventional undercarriage would need to be long (and therefore potentially weak).

The decision was therefore taken to fit a 'bicycle' type landing gear, with wheels below the fuselage and outrigger stabilisers on the wingtips. The wing itself had substantial anhedral, which was necessary in order to minimise 'dutch-roll' characteristics. This anhedral also meant the wingtips were closer to the ground, thus reducing the length of outrigger undercarriage legs.

1965

1966

English Electric Lightning T.5 Whereas the two-seat Lightning T.4 was based on the F.1 the later T.5 had its origins in the F.3 and, as such, benefited from the extra power of the Avon 301R. The first T.5 (XM967) was removed from the T.4 production line and converted at Filton; a further 21 aircraft followed it into the air. The first 'twin tub' was delivered to 226 OCU at Coltishall in April 1965 and some remained in service until 1988.

Handley Page Victor SR.2 With the V Force relinquishing its high altitude nuclear bomber role the RAF converted nine Victor B.2s for strategic recce purposes The Victor SR.2 received an array of cameras, a radar mapping system and 'sniffers' to detect particles released from nuclear testing. A single SR.2 could map a 750,000 square mile area in just six hours. The last airframe was retired in March 1975.

Hawker Siddeley HS125 Dominie The RAF ordered 20 examples of the HS125 business jet as Dominie navigation trainers and these served from 1965 until 2011. The HS125 was later modernised by British Aerospace as the BAe 125 and four of these joined 32 'The Royal' Sqn in 1971 as the BAe 125 CC.1. In 1978, two six-seat versions also joined the unit (as the CC.2) and Series 700 jets arrived from 1982 as the CC.3.

Westland Sioux HT.2 As well as the 150 Agusta-Bell/Westland 47G helicopters operated by the Army Air Corps as the Sioux the RAF also operated 15 Westland built examples in the training role. These were based with the Central Flying School at RAF Tern Hill and the first Sioux HT.2 was delivered in mid-1965. The Sioux HT.2s was used by the RAF's first helicopter display team, the Tomahawks, in 1967 and 1968.

Hawker Siddeley Andover A turboprop transport aircraft developed from the HS 748 airliner. The military version had an upswept rear fuselage and a 'kneeling' landing gear to aid ramp loading. The RAF ordered 31 Andover C.1s as cargo aircraft and six passenger carrying CC.2s (including two for the Queen's Flight). Two C.1s were converted into C.1(PR)s for photo recce duties and seven became E.3s for radio and navigational aid calibration.

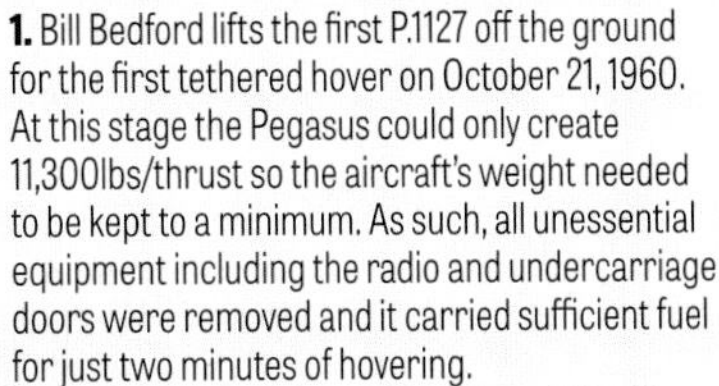

1. Bill Bedford lifts the first P.1127 off the ground for the first tethered hover on October 21, 1960. At this stage the Pegasus could only create 11,300lbs/thrust so the aircraft's weight needed to be kept to a minimum. As such, all unessential equipment including the radio and undercarriage doors were removed and it carried sufficient fuel for just two minutes of hovering.
2. Wearing Tripartite markings Kestrel XS688 poses for the camera in 1963. Today this aircraft is in the Wright-Patterson Museum in the USA.
3. Six pre-production Harrier GR.1s pictured at the manufacturer's test facility at Dunsfold aerodrome, Surrey, in 1968. **Crown Copyright**
4. Following a sortie, two Harrier GR.1s are positioned back in their hides and readied for another flight during a field deployment exercise held in March 1972. **Crown Copyright**

P.1127

In late 1959, the MoS finally awarded funding for two P.1127 research prototypes (to be registered XP831 and XP836) and XP831 was rolled out of the factory on August 31, 1960.

The aircraft performed its maiden flight on October 21, with Hawker's chief test pilot Bill Bedford at the controls. The initial flights were tethered hovers but Bedford almost lost his chance to make history. A few days before the flight he fractured his ankle in a car accident and was put in plaster. He spent the next couple of days flying two-seat aircraft to prove his abilities and he was finally signed off as fit to fly. He is probably the only pilot in history who's medical declared "Fit; *tethered hovering only*".

Testing went well with the P.1127 making its first 'conventional' forward flight and on March 13, 1961 and the first full transition from hover to forward flight on September 12.

Four extra prototypes (XP972, XP976, XP980 & XP984) were ordered but soon the project hit disaster. XP836 was destroyed on December 12 when a nozzle broke at low level, but Bedford was able to eject at the last moment. Then, on June 16, 1963, XP831 crashed at the Paris Air Show following an uncommanded nozzle rotation. Bedford was not seriously injured, but the aircraft did not fly again for more than a year.

Kestrel

On February 8, 1963, XP831 performed the first V/STOL operations from an aircraft carrier at sea, when it embarked on HMS *Ark Royal*.

RAF Fast Fact

Just a month after the Harrier joined the RAF a special celebration took place to mark the 50th anniversary of the first transatlantic crossing by John Alcock and Arthur Brown. The Daily Mail sponsored an air race between London and New York and the RAF saw this as a good way to promote its new jet's capabilities.
It was actually a race between the Post Office Tower in London to the Empire State Building in New York and each competitor had to commute to/from the nearest airfield before they could begin the aerial section of the race. This is where the Harrier had an advantage and Sqn Ldr Tom Lecky-Thompson used a coal yard next to St Pancras station in London (illustrated above) from which to take off. He then landed on the quayside of the Bristol Basin in New York just 6hrs and 11 minutes later.

By now, the US Government proposed that the P.1127 should be the subject of a joint British/American/German programme to evaluate V/STOL aircraft. This entailed both tripartite funding to help build nine aircraft and the funding of a three-nation squadron to aid test flying. Air and ground crew were drawn

1967

Short Belfast A heavy lift turboprop freighter built exclusively for the RAF. The aircraft suffered from excess drag and was unkindly nicknamed the 'Bel-slow.' In 1976, the fleet of ten was retired and sold into civilian hands. In 1982, the RAF chartered them back to carry equipment to the Falklands and in 1990 they flew to the Gulf carrying helicopters that were too large to be carried by the RAF Hercules fleet.

Vickers VC10 C.1 Developed from the civilian jetliner as a strategic transport. The RAF would ultimately receive 14 VC.10 C.1s, which combined the 'Standard' VC10 airframe with the more powerful engines and fin fuel tank of the Super VC10. Deliveries began in 1966 and the aircraft saw extensive use around the globe. By the late 1980s, the 13 remaining C.1s were fitted with refuelling pods and became C.1K tanker/transports.

Lockheed C.130K Hercules When the RAF needed a medium range transporter it ordered 66 of the then-new Hercules [see p124]. The first C-130K entered service (as the Hercules C.1) in April 1967. Defence cuts in 1975 saw the fleet reduced by 13 aircraft. Thirty C.1s were later extended by 15ft to create the C.3; the first of these arriving in 1980. Due to their high airframe hours the C-130Ks were retired in 2013.

Slingsby T.53B Created to meet a need to replace the wooden gliders used by the Air Training Corps with a new metal two-seater. The T.53B was built for evaluation and the first flew in March 1967. It had a flush riveted light alloy construction with a slightly forward swept wing; the latter to give the rear a better view. The RAF ordered 40 but the arrangement was cancelled following a fire which destroyed the Slingsby factory.

1969

BAC Jet Provost T.5 Designed as a pressurised replacement for the JP T.3 & T.4 fleet. It had a more bulbous nose and a different canopy. The wings were also strengthened to carry tip tanks. The RAF ordered 110 JP T.5s and the first joined CFS in September 1969. The fleet was updated in 1973 with new avionics and 94 had their tip tanks removed to become T.5As. T.5s were the last JPs in RAF service and finally retired in 1993. **SDB**

from the RAF, Luftwaffe, and the US Air Force, Army and Navy. All of the American pilots were test pilots, while those from the UK and Germany were from front-line squadrons.

The evaluation aircraft were dubbed the Hawker Siddeley Kestrel FGA.1 and although largely similar to the P.1127 these had a 15,000lb/thrust Pegasus. Other changes included a slightly swept wing, an anhedral tailplane (for improved longitudinal stability); a larger tail fin and two extra hard points on the wings to carry fuel tanks.

Harrier GR.1

The RAF was sufficiently impressed with the P.1127 to order six development aircraft (XV276-XV281) in February 1965. These were designed around Operational Requirement OR.356, which included the latest 19,000lbs/thrust Pegasus. The first of these flew on August 31, 1966 and early the following year the aircraft was named Harrier GR.1.

A follow up order for 60 aircraft was made on January 18, 1967 and the first production Harrier GR.1 was flown on December 28.

The first Harrier joined 1 Sqn at RAF Wittering, Cambridgeshire on April 1, 1969 and the Harrier Conversion Unit was 'stood up' at the same base on April 18.

They were soon joined by three Harrier squadrons at RAFG Wildenrath in Germany and in 1977 these moved to RAFG Gütersloh; closer to the border with Eastern Europe.

The RAF used its Harrier GR.1 fleet in the close air support, armed reconnaissance and ground-attack roles and it was particularly suitable to operations in West Germany. In the event of any potential Soviet aggression, Harriers would deploy to camouflaged rough bases in the woods and even built up areas, negating the need for operational airfields. From there they would launch attacks on advancing armour columns.

Harrier GR.3

In total, the RAF would receive 78 Harrier GR.1s 58 of which would be upgraded to GR.1 standard with a powerful Pegasus 103 engine.

In turn, a large number of Harriers were further modified to GR.3 standard in the late 1970s with improved avionics and sensors, including a laser ranging and marked target seeking (LRMTS) equipment in a lengthened nose section and radar warning receivers in the tail. A further 36 brand new GR.3 airframes were also delivered to the RAF.

The GR.3 was the first RAF Harrier variant to see combat when ten aircraft from 1 Sqn embarked on HMS *Hermes* alongside Royal Navy Sea Harriers during the Falklands War.

There was little space on the carrier deck so the MoD requisitioned container ships (*Atlantic Conveyor* and *Atlantic Causeway*) and fitted these with temporary flight decks to carry Harriers and helicopters to the South Atlantic.

Once they were in theatre the GR.3s were tasked with providing close air support to the ground forces on the Falklands and also attacked Argentine positions. Sea Harriers (SHars) were assigned the role of fleet air defence against the threat of attacking Argentine fighters. There was concern that the SHars might need back-up so while it had not been designed for air-to-air combat the GR.3 fleet was hastily modified to carry *Sidewinder* missiles.

Although the GR.3 would not see combat again, aircraft also spent several years based in Belize with 1417 Flt due to tensions over a Guatemalan claim to Belizean territory. The Harrier was the only RAF combat aircraft capable of operating from Belize's short runway.

Harrier II

Development of a second generation 'Harrier II' began as early as 1973. This was initially a collaborative effort between Hawker Siddeley and US-manufacturer McDonnell Douglas (MDD) and aimed at increasing the Harrier's range and weapons capabilities.

However, a lack of official funding for the new engine led Hawker Siddeley to withdraw from the project. The US continued it would be 1982 before the UK return to the programme.

1

2

3

1969

Beagle Husky The last in a line of Austers that traces its history back to the Taylorcraft. The Husky (originally the Auster D.5 until Beagle took over the Auster company) was a three-seater developed for the Portuguese Air Force as a training machine. It was also sold on the civil market and one was won by holiday camp owner Billy Butlin in a raffle. He donated the aircraft to the ATC in 1969 and it flew with 5 AEF until 1989. **SDB**

Blackburn Buccaneer The Royal Navy acquired the Buccaneer [see also p110] as a carrier-borne attack aircraft. When the TSR.2 and F-111K programmes ended the RAF also purchased examples; the first entering service in 1969. In 1978, the Navy retired its large aircraft carriers and its Buccaneers were transferred to the RAF as low level strike aircraft. The type saw combat during the 1991 Gulf War but was retired in 1994.

Hawker Siddeley Harrier GR.1 The first RAF squadron to be equipped with the VTOL Harrier was 1 Sqn at RAF Wittering, which received its first GR.1 in April 1969. The RAF received 61 GR.1s, powered by the Pegasus 101. It soon became obvious that the new fighter was capable but underpowered, so the GR.1A variant introduced the Pegasus 102. The RAF received 17 new-build GR.1As and 41 GR.1s were also re-engined. **Jet Art Aviation**

Hawker Siddeley Nimrod MR.1 Jet-powered maritime patrol aircraft developed from the Comet 4 to replace the Shackleton. Its primary duty was anti-submarine warfare but it could also be used for maritime surveillance, surface warfare and SAR. Power came from four Spey turbofans. The RAF ordered 46 Nimrod MR.1s and the first entered service in October 1969. MR.1s were eventually upgraded to MR.2 standard.

McDonnell Douglas Phantom Britain bought the Phantom for use with the RAF (dubbed the F-4K) and FAA (F-4M). The RAF received 28 Phantom FG.1s (fighter/ground attack) and 118 FGR.2 (fighter/ground attack/reconnaissance) from May 1969. In 1979, the FAA's Phantoms passed to the RAF and in 1984 the RAF purchased 15 ex-USN F-4Js – known as the F-4J(UK) – to bolster numbers. Phantoms had been replaced by Tornado F.3s by 1992.

1. During the conversion from GR.1 to GR.3 the Harrier gained an extended nose to accommodate laser ranging and marked target seeking equipment. **Jet Art Aviation**
2. The first of the second generation Harriers to enter RAF service was the GR.5. **Crown Copyright**
3. A Harrier GR.9 seen during a combat patrol over Afghanistan in December 2008. **Crown Copyright/ Staff Sgt Aaron Allmon**
4. Sixteen Harrier GR.9s flying from RAF Cottesmore, Rutland create a diamond formation to mark the retirement of the RAF Harrier on December 15, 2010. It marked the end of 41 years of service. **Crown Copyright/Cpl Al Crowe**
5. The end of the line. A Harrier pilot makes his way to the debriefing following a ceremony to mark the retirement of the famous aircraft. **Crown Copyright/SAC Mark Dixon**

Harrier GR.5

The first Harrier GR.5, as the Harrier II was dubbed in British service, flew on April 30, 1985 and the first examples entered RAF service in July 1987. Compared to the GR.3 the new variant had a wing that was 14% greater in area and 26% of the entire airframe comprised of carbon fibre composite materials. The GR.5 was also fitted with chaff and flare dispensers as well as a pair of 25mm Aden cannons.

The RAF received 43 Harrier GR.5s and a further 19 GR.5As; these acting as an 'interim' variant incorporating many of the changes that would appear as standard on the later GR.7.

The first GR.5 squadron was declared operational on December 1989 and the majority of the first units to receive the type were based in West Germany. By the time the first Gulf War broke out in 1991 the Harrier was considered too untested to take into combat, so it would be 1993 before Harriers were deployed to the Gulf to patrol no-fly zones over Iraq. By then the GR.5 was in the process of being replaced by an even more capable variant.

Harrier GR.7

The end of the Cold War meant the Harrier fleet was likely to be used more in an interdictor role than a ground attack capacity and the RAF realised it needed to make alterations to enable the aircraft to conduct this job better.

The resulting Harrier GR.7 was developed primarily to add a night-time operational capability and also featured improved avionics including a nose-mounted forward-looking infrared (FLIR) that linked to night vision goggles. The first GR.7 (ZD380) flew in May 1990 and was already in service by August.

In total 59 GR.5s and GR.5As were updated to GR.7 standard and a further 34 new-build GR.7s were also delivered to the RAF between May 1990 and June 1992.

In April 1993, GR.7s were deployed to Turkey to fly Operation *Warden* missions over Northern Iraq in support of the local Kurdish population. From 1995, the GR.7 also saw service in the war over Bosnia, both in the attack and reconnaissance roles. More than 126 strike sorties were carried out by Harriers, often assisted by Jaguar fighters acting as designators for laser-guided bombs.

A number of airframes were later upgraded to GR.7As with uprated engines to improve their take off and payload carrying capabilities, particularly in the hot climates where the Harrier was now routinely operating. Harrier GR.7/7As saw extensive operational RAF service including aboard Royal Navy carriers such as HMS *Invincible*. Operating alongside Navy Sea Harriers they formed Joint Force Harrier (JFH).

In 1999, a total of 12 Harrier GR.7/7As formed part of the RAF's contribution to Operation *Allied Force*, the NATO mission over Kosovo. A total of 870 Harrier sorties were carried out during the 78-day campaign.

Harriers played a reconnaissance and strike role in Operation *Telic*, the UK contribution to the Iraq War of 2003 and the type would form a valuable part of Britain's air war in Afghanistan.

Harrier GR.9

In the early 2000s the GR.7/7A fleet benefited from a further major upgrade programme that transformed the aircraft into the GR.9 (or GR.9A with the bigger engine) with significantly upgraded avionics. The GR.9 began its first operational deployment to Kandahar, Afghanistan in January 2007 and the last British Harriers left the region in June 2009.

However, the end was nigh for the Harrier. The GR.9 was expected to stay in service at least until 2018 but in a shock move it was announced on October 19, 2010 that the fleet was to be retired. This was part of a Strategic Defence and Security Review but left the UK with no fixed wing aircraft from which to operate from the Navy's two aircraft carriers until the F-35 Lightning II arrived in service.

The last RAF Harrier took its final bow on December 15, 2010; the 72 remaining airframes had been sold to the US Marine Corps for £116 million where they were stripped for spares. ■

1970

English Electric Canberra TT.18 A target-tug conversion of the Canberra B.2. The RAF received 21 Canberra TT.18s and although the first example flew in March 1966 it would be May 1970 before the type was allocated to 7 Sqn at RAF St Mawgan for duty. RAF TT.18s were flown by 7 Sqn until 1982 and then passed to 100 Sqn at RAF Leeming, which operated them until 1992 when they were replaced by Hawk T.1s.

Hawker Siddeley Harrier T.2 & T4 A need was seen for a two-seat Harrier to be used for pilot familiarisation and training. Based on the GR.1; the T.2 was stretched to accommodate a second seat and fitted with a taller fin. Most served with the Harrier OCU (the first arriving in July 1970) but some were provided to squadrons. A small number of T.4s were also built with the more powerful Pegasus 104 engine. **Jet Art Aviation**

1971

British Aircraft Corporation BAC One-Eleven Five BAC One-Elevens wore military registrations for service at the Royal Aircraft Establishment (RAE) and subsequent Defence Research Agency (DRA), Defence Evaluation and Research Agency (DERA) and QinetiQ. The five One-Elevens were used for various research projects, with the last one (ZH763) retiring in 2013 after being used in UAV trials. **SDB**

Schempp-Hirth Kestrel TX.1 Royal Air Force Gliding & Soaring Association instructors were some of the most gifted glider pilots in the world. To help them compete on a global level a pair of Schempp-Hirth Janus C gliders were acquired for contest and record breaking flights in 1971. Named the Kestrel TX.1 in RAF service, they were sold in 2000 when budget restrictions led to the disbandment of the competition fleet.

Slingsby Venture T.2 A development of the T.61 Falke motorglider. Following evaluation, an order was placed for 15 as the Venture T.2 for the ATC. They were based on the T.61E with hand-started 45hp Stamo engines but these were later modified to have electric starters; enabling the engine to be stopped and started in flight. A further 25 were later built to this standard. They were replaced by the Vigilant T.1 in 1990. **SDB**

The Mighty Hunter's Longest Sortie

In May 1982, with war in the Falkland Islands in full swing, Hawker Siddeley Nimrod XV232 played a crucial role in the battle - and set an RAF record in the process

The Falklands War of 1982 has been touched on elsewhere in this publication; but while the story of the Harrier force ("I counted them all out and I counted them all back") and the incredible tenacity of V-Force's sorties to drop bombs on Port Stanley are both well-told another aeroplane made a valuable and brave contribution to the conflict. This was the Hawker Siddeley Nimrod – and Nimrod XV232 in particular.

The remoteness of the islands meant aircraft operating in their vicinity would need to be either carrier-borne or fly from a forward-operating base. Luckily the British forces had access to a small isolated volcanic island in the equatorial waters of the South Atlantic. Ascension Island is just under 1,000 miles (1,609km) from the coast of Africa and 1,400 miles (2,253km) from the coast of South America, and is governed as part of the British Overseas Territory of Saint Helena, Ascension and Tristan da Cunha. Named after the day of its recorded discovery, Ascension Day, the island is also home to Wideawake Airfield and its 3,000m (9,842ft) runway.

During the Falklands war RAF Hercules and VC10 transports flew over 500 sorties to Ascension, carrying more than 5,000 people and 6,000 tonnes of freight. Extra transport capacity was provided by chartered Boeing 707s and five ex-RAF Short Belfast freighters.

First to Deploy

The first aircraft to deploy from Wideawake were two Nimrod MR.1 maritime patrol aircraft on detachment from 42 Sqn at St Mawgan, Cornwall. They were used to patrol Ascension Island waters and communicate with British nuclear submarines, but by late April they had been replaced by the more modern Nimrod MR.2s of 120, 201 and 206 Sqns from RAF Kinloss in Scotland.

Information on their operational deployment is still scant, but it is believed the aircraft flew more than 100 sorties from Ascension Island. In addition to providing Search and Rescue (their primary role), they also acted as radio links and coordinated air-to-air refuelling for Victor and Vulcan missions and Harrier staging flights.

1

Probed

The Nimrod was famed for its 'long legs' but with range at a premium, even the MR.2s were in need of more endurance. As such, in the space of just 18 days, eight aircraft were fitted with ex-Vulcan in-flight refuelling probes and re-designated as the MR.2P. Small swept finlets were added to the tailplane to remedy buffeting caused by the probe and the aircraft were rushed into service. The first air-to-air refuelling sortie was flown by aircraft XV229 on April 27 and the fleet were in theatre just over a week later.

One such aircraft was XV232. Built as an MR.1 and later modified to MR.2 standard, the airframe was fitted with a refuelling probe by engineers at Woodford, Cheshire by the time she reached the South Atlantic on May 9.

A number of Nimrods are recorded as operating during the conflict (MR.1s XV244 and XV258 along with R.1 XW664 and MR.2s XV227, XV228, XV230, XV232, XV243, XV247, XV249, XV255 and XV260) but XV232 had the most illustrious service record.

18hrs 50 minutes later the crew had covered a total distance of 8,453 miles

Endurance

At 08:05Z on May 15 the fully-fuelled XV232 lumbered from the runway at Wideawake, its four Rolls-Royce Spey turbofans belching smoke and using every last ounce of their combined 48,640lb of thrust to haul the aircraft into the sky. At the controls were Flt Lt Cowan and a crew from 201 Sqn. That day they would be joined by Air-to-Air Refuelling Instructors (AARIs) Sqn Ldr Rudin & Wg Cdr Emmerson, as all available expertise would be needed to

1971

Westland/Aérospatiale Puma A twin-engined transport and utility helicopter. The Puma was originally designed in France by Sud Aviation (later Aérospatiale) but RAF examples were built by Westland. The first of 48 Puma HC.1s entered service in June 1971 and the type found a niche operating with special forces. A total of 24 were upgraded to HC.2 standard in 2012 and are expected to remain in service until 2025. **SDB**

1972

Avro Shackleton AEW.2 When the FAA retired the Fairey Gannet Airborne Early Warning (AEW) the RAF no longer had 'eyes' in the sky looking for aircraft approaching its borders. As an interim measure, 12 Shackleton MR.2s were modified with the radar previously fitted to the Gannet. They were to be replaced by the Nimrod AEW.3 but cancellation of that project meant it would be 1991 before the 'Shak' could finally retire.

Hawker Siddeley Harrier GR.3 From 1972, the RAF's fleet of Harrier GR.1/1As were gradually upgraded to the GR.3 standard. This included the new 21,500lb/ thrust Pegasus 103 engine and an array of new sensors. An elongated nose housed a laser tracker and an electronic countermeasure suite was also provided. In 1982 ten operated from HMS *Hermes* on ground attack missions during the Falklands War. **Jet Art Aviation**

1973

Scottish Aviation Bulldog T.1 A military development of the civilian Beagle Pup. The airframe was strengthened to allow a full range of aerobatics to be flown but Beagle ceased trading before any aircraft were built and the rights were taken over by Scottish Aviation. The RAF ordered 130 Bulldog T.1s to replace the Chipmunk in the training role. Bulldogs flew with University Air Squadrons and Air Experience Flights until 2001. **SDB**

Scottish Aviation Jetstream T.1 When Handley Page went out of business the rights to the its Jetstream airliner were acquired by Scottish Aviation. The RAF ordered 26 as replacements for the Varsity in the multi-engine training role. A defence review in 1974 led to the Jetstreams entering storage until 1977. Eleven were then returned to the RAF and 14 transferred to the Navy. The last RAF examples retired in 2003.

1. XV232 makes her final landing on May 11, 2010. **Andrew Kitney**
2. Nimrod XV235 cruises over barren Scottish scenery on a training flight from RAF Kinloss. Although the terrain may have been similar to that on the Argentine coast it probably fair to assume the stress levels were more heightened over the South Atlantic! **Crown Copyright**
3. Before she reached the South Atlantic on May 9, 1982, XV232 was fitted with an ex-Vulcan refuelling probe by engineers at Woodford, Cheshire. Her standard crew of 12 was supplemented by a pair of Air-to-Air Refuelling Instructors, as the squadron pilots had received very little time to perfect the art of aerial tanking. **SDB**
4. The cramped cockpit of a Nimrod MR.2 on patrol. On May 21/22, 1982 the crew of XV232 covered a distance of 8,453 miles – a record for a British operational reconnaissance mission that stands to this day. **Crown Copyright**

keep the big patrol aircraft aloft for as long as possible.

XV232 was initially flown south to a point 150 miles (241km) north of Port Stanley before turning west until she was within approximately 60 miles (97km) of the Argentine coast.

The aircraft then tracked north-east at between 7,000ft (2,134m) and 12,000ft (3,658m) parallel with the enemy coast, and the crew used its *Searchwater* radar to survey a strip of sea 400 miles (644km) wide and 1,000 miles (1,609km) long: confirming that all Argentine warships were still fully blockaded in port by the threat of British nuclear-powered submarines.

Unluckily for the crew the weather was fine and visibility excellent, making them a prime target for missile target at their relatively low altitude. Thankfully an attack never came.

The Nimrod's ability to loiter on just two of its four Spey engines no doubt helped increase the mission's endurance and range, but the aircraft needed to refuel three times before it safely recovered to Ascension Island. By this time it had covered 8,300 miles and been aloft for a staggering 19hrs and 5 minutes – the longest reconnaissance mission then flown by an RAF aircraft.

Record Breaker

A number of 'extended range' reconnaissance flights were tasked over the next few days, culminating in a second record-breaking flight for XV232.

Just prior to the British beach landings in San Carlos water on May 21, XV232 was tasked with flying a similar course to her May 15 flight. This time she departed Wideawake at 17:15Z on the afternoon of May 20 and set course for the Argentine coast. Flt Lt Ford was at the helm this time, joined by a crew from 206 Sqn, and AARIs Sqn Ldr Wingate & Wg Cdr Emmerson. The crew's tasking was to search the waters between Argentina and the Falkland Islands for any enemy warships that could pose a hazard to the British beach landings.

By the time they landed back at Ascension Island at 14:05Z on the 21st (18hrs 50 minutes later) the crew had covered a total distance of 8,453 miles – a distance record for a British operational reconnaissance mission that stands to this day.

It is interesting to note that soon after these missions XV232 was despatched for modification work. By the time she returned to Ascension on June 5 her previously unused underwing hardpoints had been adapted to carry *Sidewinder* missiles, a move that allowed her to be described in the 'popular press' as the world's largest fighter. XV232 is believed to be the only Nimrod modified to carry the *Sidewinder*, although other airframes were later cleared to carry *Harpoon* missiles.

Along with her remaining brethren XV232 was retired in May 2010 and is now preserved in running order at Coventry Airport by a band of dedicated volunteers. ■

1974

SEPECAT Jaguar GR.1 An attack aircraft designed as a jet trainer but soon changed to include tactical nuclear strike and recce roles. A total of 165 single seat GR.1s joined the RAF and at its peak the 'Jag' equipped six squadrons. From 1983, 75 GR.1s were updated to GR.1A standards with new navigation systems, more powerful engines and Sidewinder missiles. 'Jags' saw combat over Bosnia and Iraq but were withdrawn in 2007.

SEPECAT Jaguar T.2 Considering the Jaguar stemmed from an original RAF requirement for a supersonic advanced trainer aircraft to replace the Gnat, it is apt that 38 were delivered as two-seat T.2 versions. These were advanced trainers equipped with a 30mm cannon and up to 10,000lbs of bombs. Some were later upgraded to T.4 standard with updated avionics. Like the GR.1A, the 'T Bird' was retired in 2007. **SDB**

Westland Gazelle The five-seat Aérospatiale Gazelle was manufactured in Britain through a joint production agreement with Westland. It was the first helicopter to feature a fenestron tail instead of a tail rotor. Britain ordered 142 for use by the RAF, Army and Navy. In RAF service 32 Gazelle HT.3s were used for pilot training. A small number were also converted for VIP communications duties with 32 (The Royal) Sqn. **SDB**

Hawker Siddeley Nimrod R.1 When the Signals Intelligence (SIGINT) Comets and Canberras of 51 Sqn retired they were replaced with three highly modified Nimrod MR.1s from May 1974. The R.1 differed from the maritime patrol aircraft by having a rotating dish of aerials in the bomb bay and others on the tail in a 'canoe' fairing. The last R.1 was retired in 2011 and was replaced by the RC-135W Rivet Joint in 2013. **SDB**

Panavia Tornado IDS The first prototype Tornado [see also p126] was the IDS (interdictor/strike) variant, which flew on August 14, 1974. The 'swing wing' aircraft was developed and built by Panavia Aircraft GmbH, a tri-national consortium consisting of British Aerospace, MBB of West Germany, and Aeritalia of Italy. The IDS would be the first of 14 prototypes and would go on to form the basis of the RAF's ground attack Tornado GR.1.

The RAF's Heavy Helicopter Force

Helicopters have played an ever greater role in RAF airpower over the last five decades; from supplying troops to searching for (and rescuing) downed aircrew or civilians in distress

Following the RAF's evaluation of the Hoverfly helicopter in the 1940s [Ed: see p73] the decision was made to explore rotary flying further.

The most obvious use for an aircraft with the ability to hover was in the Search and Rescue (SAR) role, which the RAF had been undertaking with fixed wing aircraft since 1941. The RAF's Air Sea Rescue Service utilised a number of aircraft types to look for downed airmen in the ocean, and then drop supplies and lifeboats. The use of rotary winged aircraft enabled rescue crews to hover in the proximity of survivors and the first helicopter to join the RAF in this capacity was the Westland Dragonfly.

Dragonfly

The Dragonfly was a licence-built version of the American Sikorsky S-51 helicopter and performed its maiden flight on October 5, 1948. It differed from its US-built S-51 in having a 540hp Alvis Leonides radial engine and while it served extensively with the Royal Navy a handful also saw RAF service in the SAR and casualty evacuation (casevac) role.

The first version served the Navy as the Dragonfly HR.1 and two examples flew with the RAF as the HC.2. These early machines were soon replaced by modified airframes with all-metal rotor blades (the HR.3 and HC.4 respectively), of which 71 were delivered to the Navy and 12 to the RAF.

However, the Dragonfly was underpowered and hovering low over the sea was a hazardous task. It was therefore decided that a more capable replacement was needed and for that the RAF looked to Bristol.

Sycamore

The Bristol Aeroplane Company had created a helicopter division as early as 1944 and its first project was the development of a four-seat machine intended for civil and military use.

The resulting Sycamore flew for the first time on July 25, 1947, powered by a 450hp P&W Wasp Junior. Further testing led to the Sycamore being fitted with a 550hp Alvis Leonides engine and in April 1949 the Sycamore family was granted its certificate of airworthiness; the first ever to be granted to a British helicopter.

1

The first RAF use of the Sycamore came in 1952 when examples were sent to the Air Sea Warfare Development Unit.

The British Army would evaluate the Sycamore HC.10 and HC.11 as air ambulance and communications aircraft respectively but neither entered full service. The RAF, however, was impressed with the helicopter and ordered 85 examples as the Sycamore HR.14.

In 1953, the RAF's first helicopter search and rescue squadron (275 Sqn) was established using the Sycamore and the type was used by Central Flying School (CFS) for pilot training.

The first use of RAF helicopters in conflict came during the Malayan Emergency, which began in 1948. Sycamores were used to deploy Army foot patrols into the jungle and a large number were transferred to the Far East Air Force to take part in the conflict.

RAF's helicopter fleet forms part of the tri-service Joint Helicopter Command, along with helicopters of the Army and Navy

The 'war' came to an end in 1960 but Sycamores remained in the region to support British forces in Brunei and to deter further aggression by Malayan communist guerrillas.

The Sycamore also saw combat during the Aden Emergency and it was not until 1972 that the last RAF examples were retired; the final two serving with 32 Sqn for VIP and Royal flying.

1975

Handley Page Victor K.2 Although some surplus B.1s were converted into tankers in the 1960s the definitive Victor refueller was the K.2, which could carry 91,000lb of fuel. The first of 24 conversions from B.2 and SR.2 to K.2 joined the RAF in July 1975. K.2s served with distinction during the Falklands War and eight were used during the 1991 Gulf War. The Victor was the last of the V Bombers to remain in service, but it too retired in 1993. SDB

1976

Hawker Siddeley/BAe Hawk T.1 Created to replace the Gnat and Hunter T.7 trainers, the Hawk was the first British aircraft designed using the metric system of measurement. The RAF ordered 175 Hawks and the first entered service in November 1976. In 1980 the Hawk also replaced the Gnat with the Red Arrows. Despite being replaced by the Hawk T.2 in 2012, the 'Reds' still use the T.1 and others fly with 100 Sqn in the 'aggressor' role.

Westland Sea King HAR.3 A licence built version of the Sikorsky S-61, fitted with Gnome turboshaft engines. The Sea King was ordered by the Royal Navy as a submarine hunter killer in 1966 but it would be 1978 before the RAF received its first HAR.3 variants to replace the Whirlwind in the SAR role. It carried three stretchers or 12 casuaties. The final examples retired in 2016 when the SAR service was privatised. Crown Copyright

1979

Hawker Siddeley Nimrod MR.2 The first of 35 upgraded Nimrods were re-delivered to the RAF in August 1979. The MR.2 had more modern avionics and the ASV Mk 21 was replaced with EMI *Searchwater* radar. Electronic Counter Measures were mounted on the wing-tips. The type went on to serve in the Falklands, Gulf and Afghanistan. The fleet was retired early in 2010 due to defence cuts. Crown Copyright

Panavia Tornado ADV The second variant of the Tornado to fly was the Air Defence Variant (ADV), which had been created to meet an RAF need for an interceptor to replace the Lightning and Phantom. Compared to the IDS [see p117] the ADV had a longer fuselage to house *Foxhunter* radar and four *Skyflash* missiles below the belly. The prototype flew in October 1979. The ADV flew well and led to the Tornado F.2 and F.3.

RAF Fast Fact

Out of all the RAF helicopter fleet one airframe stands out. Bravo November is the callsign for Chinook ZA718; one of the original 30 aircraft ordered by the RAF in 1978.
'BN' has been in service ever since and upgraded many times. It has also seen action in every major RAF operation since (and including) the Falklands War. As such it has served in the Falklands, Lebanon, Germany, Northern Ireland, Kurdistan, Iraq and Afghanistan. Four pilots have been awarded the Distinguished Flying Cross (DFC) for actions whilst in command of Bravo November.
In April 1982, Bravo November was loaded, along with three other Chinooks, aboard the container ship Atlantic Conveyor bound for the Falkland Islands. The ship was hit by an *Exocet* missile and sunk but BN was airborne at the time and managed to land on HMS *Hermes*. It was therefore the only serviceable heavy lift helicopter available to British forces involved in the hostilities.
Today, in 2020, Chinook ZA718 Bravo November continues to serve on active duty with the RAF.

1. British soldiers prepare to board a Bristol Sycamore. Sycamores were used to deploy Army foot patrols into the jungle in Malaya.
2. RAF Westland Dragonfly HC.2 WF311 with a stretcher pannier mounted on the fuselage side. The helicopter is one of three deployed to Malaya in 1950. **Crown Copyright**
3. The Puma (foreground) has been in RAF service since 1971 and remains a vital part of the helicopter fleet. The Merlin (rear) entered service in 2001 but was transferred to the Navy from 2012 onwards. **Sgt Jack Pritchard/ Crown Copyright**

Whirlwind

A large amount of Sycamores were ultimately replaced in service by the British licence-built version of the American Sikorsky S-55.

By 1950, Westland Aircraft already had experience of building the Sikorsky S-51 under licence as the Dragonfly and it approached the manufacturer for the rights to produce the S-55. This was granted and a Sikorsky-built example was assembled and test flown at Westland's factory in Yeovil, Somerset by June 1951.

However, as was often the way with the British military, the RAF and the Royal Navy wanted to alter the machine significantly and it would be August 1953 before the first British-built example took to the skies. Westland christened the new helicopter the Whirlwind and it would go on to serve in a variety of roles.

The prototype and the first ten production Whirlwind HAR.1s were powered by a 600hp Pratt & Whitney R-1340-40 Wasp: the limited power meant they mostly flew in non-combat roles such as SAR and communications duties with the Navy. The RAF took delivery of 33 HAR.2s with a larger 700hp Wright R-1300-3 Cyclone 7 engine and, painted bright yellow, these were used solely for SAR duties.

Some 24 HAR.4s also joined the RAF; these having various modifications to improve their capabilities in hot and high conditions. The HAR.4 entered service with 155 Sqn in Malaya in September 1954. The variant was also used by 217 Sqn, which flew them from Christmas Island during nuclear tests in the Pacific.

In 1959, a pair of Whirlwind HCC.8s were added to the Queen's Flight for VIP duties. Based on the HAR.4, these had dual controls and specially soundproofed cabins.

However, even the capabilities of the HAR.4 were limited due to their low engine power so, in 1960, Westland introduced a gas-turbine-powered Whirlwind: fitted with a 1,000hp Bristol Siddeley Gnome turboshaft, the increased power turned the helicopter into a truly useable workhorse. The transport variant could carry up to ten passengers, six stretchers or a freight load and earned great distinction for duties in Malaya, where it kept the Army supplied and evacuated casualties when required.

A pair of HAR.10s were also converted to HCC.12s for the Queen's Flight but it is in the SAR role that the Whirlwind is best remembered, patrolling the coastal waters and

1980

BAe Nimrod AEW.3 The Shackleton AEW.2s [see p116] were desperately in need of replacement even by the time they entered service in 1972. BAe proposed converting eleven Nimrods to AEW.3 standard with GEC Marconi radar in bulbous nose and tail fairings. The prototype flew in July 1980 but the project was plagued by cost over-runs and computer problems. It was cancelled in 1986 and the Boeing Sentry ordered.

Boeing-Vertol Chinook HC.1 & HC.2 Originally ordered in 1967 but cancelled. The order was reinstated in 1971 but cancelled again. Finally, in 1978 the order was finalised and the first example arrived in December 1980. The RAF ordered 41 CH.47Cs as the Chinook HC.1 and in 1983 a further eight were acquired. Later, 36 HC.1s were rebuilt to CH-47D standard (becoming HC.2s). Updated Chinook HC.4s continue to serve the RAF.

Panavia Tornado GR.1 The RAF ordered 228 Tornado IDS aircraft as the GR.1. The first entered service with the Tri-national Tornado Training Establishment in 1980. GR.1s subsequently replaced the Buccaneer in the overland strike role, the Jaguar in the counter air role and they saw combat during the Gulf War. From 1994, some were converted to GR.1Bs, carrying Sea Eagle missiles and replacing Buccaneers in the anti-shipping role.

1981

SEPECAT Jaguar ACT Jaguar XX765 was converted into the Jaguar Active Control Technology (ACT) prototype, with fly-by-wire (FBW) controls and aerodynamic alterations. The aerodynamic instability improved manoeuvrability while the FBW provided split-second corrections to compensate for the unstable configuration. The first of 96 test flights began in October 1981 and data was used in the development of the Eurofighter Typhoon.

1983

BAe 146 The RAF leased two BAe 146s in 1983 to evaluate their suitability to replace the Andover. These were subsequently returned to the manufacturer. In April 1986, the Queen's Flight received the first of three VIP configured BAe 146 CC.2s; two of which remain in service. In 2013 the RAF acquired a pair BAe 146-200QC freighters (as the C.3) for use in Afghanistan. They are fitted with countermeasures and flare dispensers.

The Whirlwind is best remembered for patrolling the coastal waters and mountain tops for the injured, lost and distressed

mountain tops for the injured or lost.

The Whirlwind soldiered on until the late 1970s with the final unit (84 Sqn in Cyprus) not relinquishing their last example until 1982.

Wessex

For its Whirlwind replacement the RAF turned to Westland once again; and Westland returned to Sikorsky for permission to produce its latest S-58 helicopter under licence.

This time the conversion from US to British was more radical and the decision was made to replace the Wright Cyclone piston engine with a gas turbine from the outset. Initial examples were powered by a single Napier Gazelle turboshaft and the type entered service with the Royal Navy as the Wessex HAS.1 in 1960.

The Wessex HC.2 entered RAF service in January 1964, with 18 Sqn at RAF Odiham, Hampshire the first to receive the new type. The RAF had ordered the Wessex to fulfil a variety of roles including SAR, tactical transport, air ambulance and even ground attack (using machine guns and Nord anti-tank missiles).

The RAF Wessex fleet was powered by a pair of coupled 1,350shp Gnome turboshafts, meaning it could carry up to 16 fully equipped troops or a 4,000lb (1,814kg) underslung load.

The Wessex HAR.2 (HC.2 with a winch above the starboard door and a bright yellow high-visibility colour scheme) was used by detached Flights of 22 Sqn for SAR duties around the UK coast from 1976.

The RAF Wessex's service career featured deployments to Hong Kong and Northern Ireland in response to terrorist operations, and in 1964 were deployed to Malaya to help fight communist guerrilla forces. More than 50 Navy Wessex helicopters were employed in the Falklands War of 1982.

Like the Whirlwind before it, the Wessex was adapted for use by the Queen's Flight. Two HCC.4 (similar to the HC.2) were delivered in 1969 and these served until 1998 [Ed: see p74].

1

2

3

Sea King

The Wessex's replacement within the RAF fell to yet another Westland produced licence-built American design. Westland manufactured the Sikorsky S-61 as the Sea King and although the British Navy ordered the type in 1966, it would be 1975 before the RAF committed to an order for 19 to replace the Wessex in SAR service.

The Sea King HAR.3 entered operational service with 202 Sqn at RAF Lossiemouth, Scotland in August 1978. Compared to the Wessex's 95 miles (153km) radius of operations the new type could operate up to 270 miles (435km) from base. It also had a winch that was four times as long and could carry up to 17 survivors or six stretchers in its cabin.

During the Falklands War a single RAF Sea King was despatched to Ascension Island, where it largely flew aerial replenishment sorties to ships supporting the task force.

The UK-based SAR Sea Kings were used for both military and civilian SAR tasks. For decades they were used to rescue civilians from the sea or flooded regions and worked with the Mountain Rescue Service in hilly terrain.

However, in February 2016 the RAF SAR force was disbanded and the role handed over to civilian contractor Bristow. Today, the Bell Griffin HAR.2s based at RAF Akrotiri in Cyprus are the RAF's only dedicated SAR helicopters, however; all military helicopter aircrew routinely train and practice for SAR missions.

1983

BAe Hawk T.1A Between 1983 and 1986 a total of 88 Hawk T.1s were upgraded to T.1A standard. These were designed to act as short-range interceptor aircraft; primarily to protect airfields in the event of war. The T.1A carried two AIM-9L *Sidewinder* missiles and a 30mm Aden cannon in a gun pod. T.1As would have worked in collaboration with Tornado F.3s, which would have used their radar to vector the Hawks towards targets.

Lockheed TriStar The Falklands War revealed the RAF lacked refuelling aircraft so the decision was made to buy five ex-British Airways and four ex-Pan Am Lockheed L-1011 TriStars and convert them to tankers. Two became pure tankers (K.1), three for solely transport aircraft (C.2) and four with tanker/transports (KC.1). The aircraft entered service with 216 Sqn in August 1983 and the last was retired in 2014. **US Navy**

Schleicher Valiant & Vanguard Based on the ASW 19, the Valiant TX.1 was a single-seat glider designed to compete in Club Class built contests. It was a glass fibre machine but was fitted with metal air brakes. Five were acquired by the RAF Gliding & Soaring Association. The RAF also evaluated ten of the two-seat ASK 21 as the Vanguard TX.1; these were used for training but lost out to the Vikings when it came to a large order.

1984

Grob Viking TX.1 The Grob G103 Twin Astir II Acro is a modified version of the earlier Twin Astir glider. It is a two-seat glass fibre airframe with strengthened spar caps and steel pushrods making it capable of more advanced aerobatics than the Twin Astir. The RAF ordered 100 Acros – as the Viking TX.1 – in 1980 for use by Volunteer Gliding Schools. Nine VGSs operate the Viking, training air cadets to a standard sufficient for them to fly solo.

Panavia Tornado F.2 Although the first Tornado F.2 joined 229 OCU in November 1984 the *Foxhunter* radar was far from ready (and already two-thirds over budget). Nevertheless, the RAF received 18 F.2s – all of which needed bags of concrete in the nose in place of the missing radar to maintain their centre of gravity! The F.2 also lacked thrust; particularly in reheat where it was 15% down compared to the later F.3.

4

4. Belvederes had a tremendous lifting capability and Aden-based examples quickly specialised in recovering downed aircraft from within the jungle. A Belvedere even lifted the spire onto the new Coventry Cathedral in April 1962.
5. In order to fulfil the need for helicopter pilots the RAF has operated a range of training helicopters including the Westland Gazelle, Eurocopter Squirrel, Bell Griffin and the current fleet of Airbus Juno and Jupiter machines. **SDB**

1. The Wessex replaced the Whirlwind in the RAF SAR role from 1976. They were on 24/7 standby to respond to an emergency anywhere within 40 miles of the British coast within 15 minutes. **Crown Copyright**
2. The Sea King – nicknamed the Big Yellow Budgie – was finally retired from RAF service in 2018. This example is from 202 Sqn's D Flight, based at RAF Lossiemouth. **SAC Harpur/Crown Copyright**
3. The Whirlwind was the RAF's first truly capable search and rescue helicopter. **SDB**

5

Heavy Lift

Increases in performance in the 1960s meant they could be used for a growing variety of missions and the RAF soon saw a need for a helicopter capable of carrying up to 20 soldiers.

For this they turned to Westland again, but this time the company looked to France for a solution. A deal was signed with Aérospatiale to produce the Puma under licence and the first of 49 Puma HC.1s joined the RAF in 1971.

Pumas became closely associated with British special forces, serving alongside them in Northern Ireland. They have also served in Iraq, Venezuela, Yugoslavia and Zaire.

The first upgraded Puma HC.2 returned to the RAF in 2012 and the type is expected to remain in service until 2025.

When the Navy requested a new anti-submarine helicopter in the late 1970s, Westland joined forces with Italian company Agusta to create the European Helicopters conglomerate. The resulting EH.101 would become the Merlin, which joined the Navy in 1997.

The RAF also ordered the type and it received the first 22 Merlin HC.3s in 2001 for troop transport use. RAF Merlins were deployed to Iraq in 2004 and Afghanistan in 2008, but in 2012 the fleet was transferred to the Royal Navy for use by the Commando Helicopter Force.

Twin Rotors

For heavy lift duties the RAF has turned to twin rotor designs from as early as the 1960s.

The Bristol Belvedere was based on the civilian ten-seat Bristol Type 173 helicopter, which first flew on January 3, 1952. The project was cancelled but Bristol later created the Type 192 for the RAF. Powered by a pair of 1,650shp Napier Gazelle turboshafts the Belvedere had two 49ft (15m) span rotors that were synchronised to prevent blade collision. This allowed the aircraft to operate on only one engine in the event of an emergency.

The RAF received 26 Belvedere HC.1s from 1961, which could carry 18 fully equipped troops. Belvederes served with 66 and 72 Sqns in the UK and 26 Sqn at RAF Khormaksar in Aden; the latter seeing combat service in the Aden Emergency and Borneo during the Indonesia–Malaysia confrontation.

Operationally, the Belvedere could lift more than the later Wessex, but the single-rotor helicopter was more robust and required less maintenance; thus the Belvedere was retired at the end of the 1960s.

By then the Boeing Vertol CH-47 Chinook was already well established in US military service but it would be 1978 before the British government decided to order the type to replace the Wessex in the heavy-lift helicopter role. Thirty Chinook HC.1s were and the first entered service in December 1980. Others subsequently joined the force and throughout their lifetime the RAF Chinooks have been regularly upgraded; the most recent programme seeing 46 airframes updated to HC.4 standard from 2008. These were augmented between 2009 and 2015 by 14 brand new Chinook HC.6s.

Of all the RAF helicopters the Chinook has seen the widest operational use, beginning with the Falklands. Since then, Chinooks have seen combat in both Gulf Wars, the Balkans, Lebanon and Afghanistan. They also served in Operation *Banner* in Northern Ireland and have been used widely in humanitarian missions.

Today, the RAF's helicopters are part of Joint Helicopter Command, which along with Army and Navy helicopters plays a vital role in the everyday operation of the British military. ■

1986

Vickers VC10 K.2 & K.3 The RAF was still in need of extra air-to-air refuelling aircraft so BAe was contracted to convert five former BOAC VC10s and four former East African Airways Super VC10s into the VC10 K.2 and VC10 K.3. Extra fuel tanks were installed in the cabin and both were fitted withg wing-mounted and centreline refuelling points. The last VC10 K.2 was retired in 2003 but some K.3s flew on until 2013.

BAe EAP The EAP (Experimental Aircraft Programme) was designed to research technologies that might be used in future European combat aircraft. It eventually formed the basis for the Eurofighter Typhoon. It was fitted with fly-by-wire, a Head-Up Display (HUD) and a Hands On Throttle-And-Stick (HOTAS) control system. To reduce costs, a Tornado tailfin was used. The sole EAP flew on August 8, 1986 and would go on to fly 250 sorties.

Britten Norman Islander CC.2 One of the most secretive and elusive of all RAF aircraft. Derived from the civilian BN-2T Islander, the first CC.2 arrived with the RAF Northolt Station Flight in May 1986. The unit's official duties were photographic mapping and light communications roles and the Islander could also be used as a transport. The unit eventually acquired two extra CC.2s but all three were retired in 2017.

Piper PA-31 Navajo Chieftain Three of the corporate/commuter aircraft were purchased for the RAE in 1986. A fourth aircraft joined the A&AEE in the same year in the communications role. The aircraft remained in service until the mid 1990s. In 2019, the Islanders with the RAF's top secret Northolt Station Flight were retired and the job given to two civilian registered FLIR-equipped PA-31 Navajos. **Mike Freer/Wikicommons**

1987

Panavia Tornado F.3 The F.3 first flew in 1985. Improvements over the F.2 included RB.199 Mk 104 engines and automatic wing sweep. The F.3 carried four underwing Sidewinder missiles rather than two and, finally, had working radar. It made its combat debut during the Gulf War. Delays in the Eurofighter project meant the F.3 was not retired until March 2011. Most were reduced to parts to keep the GR.4 fleet aloft.

Second Hand Tankers to the Rescue

The RAF has typically used outdated bombers as aerial refuellers, but when demand outstripped supply it turned its attention towards the airline world for help.

The first experiments in air-to-air refuelling (AAR) took place in the 1920s with two US Army Air Service Airco DH.4 biplanes flying in formation. A hose was passed from one aircraft to the other and fuel was poured from a hand-held tank.

Britain's Royal Aircraft Establishment also began trials in an attempt to extend the range of the flying boats that serviced the extremes of the British Empire. By the early 1930s it had created a system that could refuel from one aircraft to another, with flow controlled by an automatic valve on the hose which would cut off if contact was lost.

Probe-and-Drogue

Sir Alan Cobham's Flight Refuelling Ltd developed the probe-and-drogue AAR system that the modern day RAF uses and this was first demonstrated in 1949. During trials the RAF used a modified Lancaster and Gloster Meteor F.3 EE397 to establish a new jet endurance record. The Meteor remained airborne for 12 hours and 3 minutes, receiving 2,352 Imp Gal (10,690lit) of fuel in ten refuellings.

Although Lancaster and Lincoln bombers were used during trials work, the RAF would need to wait for the introduction of the 'V Force' before it received its first practical AAR aircraft. While in operational service some Vulcans, Valiants and Victors were converted to fly as tankers; when the latter two were retired as bombers, the remaining aircraft were pressed into service as dedicated 'flying bowsers.'

'Vicky Ten'

The Vickers VC10 – or 'Vicky Ten' to her crew – was designed as a jetliner to operate on long-distance routes from relatively short runways. Its performance meant it could cross the Atlantic in just over five hours (only Concorde was faster) and this was not lost on the RAF, which ordered five examples in 1960, even before the prototype had flown.Intending to use these as transport, a further six were ordered in 1962 and when British Overseas Airways Corporation (BOAC) cancelled an order the RAF ordered another five.

1

2

RAF VC10s combined the airframe of the standard airliner with the more powerful engines and tailfin fuel tank of the 'Super VC10.' Unlike the airliner variants, all passenger seats in the military VC10s faced rearwards for safety reasons. The type entered RAF service as the VC10 C.1 in December 1966.

With the already ageing V Bomber tankers reaching the end of their career, the RAF announced plans to form a squadron of nine VC10 AAR tankers in 1978. The decision was made to acquire ex-airline airframes and convert them to tankers: five ex-Gulf Air VC10s were converted to K.2 standard and four ex-East African Airways Super VC10s became K.3s.

Following conversion, the first K.2 was delivered to 101 Sqn at RAF Brize Norton, Oxfordshire on June 22, 1982: just too late to see service in the Falklands War. As such, it was the Victor that took the vital refuelling role in the missions to and from the South Atlantic.

When the last Victor K.2s needed replacing in the early 1990s, the RAF made the decision to convert five more VC10s for 101 Sqn. The

RAF Fast Fact

During the first Gulf War, in 1991, two RAF TriStars tankers deployed to King Khalid International Airport near Riyadh in Saudi Arabia during the 1991 Gulf War. In common with most of the RAF's fleet the aircraft were painted in desert pink. Appropriately nicknamed 'Pinky' and 'Perky', their main task was refuelling the RAF's Tornado F.3 fleet during the conflict.

1988

BAe Harrier GR.5 The first RAF variant of the Harrier II [see p112], which was a heavily modified version of the 'jump jet' with a one-piece wing (featuring leading edge extensions) and a partly glass fibre fuselage. The first of 43 GR.5s arrived in November 1988. The aircraft was only in service for a short period because the GR.7 superseded it in 1990. However, 21 GR.5As were also built, incorporating elements of the GR.7.

1989

Short Tucano T.1 A licence-built version of the Brazilian Embraer EMB-312 Tucano turboprop-powered basic trainer that was modified to use the 1,100shp Garret TPE331. In 1985 the RAF ordered 130 to replace the Jet Provost. The first examples were delivered in December 1989 and soon proved to 70% cheaper to operate than the JP. The Tucano was eventually retired in October 2019 and has been replaced by the T-6 Texan II.

1990

BAe Harrier GR.7 Distinguishable from the earlier GR.5 by the addition of a bulged fairing over a Forward Looking Infrared Radar (FLIR) in the nose, the GR.7 was also equipped for flying with night vision goggles. The variant had updated avionics including a digital colour map display. In total, 59 GR.5s were upgraded to GR.7 standard and 34 were built from new. The aircraft were later given larger engined and re-designated GR.7A.

1991

Boeing Sentry AEW.1 Purchased as an urgent replacement for the Shackleton AEW.2, following the cancellation of the Nimrod AEW.3. The Boeing E-3 entered USAF service in 1977 and is developed from the Boeing 707 airliner. The RAF received the first of seven in March 1991 and they were declared operational a year later. The type is named Sentry in RAF service and carries a large rotodome radar antenna atop the fuselage.

Grob Vigilant T.1 A development of the civilian Grob G109B motorglider purchased by the RAF to replace the Venture in service with Volunteer Gliding Squadrons (VGS) around the UK to train Air Training Corps and Combined Cadet Force cadets. The Vigilant had a 95hp engine, a T-tail and 57ft span wings. The first of 53 was delivered in 1991 and they equipped eleven VGS until they were retired in May 2018.

1. RAF TriStars tankers were delivered in the standard white scheme applied to its cargo aircraft. **Crown Copyright**
2. The first VC10 tanker, ZA141, was painted in a grey-green camouflage but the remaining K.2s were painted in a hemp-like colour. Eventually all the VC10s gained a new low visibility grey scheme. **Crown Copyright**
3. A Typhoon flies off the tail of a 216 Sqn TriStar in 2012. The aircraft is wearing the later grey scheme. **USAF/Sgt Austin May**
4. Both the TriStar and the VC10 (illustrated) could refuel each other to extend range. **Crown Copyright**

airframes were former British Airways Super VC10s (which became K.4s) and to help meet demand the 13 surviving VC10 C.1s were also converted to C.1K standard by adding two wing mounted refuelling pods.

Active Service

Although they were too late to see service in the Falklands, RAF VC10s deployed to the Middle East in 1991 as part of Operation *Granby*. They also saw action flying from Southern Italy in 1999, refuelling NATO aircraft as part of Operation *Allied Force* over Yugoslavia.

The new millennium saw VC10s flying over Afghanistan in 2001 and Libya in 2011.But by now the clock was ticking and the VC10s final flight took place on September 24, 2013: bringing to a close nearly five decades of service.

Second-Hand TriStars

The Falklands War had revealed the RAF's lack of AAR capacity in a very public way and the imminent retirement of the Victor K.2 fleet made it apparent that a new aircraft was urgently needed.

Budget dictated that the new aircraft would also need to augment the VC10 fleet as a long-range transport and although a number of options were considered the decision was made to buy second-hand Lockheed L-1011 TriStars.

These were wide-body aircraft powered by three Rolls-Royce RB211 engines and their similarity to the USAF's KC-10 fleet offered the RAF the possibility of a relatively easy AAR conversion. The decision was also influenced by British Airways' desire to offload its fleet of L-1011-500 TriStars.

The decision was made to acquire ex-airline airframes and convert them to tankers

Six aircraft were purchased in December 1982, converted for RAF use by Marshall's of Cambridge. Two became passenger/tanker aircraft (designated TriStar K.1s) and the other four were designed to operate in the tanker, cargo or passenger role as the KC.1. The latter differed from the K.1 in having a large cargo door fitted to the fuselage.

The initial order was increased in 1984 with the purchase of three ex Pan Am airframes. These would be operated as passenger, freight and medevac aircraft and were designated C.2 and C.2A – the difference being the avionics fit.

The first TriStar tanker arrived with 216 Sqn at Brize Norton in March 1986 and the type saw extensive service with the RAF including involvement in the wars in the Gulf, Kosovo, Afghanistan and Libya.

RAF TriStars had originally been due to remain in service until the late 2010s but this was brought forward and the nine aircraft were retired in 2014 and sold.

Both the VC10 and the TriStar were replaced in RAF service by the Airbus Voyager; the RAF's first ever purpose-built AAR tanker. ■

1994

Eurofighter EF2000 Although the Future European Fighter Aircraft programme began in 1983 – and the EAP flew in 1986 – delays meant it would be March 27, 1994 before the first EF2000 took to the skies. The first British development aircraft flew on April 6. The French eventually left the project and the end of the Cold War also saw the impetus slow. It would therefore be 2006 before the RAF Typhoon became operational.

Vickers VC10 K.4 The RAF purchased 14 ex-British Airways Super VC10s in 1981 for spares. A need for more tankers arose in 1989 and the decision was made to convert five of them into VC10 K.4s. The absence of a forward freight door meant extra tanks could not be fitted in the cabin; thus reducing the range compared to the K.3. The first K.4 entered service with 101 Sqn in April 1994 and the last remained in service until 2013.

1995

BAe Harrier T.10 & T.12 Just as the Harrier T.2s and T.4s were used as conversion trainers for the first generation VTOL fighter so the T.10 performed a similar role for the Harrier II. Based on the USMC TAV-8B, the T.10 was combat capable and could be used alongside single-seaters if need arose. The RAF received 13 T.10s from 1995 but the advent of the Harrier GR.9 in 2006 meant some were upgraded to T.12

Slingsby T67M Firefly A basic military trainer variant of the Fournier RF-6. In the 1990s the civilian operated Joint Elementary Flying Training School (JEFTS), which provided basic training to RAF, FAA andAAC pilots selected the T67M260 variant and the first of 51 was delivered in 1995. In 2003, the RAF opted to provide elementary flying training through UASs and the Fireflies were replaced by Grob Tutors.

1996

Eurocopter Squirrel The Gazelles that had been service with 32 (The Royal) Sqn from 1976 were replaced in the VIP communications role in 1996 by the first of three Aérospatiale AS355 Twin Squirrel helicopters. A year later, the first of 26 single-engined AS350 Squirrel HT.1s joined the Defence Helicopter Flying School to replace the Gazelle in the helicopter training role. The Squirrel remained in service until 2018.

Fat Albert's Humanitarian Role

The Lockheed C-130 Hercules has served the RAF from the 1960s to the present day and continues to play a vital role in wartime and peacetime operations around the world

By the end of the 1960s it became clear that the RAF's Handley Page Hastings and Blackburn Beverleys were approaching the end of their working lives. Although the Armstrong Whitworth Argosy joined the force in 1961, the service was in need of a new medium-range tactical airlifter.

Armstrong Whitworth had been working on the AW.681 Vertical Take Off & Landing (VTOL) military transport, but sadly this ambitious (albeit feasible) project was cancelled by the new Labour Government in January 1965, forcing the RAF to look elsewhere. For expediency that search extended overseas and the US-based Lockheed Corporation pitched its C-130 Hercules for the contract.

Hercules

Known to many by its 'Fat Albert' nickname, the C-130 had performed its first flight on August 23, 1954 and entered USAF service just over two years later. By the mid-1960s hundreds were in American service as well as with a host of air forces across the globe.

At the time it was considered to be the best aerial transporter on the market and the RAF seized the opportunity to order 66 of the C-130K variant. These were to be designated as the Hercules C.1 in RAF service and the first (XV176) performed its maiden flight on October 19, 1966 at Marietta, Georgia.

The Hercules C.1 first entered service with 242 OCU at Thorney Island, Sussex in April 1967, followed by the first operational unit (36 Sqn) which replaced its Hastings at RAF Lyneham, Wiltshire on August 1, 1967.

A further six units, (24, 30, 36 and 47 Sqns at home, 48 Sqn in Changi, Singapore and 70 Sqn at Akrotiri, Cyprus) received the Hercules C.1 and from 1970, all UK-based aircraft were centralised at RAF Lyneham.

However, further defence cuts in 1975 saw the fleet reduced by 13 aircraft and 36 and 48 Sqns both disbanded.

1

Extended Fuselage

Losing 13 aircraft hampered the RAF's load carrying capabilities but a novel solution was announced in 1978. By extending the fuselage with the addition of a 15ft 'plug' a further 20,000lb (9,072kg) of cargo could be carried and, furthermore, the modification also increased the aircraft's cruise speed.

The fuselage components were produced by Lockheed and shipped over to Marshall's of Cambridge for conversion; the first stretched aircraft flying from Cambridge on January 10, 1980. The last of 30 – by now dubbed the Hercules C.3 – was delivered to Lyneham on November 25, 1985.

During the Falklands War, there was a need to extend the range of the fleet, so the airframes were converted for aerial refuelling (both giving and receiving). The tankers were designated as the C.1K and the receivers renamed as C.1P and C.3P ('P' for probe).

The only substitute for a Hercules turned out to be another Hercules!

Operation Bushel

Perhaps the RAF Hercules' most famous exploits came in 1984 and 1985 when they were deployed to Africa to delivery much-needed aid to the famine-stricken population of Ethiopia.

When BBC journalist Michael Buerk's heartrending report highlighted the plight of the starving Ethiopians, it kick-started a worldwide humanitarian appeal for help.

Bob Geldof gathered popstars together to record the famous *'Do they know it's Christmas'* charity single, but the RAF was providing more direct help. Between November 1984 and December 1985 the Lyneham-based Hercules'

1997 — **2000**

Bell 412 Griffin A much developed version of the Bell UH-1 'Huey'. The RAF operated two variants of the Bell 412 as the Griffin. The HT.1 was flown by flown by 60(R) and 202(R) Sqns as part of the Defence Helicopter Flying School and used for multi-engined training. The 60 (R) Sqn Griffins were retired in 2018. The HAR.2 continues to fly with 84 Sqn in Gibraltar and can carry six troops, be used for SAR or firefighting. **SDB**

Panavia Tornado GR.4 Re-tasking the GR.1 from low to medium level operations meant modifying it with FLIR and NVG capability. The upgrade to GR.4 standard also saw the jets adapted to carry *Storm Shadow* missiles, *Brimstone* anti-tank missiles, *Paveway* IV laser-guided bombs and RAPTOR recce pods. The first was delivered to the RAF in October 1997 and GR.4s flew combat over Iraq and Afghanistan. The Tornado retired in 2019.

Grob Tutor When the RAF retired its Bulldogs the MoD decided the replacement aircraft should be owned and operated by a civilian contractor and leased under a Private Finance Initiative (PFI) scheme. The contract was awarded to Babcock, which provided a fleet of 99 Grob 115E Tutor T.1s from 1999. The aircraft carry civilian registrations as well as RAF roundels. All RAF pilots receive their elementary training on the type.

Lockheed C-130J Hercules In 1994, the RAF ordered 25 of the latest C-130Js with new Rolls-Royce engines, Dowty composite propellers and a digital cockpit to replace C-130Ks. Ten were the standard C-130J (known as the Hercules C.4) and 15 were the stretched C-130J-30 (Hercules C.5). The first example arrived in 1999. They were due to be retired when the A400M entered service but are now expected to remain until 2030.

Dassault Alpha Jet In 2000, twelve ex-Luftwaffe Alpha Jets joined the Defence Evaluation and Research Agency (DERA). These were to be used for testing and trials work as the RAF could no longer spare any Hawk airframes. All 12 were allocated RAF serial but only seven were flown. In 2001, DERA was privatised and became QinetiQ but the Alpha Jets kept their RAF serials until they were retired in January 2018. **QinetiQ**

RAF Fast Fact

The RAF's first female pilot was a Hercules captain. Flt Lt Julie Gibson flew the HS Andover with 32 Sqn at RAF Northolt, London before being promoted to captain and moving to RAF Lyneham to fly the C-130K.
She had learned to fly while attending City, University of London, from which she qualified with a BSc in Aeronautical Engineering in 1983. Upon joining the RAF in 1984 she completed officer training, was posted to RAF Honington, Suffolk and commanded 75 engineers at the tactical weapons unit. She later successfully applied for pilot training, going on to train in the Advanced Flying Training Wing. She graduated as the RAF's first female pilot on June 14, 1991.

1. The Hercules fleet flew 2,152 sorties and dropped 32,000 tonnes of supplies during Operation *Bushel*.
2. In an attempt to appease British unions -a deal was made for Scottish Aviation produce fuselage sections for the RAF's C-130Ks. It is unclear how cost effective this was as it involved the sections being shipped by sea and land to Georgia in the USA before being incorporated into the aircraft and then flown back to UK.
3. Members of 34 Sqn RAF Regiment and a C-130J taking part in Exercise *Lions Dawn* in 2016.
All: Crown Copyright

completed 2,152 sorties and delivered 32,000 tonnes of supplies during Operation *Bushel*.

Six C-130Ks operated out of the capital city Addis Ababa and the crews flew four to five sorties a day, often in difficult conditions.

The Hercules' 'flying truck' qualities made it perfect for the job as it could land on short, dusty strips to deliver supplies to remote places. However, some of the most affected areas were high into the mountains with only rough landing strips so on occasion the crews would resort to air dropping the aid on pallets from its rear loading ramp at an altitude of just 15ft.

This was just the first of many humanitarian missions that have been supported by the RAF 'Fat Albert' fleet. The longest running of these was Operation *Cheshire*, the relief effort in the Balkans which ran from July 1992 to January 1996. The operation, designed to keep the inhabitants of Sarajevo alive, was initiated by the UN as road and rail networks had been destroyed during the civil war.

RAF Hercules' would conduct three or four air drops each day and by the end of the operation 26,577 tonnes of supplies had been delivered from bases in Zagreb, Croatia and Ancona in Italy. Unlike Ethiopia, this was a warzone and RAF crews were regularly targeted by small arms fire and mortar shells.

In more recent years, RAF C-130s have delivered much needed humanitarian aid (including jerry cans of drinkable water, tents and solar lights that can also recharge mobile telephones) to refugees on Mount Sinjar in Iraq.

New Generation

In late 1993 the RAF found itself in need of a replacement for its ageing Hercules fleet. It soon realised the only substitute for a Hercules was indeed another Hercules.

The new generation of C-130J was fitted with new engines and Dowty composite propellers as well a new suite of digital avionics alongside a host of other updates. The RAF ordered ten C-130J aircraft and 15 of the longer C-130J-30 in December 1994. The first example reached RAF Lyneham on November 21, 1999.

In RAF use the C-130J-30 is known as the Hercules C.4 and is a similar size to the C.3. The C-130J Hercules C.5 is the same size as a C1.

Intensive use in Operations *Telic* and *Herrick* meant the C-130 fleet accumulated flying hours more rapidly than projected so in the 2010 Strategic Defence and Security Review (SDSR), the decision was made to retire the C-130Ks by the end of 2013 and bring the C-130J/J-30 retirement forward a decade to 2022. The plan was to replace the aircraft with the new Airbus A400M Atlas but it was eventually realised that the Hercules could operate neatly alongside the Atlas, so the 2015 SDSR made allowances for 14 C.4s to remain in service until 2030.

The RAF has now operated the C-130 for five decades; will that actually end in 2030? ■

2001

AgustaWestland Merlin When the Navy requested a new anti-submarine helicopter in the late 1970s, Westland joined forces with Agusta to create the Merlin, which joined the Navy in 1997. The RAF received the first of 22 Merlin HC.3s in 2001 for troop transport use. Merlins were deployed to Iraq in 2004 and Afghanistan in 2008, but in 2012 the fleet was transferred to the Royal Navy for use by the Commando Helicopter Force.

Boeing C-17 Globemaster III A long range, heavy-lift strategic transport aircraft. In 2000, the MoD entered into a seven-year 'lease and support' contract with Boeing (and the USAF) for four C-17s; which were to be used for military and humanitarian missions. The first arrived in 2001 and in 2006 the RAF opted to buy the four aircraft and order a fifth. By 2012 the fleet had grown to eight examples of the Globemaster III.

2003

Eurofighter Typhoon F.2/FGR.4 After a protracted development the first Typhoon F.2 entered RAF service in 2003. The F.2 replaced the Tornado F.3 on Quick Reaction Alert (QRA) duties in 2007. The following year the multi-role FGR.4 was declared combat ready. The type has seen action in Libya and Syria and the last of 160 RAF airframes was delivered in September 2019. The type is expected to remain in service until 2040.

Eurofighter Typhoon T.1/T.3 The two-seat Typhoon entered service with 17 Sqn in December 2003. Some T.1s were later upgraded to T.3 standard, with updated avionics, but as they were Tranche 1 airframes their update capability was limited. As such, it was announced in 2018 that 16 twin-seat Typhoons would be reduced to spares to keep other aircraft aloft. In part, this reflected the greater use of training simulators.

2004

BAe Nimrod MRA.4 Created as a successor to the Nimrod MR.2. The programme took existing airframes and rebuilt them with more efficient Rolls-Royce BR700 turbofans and new avionics and radar systems. An order for 21 was placed in 1996 but it would be August 2004 before the prototype flew. Further delays and cost overruns meant the contract was cancelled in 2010. It was £789 million over-budget.

European Tonka Jet

The Panavia Tornado served the RAF in both interceptor and ground attack roles until 2011 and 2018 respectively

In the late 1960s, the RAF was looking for a replacement for its Vulcan and Buccaneer strike aircraft. The BAC TSR.2 had been cancelled, as had its American F-111K replacement, so a call was issued for a new aeroplane.

Britain and France began working on the AFVG (Anglo French Variable Geometry) aircraft in 1965. The idea behind a variable-geometry (VG) wing is to blend the manoeuvrability and slow handing of a straight wing with the aerodynamic speed of a swept wing. However, the programme ended two years later when the French withdrew from it.

Later in the decade, Belgium, Canada, Italy, the Netherlands and West Germany began looking for a replacement for their Lockheed F-104 Starfighters. Britain joined in 1968, by which time the AFVG was referred to as the Multi Role Combat Aircraft (MRCA) – although some in the RAF quipped that the acronym really stood for 'Must Refurbish Canberra Again'!

It soon became obvious that such a diverse range of nations wanted very different things from the aircraft. As such, Britain, West Germany, the Netherlands and Italy began collaboratively working on their own aircraft in May 1969 under the Panavia name. The aim was to produce an aircraft capable of undertaking tactical strike, reconnaissance, air defence and maritime roles during the Cold War.

The resulting design had a wing that could sweep between 25 and 67 degrees; the aircraft was also fitted with full span flaps and thrust-reverser 'buckets' over the engine nozzles to help reduce the landing distance.

The Dutch pulled out of the project in 1970, so the UK and West Germany were each allocated 42.5% of the workload and financing, with Italy conducting the remaining 15%. Similarly, a tri-national company (Turbo-Union) was established in June 1970 to develop and build the RB199 engines for the aircraft, with 40% of the ownership going to Rolls-Royce in the UK. Initially referred to as the Panavia Panther, the name soon changed to Tornado.

Tornado IDS

The first prototype Tornado IDS (Interdictor Strike) took off from Manching, Germany on August 14, 1974 with test pilot Paul Millett at the controls.

The first orders were signed by the partner countries in July 1976 and on June 5, 1979 the first examples joined the RAF and the German Luftwaffe. The first Italian Tornado was delivered on September 25, 1981; the same year that the Tri-national Tornado Training Establishment (TTTE) officially opened at RAF Cottesmore, Rutland to train pilots and navigators for all nations.

1. Two Tornado F.3s of 1435 Flight based at Mount Pleasant, patrolling the skies over the Falkland Islands. **Crown Copyright/Cpl Darren Smith**

In RAF service the Tornado IDS was referred to as the GR.1 and affectionately known as the 'Tonka' by virtue of its substantial size.

The first British prototype (XX946) flew on October 30, 1974 and the first production GR.1 was delivered on July 1, 1980. TTTE-qualified RAF crew went onto the Tornado Weapons Conversion Unit (TWCU) at RAF Honington, Suffolk before being posted to a front-line squadron; the first of which to become operational being IX(B) Sqn at RAF Marham, Norfolk. In time, 27 and 617 Sqns would also form on the 'Tonka' at Marham.

The Tornado GR.1 fleet also served with RAF Germany (RAFG), with XV Sqn receiving its first examples in September 1983 at RAFG Laarbruch, followed 16 and 20 Sqn in 1984. Elsewhere, 14, 17 and 31 Sqn started to arrive at RAFG Brüggen in 1984 and the following year IX Sqn moved from Marham to join them.

Luckily, the aircraft were never called upon to fulfil their nuclear role, but 1991 saw RAF Tornados deployed operationally for the first time. Almost 60 Tornado GR.1s were part of the British contribution to Operation *Granby;* deploying to Bahrain and Saudi Arabia for the first Gulf War. They flew extensive missions and six examples were lost in combat.

In 1994 the fleet was subjected to a Mid-Life Upgrade (MLU) from GR.1 to GR.4 standard and the GR.4 soon made its operational debut in Operation *Southern Watch*; patrolling Iraq's southern airspace from bases in Kuwait.

2004

Beechcraft King Air T.1 The Beechcraft B200 King Air executive turboprop was chosen to replace the Jetstream as the RAF's multi-engine trainer. The aircraft were operated by 45 (R) Sqn and used to provide the multi-engine lead-in (MELIN) course for pilots destined to fly aircraft such as the C-130. Weapon systems officers (WSOs) also trained on the King Air until 2018 when it was replaced by the Phenom [see p129].

2006

AgustaWestland A109E Power Developed from original Agusta A109 helicopter that first flew in 1971. Although two ex-Argentinian A109s (captured in the Falklands) were operated by the Army in support of the SAS it would be 2006 before the type joined the RAF. In 2006, three AW109E Power variants were leased for use by 32 (The Royal) Sqn as VIP transports. Two were retired in 2011 but one continued until 2016.

BAe Harrier GR.9 The final RAF version of the Harrier. GR.9s were GR.7s with upgraded avionics, communications and weapons capabilities; including the AGM-65 *Maverick* air-to-ground missile. The type was expected to stay in service until at least 2018 but defence cuts meant the last flight took place on December 15, 2010. The remaining 72 GR.9s were sold to the United States Marine Corps for £116 million to be stripped for spares.

2007

General Atomics MQ-9A Reaper The RAF ordered two armed MQ-9A Reaper UAVs and the type was initially operated from Creech AFB in Nevada before moving to RAF Waddington, Lincolnshire. Flights over Afghanistan began in 2007 and the RAF eventually received ten airframes. Reapers were due to retire in 2015 but have remained in service and in 2016 an order for 26 Predator B versions was placed, with options for another ten.

2008

Diamond DA-42 MPP Developed from the DA-42 TwinStar training aircraft. Three joined the RAF in 2008 and are fitted with electro-optical and infrared cameras. The 'multi-purpose platforms' are operated by DO Systems on behalf of the RAF. Compared to the civilian version, the aircraft has a bubble canopy along with a myriad of sensors and scanners and an exhaust muffler that make it hard to hear from the ground.

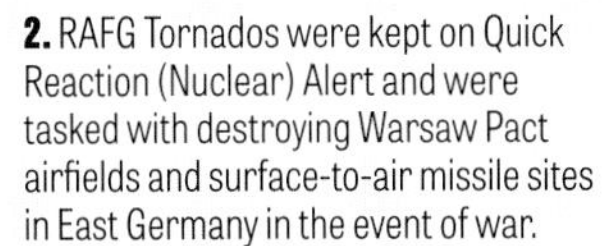

2. RAFG Tornados were kept on Quick Reaction (Nuclear) Alert and were tasked with destroying Warsaw Pact airfields and surface-to-air missile sites in East Germany in the event of war.
3. Almost 60 RAF Tornado GR.1s deployed to Bahrain and Saudi Arabia during the first Gulf War. They flew extensive missions and six examples were lost in combat.
4. Tornado GR.4s returning to RAF Marham following their participation in Operation *Ellamy* in 2011. Tornados flew 1,400 sorties over Libya.
Crown Copyright/SAC Andy Mason

5. The Tornado was designed to fly at high speed at low-level in order to penetrate deep into enemy territory. This aircraft is practicing through one of the Welsh valleys on the LFA-7 'Mach Loop' in 2013.
Crown Copyright/SAC Tim Laurence

The aircraft also took part in the Kosovo War in 1999 and in 2003 GR.4s were heavily used in Operation *Telic*, Britain's contribution to the 2003 invasion of Iraq.

Britain withdrew the last of its Tornados from Iraq in June 2009, by which time they were already in use in Afghanistan. They would remain there until November 2014.

In 2011, GR.4s were part of the RAF effort to enforce a no-fly zone in Libya and in 2015 Tornados conducted airstrikes in Iraq.

The RAF Tornado's swansong would come in 2018 when GR.4s took part in Operation *Shader* against Syrian military targets. The final mission was flown on January 31, 2019 after which the jets flew back to RAF Marham and the type finally retired on March 14.

Tornado ADV

In the 1980s, the RAF also needed an interceptor to replace its ageing Lightnings and Phantoms, so it asked British Aerospace to create the Tornado ADV (Air Defence Variant).

The requirements demanded that the aircraft had the ability to fly Combat Air Patrols (CAP) in all weathers up to 350 miles (563km) from its home airfield and be able to fire missiles using 'look-down, shoot-down' capability at a range of up to 25 miles (40km).

The airframe was lengthened by 5ft (1.54m) to accommodate the AI.24 *Foxhunter* airborne radar and upgraded RB199-34 Mk.103D engines gave 10% more power. Weaponry included a 27mm Mauser cannon, four *Sky Flash* missiles and a pair of AIM-9s.

The prototype was rolled out on August 9, 1979 and it for the first time on October 28, by which time it was known as the Tornado F.2.

The Foxhunter radar was far from ready (and already two-thirds over budget) when the first production F.2 (ZD900) flew on March 5, 1984 so the first 18 aircraft were delivered without radar. Amazingly, to make up for the missing radar, the noses of the jets were filled with concrete to maintain their centre of gravity!

All subsequent aircraft were updated to F.3 standard with RB199R Mk.104 engines and improved avionics. The F.3 also had an additional pylon for two extra AIM.9 missiles.

The type made its combat debut during the 1991 Gulf War when 18 aircraft deployed to Dhahran, Saudi Arabia. Following further upgrades, F.3s were used as escort fighters over Bosnia in 1993; they also flew during Operation *Allied Force* in 1999. In 2003, the F.3 was used in Operation *Telic* in Iraq but a year later the decision was made to start reducing the fleet. By 2011 it had been completely replaced by the Eurofighter Typhoon. ■

2009

Mil Mi-17 In 2008 the MoD purchased two ex- Bulgarian Air Force Mil Mi-17 *Hip* helicopters. They were upgraded in Lithuania and delivered to Boscombe Down for training Afghan pilots. Registered ZB697 and ZB698, the aircraft were painted in a 'raspberry ripple' red, white and blue scheme. By 2010, some 18 pilots and nine flight engineers were trained. The helicopters were then gifted to the Afghan Air Force. **Philip Stevens**

Raytheon Sentinel A long-range battlefield surveillance and intelligence gathering aircraft. Based on the Global Express business jet the Sentinel can track targets and pass information to other forces in real time. The first of five joined the RAF in 2008 and they have been used in support of operations in Afghanistan, Iraq, Libya, Mali and Syria. The fleet was cut to four in 2017 but the out of service date extended to 2021.

BAe Hawk T.2 The Hawk T.2 is very different to the T.1. It is developed from the Hawk 128 and has a more powerful engine, a new wing and revised airframe with a glass cockpit and fly-by-wire. The T.2 was selected by the RAF in 2003 and the MoD partnered with Ascent Flight Training to provide the UK Military Flying Training System (MFTS). The 28 T.2s are part of this and use data links to simulate combat scenarios.

Beechcraft Shadow R.1 An intelligence gathering aircraft based on the King Air 350. The Shadow uses electro-optical and electronic surveillance techniques to gather data and has a live satellite link to upload and download information mid-flight. The Shadow similar is also fitted with various defensive aids. The first of six joined V(AC) Sqn in 2009 and some later moved to 14 Sqn. The fleet is set to increase by three.

Boeing Chinook HC.3 In 1995, the RAF ordered eight MH-47E Chinooks for £259 million as dedicated special forces helicopters. The HC.3 had an in-service date of 1998. They were eventually delivered in 2001 but it was impossible to certify the avionics software and they were stored in heated hangars until 2008 when they were fitted with HC.2 style avionics. The first HC.3 flew in 2009 at a programme cost of £500 million.

The RAF in 2020

As it enters its second century the RAF continues to defend the UK and its overseas interests

Today, in 2020, the RAF describes its mission statement as "To provide an agile, adaptable and capable Air Force that, person for person, is second to none, and that makes a decisive air power contribution in support of the UK Defence Mission." To do this, the RAF maintains an operational fleet of more than 800 aircraft of diverse types.

Fast Jets

The RAF currently has eight squadrons of Eurofighter Typhoons as its primary multi role air defence and ground attack fighter aircraft. Their main task is to defend UK airspace on Quick Reaction Alert (QRA), offering around-the-clock fighter coverage. With the retirement of the Tornado GR.4 in April 2019, the Typhoon FGR4 took over ground attack duties.

The first of the RAF's new Lockheed Martin F-35B Lightning II aircraft arrived in the UK in June 2018 and 617 Sqn was declared combat ready in January 2019. The BAe Hawk T.1s of 100 Sqn at RAF Leeming, Yorkshire act as aggressor aircraft, fulfilling the role of enemy aircraft in air combat training.

Intel & Reconnaissance

In the Intelligence, Surveillance, Target Acquisition and Reconnaissance (ISTAR) role the RAF operates a fleet of four Boeing Sentry AEW.1s to detect incoming enemy aircraft and to co-ordinate the aerial battlefield. In March 2019, five Boeing E-7 Wedgetails were ordered to ultimately replace Sentry from 2023.

The Raytheon Sentinel R.1 provides an airborne ground radar-surveillance capability and in 2009 these were supplemented by five Beechcraft Shadow R1 aircraft equipped for the ISTAR role over Afghanistan.

Three Boeing RC-135W Rivet Joint replaced the Nimrod R.1 fleet in the Signals Intelligence (SIGINT) role from 2014 and these were first deployed to the Middle East in August of that year. They have since flown missions over Iraq and Syria as part of Operation *Shader*.

A fleet of MQ-9A Reaper Unmanned Aerial Vehicles (UAVs) also support operations in Iraq and Afghanistan; they are operated by 39 Sqn at Creech AFB, Nevada and XIII Sqn at RAF Waddington, Lincolnshire.

In 2015, it was announced that the RAF was to receive nine Boeing P-8 Poseidon maritime patrol aircraft to replace the Nimrod after its disposal in 2010. The aircraft will include an overland surveillance capability so they can operate alongside other RAF ISTAR platforms. The first Poseidon is due to join 120 Sqn at Lossiemouth in 2020.

On April 1, 2019 the British Army's fleet of Britten-Norman Defender AL.2 surveillance aircraft and Islander AL.1/CC.2 surveillance and utility aircraft transferred to the RAF. The aircraft had previously been part of 651 Sqn AAC but now fall under the direction of the RAF's No 1 Group. To simplify this process, 651 Sqn has become an RAF unit but remains at its base at RAF Aldergrove in Northern Ireland.

The unit provides ISTAR support to UK special forces operations with the Islander and Defender fitted with a low light level television or infrared camera positioned in a turret mounted beneath the nose. The aircraft also have door- and floor-mounted cameras, radar and COMINT (COMmunications INTelligence) gear for listening in on radio signals.

1

2

3

2011

Airbus Voyager Replaced the RAF's TriStar and VC10 refuellers and transport aircraft. The MoD signed a deal with the AirTanker consortium to lease 14 Airbus A330 MRTTs under a PFI arrangement. From 2011, the aircraft was delivered in two versions: Voyager KC.2 and KC.3. The 'surge capacity' deal allows Air Tanker to lease Voyagers to the civil market as airliners when not needed operationally by the RAF.

2012

Avro RJ70 & RJ100 Developed from the BAe 146 [see p119] the Avro RJ project began in 1992. In 2010, defence contractor QinetiQ acquired an RJ70 and RJ100 to replace the BAC 1-11 used at the Empire Test Pilots' School. The RJ100 (originally G-BZAY and later QQ101) and RJ70 (G-BVRJ/QQ102) entered service in 2012. In 2019, the aircraft reverted to civilian registrations as G-ETPL and G-ETPK but continue in the same role.

Boeing Rivet Joint A derivative of the USAF RC-135W Signals Intelligence aircraft, ordered to replace the Nimrod R.1 [see p117]. Three ex-USAF KC-135R tankers were purchased and converted to RC-135Ws under the Airseeker project. It has sensors which the RAF says "soak up electronic emissions from communications, radar and other systems". The first of three was delivered in 2013 and is expected to remain in service until 2045.

2014

Airbus Atlas The Airbus A400M turboprop-powered airlifter was developed as a multinational project. The type entered RAF service in November 2014 and 20 of the 22 on order have so far been delivered. In RAF service the type is called Atlas and carry a 37 tonne payload more than 2,000 miles and land on unprepared airstrips. It can also accommodate 116 fully equipped troops or a Chinook inside its cabin.

Boeing Chinook HC.6 The first of 14 HC.6s joined the RAF in 2014. Based on the CH-47F they are a vastly modernised version of the helicopters that have served the RAF since 1980 [see p119]. It has the Boeing Digital Automatic Flight Control System (DAFCS – pronounced 'Daffics'), which improves handling in low visibility As of 2020 the RAF Chinook force consisted of 38 HC.2/2A/4s, eight HC.3/5s and 14 of the new HC.6s.

RAF Fast Fact

In 2019 there were just over 28,000 men serving in the Royal Air Force and 4,760 women.

1. The RAF currently has eight squadrons of Eurofighter Typhoons as its primary multi role air defence and ground attack fighter aircraft. These two 6 Sqn jets are carrying dummy *Paveway* II laser guided bombs. **Crown Copyright/SAC Ash Reynolds**
2. The first Boeing P-8 Poseidon MRA.1 (ZP801) Pride of Moray performed its maiden flight on July 13, 2019. The fleet of nine will eventually be based RAF Lossiemouth with 120 and 201 Sqns. **Boeing**
3. The first of the RAF's new Lockheed Martin F-35B Lightning II aircraft arrived in the UK in June 2018 and 617 Sqn was declared combat ready in January 2019. **Crown Copyright**
4. The largest airlifter in RAF service is the Boeing C-17 Globemaster III; nine of which are based at RAF Brize Norton. Here, personnel from 904 Expeditionary Air Wing based at Kandahar Airfield in Afghanistan head back to the UK aboard a C-17 at the end of their tour of action. **Crown Copyright/Cpl Andrew Morris**

Air Mobility

For heavy strategic airlifting duties the RAF operates a fleet of eight Boeing C-17 Globemaster IIIs from RAF Brize Norton.

Strategic airlift tasks are also carried out by the Airbus Voyager, which arrived in April 2012, and is also now the RAF's only air-to-air refuelling aircraft. Tactical airlifting over a shorter range is conducted by the C-130J Hercules and the Airbus A400M Atlas.

The Queen's Flight was replaced by 32 (The Royal) Sqn in 1995 and currently operates the Agusta A109 and BAe 146 CC.2 in the VIP transport roles from RAF Northolt in West London. Two additional second-hand BAe 146 freighters were purchased and converted into tactical freight and personnel transports. Designated as the BAe 146 C.3, the first arrived in Afghanistan in April 2013. The RAF also operates Puma and Chinook helicopters as part of Joint Helicopter Command [Ed: see p118].

Training

In recent years the UK military flying training programme has been civilianised through a public-private partnership with the Ascent Flight Training corporation.

Following basic training on the Grob G.120P Prefect, students pass through the Beechcraft T-6 Texan II or the Embraer Phenom 100 multi-engine trainer depending on whether they are destined for fighter or cargo aircraft.

Basic fast jet training is undertaken on the Texan II before an advanced programme is conducted on the BAE Systems Hawk T.2 at RAF Valley, Anglesey. A growing emphasis is also placed on simulators and other 'synthetic' training to deliver aircrew to the front line.

Rotary wing students are taught on the Airbus H135 Jupiter and Airbus H145 Juno helicopters at RAF Shawbury, Shropshire before advancing to the Bell Griffin HT.1.

The Grob Tutor equips the 14 University

5. The proposed BAE Systems Tempest is intended to enter RAF service from 2035 replacing the Eurofighter Typhoon (in the same way that the Hawker Tempest replaced the Typhoon in World War Two). The new Tempest will be able to fly manned or unmanned and use swarming technology to control drones.. **BAE Systems**
6. One of the latest aircraft to join the RAF is the Beechcraft Texan II, which took over the basic fast jet training role from the Tucano T.1 in 2019. **Crown Copyright**
7. The RAF operates four Boeing Sentry AEW.1s in the ISTAR role but these are due to be replaced by five Boeing E-7 Wedgetails from 2023. **Crown Copyright**
8. Via a public-private partnership with Ascent Flight Training, RAF pilots now receive basic instruction on the Grob G.120P Prefect. **SDB**

2016

Embraer Phenom T.1 Based on the Phenom 100 business jet. The new aircraft took over multi-engine aircrew training from the King Air [see p126] and is a much more modern machine. It has a touchscreen cockpit and a cockpit layout far closer to the frontline types that students will go on to fly operationally. The five Phenoms are operated by Ascent under a PFI agreement and based at RAF Cranwell as part of the UK MFTS.

Grob Prefect T.1 A turboprop development of the Grob 115 Tutor, [see p124]. The G120TP prototype first flew in 2010 and has a composite airframe, glass cockpit and a Rolls Royce M250 powerplant. As part of MFTS, Ascent is providing 23 Prefect T.1s to replace Tutors in the elementary flying training role at RAF Cranwell. The first was delivered in 2016 and training flights began in 2017. **Crown Copyright**

Leonardo AW109SP GrandNew The latest version of the Agusta A109. In 2016, AgustaWestland was absorbed by parent company Finmeccanica – which then changed its name to Leonardo. A single AW109SP GrandNew joined 32 (The Royal) Sqn in 2016 to replace the existing AW109Es. It can be flown by a single pilot in all weather conditions, by day or night. It is used to transport military commanders and government ministers.

2017

Airbus H135 Juno T.1 Replaced the Squirrel [see p123] in the rotary wing training role with the Defence Helicopter Flying School at RAF Shawbury. Based on the Eurocopter EC135, it has a glass cockpit. It also the quietest helicopter in its class. When Ascent was chosen to provide the UK's MFTS helicopter tuition it ordered 29 H135 Juno T.1s; the first of which arrived on April 3, 2017. Training flights began in mid 2018.

Airbus H145 Jupiter T.1 Based on the Eurocopter EC145 (itself based on the Bolkow/Kawasaki developed BK117 of 1977) the H145 has replaced the Bell 412 Griffin in the advanced helicopter training role. Three have been acquired by Ascent to provide tuition at RAF Shawbury and RAF Valley. The first arrived in 2017 and the first courses began in April 2018. Like the Juno, the Jupiter is operated via a PFI deal but carry military registrations.

Air Squadrons. These are co-located with Air Experience Flights, which share the same aircraft and facilities to provide 'taster' flights to the Air Training Corps. The Volunteer Gliding Squadrons also provide air experience flying to cadets using the Grob Viking T.1 glider.

Future Flight

In July 2019, a joint US-UK team (Team ARTEMIS) was announced to launch and retrieve small military satellites. As such, 23 Sqn is set to become the RAF's first Space Squadron.

In 2015 it was announced that QinetiQ was developing the solar-powered Zephyr UAV for RAF use. According to then Prime Minister David Cameron, this is "designed to fly at the edge of the atmosphere for weeks on end."

Other UAV developments include a February 2019 announcement by the government that the UK will develop "swarming drones" to defeat enemy air defences. It is believed 216 Sqn will be stood up to specifically control these UAVs.

Other futuristic applications including the Protector programme aim at delivering a next-generation medium-altitude, long-endurance (MALE) UAV to replace the current Reapers. It is thought these will be based upon the USAF's armed Predator B aircraft with an endurance of over 40 hours. The RAF's first Protector RG.1 is slated to be delivered by 2024.

During the 2018 Farnborough Airshow, a joint programme consisting of government divisions alongside BAE Systems, Leonardo, MBDA and Rolls-Royce was announced. Dubbed 'Team Tempest', the group was tasked with developing a new RAF fighter by 2035.

1. New RAF fast jet pilots now progress from Grob Prefect to the Texan II and then onto the Hawk T.2 (illustrated) **Crown Copyright**
2. The Lightning II is a VTOL aircraft and is seen here transitioning from the hover during a demonstration flight. **Crown Copyright/Cpl Tim Laurence**

Legacy

Many of the 'hotspots' of today's world would have been very familiar to members of the RAF nearly a century ago. The Typhoons and Reapers operating over Iraq and Syria today are doing much the same job as the Bristol F2Bs and de Havilland DH.9As of the 1920s; when Typhoons were attacking enemy tanks in the Libyan desert in 2011, they were following in the wake of the Hurricanes which did so in 1942. Whatever the future holds, the RAF will be building on a strong heritage and the unwavering loyalty of the British Public. *Per Ardua ad Astra ("Through Adversity to the Stars")* ■

2018

Beechcraft Texan T.1 Replaced the Tucano [see p122] in the fast jet training role. RAF students now progress from Prefect to Texan to Hawk T.2. The Texan replaces the analogue cockpit of the Tucano with a digital glass cockpit that is capable of generating simulated air-to-air targets. The aircraft is based on the USAF's Texan II and an order for ten was placed by Ascent in 2016. The aircraft are based at RAF Valley as part of MFTS.

Lockheed Martin F-35B Lightning II The short take off and vertical landing variant of the Joint Strike Fighter. The X-35 first flew in October 2000. The Lightning II is a single-engined, all-weather, stealth, fifth-generation, multirole combat aircraft designed for both ground-attack and air-superiority missions. The RAF plans to operate the F-35B from both land bases and carriers and the first of 48 aircraft arrived in 2018.

2019

Britten-Norman Defender R.2 The Army Air Corps fleet of Britten-Norman Defender AL.2 surveillance aircraft transferred to the RAF on April 1, 2019. Developed as a dedicated military version of the Islander, the Defender was built for counter-insurgency, forward air control and reconnaissance duties. Defenders are fitted with an electro-optical turret under the nose. Eight are thought to have transferred to the RAF.

Britten-Norman Islander R.1 As part of the transfer of assets between the AAC and RAF on April 1, 2019 three Islander AL.1s joined the RAF. The Army used the Islander for communications and reconnaissance duties; notably in Northern Ireland. The RAF will now operate the type under the direction of No 1 Group. The AAC's 651 Sqn has transferred to the RAF but the aircraft and personnel remain at Aldergrove.

2020

Boeing Poseidon MRA.1 The RAF ordered nine P-8 Poseidons in 2015 to replace the Nimrod MR.2 (and the cancelled MRA.4). Based on the Boeing 737-800ERX airliner the P-8 is used in the anti-submarine warfare, anti-surface warfare, and anti-shipping roles. The nine RAF Poseidons will be delivered in batches and the first is expected to enter service with 120 Sqn at RAF Lossiemouth in the summer of 2020. **Boeing**